D0079368

INEQUALITY, COOPERATION, AND ENVIRONMENTAL SUSTAINABILITY

INEQUALITY, COOPERATION, AND ENVIRONMENTAL SUSTAINABILITY

Edited by

JEAN-MARIE BALAND,

PRANAB BARDHAN, AND

SAMUEL BOWLES

RUSSELL SAGE FOUNDATION
NEW YORK

PRINCETON UNIVERSITY PRESS
PRINCETON AND OXFORD

Copyright © 2007 by Russell Sage Foundation

Requests for permission to reproduce material from this work should be sent to
Permissions, Princeton University Press

Published by Princeton University Press, 41 William Street, Princeton, New Jersey 08540

In the United Kingdom: Princeton University Press, 3 Market Place, Woodstock,
Oxfordshire OX20 1SY

And the Russell Sage Foundation, 112 East 64th Street, New York, New York 10021

Library of Congress Cataloging-in-Publication Data

Inequality, cooperation, and environmental sustainability / edited by Jean-Marie Baland,
Pranab Bardhan, and Samuel Bowles.
   p. cm.
  Includes bibliographical references and index.
  ISBN-13: 978-0-691-12879-5 (cloth : alk. paper)
  ISBN-10: 0-691-12879-0 (cloth : alk. paper)
   1. Sustainable development—Case studies. 2. Natural resources, Communal—Case
studies. 3. Commons—Case studies. I. Baland, Jean-Marie. II. Bardhan, Pranab K.
III. Bowles, Samuel.

  HC79.E5I5146 2007
  338.9'27—dc22   2006044988

British Library Cataloging-in-Publication Data is available

This book has been composed in Sabon

Printed on acid-free paper. ∞

www.russellsage.org

pup.princeton.edu

Printed in the United States of America

1   3   5   7   9   10   8   6   4   2

10   9   8   7   6   5   4   3   2   1

CONTENTS

PREFACE

Jean-Marie Baland, Pranab Bardhan, and Samuel Bowles

This book originated as a project of the Research Network on the Effects of Inequality on Economic Performance, headed by Bardhan and Bowles. It is part of our exploration of the ways that differences in wealth, status, and rights may influence the economic performance of firms, farms, communities, and nations. We are grateful to the other members of the network for their comments on the studies included in this book, many of which were discussed at Network meetings. We would like to thank the MacArthur Foundation for its generous funding of the Network, which allowed a rather ambitious program of field studies and theoretical work, the results of which are included here. Caren Grown at the Foundation assisted greatly in our work, and we are grateful for her help.

A grant from the Russell Sage Foundation to the Santa Fe Institute to study "Persistent Inequality in a Competitive World" allowed us to convene a workshop of the authors to discuss initial drafts of the papers. Other projects funded by that grant include studies of the intergenerational transmission of economic status, the poverty traps contributing to persistent inequality among families, nations, and ethnic groups, and the impact of globalization on egalitarian redistribution by nation-states. We are grateful to the Russell Sage Foundation for their generous support, and to Andi Sutherland and the staff of the Santa Fe Institute for their contributions to this project.

Jean-Marie Baland, Pranab Bardhan, and Samuel Bowles
Santa Fe, New Mexico
March 2004

INEQUALITY, COOPERATION, AND ENVIRONMENTAL SUSTAINABILITY

Chapter 1

INTRODUCTION

Jean-Marie Baland, Pranab Bardhan, and Samuel Bowles

Does inequality exacerbate environmental problems? Would an equalization of wealth, social status, and political power contribute to environmental sustainability? Or is environmental degradation a likely byproduct of efforts to advance the economic, social, and political interests of the less well-off? In this book, we investigate the impact of inequality on environmental sustainability. We focus on local commons as they are essential to the livelihoods of many of the world's poorest people, and because recent research illuminates how private incentives, group governance, and government policies might combine to better protect these essential resources. At a local level users interact in a structure called social dilemmas, in which the pursuit of individual material gain in exploiting the commons enters into conflict with the general interest. Local environmental degradation often results from a failure by members of the community to cooperate in its protection. For this reason we give special attention to the effect that inequality may have on cooperation.

The problem is often termed the "tragedy of the commons." However, many communities have managed common resources with great success over hundreds of years. Maine lobstermen limit their catch by means of local restrictions on who can set traps where. Turkish fishermen allocate fishing spots by lot and then rotate them (Ostrom 1990, Acheson 1988). Successful cooperation to protect forestry and water resources has also been documented (Bromley and Feeny 1992). But failures are also too common. Moreover, many studies of "collective action" potentially suffer from a selection bias, as failures are often harder to observe. "Success stories" of local cooperation may thus be overrepresented.

1.1. Collective Action and the Tragedy of the Commons

To blame inequality when the tragedy of the commons unfolds, one needs to know how inequality affects the ability and the incentives of group members to cooperate. Olson (1965) suggested that inequality promotes cooperation by increasing the likelihood that a few wealthy individuals will be able to capture enough of the benefits to induce them to provide the public good independently of the actions of the others. The first two chapters in this volume provide an approach based on individual incentives to assess the relevance of this argument.

In chapter 2, Baland and Platteau present a survey of simple models of voluntary contributions to a common good, or voluntary participation to a regulatory structure, as a guide to studying the mechanisms linking inequality to collective action. The effects of various dimensions of inequality (income, assets, stakes, . . .) are analyzed and some related empirical evidence is presented. In chapter 3, Bardhan, Ghatak, and Karaivanov propose a general model in which producers voluntarily contribute to a collective input, such as irrigation, which is complementary in production with privately owned inputs, for example, private land. Private inputs are unequally distributed among the producers, giving them differing incentives to contribute to the public good. The challenge is to identify the distribution of private inputs leading to the least inefficient outcome.

The lessons one can draw from these two chapters are close. In equilibrium, cooperators voluntarily contribute to the common good while free-riders choose not to contribute. If incentives to contribute are increasing with wealth, free-riders are less well-off and cooperators are wealthier, so that disequalizing transfers from the former to the latter increase total contributions and Olson's argument about a larger "internalization" effect is right. Both chapters however stress the ambiguity of this result along a number of dimensions. Thus, results can differ widely when benefits are measured in terms of output, surplus, or utility. Results also depend on the technological assumptions made and on the particular type of public good under concern.

These two chapters also illustrate how inequality generates contradictory effects on cooperation, such as:

1. A higher income level increases an agent's demand for the environmental good (an income effect), but also increases the opportunity cost of the time spent collecting the good (a substitution effect).

2. Lower assets may reduce the stakes members have in the resource, but also their ability to extract large amounts. Thus a smaller fisherman is less interested in protecting future catches, but also cannot really overfish.

3. Alternative income opportunities may prompt the user to exhaust the resource before changing occupation, but also make it more costly to spend time exploiting the resource.

4. For collective regulation of the commons, inequality may provide leaders with enough incentives but may also discourage poorer individuals to participate at all.

1.2. The Dimensions of Inequality

Various dimensions of inequality are relevant. Income inequality may affect the households' demand for goods provided by the commons, their opportunity cost of time, or their demand for regulation. But asset inequality also matters: land ownership determines one's gains from the collective irrigation scheme; the number of fishing boats owned affects one's long-term gains from voluntary reductions in fishing efforts.

Ethnic and social heterogeneity are also relevant, particularly where collective rules and organizations have to be set up (Alesina and La Ferrara, 2000). Baland et al. in chapter 10 find that caste conflicts reduce the effectiveness of the forest management committees in the Himalayan forests. Gender inequality also affects the performance of cooperation in the Indian forest along various mechanisms described by Agarwal in chapter 11. Technique and skill differences do matter. Thus, following Bardhan and Dayton-Johnson (chapter 5), the position of a farmer at the top-end or the tail-end of the irrigation network crucially affects his incentives to participate in the scheme. In chapter 7, Gaspart and Platteau show how differences in fishing techniques led to conflicts in the management of a shared fishery in Senegal.

1.3. Environmental Outcomes without Collective Action

Inequality has an impact on the environment even in the absence of collective action. The most obvious mechanism is the "consumption" of environmental goods. Thus, redistribution of income from the rich to the poor could worsen the environment if the consumption foregone by the rich had little environmental impact, while the increased consumption of the poor imposed substantial environmental cost. This requires that the marginal impact on the environment decreases with income.

Chapter 10 by Baland et al. is an attempt to separate out this "direct" impact of inequality from its indirect impact via collective action. They find in Nepal evidence of a concavity effect in firewood consumption, which implies that, ceteris paribus, were the poor to become a bit richer and the rich a bit poorer, more firewood in aggregate would be extracted. Having identified this effect, they subsequently analyze the remaining unexplained component of firewood collection, as reflecting the nature of collective action at the village level, and find a negative impact of caste heterogeneity on forest conservation.

More generally, however, the evidence for concavity effects is mixed. Data from a study by the U.S. Congressional Budget Office indicate that the relationship between income and "carbon-intensive consumption" shows no strong concave effects and may even be somewhat convex, depending on the method of estimation (Dinan and Lim 2000). Moreover, the effects of inequality may operate by shifting the relationship between income and environmental exploitation, such as under the "pecuniary emulation" discussed by Thorsten Veblen (1899/1934). If the standard of a decent lifestyle is influenced by the consumption of the rich, then increasing inequality between the rich and the rest of the society may stimulate efforts to catch up through working more and consuming more, thereby accelerating environmental degradation (for related evidence for ten OECD countries, see Bowles and Park 2005). Another possible mechanism follows from the undersupply of leisure-enhancing goods. Highly unequal societies may fail to provide adequate public goods complementary to the use of free time (libraries or public recreational facilities). As free time is thus less valuable relative to the consumption of commodities, consumer choices are biased toward less environment-friendly consumption goods. A third mechanism discussed by James Boyce in chapter 12 is based on two hypotheses. First, social decisions on environmental protection issues favor some groups over others. Second, a less equal distribution of power results in more environmental degradation as wealthier people can better insulate themselves from its consequences by purchasing private environmental quality. This process is illustrated with the example of the hazardous waste disposal policy in the United States, which is biased against low-income areas with a high percentage of African Americans and other minorities.

1.4. COOPERATION

Much of the literature describes as "cooperative" a behavior through which one agent internalizes some of the externalities he imposes on other users, and refrains his own use below what would maximize his individual profits. Cooperation in this setting therefore does not imply any voluntary creation of a collective "institution," but simply results from an uncoordinated spontaneous reduction in the use of a resource. Even in this simplified setting, the issue is potentially complex as the discussion of games of appropriation in chapter 2 reveals.

In chapter 8 Cardenas brings behavioral experiments typically performed in university laboratories into the field, by letting Colombian farmers whose livelihood involves exploiting a common forest play common resource experiments. In this setting, individuals freely set their levels of extraction, and are fully informed of the impact of their use on the other users in the group. Cardenas shows that wealth distance increased overexploitation of the experimental commons. This is surprising, as the game was designed so that individual incentives were independent of the characteristics of the members of the group. Cardenas was able however to pinpoint why wealth inequality may matter. In experiments in which no communication was allowed, the more homogeneous groups did no better than the groups with unequal wealth, but when communication was allowed, they were much more successful. By contrast, Cardenas did not find that poverty as such was a major obstacle: poor but homogenous groups displayed significantly higher levels of spontaneous cooperation than wealthier homogeneous groups

Cooperation however often requires collective action, a coordinated effort to regulate the use of the resource. Users then have to create collective institutions to this end. Chapter 2 analyzes the individual incentives to contribute to this coordinated effort, as well as to abide by these rules. In chapter 4, Janssen and Ostrom present an alternative theoretical approach to the creation and the adoption of collective rules, based on agent-based computational modeling. In the evolutionary dynamic their model captures, some rules are copied more than others and proliferate, while others do not diffuse and are eliminated. By simulating repeated interactions between agents, they show that high levels of heterogeneity undermine the building up of trust, a necessary condition for the emergence of conservation rules. Heterogeneity leads to the development of different identities, and to mentalities of "us" versus "them," which reduce the levels of cooperation and the overall performance of the society.

Many of the empirical studies in the present book investigate various aspects of collective action. For instance, in chapter 5 Bardhan and Dayton-Johnson present the main results of two large-scale empirical studies of irrigators' communities, one located in South India and the other in Mexico. They investigate how inequality affects the design of local rules for managing irrigation resources, and in turn how the rules in place themselves affect the level of cooperation. They find that inequality in landholdings is associated with lower maintenance and greater incidence of water-related conflicts, and also find that social heterogeneity—caste differences in India—reduces cooperation. They also show how rule compliance in these communities depends on the farmers' perception of the process by which these rules were created. Thus, in South India, maintenance rules are often broken because farmers believe that they were crafted by the local elite. Rules made by governmental officials who are not villagers are particularly prone to noncompliance.

In chapter 7 Gaspart and Platteau analyze attempts by Senegalese fishermen to regulate catches in the 1990s. They find that even though skill and technical heterogeneity are important obstacles to collective organization, they can often be overcome through the design of differentiated and adaptable rules. Wealthy local elites sometimes plays a leading role in the organization of collective action. By contrast, as noted above, a long history of conflicts characterizes villages where migrants and local fishermen compete and make use of different equipment and fishing methods. In addition, where poor fishers were indebted to fish sellers, efforts by the fishers to restrict the catch generally failed.

In chapter 9 Somanathan, Prabhakar, and Mehta use data on the Himalayan forests in North India based on satellite imagery. They investigate the impact of caste heterogeneity and land inequality on forest conservation. As these forests are managed by local village councils, they also examine the effect of female participation in such councils. There is no evidence of an impact of caste heterogeneity and female participation on collective action, nor on the state of the forest. There is some partial evidence that land inequality plays a negative role, but the evidence is not systematic.

1.5. COOPERATION AND ENVIRONMENTAL SUSTAINABILITY

The causal relationship going from "cooperation" to the state of the resource is not simple either. First, even when a well-identified group has an exclusive use of the resource (i.e. collective property rights are well-defined), and the user group is potentially well organized, it is not clear that users have a correct perception of the optimal use of the resource. For example, the idea that hunting pressure could reduce populations in the long run was absent in many traditional societies (see Baland and Platteau 1996).

Second, even where users realize that their current actions have a direct impact on the state of the resource, it may not be optimal to preserve the resource. Thus, conversion of forests to agricultural land may often correspond to an "optimal use path" in densely populated rural areas. In some instances, collective action may even be initiated to degrade the resource, as a reaction to a feeling of dispossession of local communities by state authorities. In northern India, Ho tribesmen who lost rights to forest lands developed a "forest cutting movement . . . as a means of asserting their rights to use the lands which forestry laws denied them" (Colchester 1994:83).

Third, the measurement of the "environmental outcome" is not in itself an easy task. Some studies focus on a measure of current flows or catches (e.g., the number of loads of firewood taken from a forest in a week, such as in Baland et al., chapter 10), while others rely on measures of stocks (e.g., forested areas, and measures of crown cover per species, such as in Somanathan et al., chapter 9). Other authors, such as Gaspart and Platteau (chapter 7) even rely on subjective perception of the state of the resource. In a stationary equilibrium, the flow and the stock should vary in the same way. However, in most cases the environment studied is far from a "stationary path." As a result those two measures do not coincide, and the simultaneous use of both should be recommended. Even where the resource is well defined, good measures of the current use and stock are often multidimensional. Thus, in a degrading forest, one should look not only at the amount of firewood taken (a flow measure), or the forested area and the crown cover (a stock measure), but also at the various indicators of forest biomass and growth potential: basal area, girth, height, cutting practices, species composition, density of seedlings, ratio of branches and twigs to the trunk, and so on.

Moreover, collective action need not produce a unique type of outcome. The nature of this outcome may also vary with inequality. For instance, as also stressed by Boyce in chapter 12, the type of public good desired depends on income, so that the type and the amount of public good produced collectively varies systematically with income distribution (see also Alesina, Baqir, and Easterly 1999). In chapter 11 Agarwal provides a striking illustration of the way gender inequalities, through the action of village forest committees in India, translate into widely different forest management practices. Based on her field investigations in five states of India and additional data drawn from other studies, she shows that male dominated committees are tempted to impose seasonal bans on firewood collection in order to increase the stock of timber, the proceeds of which they control; the cost of such restriction is almost exclusively borne by the women, who are in charge of collecting firewood. Moreover, women's lack of involvement in the decision-making processes also reduces their ability as well as their incentive to cooperate in local forest management.

Finally, collective regulation has a distributive impact, the pattern of which depends on the initial differences across users. The larger those differences, the more likely some users will oppose a particular regulation, producing a status quo bias. Sara Singleton in chapter 6 analyzes the critical role played by distributional conflicts in the history of the Pacific Northwest salmon fishery. By reviewing intertribal negotiations, she describes how the acceptability of an agreement depended on its (perceived) distributional consequences. Thus, despite an urgent need for a coordinated management scheme, no general scheme for solving intertribal allocation rules could be found because each proposed rule disadvantaged at least one of the user group. And some measures that benefited everyone were opposed by some groups because alternative rules would give them higher returns. Gaspart and Platteau in chapter 7 also provide a striking illustration of the importance of the redistributive impact of a given rule for its acceptability among users. They also show how collective action was more likely where more immediate returns were visible.

1.6. Some Concluding Comments

Our book is devoted almost entirely to the question of the sustainability of local commons, and the impact that inequality may have on the kinds of cooperation necessary to deter environmental degradation at the local level. Our findings suggest that the effect of inequality on environmental sustainability depends critically on the institutional setting that structures interactions among agents and the technical nature of the environmental asset in question. We find little evidence in any of our studies that poverty per se contributes to environmental degradation.

Our research provides evidence that in many settings inequality does indeed inhibit mutually beneficial approaches to the governance of the commons. Redistributive policies (like land reform or expansion of mass education) may then have important beneficial side effects on common resources that are often ignored in the literature on land reforms or education. Other studies in this book also offer a more skeptical view. In forest management in Asia, the effect of inequality, if any, is minor compared to the impact of population growth, income growth, or modernization. In general, the studies in this volume make us more aware of the complexities in the relation between inequality and collective action, and of the need for more context-specific empirical investigations into the different types of alternative mechanisms through which the relevant processes may operate.

References

Acheson, James. 1988. *The Lobster Gangs of Maine*. Hanover, N.H.: New England Universities Press.

Alesina, Alberto, Reza Baqir, and William Easterly. 1999. "Public goods and ethnic divisions." *Quarterly Journal of Economics* 114(4): 1243–84.

Alesina, Alberto, and Eliana La Ferrara. 2000. "Participation in heterogeneous communities." *Quarterly Journal of Economics* 115(3): 847–904.

Baland, Jean-Marie, and Jean-Philippe Platteau. 1996. *Halting Degradation of natural resources. Is there a role for rural communities?* Oxford, Clarendon Press.

Bowles, S., and Yong-jin Park. 2005. "Inequality, Emulation, and Work Hours: Was Thorsten Veblen Right?" *The Economic Journal* 115(507): F397–F412.

Bromley, Daniel W., and David Feeny. 1992. *Making the Commons Work: Theory, Practice, and Policy*. San Francisco: ICS Press.

Colchester, Michael. 1994. "Sustaining the forests: the community-based approach in South and South-East Asia." *Development and Change* 25(1): 69–100.

Dinan, Terry, and Diane Lim. 2000. "Who gains and who pays under carbon-allowance trading?" Washington, D.C.: Congressional Budget Office.

Olson, Mancur. 1965. *The Logic of Collective Action: Public Goods and the Theory of Groups.* Cambridge, Mass.: Harvard University Press.

Ostrom, Elinor. 1990. *Governing the Commons: The Evolution of Institutions for Collective Action.* Cambridge: Cambridge University Press.

Veblen, Thorsten. 1899/1934. *The Theory of the Leisure Class.* New York: Modern Library.

Chapter 2

COLLECTIVE ACTION ON THE COMMONS:
THE ROLE OF INEQUALITY

Jean-Marie Baland and Jean-Philippe Platteau

During the last decades, collective initiatives in matters of common-property resource management have been documented in numerous empirical studies. A theme that has received particular attention in this literature is the impact of inequality on collective-action capacities. Conclusions from these studies are far from univocal, as some studies stress the positive role of inequality while others point in the opposite direction (contrast for instance Wade 1988 with Cernea 1989). One should, however, avoid the temptation to conclude that nothing definite can then be said about the role of inequality. As a matter of fact, the relations tested differ across the available studies in terms of measurement of the crucial variables, in terms of the interpretation of the results, and in terms of the precise characteristics of the underlying environment.

Regarding the first source of ambiguity, it is obvious that inequality is not unidimensional and, therefore, it is possible that some dimensions of inequality are conducive to collective action whereas others are detrimental to it. Moreover, confusion is likely to arise if the dimension of inequality that the researcher is intending to test is in fact combined with some other dimension that does not have the same effect on collective action. To illustrate, two studies assessing the impact of inequality in income or wealth may well reach divergent conclusions because in one case, such inequality is combined with caste polarization or a rigid social polarization, while in the other case, income inequality is accompanied by a rather fluid social structure (Hayami and Kikuchi 1981). Measurement problems can also arise because the type of collective action considered is not the same. Indeed, collective action can be reflected in the willingness of group members to voluntarily contribute to the construction of a collective infrastructure, such as a drain in a watershed or a water control structure in an irrigation scheme (see, e.g., Gaspart et al. 1998), or to the conservation of a resource implying self-restraint behavior. Or, alternatively, it can take on the form of people's participation in the setting up of a regulatory agency endowed with powers to collect fees, impose contributions on members, lay down rules, and punish deviant behavior (see, e.g., McKean 1986 or Edmonds 2000). In the latter case, moreover, collective action is sometimes measured by various management actions (existence of management rules, of sanctioning and monitoring activities, incidence of rule-breaking, etc.), sometimes by their impact on efficiency in the use of the managed resource (as measured, for instance, by the rate of deforestation, the progression of sand dunes, the size and maturity of the fish caught), and sometimes by both.

An important source of interpretative ambiguity arises when authors infer that inequality is conducive to collective action because they find that richer users bear a larger share of the costs involved. As we shall argue below, while an increase in inequality may well enhance the incentives of the rich users to contribute more to collective action, such increase may simultaneously reduce the incentives of the poor. As a result, one cannot be sure that increased participation of the rich users will better contribute to the efficient management of a resource than a situation in which there is a more balanced pattern of contributions by both the rich and the poor (see Baland and Platteau 1999, and the chapter by Bardhan, Ghatak, and Karaivanov in the present volume).

Moreover, most studies focusing on "inequality and collective action" stress the causal mechanisms through which inequality has an impact on collective action. The literature is, however, subject to biases and misinterpretations as researchers often are not careful enough to properly control for the impact of a number of endogenous variables, such as the level of income, which themselves depend on collective action. Reverse causations, say from collective action to the level and distribution of income, cannot be excluded, and an appropriate methodology is therefore necessary.

Lastly, most empirical studies about collective management of common-property resources implicitly refer to a unitary model of the commons, the archetype of which is the grazing problem depicted by Hardin. This is misleading, however, insofar as collective-action outcomes depend on the incentive structure available to the users and the type of interactions among them, which are themselves determined by the characteristics of the resource and the technology used. In particular, it is essential to distinguish between situations in which agents have a predetermined stake in the commons and those in which such stakes are the result of a voluntary decision.

In the following, we consider the impact of inequality in wealth or income abstracting from other forms of inequality that might possibly accompany it. Attention is deliberately focused on two central issues mentioned above, that is, the necessity to distinguish between various models of the commons on the one hand, and between voluntary contributions and participation in a regulatory structure, on the other.[1] These two issues will be examined successively in sections 1 and 2.

2.1. MODELING THE COMMONS

Since in reality a wide variety of common-property situations exist, it is impossible to account for all of them in terms of a unique analytical model. Two main models will be considered below. The first, labeled the common-good model, examines a situation where users share the benefits from joint exploitation of a common-property resource in proportion to their share or stake in it, which is predetermined. In the second type of model, users benefit from the commons in direct proportion to the relative amounts of their appropriation efforts which they freely decide. We refer to this case as the appropriation model.

2.1.1. The Common-Good Model

In the common-good model, due to different endowments in the relevant asset, agents draw unequal benefits from the common resource or the public good produced. Think of the harvesting of immature fish by means of small mesh nets in a common fishery, or the building and maintenance of anti-erosive barriers in a hilly area, or the collective-maintenance of irrigation channels. In all these situations, the benefits of the "public good" provided are not enjoyed by all agents in the same proportion. For instance, it is the fisherman with the largest fleet, and therefore the largest share in total fish catches, who benefits most from the protection of juveniles through the adoption of appropriate mesh sizes.

In these circumstances, a public good is produced (or a public bad avoided) with the help of the voluntary and decentralized contributions by individual users. The latter benefit from the public good in proportion to their share or "interest" in the good (which is called common good in what follows). This share is often directly related to their ownership of the relevant factors of production. Thus, in the case of a fishery composed of n fishermen, the share of fisherman i, s_i, can be thought of as being equal to the number of boats he owns, B_i, in proportion to the total number of boats in the fishery, if we assume that only one type of boat technology is available. Similarly, the share of peasant i in the collective irrigation system, s_i, is (at least for the sake of many of the relevant issues) equal to the ratio of his landholdings to the total service area operated under this system. The question considered here is thus, given his predetermined share, s_i, how much agent i contributes to the common good.

Consider first a situation under which agents maximize their profits, Π_i, by contributing an amount, g_i, to the production of a common good, $G(\Sigma g_j)$. Profits to agent i are then equal to the difference between his gross benefit, proportional to his share, and the cost of contributing:

$$\max \Pi_i = s_i G(\Sigma g_j) - g_i \qquad with \qquad g_i \geq 0$$

By maximizing profits, each agent equalizes the marginal benefit to himself of the amount he contributes to his marginal cost, which is here constant, equal to 1 (and identical across all agents). But the agent with the largest marginal benefit is the one with the largest share, and that agent is the most incited to contribute. As a result, the Nash equilibrium is such that only the largest user contributes: given the contribution made by the largest user, the individual marginal benefit to all other users is necessarily smaller, as they all have smaller shares, but they all face the same marginal cost, equal to one. As the marginal cost then exceeds their marginal benefit, they decide to contribute nothing (if they could do so, they would even contribute negative amounts). But, if all smaller agents decide not to contribute anything, the largest one has no other choice than to contribute the amount he would have picked up if he were alone. As no agent has an incentive to change, this situation is a Nash equilibrium. The largest user contributes alone to the common good, and all other users choose to free-ride (see Baland and Platteau 1997b: 458–61). As is well known, this situation is inefficient as the public good is underprovided. This is because the large user adjusts his own contribution so as to equate the marginal cost to contribute, 1, to his own marginal benefit, thereby neglecting the positive effects of this contribution on all other users.

In this type of case, the nature of the equilibrium is such that, by transferring shares from the noncontributing to the contributing agent, the level of the common good provided is increased. In other words, the common good is more efficiently produced when inequality is deepened. In conformity with Olson's (1965) well-known conclusion, the largest and most efficient voluntary provision of the common good obtains when all the shares are concentrated in the hands of a single agent.

The use of a simple profit function as the objective pursued by the agents implies that income effects are ruled out and the distribution of income, y_i, is irrelevant. This is no more true if we instead consider that the common good and the individual contribution enter into the objective function in a nonadditive way. This assumption is more adequate to analyze situations in which the amounts contributed cannot be freely bought and sold on a (perfect) market, for instance, if contributions are made in terms of hours of work, and the labor market is imperfect.[2] Suppose then that agents maximize the following objective function:

$$U = U(y_i - g_i, s_i G(\Sigma g_j))$$

We assume that the common good is a strictly normal good, and that the production technology for the common good, $G(.)$, is a normal production function (increasing and concave). In fact, the model is then very close to a pure public-good model, with G being the amount of public good produced, and the difference of shares between two agents being taken to reflect a difference in preferences. The first term in the utility function, $y_i - g_i$, represents expenditures on all other goods, once the contribution, g_i, has been substracted from the original income, y_i.

First consider the effects of changes in the distribution of income, y_i. In this case, one can directly apply the results from the public-good literature. First, it can be shown that, when agents voluntarily contribute to the production of a public good, the (inefficient) amount produced is independent of the extent of inequality among contributing users (Bergstrom, Blume, and Varian in their seminal paper 1986). In other words, the distribution of income between contributing agents is irrelevant. (The intuition behind this apparently paradoxical result, known as the *neutrality result*, is given in the next chapter of this book.) Moreover, when some agents choose not to contribute, a transfer from noncontributors to contributors will increase the level of the public good produced, provided it is a normal good (a good the desired consumption of which increases with income). In the same logic, any change in the distribution of income that increases the aggregate wealth of the contributing agents increases the equilibrium amount of public good provided (see proposition 4 in Bergstrom et al. 1986).[3]

Let us now turn to the more relevant problem of the impact of the distribution of shares, s_i. (Indeed, it is to that type of asset inequality that most empirical work is related.) Assume that agents differ only in their shares in the common good (while they have the same preferences and face the same constraints). In this setting, individual contributions at equilibrium will always be higher for agents with larger shares and it is of course possible that the poorest users make no contribution at all. Not surprising, therefore, is the oft-observed result in the empirical literature that richer users (big landowners, fishermen owning many boats and nets, etc.) contribute significantly more than poorer ones to the management of common-property resources or to the construction and maintenance of collective infrastructures.

In the same setting, a disequalizing transfer of shares from someone who does not contribute to another who contributes increases the overall provision of the public good. From here, it is tempting to infer that greater inequality is more conducive to collective action. This is not a correct inference because the impact of transfers between contributors is in fact ambiguous. It will actually depend on whether the increased contribution by the winning agent outweighs the reduction by the losing agent. One may easily construct examples such that, starting from an equal distribution of shares where everyone contributes, inequality first prompts the smaller users to stop cooperating, thereby leading to a fall in the amount of common good provided. Higher inequality, by transferring shares from noncontributing to contributing agents, will then increase the production of the common good. A U-shape relationship between inequality and the provision of common good can thus be expected (see for instance Dayton-Johnson and Bardhan 2001). Olson's conjecture holds, however, and the largest level of the common good is still provided when one agent concentrates all the shares.

In their analysis of irrigation systems in Mexico and South India presented in chapter 5, Bardhan and Dayton-Johnson find some evidence of a U-shape relationship between landholding inequality (that can be interpreted as inequality of shares in a common good) and voluntary provision to the common good, such as the maintenance of the collective channels.[4] Their evidence also supports the idea that inequality induces larger agents to support a bigger share of the collective costs in conformity with the prediction of the model (see also Tang 1991; Dayton-Johnson 1998; and Bardhan 2000).

We have so far assumed that the unit price of the voluntary contributions is uniform across all agents: one unit contributed costs one unit of income. In many realistic settings, the unit cost of contribution is nevertheless variable. Thus, when contributions take on the form of labor time spent in the production or maintenance of the common good, one expects them to be costlier for the rich since the opportunity cost of their time is higher. Under such conditions, one can no more be sure that the larger users will contribute more than the poorer users to the production of the common good. If the distribution of shares, s_i, is correlated with that of the opportunity costs of time, the two effects run in opposite directions: larger shares provide more incentives to participate in the collective undertaking, while a higher opportunity cost of time discourages such participation.[5]

Labor inputs are not the only possible form of contributions, though. When contributions can be made in cash, the expectation is that agents with a higher opportunity cost of time will prefer this form of contribution. It is revealing that cash contributions are usually propounded by richer users, while labor contributions are the preferred option of the poor. Also revealing is the fact that in many schemes, richer users are allowed to send wage laborers in their place to contribute to the collective undertaking. When the type of contributions is thus left free, the effect on participation of differential costs of contributing is neutralized (see Sengupta 1991).

In the foregoing discussion of the common-good model, we assumed that contributors do not derive benefits from their own individual contributions as such, but only through their impact on the common good. This assumption is relaxed in chapter 3 of this book, in which Bardhan, Ghatak, and Karaivanov investigate its implication in detail. By allowing private benefits to depend not only on the level of the common good and private endowments (or share), but also on the contribution made by the agent, they show that the neutrality result fails to hold, in the sense that equality among contributors, as well as between noncontributors, increases efficiency, while some inequality between contributors and noncontributors is desirable.

We have also assumed the absence of nonconvexities since the production function transforming the aggregated individual contributions into the common good is smooth, increasing, and concave. Yet, there exist a number of situations related to common-property resources where technology displays a nonconvexity such as a threshold phenomenon,[6] for instance because of setup costs in the building of a common infrastructure, or because of a minimum threshold level beyond which the resource cannot reproduce itself and therefore disappears. Consider the following example. Agents decide voluntarily to contribute an amount g_i to the building of a common infrastructure such that aggregate contributions must reach a critical level for the public good to yield any benefit: $G(\sum_i g_i) = 1$ if $\sum_i g_i$ is greater or equal to a constant C, and $G = 0$ otherwise.

If no share in the benefits of the common good is large enough for an agent to have the incentive to produce alone $(s_i < C)$, there is a Nash equilibrium under which no agent contributes: no one starts contributing because no other user is contributing, making the marginal value of one's own contribution equal to zero. Simultaneously, if enough agents contribute something, another agent might be induced to provide the necessary contribution so as to reach the critical level required. There are thus many potential equilibria, but there are two generic outcomes: whereas in one type of equilibrium nothing is produced, in the other a subset of agents contribute so as to cover the setup cost. This type of situation is known as a *coordination problem*: if agents could easily coordinate their contributions, the common good would always be provided. It is therefore evident that nonconvexities give rise to more complex possibilities than those yielded by the simple representation of free-riding behavior by the Prisoner's Dilemma. Moreover, as only a limited number of contributions are needed, there is in fact a continuum of Nash equilibria under which the common good is produced, where some agents may contribute more or less depending on the others' contributions. Whereas it is true that agents with larger shares will tend to appear more frequently in the possible equilibria, and that their equilibrium contributions will on average be more important, no further precise prediction can be inferred from this setting (see Gaspart et al. 1998). In particular, one can easily construct examples of equilibria in which only the smallest agents contribute to the public good. Also, given the multiplicity of equilibria, it is hard to obtain meaningful comparative statics results.

2.1.2. The Appropriation Model

In many situations, agents jointly exploit a common-property resource by individually choosing their individual level of harvesting. Villagers thus decide the number of hours they spend in the forest gathering fuelwood, fishermen decide the number of boats they operate in a common fishery, or, to refer to Hardin's (1968) celebrated example, herders decide on the number of animals to let graze on the common pasture. In all these situations, the level of harvesting effort decided by an individual agent has an impact not only on the collective level of exploitation of the resource, but also on his share in collective harvest which is usually directly proportional to his effort level. Shares are therefore endogenous and no more predetermined.

To get a vivid idea of the problem, consider a fishery in which a fixed number of fishermen (say, four people) freely decide the number of boats to put out at sea. Each of them has free access to the fishing ground. A fisherman's choice typically will be based on a comparison between the price of entry which he has to bear (say, the rental price of fishing gear) and his expected income. As long as the net expected benefit on his own gear is positive, he decides to put in an additional unit of fishing effort. As long as average productivity increases, there is in fact no problem as, by adding an additional fishing unit, he increases the return on existing gears, and everyone is better off. The problem comes in the decreasing phase of the average returns, when the addition of a new boat imposes a negative externality on the operating fishing units because it reduces the amount of fish caught by each of them. Total net income, or profit, is defined as the difference between the value of aggregate catches and the total operating costs obtained by multiplying the number of boats and their unit price assumed to be equal to one. The relationship between the total number of boats, total output, total profits,

TABLE 2.1
Relationship between Total Level of Appropriation Efforts and Total Profit on a CPR with Decreasing Returns

Number of Boats	1	2	3	4	5	6	7	8	9	10	11
Total output	2.00	8.00	12.00	15.00	17.00	17.50	17.60	17.10	16.30	15.50	11.55
Total profits	1.00	6.00	9.00	11.00	12.00	11.50	10.60	9.00	7.30	5.50	0.55
Profit per boat	1.00	3.00	3.00	2.75	2.40	1.92	1.51	1.12	0.81	0.55	0.05

and average profits per boat, as considered in our hypothetical example, is given in table 2.1.

Given the technology described in the table, the game has a unique Nash equilibrium (2,2,3,3) in which 2 fishermen put out 2 boats each while the other 2 put out 3 boats. Consider a fisherman with 2 boats. Given that the 3 other fishermen operate 8 boats in total, he earns a net income of 0.55 on each of his boats, yielding a total income of 1.10. Putting 1 more boat would reduce the average income per boat from 0.55 to 0.05, so that his total income would fall to 0.15. On the other hand, if he puts out only 1 boat, he would get an income of 0.81. He therefore decides to put out 2 boats, which bring him more income than any other alternative. The same reasoning can be made for the 3 other fishermen, and the conclusion is reached that no one has any interest to change his number of boats. As a result, (2,2,3,3) is a Nash equilibrium.

It is a unique equilibrium. For instance, (4,2,2,2), which also totals 10 boats, is not an equilibrium as the fisherman operating 4 boats earns $4 \times 0.55 = 2.2$ units of income, while by reducing his fleet to 3 boats, he would be better off, as he would then earn $3 \times 0.81 = 2.43$ units of income. This cannot therefore be a Nash equilibrium: given what the others do, the big fisherman has an incentive to change his decision.

It is clear that the total number of boats thus operated in the fishery (10) is in excess of the social optimum, which requires that only 5 boats be used to maximize aggregate profits. This is the number of boats that a well-managed fishing cooperative would choose, or that an individual fisherman would choose if he was alone in the fishery. The problem is that, with more than one decision-maker and in the absence of contracts and long-term commitments, no one, individually, has any interest to deviate from his Nash equilibrium decision.

Let us now introduce inequality among the different fishermen. For instance, consider an external constraint—say, a credit constraint—that

TABLE 2.2
Impact of Heterogeneity on the Total Amount and the Distribution
of Appropriation Efforts When Increased Efforts Are Impossible

Distribution of Credit Constraints	Gini Index of the Distribution of Credit Constraints	Equilibrium Allocation of Boats	Index of Efficiency in the Final Allocation (%)	Income of the Poorest Fisherman
1 1 1 7	0.45	1 1 1 4	88.00	1.51
1 1 2 6	0.40	1 1 2 3	88.00	1.51
1 1 3 5	0.35	1 1 3 3	75.00	1.12
1 1 4 4	0.30	1 1 3 3	75.00	1.12
1 2 2 5	0.30	1 2 2 3	75.00	0.81
1 2 3 4	0.25	1 2 3 3	58.00	0.85
2 2 2 4	0.15	2 2 2 3	58.00	1.10
2 2 3 3	0.10	2 2 3 3	45.00	1.10

has the effect of limiting the number of boats which some fishermen can own. The question is whether such a constraint is susceptible to reducing the extent of overexploitation of the fishery by altering the distribution of access rights.

Typically, rationing on the credit market deprives a number of operators of the funds necessary to acquire as many boats as they would like. In table 2.2, the first column shows all the possible configurations of a constrained access by fishermen to boat ownership, under the assumption that the total credit available allows the financing of at most 10 boats. For example, (1,1,1,7) means that 3 fishermen can buy only 1 boat, while the last one can buy up to 7 boats. The second column gives the respective values of the Gini coefficients pertaining to all possible distributions of the credit constraints. The resulting Nash equilibria of the instantaneous game where, given his credit constraint, each fisherman has to choose the number of boats to operate are described in the third column. These equilibria are computed in the same way as indicated above with respect to table 2.1. Thus, in the situation where the credit constraint is (1,1,1,7), the Nash equilibrium is such that the large fisherman chooses to operate 4 boats, given that the 3 others operate 1 boat each: indeed, if he would choose 3 boats instead, he would earn 5.76 units of income (3 × 1.92), which is smaller than the 6.04 units of income he earns by operating 4 boats (4 × 1.51). Clearly, if the larger user chooses 4 boats, a small fisherman prefers to put in 1 boat to operating none. As a result, with (1,1,1,4) boats in operation, no fisherman has an interest to change his decision and what we have is therefore a Nash equilibrium. What is shown in the last column is an efficiency index of the Nash equilibria: it is calculated as the ratio of the total net income obtained in the final situations to the (first-best) optimum.

The striking feature that emerges from table 2.2 is the following: given the users' inability to reach a binding agreement together, the most desirable situations obtain when the distributions of credit constraints are the most skewed. In these cases, indeed, the value of the efficiency index works out to be 88 percent, which means that maximum inequality leads to an outcome that is remarkably close to the optimum. This represents a significant improvement, since the value of this index in the unconstrained Nash equilibrium (2,2,3,3) is as low as 45 percent. Furthermore, a comparison of the second and fourth columns reveals that there is a perfect rank correlation between the measure of efficiency in the equilibrium situations and the skewness of the distribution of credit constraints (as measured by the Gini coefficient). This is because users with larger credit endowments have a strong incentive to exercise self-restraint and to leave part of their credit capacity unused. Such an outcome follows from the fact that smaller users, bound by their credit constraints, cannot increase their rates of use of the fishery by multiplying their boats.

Equally noticeable is the fact that the poorest fishermen earn a higher income in the most inequitable situation (1.51) than in the most equitable one (2×0.55) although they operate fewer boats. Rather paradoxically, therefore, constraints or factor market imperfections that limit the access of some users to capital or other critical inputs may thus allow inequitable distributions of endowments to increase the incomes of the most constrained users.

A wide array of constraints actually exist that can yield the above effect. The administrative distribution of harvesting licenses by a central authority provides an interesting application of our central argument. Indeed, if the state distributes the available licenses in an unequal way among the operating fishermen, it would create a situation in which the bigger license-holders have an incentive not to use all their licenses, which can even lead to an improvement of the incomes of the small license-holders.

The above argument can be generalized as follows. Consider n agents who jointly exploit a common-property resource and share their benefits in direct proportion to the relative amount of appropriation efforts they have chosen to put in. Let g_i stand for the appropriation effort of agent i. Total output can then be written as:

$$G = G\left(\sum_i g_i\right)$$

where $G'' < 0$ and G' is first positive, then negative. For the sake of simplicity, we assume that the cost per unit of effort is constant and equal to 1, so that the profit accruing to agent i can be written as:

$$\Pi_i = \left(g_i \Big/ \left(\sum_{j=1}^{n} g_j \right) \right) G \left(\sum_j g_j \right) - g_i = s_i G - g_i$$

In a Nash equilibrium, each agent maximizes his profit by choosing his own level of effort, taking the level of effort provided by others as given. Raising the level of effort has two separate effects on profit: it may increase (or reduce) the aggregate output to be shared by all users, and it increases the individual's share in aggregate output. This is expressed in the first-order condition for profit maximization:

$$\frac{\partial \Pi_i}{\partial g_i} = \frac{\partial s_i}{\partial g_i} G + s_i \frac{\partial G}{\partial g_i} - 1$$

$$= \left(\sum_{k \neq i} g_k \Big/ \left(\sum_{j=1}^{n} g_j \right)^2 \right) G \left(\sum_j g_j \right)$$

$$+ \left(g_i \Big/ \sum_j g_j \right) \left(G' \left(\sum_j g_j \right) \right) - 1 = 0$$

In the above equation, the first term is always positive: by increasing his level of effort, an agent always increases his share (which actually corresponds to the ratio of his effort to total effort). The second term can be positive or negative and represents the increase (decrease) in total output that is generated by the additional unit of effort, agent i receiving a share $\left(\dfrac{g_i}{\sum_j g_j} \right)$ of this increase (decrease). The last term, 1, is the marginal cost of an additional unit of effort. The above expression summarizes well the problem for an individual user: by adding 1 unit of effort, he increases his costs, he increases or decreases total output, and he increases his share in total output. The social optimum would require that the marginal benefit to all users is equal to the cost, implying that $\dfrac{\partial G}{\partial g_i} - 1 = 0$. In the Nash equilibrium, the level of exploitation of the common resource is inefficiently high. This is because the "share effect" always dominates, so that at the efficient point where marginal productivity is equal to marginal cost, agents have an incentive to increase their effort level since it increases their share in aggregate output. More formally, rearranging terms in the above expression, one gets:

$$
\frac{\partial \Pi_i}{\partial g_i} = \left(\sum_{k \neq i} g_k \Bigg/ \left(\sum_{j=1}^{n} g_j \right)^2 \right) G \left(\sum_j g_j \right)
$$

$$
- \left(\sum_{k \neq i} g_k \Bigg/ \sum_j g_j \right) \left(G' \left(\sum_j g_j \right) \right) + \left(G' \left(\sum_j g_j \right) \right) - 1 = 0
$$

$$
= \left(\sum_{k \neq i} g_k \Bigg/ \sum_j g_j \right) \left(\frac{G\left(\sum_j g_j \right)}{\sum_{j=1}^{n} g_j} - G'\left(\sum_j g_j \right) \right)
$$

$$
+ G'\left(\sum_j g_j \right) - 1 = 0
$$

Because of concavity, the average is always greater than the marginal, which implies that the first term above is positive. Hence, the second term is negative, which implies that at the Nash equilibrium agents set the total amount of effort in such a way that its marginal productivity is below marginal cost.[7]

Consider the situation under which the distribution of wealth translates into a distribution of the maximal amount of effort that an agent can choose.[8] While the constraint is not binding for wealthier agents in the choice of their effort level, it is binding for poorer ones. Consider a disequalizing transfer from (i) an agent who was previously unconstrained and is now constrained, or (ii) from an agent who was previously constrained. Such a transfer has the effect of reducing the aggregate level of effort, thereby making the use of the common-property resource more efficient.

Suppose that the transfers benefited an unconstrained agent.[9] The constrained user, who lost from the transfer, reduces his own level of effort (by an amount equal to the change in his constraint). The question is then whether, after the transfer, the benefiting user will increase his effort level enough to make the aggregate level unchanged. The answer is no, and the intuition behind this result is that the benefiting user now has a larger share, and thus better internalizes the negative impact of his over-fishing (or, loosely speaking, his behavior is now closer to an optimal one).

More formally, if the aggregate level of effort remains constant, the derivative of the profit function given above for the benefiting user is negative. Hence, the post-transfer level of effort chosen by this agent will never be such that the aggregate level (increases or) remains constant. As can be checked from the F.O.C. above, he does increase his level of effort (i.e., efforts by the agents are strategic substitutes in this model), but this increase is smaller than the reduction in the effort levels of the losing agent. It also should be noted that, in some circumstances,[10] a disequalizing change in the distribution of wealth may have such an impact on the aggregate level of effort that the welfare of all users is increased.

By using the profit function above as describing the objective of the agents, we have assumed that individual benefits are linear in the quantities harvested, as though they could be freely sold on the market. However, in some important instances, such as the collection of firewood in the common forest, or of water in the common well, the resource is usually harvested for the exclusive purpose of self-consumption. In such instances, the individual benefits derived from the use of the resource are not linear in the quantities used. To analyze this issue, let us first maintain the assumption that the cost of harvesting the resource is constant in monetary terms and equal to 1. The amounts of, say, firewood harvested from the common forest directly enter into the agent's utility function as a consumption good:

$$U = U(y_i - g_i, f_i)$$

where y_i represents agent i's income (so that $y_i - g_i$ represents the expenditures on other goods), and f_i is the amount of firewood harvested (and consumed):

$$f_i = \left(g_i \middle/ \left(\sum_{j=1}^{n} g_j \right) \right) G\left(\sum_j g_j \right)$$

We assume that firewood is a normal good (its demand increases with income because it is presumably complementary to the amount of food consumed, and it is also used for heating). Transferring income from agent i to agent j, where $y_j > y_i$, increases firewood consumption of agent j but reduces that of agent i. Whether or not it increases the total amount of firewood harvested and consumed depends on whether firewood consumption is a convex or a concave function of income, that is, whether firewood is a luxury good or not. If it is a luxury good, the marginal propensity to spend on firewood is higher for higher income classes, and greater inequality in income increases the aggregate amount of firewood harvested. By contrast, if firewood is not a luxury good, a more equal distribution is associated with a higher aggregate level of firewood consumption.

However, by assuming that the cost of collecting firewood is constant, we fail to capture another important mechanism through which inequality impacts on the use of the commons. Indeed, if we consider that agents differ in their wage rates, so that y_i now represents the wage rate of agent i (his time endowment equals 1) and hence the opportunity cost of the amount of time g_i spent in the forest collecting firewood, the income available to spend on other goods is now equal to $y_i(1 - g_i)$.

An increase in agent i's wage rate has two effects: an income effect through which it causes his propensity to consume and, therefore, to collect firewood to rise, and a substitution effect, since firewood is more expensive due to the higher value of the time needed to collect it. The net impact on the amount of firewood collected and the time spent in the forest collecting it are therefore indeterminate. As a result, depending on the relative strength of these two effects, poverty may or may not lead to a higher level of appropriation in the commons. The effect is theoretically ambiguous.[11]

Since no clear relationship can be established between wage rates and collection levels, the aggregate impact of transfers between agents is ambiguous, and a fortiori so. As the study by Baland et al. presented in chapter 10 shows in the case of firewood collection in rural Nepal, the income effect may dominate at the individual level, so that richer households tend to collect more firewood. Whether or not higher equality would lead to higher aggregate levels of collection or not depends once again on the concavity of the relationship between collection and income.

2.1.3. Some Limits of the Analysis

It bears noting that we have so far limited our attention to a very simple setting which allowed us to focus on well-defined causal mechanisms, while not necessarily doing justice to the complexity of some situations. Thus, in more realistic situations, games may well be interlinked, in the sense that what happens between two agents in one situation has an impact on the interaction process in other situations. Interlinked games are more likely to arise in small village communities in which people are related through dense and multiplex relationships. In such circumstances, defection in one sphere of social or economic life is punishable in other spheres, which makes "cooperative" outcomes more likely to be established.

Two chapters in this book follow alternative approaches to deal with the potentially complex nature of the relationships between users on the commons. In chapter 4, Janssen and Ostrom propose a methodology based on neural networks to model complex interactions between agents. While still exploratory, their results tend to show that heterogeneity, in the sense of agents carrying different symbols, might undermine trust and lower the likelihood of successful collective action.

In another alternative approach, Cardenas carried out a fascinating series of experiments in rural communities of Colombia (see chapter 8 of this book). He invited groups of villagers to play a given number of rounds of an appropriation game, where each participant had to choose his own level of appropriation. Interestingly, while payoffs and game structures were identical across all groups, his results suggest that the actual outcome of the game depends on the level of inequality between the participants. More precisely, wealth inequality undermined cooperation even when face-to-face communication was allowed. This runs counter to the theoretical prediction that generalized defection should be observed in all groups. As is often the case with experimental evidence, the work of Cardenas tends to cast doubt on the ability of simple game-theoretical analyses to explain all aspects of collective action. It thus points to the need of other approaches in order to improve our understanding of the determinants of human behavior.

2.2. REGULATING THE COMMONS

2.2.1. Wealth Inequality and the Formation of a Regulatory Authority

In the previous section, agents interacted in a completely decentralized manner. In numerous field situations, however, there often exists a local authority charged with laying down and enforcing rules for the use of the CPRs (for more details, see Baland and Platteau 1996; chap. 12). The question then immediately arises as to how the cost of collective regulation, that is, the cost of initiating and performing regulatory tasks, is borne within the group of users.

The logic of the argument here is the same as that underlying our discussion of nonconvexities. Indeed, in most instances, the creation of a regulatory authority can be interpreted as a public or common good for which costs have to be incurred. These costs partly consist of the time and other resources devoted to collectively organize regulation and to ensure its proper implementation (mobilization of users, monitoring and sanctioning activities, dispute settlements, rule revision, etc.). Moreover, for collective action to succeed, a minimum aggregate amount of effort must be put in, lest individual efforts should be spent in vain. Benefits from such action can be thought of as increasing with intensity of use of the resource, which is itself related to wealth endowment. Therefore, the incentives to bear the above costs can be considered as rising with wealth. Inequality may thus play a useful role by giving better-endowed members sufficient incentives to incur the costs involved (see also Bardhan 1993: 638).

There is abundant evidence to support the hypothesis that the costs of initiating collective action are largely borne by the economic elite. Thus, in his in-depth study of irrigation systems in South Indian villages, Wade cogently argues that the effectiveness of a local irrigation council "depends on its councillors all having a substantial private interest in seeing that it works, and that interest is greater the larger a person's landholding" (Wade 1987: 230). The claims that big landowners can make "are sufficiently large for some of them to be motivated to pay a major share of the organisational costs" (Wade 1988: 190). To give another example, in Ha Nchele, a lowland village in Lesotho, rotational grazing has been successfully introduced on village grazing lands as an alternative to taking animals to a cattle post in the mountains, mainly because the village chief held the greatest number of livestock, and thereby took a predominant part in the development of the project (Swallow and Bromley 1995); in the same vein, see Braverman et al. (1991), Laitos (1986), Garcia-Barrios and Garcia-Barrios (1990), Menzies (1994), Heckathorn (1993), Peters (1994), and Gaspart and Platteau (chapter 7 in this book).

As has already been emphasized in another context, the fact that better endowed agents tend to be more involved in the collective action process does not imply that increased wealth inequality necessarily increases the likelihood of successful emergence of regulatory mechanisms. It indeed narrowly depends on the political or social "technology" of collective action. For example, if the starting of regulation requires the personal commitment of a single individual user (or of a few of them), it is crucial for the success of collective action that this (these) user(s) can internalize a sufficiently large share of the expected benefits.

Conversely, if the active support of all users is socially needed, reduced incentives for the smaller users to participate may undermine regulation. Interestingly, many empirical studies document cases in which collective action fails because some users are so small or attach so little weight to their resource endowment that they have no real stake in participating in it. Defecting users are often wealthy agents who enjoy access to rewarding alternative opportunities (Zufferey 1986). Their lack of interest in the commons has serious consequences insofar as they do not, or do not any more, perform their expected leadership role required to coordinate collective action among all users.

A remarkable illustration of this possibility concerns the arid areas of Western Rajasthan. Before independence, communal grazing lands used to be under the effective control of big landlords known as *jagirdars*. By virtue of their dominating position, they could appropriate a large share of the benefits accruing from the exploitation of the common-property resources (the best pastures were indeed earmarked for the animals owned by them). It is therefore not surprising that they took upon themselves the task of deciding and implementing "conservation measures which ensured considerable stability to these resources" (Shanmugaratnam 1996: 172). Such measures had the effect of conserving perennial grass species and trees and of allowing effective rotational grazing thanks to proper maintenance of water points (Jodha 1987, 1989).

After independence, following a land reform that resulted in the privatization of a large part of the village grazing areas and in the dissolution of the *jagirdari* rule and its replacement by the *panchayat* system, collective maintenance of the commons was discontinued. Degradation followed as evidenced by poor growth of grass, spread of sand dunes, and death of trees. The problem is that in the new circumstances the biggest landowners are able to produce a large part of their fodder needs on their private land (crop residues are privatized since farms are opened after harvest only after the owner's livestock has grazed the bulk of the crop residues) and have the wherewithal to buy from the market the supplementary feed needed. Given their high degree of self-sufficiency in fodder, they tend to be uninterested in the management of the remaining common. In contrast, poorer farm owners depend greatly on these commons for access to fodder yet prove unable to coordinate their actions so as to prevent resource degradation (Gupta 1986: 312; Shanmugaratnam 1996: 173–8).

Wealthier users can not only refrain from participating in resource-preserving collective actions, but they may also attempt to undermine such actions in order to further their own private interests. In Mali, for example, the emergence of absentee herd owners with outside economic opportunities appears to be a major stumbling block on the way toward pastoral institution-building for sustainable rangeland management. This was a result of the great Sahelian droughts in the seventies when pastoralists were forced to sell their livestock to farmers or, more generally, to wealthier town-dwellers like traders and civil servants. According to a recent evaluation study of the Mopti Area Development Project, "Absentee herd owners favour open access rangelands so that their herds can graze anywhere. They may even use their political influence to prevent pastoral associations receiving legally defensible land rights" (Shanmugaratnam et al. 1992: 20).

2.2.2. Regulation through Transfers, Quotas, and Taxes

The impact of inequality on collective regulation has been little discussed in the literature on appropriation. There are, however, a number of argu-

28 BALAND AND PLATTEAU

ments to support the view that wealth or skills inequality between users makes regulation less efficient.

First, the economic elite may decide to participate with a view to influencing the collective action in a direction suitable to their private interests. This argument is at the heart of the power-weighted social decision rule discussed by Boyce, in chapter 12. In their analysis of sugar cooperatives in Maharashtra, Banerjee et al. (2001) show how the weight of wealthy and influential users in collective decision-making tends to distort collective regulation toward their interest, at the cost of efficiency. Their empirical estimates show that distortions (and inefficiency) in collective regulation tend to be highest when inequality is large among users. Sharing of costs is specially asymmetrical when a group of low social status which hardly benefits from the village commons is required to bear costs in the same manner as those who draw sizeable gains from the resource use. Thus, for example, in the irrigation system of the Ziz Valley located to the south of the eastern High Atlas mountains (Morocco), there prevails the rule that the Haratine, a group of people of dark complexion and subservient status, must participate in the operation and maintenance of the irrigation infrastructure of the village even though they do not own any land. Moreover, "they are denied the right of use of wild grass and forbs patches found on the banks of the river canals as well as on field boundaries" (Ilahiane 2001: 106). As for others, the rule provides that in normal times the labor provided by each holder is a function of his holdings except for religious authorities who are exempt from manual work on the grounds of their divine power (ibid.).

In their study of irrigation schemes in Mexico and India, Bardhan and Dayton-Johnson (see chapter 5 of this book) find that higher inequality is strongly associated with proportional water allocation and equal division of costs which directly favors large landowners. Interestingly, in the same study, they also find that, in South Indian irrigation schemes, maintenance is lower where many farmers believe that the rules have been crafted by the local elite. Relatedly, in her study of forest management decentralization in Nepal and India (see chapter 11 of this book), Agarwal argues that men, by dominating the local forestry councils, adopt forest management schemes that directly hurt the interest of women in the village.

This discussion allows us to provide an alternative motivation for the economic elite to bear the costs of collective action. Indeed, as the elite usually consists of agents for whom the benefits of collective action are potentially the most important, they often involve themselves actively in the setting of collective management schemes with a view to tipping the balance in their favor. Smaller agents basically have less to lose, even if the regulation is detrimental to them, than larger users. This prompts the latter to initiate processes of collective action, anticipating that they can influence the regulatory scheme to increase their own individual benefits at the expense of the smaller, and less involved, users.

Second, in the presence of inequality, regulation is more difficult to design and implement because regulatory instruments are imperfect[12] and often limited to uniform quotas, or constant tax rates (see Baland and Platteau 1998a; Kanbur 1992). The problem with such instruments is that they cannot be tailored to the particular situation of each user, and must be calibrated for average characteristics. Consequently, the second-best regulated outcome tends to deviate all the more from the first-best (with individual-specific regulation) solution as resource users are more heterogeneous. Absent compensatory transfer schemes, it is also more likely that some of the users will be hurt by the regulation proposed. Therefore, if we require the regulated solution to Pareto-dominate the ex ante unregulated situation, the Pareto-dominating regulation tends to be all the less efficient as inequality or heterogeneity is greater among users.

In her case study of salmon fisheries management on the Pacific coast of the United States, Sara Singleton (see chapter 6 of this book) offers a vivid illustration of this issue. As she convincingly argues, the lack of flexibility in the set of rules considered and the need for a consensus among all tribes undermined all efforts toward establishing a joint management scheme. It is precisely because of the expected distributional impact of the various measures (mostly quotas) that were proposed and discussed, that, for the past twenty years, fishing tribes have not been able to agree on a set of rules. To solve their most urgent problems, tribes are therefore compelled to resort to ad hoc and day-to-day measures.

That the regulated outcome may not be efficient is an important conclusion that invites us to critically assess field experiences with resource management schemes. Such a step is all the more necessary as there is a general tendency in the empirical literature to confuse the means with the end by inferring from the simple existence of regulatory instruments that the resource concerned is properly managed or conserved. Field enquiries typically focus on the question of whether rules have been laid out and whether they are effectively enforced (what are the detection and monitoring methods used, what is the incidence of rule violation, etc.). For example, studies dealing with forestry or irrigation schemes have a tendency to describe in considerable detail the various rules established by a user community to regulate access to the forest or water as well as the monitoring and sanction systems created toward the purpose of enforcing them (see Ostrom 1990, 1992; and Baland and Platteau 1996). An effort is then generally undertaken to identify the characteristics of the user communities relatively successful in devising and applying membership or use rules as though these rules were necessarily conducive to efficient management of local-level resources. Typically, the possibility is rarely contemplated that rules do not support an efficient outcome or that they are infringed because they are inefficient or hurting the interests of violators.

That regulation tends to be more difficult to implement in the presence of inequality[13] is supported by the well-known analysis of shrimp fishery in Texas by Johnson and Libecap (1982)

> Contracting costs are high among heterogeneous fishermen, who vary principally with regard to fishing skill. The differential yields that result from heterogeneity affect the willingness to organize with others for specific regulations . . . regulations that pose disproportionate constraints on certain classes of fishermen will be opposed by those adversely affected. (. . .) Indeed, if fishermen had equal abilities and yields, the net gains from effort controls would be evenly spread, and given the large estimates of rent dissipation in many fisheries, rules governing effort or catch would be quickly adopted. (. . .) For example, total effort could be restricted through uniform quotas for eligible fishermen. But if fishermen are heterogeneous, uniform quotas will be costly to assign and enforce because of opposition from more productive fishermen. Without side payments (which are difficult to administer), uniform quotas leave more productive fishermen worse off. (Johnson and Libecap 1982: 1006–10)

Evidence from Senegal artisanal fisheries confirms that fishermen are reluctant to differentiate fishing quotas according to individual skill levels or performance. As noted by Gaspart and Platteau (see chapter 7 in this book), many fishermen actually denied that skill differentials exist in their community and they "actually took pains to explain that better performances on the part of some fishermen are only transient phenomena likely to be reversed as soon as luck turns its back on them to favour other fishing units" (p. 00). The difficulty of measuring relative skill levels in a way that would be accepted by everybody undoubtedly explains why the only feasible regulatory system is one of skill-neutral quotas.

Note that uniform quotas do not necessarily run counter to the interests of the rich insofar as they can be specified per unit of physical assets owned. Thus, in the fishing communities studied by Gaspart and Platteau (see chapter 7), effort regulation is achieved by fixing a number of sea trips or a quantity of fish landings per boat unit and not per fishing household. Moreover, if uniform quotas may hurt the interests of the rich, uniform costs may work to their advantage, as discussed earlier in the case of Mexican irrigation management schemes (Bardhan and Dayton-Johnson, chapter 5 in this book).

2.3. CONCLUDING REMARKS

By distinguishing between two central models of the commons, on the one hand, and between making voluntary contributions and participating in a regulatory structure, on the other hand, we have been able to differentiate the impact of inequality on efficiency in the use of the commons. Economic analysis thus allows us to clarify the conditions under which inequality impinges upon the use of the commons in different manners.

In particular, we find that inequality is more likely to encourage efficient use of common-property resource when it facilitates the establishment of a regulatory authority and, in appropriation problems, when it has the effect of reducing the aggregate level of use of the resource, by placing constraints on the individual harvesting efforts of the smaller users. By contrast, when the gamut of available regulatory instruments is limited, inequality between users makes collective agreement and effective enforcement of regulatory schemes more difficult to achieve. In games of voluntary contributions to a common good, the impact of inequality is more ambiguous: while it is generally true that larger users tend to contribute more to the common good, increased inequality also reduces the incentives of small users to contribute. As we have repeatedly emphasized, however, the precise impact of inequality crucially depends on the specific problem that is being considered. As a result, researchers should be encouraged to carefully assess the characteristics of the community, of the common-property resource, and of the environment which they study to be in a position to interpret the empirical evidence at hand in a meaningful way.

Despite their limited explanatory power, particularly with reference to available experimental evidence (see chapter 8), the theoretical models reviewed in section 1 provide useful guides that direct our attention to the critical factors determing the direction of the effect of inequality on resource management. Among the factors highlighted by our discussion are the incentive structure facing participants in their peculiar management problem, the nature of the constraints that limit individual behavior, the technology of production in the common property, the range of available regulatory instruments (themselves influenced by the prevailing social structure), and the degree of repetition and complexity in human interaction processes.

Notes

1. See in particular the empirical analysis by Bardhan and Dayton-Johnson (see chapter 5 of this book) in which they carefully distinguish between these two separate issues.

2. Note also that the distribution of income is relevant even with a linear objective function, if individual income has an impact on the benefits one agent enjoys from the collective good. Bardhan, Ghatak and Karaivanov (see chapter 3) is an explicit attempt to highlight this result.

3. However, as consumers can differ in their preferences, the redistribution of income discussed here cannot be directly related to inequality. Indeed, nothing so far prohibits a situation in which poor consumers, who have a "strong" preference for the public good, contribute while the rich consumers, with other preferences, do not have an income high enough to prompt them to contribute. In such a situation, redistributions of income that would increase the aggregate provision of the public good are equalizing.

4. Strictly speaking, in their estimates, the U-shape is not rejected, but the turning back of the U does not take place in the relevant range of the Gini coefficients (see their chapter below).

5. If opportunity costs of time are perfectly correlated with shares, and if individuals maximize their net incomes (or profits), equilibrium contributions will be identical among them.

6. See in particular Baland and Platteau (1997a) for a discussion of nonconvexities in the realm of common-property resources.

7. For a counterargument with imperfect competition, see Cornes et al. (1986).

8. In a more sophisticated model, instead of assuming an upper bound to the level of effort chosen by the agents, one may assume that income or wealth affects the marginal cost of effort. This is what Cornes and Sandler (1993) do to show that the neutrality theorem, which holds for a pure public good, does not apply to the type of "commons" problem discussed in this section (see below, however).

9. If the transfer benefited a constrained agent, the discussion is basically unchanged. If more than one agent benefits from the transfer, one can always decompose the transfer as the sum of successive transfers to a single agent. Similarly, if the transfer originates from more than one agent, one can always decompose such a transfer as the sum of transfers from each agent.

10. Clearly, a bilateral transfer from a constrained to an unconstrained user can only make the constrained user worse off. It is only if the total level of use of the resource by the other agents falls that his welfare can increase, and this never happens in the case of a bilateral transfer, but may happen when multiple simultaneous transfers from constrained to unconstrained users are considered.

11. Note that, even if richer agents collect more firewood, it may still be true that poorer agents depend relatively more on the commons, as firewood collected may represent a higher proportion of their total income. For this to be true in the case of a uniform cost of collection c, it suffices that the firewood collected is a normal but not a luxury good.

12. For a thorough discussion of the limitations in the use of such instruments in the case of common-property resources, and in particular the importance of equal treatment of community members and the prohibition of monetary compensations, see Baland and Platteau (1998b: 782–4).

13. In a detailed and careful empirical study of forest cover in Indian Himalaya, Somanathan, Prabhakar, and Mehta (see chapter 9 of this book) do not support the idea that inequality would tend to make collective regulation of forest resources more difficult. They indeed show that the state and quality of forests managed by local forest councils are basically not affected by the level of

inequality (in landholding) or caste heterogeneity within villages. By contrast, there is some support for the hypothesis that higher population density has the effect of reducing the stock and quality of the common forest.

REFERENCES

Baland, J. M., and J. P. Platteau. 1996. *Halting Degradation of Natural Resources—Is There a Role for Rural Communities?* Oxford: Clarendon Press.
———. 1997a. "Coordination problems in local-level resource management." *Journal of Development Economics* 53: 197–210.
———. 1997b. "Wealth inequality and efficiency in the commons, Part I: The unregulated case." *Oxford Economic Papers* 49(4): 451–82.
———. 1998a. "Wealth inequality and efficiency in the commons, Part II: The regulated case." *Oxford Economic Papers* 50(1): 1–22.
———. 1998b. "Dividing the commons—A partial assessment of the new institutional economics of property rights." *American Journal of Agricultural Economics* 80: 644–50.
———. 1999. "The ambiguous impact of inequality on local resource management." *World Development* 27(5): 773–88.
Banerjee, A., D. Mookherjee, K. Munshi, and D. Ray. 2001. "Inequality, control rights and efficiency: A study of sugar cooperatives in Western Maharashtra." *Journal of Political Economy* 109: 138–90.
Bardhan, P. 1993. "Analytics of the institutions of informal cooperation in rural development." *World Development* 21(4): 633–9.
———. 2000. "Irrigation and cooperation: An empirical analysis of 48 irrigation communities in South India." *Economic Development and Cultural Change* 48(4): 847–65.
Bergstrom, T., S. Blume, and H. Varian. 1986. "On the private provision of public goods." *Journal of Public Economics* 29: 25–49.
Braverman, A., J. L. Guasch, M. Huppi, and L. Pohlmeier. 1991. "Promoting rural cooperatives in developing countries: The case of Sub-Saharan Africa." *World Bank Discussion Papers* 121, Washington, D.C.: World Bank.
Cernea, M. 1989. "User groups as producers in participatory afforestation strategies." *World Bank Discussion Papers* 70, Washington, D.C.: World Bank.
Cornes, R., S. Mason, and T. Sandler. 1986. "The commons and the optimal number of firms." *Quarterly Journal of Economics* 101(3): 641–6.
Cornes, R., and T. Sandler. 1993. *The Theory of Externalities, Public Goods and Club Goods.* Cambridge, Mass.: Cambridge University Press.
Dayton-Johnson, J. 1998. Rules and cooperation on the local commons: Theory with evidence from Mexico. Ph.D. dis., University of California, Berkeley.
Dayton-Johnson, J., and P. Bardhan. 2001. "Inequality and conservation on the local commons: a theoretical exercise." *The Economic Journal* (forthcoming).
Edmonds, E., 2000, "Building community institutions to manage local resources: An empirical investigation." Dartmouth College: mimeo.

Garcia-Barrios, R., and L. Garcia-Barrios. 1990. "Environmental and technological degradation in peasant agriculture: A consequence of development in Mexico." *World Development* 18(11): 1569–85.

Gaspart, F., M. Jabbar, C. Melard, and J. P. Platteau. 1998. "Participation in the construction of a local public good with indivisibilities: An application to watershed development in Ethiopia." *Journal of African Economies* 7(2): 157–84.

Gaspart, F., and J. P. Platteau. "Heterogeneity and collective action for effort regulation: Lessons from Senegalese small-scale fisheries." Chapter 7 in this volume.

Gupta, A. K. 1986. "Socioecology of stress—Why do common property resource management projects fail? In National Research Council," *Proceedings of the Conference on Common Property Resource Management.* Washington, D.C.: National Academy Press.

Hardin, G. 1968. "The tragedy of the commons." *Science* 162: 1243–48.

Hayami, Y., and M. Kikuchi. 1981. *Asian Villages at the Crossroads.* Tokyo: University of Tokyo Press, and Baltimore: John Hopkins Univeristy Press.

Heckatorn, D. W. 1993. "Collective action and group heterogeneity: Voluntary provision versus selective incentives." *American Sociological Review* 58: 329–50.

Ilahiane, H. 2001. "The ethnopolitics of irrigation management in the Ziz Oasis, Marocco." In *Communities and the Environment: Ethnicity, Gender and the State in Community-Based Conservation,* ed. A. Aggrawal and C. C. Gibson, 89–110. New Brunswick, N.J. and London: Rutgers University Press.

Jodha, N. S. 1987. "A case study of the degradation of common property resources in Rajasthan. In *Land Degradation and Society,* ed. P. Blaikie and P. Brookfield, 196–207. London and New York: Methuen.

Jodha, N. S. 1989. *Fuel and Fodder Management Systems in the Arid Region of Western Rajasthan.* International Centre for Integrated Mountain Development, Kathmandu, Nepal.

Johnson, R. N., and G. D. Libecap. 1982. "Contracting problems and regulation: The case of the fishery. *American Economic Review* 72(5): 1005–22.

Kanbur, R. 1992. "Heterogeneity, distribution and cooperation in common property resource management." Policy Research Working Papers, The World Bank, Washington, D.C.

Laitos, R. 1986. "Rapid appraisal of Nepal irrigation systems." Water Management Synthesis report, 43. Fort Collins: Colorado State University.

McKean, M. A. 1986. "Management of traditional common lands (Iriaichi) in Japan." In National Research Council, *Proceedings of the Conference on Common Property Resource Management,* Washington, D.C.: National Academy Press, 533–89.

Menzies, N. K. 1994. *Forest and Land Management in Imperial China.* London: St. Martin's Press.

Olson, M. 1965. *The Logic of Collective Action.* Cambridge, Mass.: Harvard University Press.

Ostrom, E. 1990. *Governing the Commons: The Evolution of Institutions for Collective Action,* Cambridge: Cambridge University Press.

Ostrom, E. 1992. *Crafting Institutions: Self-governing Irrigation Systems.* San Francisco: ICS Press.

Peters, P. E. 1994. *Dividing the Commons—Politics, Policy, and Culture in Botswana*. Charlottesville and London: University Press of Virginia.

Sengupta, N. 1991. *Managing Common Property—Irrigation in India and the Philippines*. New Delhi: Sage Publications.

Sethi, R., and E. Somanathan. 1996. "The evolution of social norms in common property resource use. *American Economic Review* 86(4): 766–88.

Shanmugaratnam, N. 1996. "Nationalization, privatization and the dilemmas of common property management in Western Rajasthan. *Journal of Development Studies* 33(2): 163–87.

Shanmugaratnam, N., T. Veveld, A. Mossige, and M. Bovin. 1992. "Resource management and pastoral institution building in the West African Sahel." World Bank Discussion Papers, 175, World Bank, Washington, D.C.

Swallow, B., and D. Bromley. 1995. "Institutions, governance and incentives in common property regimes for African Rangelands. *Environmental and Resource Economics* 6(1): 99–118.

Tang, S. 1991. "Institutional arrangements and the management of common-pool resources." *Public Administration Review* 51(1): 42–51.

Wade, R. 1987. "The management of common property resources: Finding a co-operative solution." *World Bank Research Observer* 2(2): 219–34.

———. 1988. *Village Republics: Economic Conditions for Collective Action in South India*. Cambridge: Cambridge University Press.

Zufferey, F. S. 1986. *A Study of Local Institutions and Resource Management Inquiry in Eastern Central District*. Land Tenure Center, LTC paper No. 88, University of Wisconsin–Madison.

Chapter 3

INEQUALITY AND COLLECTIVE ACTION

Pranab Bardhan, Maitreesh Ghatak,
and Alexander Karaivanov

While the literature on collective action in political science and economics is large, its interrelationship with economic inequality is a relatively underresearched area. Yet this is important in the management of environmental resources. If underlying economic or social inequalities make collective action difficult, community cooperation on efforts to conserve resources becomes harder to achieve. For example, an important policy question to ask may be: how does the reduction of land inequality through, say, a land reform, affect agricultural productivity by changing the provision of collective goods like irrigation? Similarly, if the market process increases the inequality of ownership of different boat sizes in a fishing community, how does it affect their total catch and profits in an unregulated fishery? (Similar questions arise in the collective use of other public resources: e.g., does inequality in property holdings in an urban residential area help or hinder in the operation of neighborhood crime watch groups?) In this chapter we address such questions about the effects of private wealth inequality on collective action in the sense of the voluntary provision or use of collective goods. We do not discuss the collective-action problem involved in formulating or enforcing social rules for their use; in the preceding chapter Baland and Platteau discuss the theoretical issues involved in collective participation in social rules as well, and in chapter 5 Bardhan and Dayton-Johnson refer to some of the empirical issues in such rules in the context of water allocation.

A collective-action problem arises whenever externalities are present. Externalities arise whenever an individual does not internalize the full consequences of his or her actions. They are quite pervasive in all walks of life.

We thank the editors Jean-Marie Baland and Sam Bowles for very helpful comments. We aslo thank Abhijit Banerjee, Timothy Besley, Pierre-Andre Chiappori, Avinash Dixit, Paul Seabright, and workshop participants in Chicago, London School of Economics, the Conference on Inequality, Cooperation and Environmental Sustainability at the Santa Fe Institute, 2001, and the NEUDC 2001 Conference at Boston University for useful feedback. However, the responsibility for all errors and shortcomings lies only with us.

These could be both positive or negative. For example, by donating money to a particular cause we typically do not internalize the positive effect our contribution has on others who support the cause, and this leads such contributions to be less than what is socially optimal. In contrast, if we operate a vehicle or some other machinery which creates pollution, we do not internalize the negative effect our contribution has on others and this leads to such activities being carried out at a level that is higher than socially optimal. Whether an action is subject to externalities depends, among other things, on the nature of the action (supplying labor in the market versus voluntary work) and the institutions or rules of the game (farming can be undertaken by an individually owned farm or a cooperative, and in the latter case the actions of the members would be subject to externalities).

Although our framework is relevant to a general class of problems relating to voluntary provision or use of collective goods, for the sake of a common concrete anchor we shall often use the example of land reform in our subsequent exposition. Suppose producers use as inputs one private good (say, land) and one collective good (say, irrigation water) to produce a private good (say, rice). The private and collective inputs are complements in the production function. This collective good may be a public good (with positive externalities) like a public irrigation canal, or a common-property resource (henceforth, CPR), like a community pond or forest, with negative externalities.

The assumption of decreasing returns, a standard one in most economic contexts, implies that the more scarce an input is in a given production unit, the higher is its marginal return. As a result, one would expect a more equal distribution of this input across production units to improve efficiency, as land goes from low-return farms to high-return farms. If the market for this input operated well, then the forces of arbitrage would make sure it is allocated equally to maximize efficiency. However, there is considerable evidence to suggest that the market for inputs such as land or capital does not operate frictionlessly to bring this about, and the private endowment of an individual determines how much of that input she can use in her production unit.[1] There is a large literature showing that small farms are more efficient than large farms in agricultural sectors of developing countries. This is typically advanced as one of the main arguments for land reform in terms of efficiency.[2] Some authors (e.g., Bardhan 1984; Boyce 1987) have gone one step further and argued that a more egalitarian agrarian structure is also more likely to solve collective-action problems, especially those related to irrigation.[3]

But in the presence of collective-action problems, inequality of private endowments such as land or wealth may pull in the opposite direction. Indeed, in his pioneering work on collective action, Olson (1965) makes the following case in favor of inequality:

In smaller groups marked by considerable degrees of inequality—that is, in groups of members of unequal "size" or extent of interest in the collective good—there is the greatest likelihood that a collective good will be provided; for the greater the interest in the collective good of any single member, the greater the likelihood that the member will get such a significant proportion of the total benefit from the collective good that he will gain from seeing that the good is provided, even if he has to pay all of the cost himself. (p. 34)

We can interpret the "size" of a player by her endowment of the private input if it is complementary with the collective good in production.[4] Olson considered pure public goods only, which indeed have the property that only the largest (richest) player contributes. Our chapter is concerned with the following questions. Is this property pointed out by Olson true for a more general class of collective goods that include both impure public goods (i.e., collective goods where individual benefits are not independent of how much she contributes) and CPRs (with negative externalities)? If we look at welfare instead of the level of the provision of the collective good, is it possible that some degree of inequality may yield a higher level of joint surplus than perfect equality? Furthermore, is it possible for the allocation under some degree of inequality to Pareto-dominate the allocation under perfect equality?[5] If more than one player is involved in the provision of the public good, how would inequality *within* the class of contributors affect efficiency and how would inequality *between* the class of contributors and noncontributors affect efficiency?

Since the private and collective inputs are complementary in our framework, the marginal return from contributing to the public good is increasing in the amount of the private input an agent has and which we are going to refer to as "wealth" in the rest of this chapter. As a result, there will exist a threshold level of the amount of the private input such that only agents who have a level of wealth higher than this threshold will participate in providing the collective good, while those with a lower level will free-ride on the former group.[6] This means that redistributions that increase the wealth of the richer players at the expense of noncontributing poorer players would achieve a greater amount of the public good, and *other things being constant*, this should increase joint surplus. In our framework, this is how Olson's original argument shows up. However, his argument focuses only on the total amount of the public good and not on joint surplus. In particular, the gain from increasing the size of the collective input has to be measured against the cost arising from worsening the allocation of the private input in the presence of decreasing returns.

We show that the amount of contribution toward the provision (in the case of common property resources this has to be interpreted as extraction) of the collective input is a concave function of the endowment of the private input of the player for most well-known production functions (e.g., the Cobb-Douglas and the CES) and also that the equilibrium level of joint surplus (of both contributing and noncontributing players) is a concave function of the wealth distribution and hence displays inequality aversion. In addition, the total amount of the collective input is a concave function of the wealth distribution *among contributing players*. This means that initial asset inequality lowers the total provision of (pure and impure) public goods, and lowers the total extraction from the CPR. We provide a precise characterization of what the optimal distribution of wealth that maximizes joint surplus is in the case of imperfect convertibility between the private input and contribution to the collective input. We show that the joint surplus maximizing wealth distribution under private provision of the public good involves equalizing the wealth levels within the group of all noncontributing players at some positive level and also within the group of all contributing players. The contrast with the conclusions of both Olson and what we refer to as the distribution neutrality literature in the next section is quite sharp. The key assumptions leading to our result are: market imperfections that prevent the efficient allocation of the private input across production units, and some technical properties of the production function that are shared by widely used functional forms such as Cobb-Douglas and CES (constant elasticity of substitution) under decreasing returns to scale.

The above result takes the number of contributors to the collective input as given. It is difficult to characterize the optimal distribution of wealth when the number of contributors can be chosen. A key question of interest is: does perfect equality among all players maximize joint surplus? We provide a limited answer to this question. It turns out that perfect equality among all players (i.e., intergroup inequality in addition to intragroup inequality) is not always optimal. If wealth was equally distributed among all players, the average wealth of contributing players is low and this could reduce the level of the collective good. In contrast, concentrating all wealth in the hand of one player will maximize the average wealth of contributors, but will involve significant losses due to the assumed decreasing returns in the individual profit function with respect to wealth. The optimal distribution of wealth characterized above achieves a compromise between these two different forces.

The plan of the chapter is as follows. In the next section we provide a brief review of the literature in economics that deals with similar issues. In section 3.2 we provide a formal analysis of a simple model and briefly discuss the implications of relaxing some of our main assumptions. Our main results are presented in section 3.3. Finally, in section 3.4 we provide some concluding observations.

3.1. A REVIEW OF THE EXISTING LITERATURE

The public economics literature has addressed the question of inequality among contributing players in some detail. A key finding is the surprising "distribution-neutrality" result for a particular class of collective-action problems, namely, the provision of *pure* public goods.[7] These are public goods where individual contributions are perfect substitutes in the production of the public good and everyone gets the same benefit from the public good irrespective of the level of their contributions. Then, in a Nash equilibrium, the wealth distribution within the set of contributors does not matter for the amount of public-goods provision. The intuition behind this result is explained very clearly by Bergstrom, Blume, and Varian (1986). Suppose after the redistribution every player adjusts his contribution to the public good by exactly the same amount as his change in wealth and leaves the consumption of the private good unchanged. In that case the amount of the public good is the same as before and so the initial allocation is still available to all players. Those who have lower wealth because of the redistribution have a restricted budget set and would clearly prefer the previous allocation if it is still available. The budget set of those who have higher wealth because of redistribution expands, but not in the neighborhood of the original choice. In particular, now the extra options available to the player which are not dominated by options in the previous budget set involve a lower level of the public good compared to what she would receive if she did not contribute before, and higher levels of the private good. But she did contribute before, and so she is also better off with her previous choice.

Subsequent work has shown that the neutrality result depends crucially on the individual contributions being perfect substitutes in the production of the public good, the linearity of the resource constraints, the absence of corner solutions, and the "pureness" of the public good (i.e., the benefit received by a player must depend only on the total level of contributions, but not on her own contribution; see Cornes and Sandler 1996: 184–90 and 539; Bergstrom et al. 1986; Cornes and Sandler 1994).[8] In this chapter[9] we consider three points of departure from the distribution-neutrality framework. First, we adopt the framework of a generalized collective good of which pure and impure public goods with positive externality (e.g., roads, canal irrigation, law and order, public R&D, public health and sanitation) are particular cases. We also analyze collective goods with negative externality (e.g., forestry, fishery, grazing lands, surface or groundwater irrigation).

Second, another point of departure from the standard literature on voluntary provision of public goods is that we look not only at the level of provision of the collective good in question, but also at the total surplus from the good, net of costs.

Third, the distribution-neutrality result assumes that the contributions toward the public good and the private input are fully convertible.[10] In practice, particularly in the building of rural infrastructure in developing countries, the contribution toward the public good often takes the form of labor. To fix ideas, let us think of the private input as capital. Then this assumption bypasses an important issue of economic inequality: labor is not freely convertible into capital. Typically, labor and capital are not perfect substitutes in the production technology, and because of credit market imperfections capital does not flow freely from the rich to the poor to equate marginal returns. We take this more plausible scenario as our starting point and examine the effect of distribution of wealth among members of a given community on allocative efficiency in various types of collective-action problems (involving public goods as well as common-property resources, or CPR) in the presence of missing and imperfect capital markets. This is particularly important in less developed countries where the life and livelihood of the vast masses of the poor crucially depend on the provision of above-mentioned public goods and the local CPR (particularly when it is not under commonly agreed-upon regulations[11]), and where markets for land and credit are often highly imperfect or nonexistent. In poor countries where property rights are often ill-defined and badly enforced, even usual private goods sometimes have certain public-good features attached to them, and due to ongoing demographic and market changes the traditional norms and regulations on the use of CPR are often getting eroded. In such contexts, inequality of the players may play a special role.

Our work is also motivated by the growing empirical literature on the relationship between inequality and collective-good provision. For example, in an econometric study of forty-eight irrigation communities in south India, Bardhan (2000) finds that the Gini coefficient for inequality of landholding among the irrigators has in general a significant negative effect on cooperation on water allocation and field channel maintenance but there is some weak evidence for a U-shaped relationship. Similar results have been reported by Dayton-Johnson (2000) from his econometric analysis of fifty-four farmer-managed surface irrigation systems in central Mexico. Chapter 5 in this book summarizes those findings from south India and central Mexico. In a different context, using survey data on group membership and data on U.S. localities, Alesina and La Ferrara (2000) find that, after controlling for many individual characteristics, participation in social activities is significantly lower in more unequal localities.

3.2. THE MODEL

Suppose there are $n > 1$ players. Each player uses two inputs, k and z, to produce a final good. The input k is a purely *private* good, such as land, capital, or managerial inputs. We assume that there is no market for this input and so a player is restricted to choose $k \leq w$ where w is the exogenously given endowment of this input of a player. While we will focus on this interpretation, there is an alternative one which views w as capturing some characteristic of a player, such as a skill or a taste parameter.[12] In contrast, z is a *collective* good in the sense that it involves some externalities, positive or negative. We assume that each player chooses some action x which can be thought of as her effort that goes into using a common-property resource or contributing toward the collective good. Let $X \equiv \sum_{i=1}^{n} x_i$ be the sum total of the actions chosen by the players where x_i denotes the action level of player i. The individual actions aggregate into the collective input in the following simple way: $z_i = bx_i + cX$. The production function for the final good is given by $f(w_i, z_i)$ and thus the profit (surplus) function of player i is $\pi_i = f(w_i, z_i) - x_i$.[13]

Note that the input x_i appears twice in the profit function, once on its own as a private input, and once in combination with the quantities used or supplied by other agents. This implies that the private return to a player always exceeds the social return as long as $b > 0$. The input X can be a good (e.g., R&D, education) or a bad (e.g., any case of congestion or pollution). This formulation allows each player to receive a different amount of benefit from the collective input which depends on the action level they choose. In contrast, for pure public goods every player receives the same benefits irrespective of their level of contribution. This case, as well as many others (involving both positive and negative externalities), appear as special cases of our formulation as we will see shortly. Following the distribution neutrality literature we assume that the cost of supplying one unit of the collective input is simply one, and that the production function, f, exhibits decreasing returns to scale[14] with respect to the private and the collective inputs x_i and z_i (possible examples include the Cobb-Douglas production function or the CES production function).

We allow c to be positive, negative, or zero. For technical reasons, when c is negative we need to assume that the absolute value of c is not too large.[15] When $c = 0$ we have the case of a pure private good—there are no externalities. For $b = 0$ and c positive we have the case of pure public goods, that is, the one on which most of the existing literature has focused. For b and c positive we have the case of impure public goods as

TABLE 3.1
Type of Good under 4 Sets of Parameter Values

Case	Description	Type of Good
$c < 0$ and $b > 0$	Negative externalities	Commons (forestry, fishery)
$c = 0$ and $b \geq 0$	No externalities	Pure private good (supplying labor in own farm)
$c > 0$ and $b = 0$	Positive externalities	Pure public good (quality of air or water)
$c > 0$ and $b > 0$	Positive externalities	Impure public goods (roads, canal irrigation)

defined by Cornes and Sandler (1996). For b positive and c negative we have a version of the commons problem: by increasing her action relative to those of the others an individual gains. These cases are summarized in table 3.1.

3.3. The Decentralized Equilibrium

Let us consider the decentralized Nash equilibrium allocation. By decentralized we mean there is no planner who coordinates the actions of the different players. Each player behaves independently. In a Nash equilibrium each player is choosing an action optimally given the action choices of others. Formally speaking, player i takes the contribution of the other players as given and solves:

$$\max_{x_i \geq 0} \pi^i = f(w_i, z_i) - x_i.$$

Let the function $g(w_i) > 0$ denote the value of z_i that solves the first-order condition of the above problem taken as equality:

$$f_2(w_i, g(w_i))(b + c) = 1$$

Thus, $g(w)$ represents the level of the collective input z_i that player i would like to choose if her wealth were w_i. Notice that a player can affect the level of the collective input only partly through her own contribution, the rest depending on the contribution of the other players. This function merely gives the desired level of the collective input of a player as a function of her wealth level. Under some technical assumptions[16] we make the following observation which follows upon inspecting $(g(w))$:

Observation 1: *The desired level of the collective input for a player is increasing in her wealth level. If the production function displays constant returns to scale, then the desired level of the collective input for a player is an increasing and linear function of her wealth. For most production functions displaying decreasing returns to scale (e.g., the Cobb-Douglas, the CES), the desired level of the collective input for a player is an increasing and a strictly concave function of her wealth.*

This property follows directly from the complementarity between wealth and the collective input in the production function (i.e., a higher level of wealth raises the marginal return from the collective input) and diminishing returns with respect to the collective input. An increase in the wealth level raises the marginal return of the collective input relative to its marginal cost, which is assumed to be constant and equal to one. To restore equilibrium at the individual level, given diminishing returns, the amount of the collective input must increase. It immediately follows that the collective input for a player would be increasing in her wealth level. Suppose we take a unit of wealth from a rich person and give it to a poor person. We know that the contribution of the former to the collective input would increase and that of the latter would fall. Can we say which effect is going to be larger, that is, what is the net effect? It turns out that if the production function displays constant returns to scale, then the net effect is zero. The technical property of constant returns to scale implies that if both the wealth of a player and the amount of the collective input received by her are increased proportionally, the marginal return from contributing remains unchanged. As a result, the desired level of the collective input for a player is going to be a linear function of her wealth. If there are decreasing returns to scale, then a proportional change in the wealth of a player and the amount of the collective input received by her lead to a change in the marginal return from contributing. For most well-known cases of decreasing returns to scale production functions (such as the Cobb-Douglas, CES), the marginal return falls.[17] This means the poor person increases her contributions by an amount greater than the amount by which the rich person cuts her contribution down. In other words, the desired level of the collective input for a player is an increasing and a strictly concave function of her wealth. Notice that the level of the collective input is strictly increasing in the contribution of a player. Given that the desired level of the collective input is increasing in the wealth level of a player (Observation 1), it follows that irrespective of whether we have positive or negative externalities, for a given level of contribution of other players, a richer player has a higher marginal profit from contributing than a poorer player. Then the following observations follow directly.

Observation 2: *(i) For the case of a pure public good, the amount of the collective input enjoyed by each player is the same, whether the player contributes or not. Therefore, only the richest player contributes. This implies that even when the difference in the wealth between the richest player and second richest player is arbitrarily small, the former provides the entire amount of the public good.*

(ii) For the case of impure public goods or CPRs, the amount of the collective input enjoyed by each player is different. Therefore, even if a player's marginal return from contributing is less than that of the richest player, she can contribute less and enjoy a lower level of the collective input and thereby still attain an interior optimum.

(iii) For the case of pure private goods, there are no externalities of any kind. In this case, as long as the wealth level is positive, each player will choose a positive level of the action.

Let us denote by $\hat{x}_i$ the optimal action choice of player i. Given that the richest player has a higher marginal return from contributing to the collective input than the poorer players, and since the marginal return from the collective input becomes arbitrarily large as its level goes to zero, *the richest player will always contribute* so long as her wealth level is positive. Given the definition of $g(w_i)$, the optimal contribution of a contributing player can be written as:

$$\hat{x}_i = \frac{g(w_i) - cX}{b} \tag{1}$$

We characterize the decentralized equilibrium in the following two steps. First, for a given distribution of the private input we solve for the optimal contributions of each agent, $\hat{x}_i$, the total contribution X, and the joint surplus, Π. Second, we look for the distributions of w_i which maximize the total contribution and joint surplus to be able to analyze the effects of inequality on these two variables.

3.3.1. Effect of Wealth Inequality on Total Contributions and Joint Profits

From equation (1):

$$X = \frac{\sum_{i=1}^{m} g(w_i)}{b + mc}$$

where m is the number of contributing agents in equilibrium. Notice that then Observation 1 implies that X is the sum of m concave functions and as such is a concave function itself. Moreover, as these functions are identical and receive the same weight, if we hold the number of contributors constant, total contribution is maximized when all contributing agents have equal amounts of the private input. Therefore we have:

Result 1: *The total contribution is strictly concave in the private input endowments and is maximized when all contributing agents have equal amounts of the private input.*

Recall that our assumptions above imply that diminishing returns with respect to the collective input used by the i-th individual set in at a faster rate at a higher wealth level, and so the optimal level of the collective input is a concave function of the wealth level. Result 1 follows from this assumption, and the fact that the collective input used by the i-th individual is a linear function of the individual's own contribution and the contribution of other players.

　To see this more clearly, consider the two-player version of the game where player 1 has wealth $w + \varepsilon$ and player 2 has wealth $w - \varepsilon$ where $\varepsilon > 0$. By changing ε, we can study the effect of greater inequality on the contributions of the two players. Naturally, the higher ε is, the higher will be the contribution of player 1 and the lower will be the contribution of player 2. But if one player increases her contribution and the other player decreases hers, these will lead them to further adjust their contributions, and so on. To get a concrete answer, we need to consider the reaction functions of the players which tell us how much one wants to contribute as a function of the contribution of the other player. They are derived from the first-order conditions of the players, and are as follows:

$$x_1 = \frac{1}{b+c} \{g(w + \varepsilon) - cx_2\}.$$

$$x_2 = \frac{1}{b+c} \{g(w - \varepsilon) - cx_1\}.$$

Assume that both players are contributing in equilibrium and consider the effect of an increase in ε to ε'. The direct effect is to increase x_1 and reduce x_2. For the case of positive externalities ($c > 0$), the indirect effects which work through the other player's contribution move in the same direction, while for the case of negative externalities, the indirect effects move in the opposite direction. The former case is illustrated graphically in figure 3.1. Since $c > 0$ the reaction functions of both players are downward sloping. Suppose we start with an equilibrium at point A. An increase in inequality leads to a downward parallel shift of the reaction

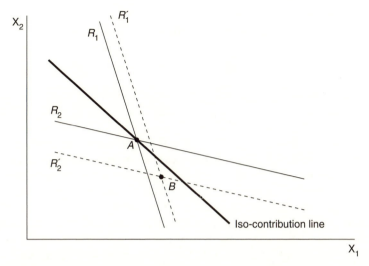

Figure 3.1. The impact of inequality on the equilibrium contributions: The case of positive externalities.

function of player 2 (denoted by R_2 and R'_2) and an upward parallel shift of the reaction function of player 1 (denoted by R_2 and R'_2). Notice that since the function $g(.)$ is concave under our assumptions, the difference between $g(w - \varepsilon)$ and $g(w - \varepsilon')$ is bigger than that between $g(w + \varepsilon)$ and $g(w + \varepsilon')$, in other words, the loss in total surplus resulting from reducing 2's contribution would be bigger than the gain from increasing 1's contri-bution.[18] This implies that the new equilibrium (point B) lies to the south-west of the iso-contribution line through A (the heavy solid line in figure 3.1) and hence the total contribution, X, is decreasing in inequality, ε.

The effect of wealth inequality on X has implications which are quite different from those available so far in the public economics literature. Our analysis shows that greater equality *among those who contribute toward the collective good* will increase the value of X. Therefore, a more equal wealth distribution among contributors will increase the equilibrium level of the collective input. In addition, any redistribution of wealth from noncontributors to contributors that does not affect the set of contributors will also increase X.[19] In terms of the two-player ex-ample, this implies that as long as both players contribute, any inequal-ity in the distribution of wealth reduces X. But with sufficient inequality, if one player stops contributing then any further increases in inequality will increase X.

Let us now turn to the normative implications of changes in the distri-bution of wealth. Under the first-best, which can be thought of as a centralized equilibrium where players choose their contributions to maximize joint surplus, the first-order condition for player i is:

$$f_2(w_i, z_i)(b + nc) \leq 1.$$

The difference with the decentralized equilibrium is that now individuals look at the social marginal product of their contribution to the collective input, that is, $f_2(w_i, bx_i + cX)(b + nc)$ as opposed to the private marginal product, that is, $f_2(w_i, bx_i + cX)(b + c)$. Then it follows directly that those who will contribute will contribute more (less) than in the decentralized equilibrium if $c > 0$ ($c < 0$). Also, the number of contributors will be higher (lower) than in the decentralized equilibrium if $c > 0$ ($c < 0$).

Therefore, for the case of positive externalities, the total contribution in a decentralized equilibrium is less than the efficient (i.e., joint surplus maximizing) level. Conversely, for the case $c < 0$, total contributions exceed the socially efficient level. From this one might want to conclude that greater inequality among contributors increases efficiency in the presence of negative externalities and reduces efficiency if there are positive externalities.[20] Indeed, the literature on the effect of wealth (or income) distribution on collective-action problems has typically focused on the size of total contributions. However, that is inappropriate as the correct welfare measure is joint surplus, Π.

In the presence of decreasing returns to scale, the distribution of the private input across agents will have a direct effect on joint surplus irrespective of its effect on the size of the collective input. In particular, greater inequality will reduce efficiency by increasing the discrepancy between the marginal returns to the private input across different production units. In the case of negative externalities, these two effects of changes in the distribution of the private input work in different directions, while in the case of positive externalities, they work in the same direction. The following result characterizes the joint surplus maximizing wealth distribution for a given number of contributors (users), m.

Result 2: *Suppose we have either positive externalities, or a small degree of negative externalities. For a given number of contributors the joint surplus maximizing wealth distribution under private provision of the public good involves equalizing the wealths of all noncontributing players to some positive wealth level and also those of all contributing players to some strictly higher wealth level.*

This result shows that maximum joint surplus is achieved for both contributors and noncontributors, if there is no intragroup inequality. This is a direct consequence of joint profit of each group being concave in the wealth levels of the group members. The contrast with the conclusions of both Olson and the distribution neutrality literature is quite sharp. The key assumptions leading to the result are market imperfections that prevent the efficient allocation of the private input across production units, and some technical properties of the production function that are shared by widely used functional forms such as Cobb-Douglas and CES under decreasing returns to scale.

In the above result we did not talk about intergroup inequality. Formally, we took m as given while considering alternative wealth distributions. An obvious question to ask is, what is the joint profit maximizing distribution of wealth when we can also choose the number of contributors, m? For example, does perfect equality among all players maximize joint surplus? This turns out to be a difficult question in general. Below we provide detailed analysis for the various possible cases of both positive and negative externalities. Let us first look at the case of positive externalities $(c > 0)$. Suppose all players are contributing when wealth is equally distributed. Then from Result 2 we know that limited redistribution that does not change the number of contributors cannot improve efficiency. This immediately suggests the following:

Corollary to Result 2: *Suppose all players contribute under perfect equality. Then if after a redistribution all players continue to contribute, joint surplus cannot increase.*

But suppose we redistribute wealth from one player to the other $n - 1$ players up to the point where the former stops contributing. Recall that when the group size is $m < n$, $X = \dfrac{mg(\hat{w})}{b + mc}$. It is obvious that an increase in the average wealth of contributing players keeping the number of contributors fixed will increase X. It turns out that an increase in m holding the average wealth of contributors constant will always increase X.[21] However, if we simultaneously decrease m from n to $n - 1$ and increase the average wealth of contributors, it is not clear whether X will go up or not. If X goes down then we can unambiguously say that joint profits are lower due to this redistribution (for $c > 0$) since the effect of this policy on the efficiency of allocation of the private input across production units is definitely negative. However, if X goes up then there is a trade-off: the increase in X benefits all players (since $c > 0$), including the player who is too poor to contribute now, but this has to be balanced against the greater inefficiency in the allocation of the private input.

To analyze the effect of wealth distribution on joint profits when some players do not contribute, we restrict attention to the comparison between joint profits under perfect equality (i.e., when all players have the same wealth) and the wealth distribution that is obtained by a redistribution that leads to m contributing and $n - m$ noncontributing players.

From the discussion above, we know that under our assumptions all players contribute under perfect equality. We focus on studying only the efficient wealth distributions, that is, ones which achieve maximum joint surplus. Since any intragroup inequality among the contributors and noncontributors reduces joint surplus, we assume that all m contributors have equal wealths and all $n - m$ noncontributors have equal wealths after the redistribution. We are then able to show that:

Result 3: *(a) For pure public goods perfect equality among the agents is never joint surplus maximizing. (b) For pure private goods perfect equality is always joint surplus maximizing.*

We noted a special property of pure public goods in the previous section (Observation 2(i)), namely, even if the difference in the wealth between the richest player and the second richest player is arbitrarily small, the former provides the entire amount of the public good with everyone else free-riding on her. This property is the key to explain why perfect equality is not joint surplus maximizing in this case. Start with a situation where all players except for one have the same wealth level, and this one player has a wealth level which is higher than that of others by an arbitrarily small amount. As a result, this player is the single contributor to the public good. A small redistribution of wealth from other players to this player, keeping the average wealth of the other players constant, will have three effects on joint profits: the effect due to the worsening of the allocation of the private input, the effect of the increase in X on the payoff of the noncontributing players, and the effect of the increase in X on the payoff of the single contributing player. The result in the proposition follows from the fact that the first effect is negligible since by assumption the extent of wealth inequality is very small, the second effect is positive, and the third effect can be ignored by the optimality conditions. It should also be noted that this result goes through for both constant and decreasing returns to scale. The second part of Result 3 follows from the fact that when $c = 0$ a player will always choose $x_i > 0$, however small her wealth level, as the marginal product of contributing is very high. Then all players are contributors so long as they have nonzero wealth and it follows directly from Result 2 that perfect equality will maximize joint profits.

For the case of impure public goods ($b, c > 0$) under decreasing returns to scale we can provide only a partial characterization. We show that:

Result 4: *Consider the case of impure public good subject to decreasing returns to scale.*
(a) For a given number of players and a given level of externalities, perfect equality is always joint surplus maximizing for high values of the

private marginal return from the action of a player. For low values of the private marginal return from the action, perfect equality is never joint surplus maximizing.
(b) For a given number of players and a given level of the private marginal return from the action of a player, perfect equality is always joint surplus maximizing when the level of externalities is low.

Two opposing forces are at work in this case—the "decreasing returns to scale" effect calling for equalizing the wealth of agents and the "dominant player" effect due to the positive externality calling for redistribution toward the richest players as there is a positive effect on the payoffs of the noncontributing players. Each of the two effects can dominate the other depending on the parameter values. The direct effect of an increase in the richer player contribution on her own payoff can be ignored because of the optimality conditions.

While we cannot provide a full characterization of the case of decreasing returns, due to the existence of these two opposing forces, we can provide some illustrative examples using the Cobb-Douglas production function $f(w, z) = w^\alpha z^\beta$ for a two-player game. In figures 3.2 and 3.3, we plot how the difference between joint surplus under perfect equality and under inequality (where the degree of inequality is chosen to maximize joint profits given that only one player contributes) varies with b and c for several alternative sets of values of the parameters α and β. As we can see from the figures: (a) there is a unique threshold value for b such that perfect equality leads to higher surplus for b higher than this value and the opposite is true for b lower than this threshold; and (b) there is a unique threshold value for c such that perfect equality leads to higher joint surplus for c higher than the threshold and the opposite holds if c is lower.

Finally, we turn to the case of negative externalities, that is, $c < 0$. We show that:

Result 5: *When there are strong negative externalities, perfect equality is never joint surplus maximizing.*

Intuitively, joint surplus is the sum of individual surpluses ignoring the externality of a player's action on others, and the sum total of the externality terms. The former is concave in the wealth distribution but in the case of negative externalities, the latter is convex. For c close to zero the decreasing returns to scale effect dominates, in other words, joint profits are maximized at perfect equality but for low enough c (large in absolute value) the "cost of negative externality" term, which is convex, dominates and so greater inequality leads to higher joint profits.

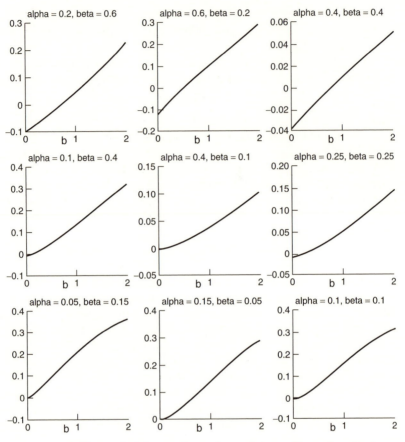

Figure 3.2. Difference in joint surplus under perfect equality and optimal inequality.

3.3.2. Extensions

It is important for our result that x_i and w_i are different types of goods and one cannot be freely converted into the other. Suppose instead that the individual can freely allocate a fixed amount of wealth between two uses, namely, as a private input and as her contribution to the collective input. This is the formulation chosen by the literature on distribution neutrality (e.g., Warr 1983; Bergstrom et al. 1986; Cornes and Sandler 1996; and Itaya et al. 1997). This literature focuses on pure public goods, that is, where $z_i = cX$. We show[22] that in the more general case of impure public goods the neutrality result does not go through except in some special cases. More specifically, our analysis shows that in this case, re-

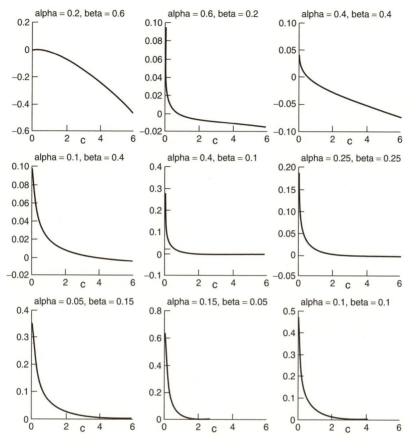

Figure 3.3. Difference in joint surplus under perfect equality and optimal inequality.

laxing the assumption of perfect convertibility of the private input and the contribution to the collective input implies that the distribution neutrality result no longer holds. Greater equality among contributors always improves efficiency for impure public goods (i.e., $c > 0$) while for collective inputs subject to negative externalities, the effect of inequality on efficiency is ambiguous. In the latter case, we characterize conditions under which we can sign the effect of inequality on efficiency. Our results do not depend on the production functions being homothetic, but in the general case even with free convertibility, distribution neutrality can break down if the collective input is not a pure public good, as is well recognized in the literature (see, e.g., Bergstrom et al. 1986 and Cornes and Sandler 1996).

Above, we assumed that the private input and the public good are complements in the production function. In Bardhan, Ghatak, and Karaivanov (2002) we have also examined the implications of these two inputs being substitutes. As before, joint surplus goes up if wealth is equally distributed among noncontributors. Also, we cannot say for sure whether the optimal distribution of wealth involves perfect equality, or some inequality among the contributors (the poorest agents in this case) and the rest. For the intuition behind this result, notice that those who contribute use the efficient amount of the input. Other players have more than the efficient level of the input in their production units. Any redistribution from the poor to the rich players does not affect the profit of the former as they exactly compensate for this by increasing their contribution. Since rich players have more than the efficient level of the input in their firms, normally a transfer of an additional unit of wealth would reduce joint profits since the marginal gain to the rich player is less than the marginal cost to the poor player. But every extra unit of wealth received by the rich player increases the input received by her firm by *twice* the amount because of the increase in the effort by the poor player, and as a result it is not clear whether joint profits increase or decrease.

Finally, in our main exposition we studied the case where the player's own contribution and the total contribution of all players are perfect substitutes in determining the benefit from the collective input enjoyed by a player. We have also considered an alternative formulation in which they can be complements. Analytically, this case turns out to be quite hard to characterize even when we assume a specific form of the production function, namely Cobb-Douglas, and consider a two-player game. We show that if we compare the allocations under perfect equality (both players have the same level of wealth) and perfect inequality (one player has all the wealth and the other player has nothing), joint surplus is always higher under perfect equality for nonnegative externalities. However, if there are substantial negative externalities, then under some parameter values joint surplus will be higher under perfect inequality. The intuition for this result lies in the fact that when the negative externality problem is very severe, then under perfect equality the players choose their actions related to the collective input at too high a level relative to the joint surplus maximizing solution. Perfect inequality converts the model to a one-player game and hence eliminates this problem. On the other hand, due to joint diminishing returns to the private input and the collective input, joint surplus is lower under perfect inequality compared to perfect equality if there were no externalities. What this result tells us is that perfect inequality is desirable only when the negative externality problem is severe and when the extent of diminishing returns is not too high.

3.4. CONCLUDING REMARKS

In this chapter we analyze the effect of inequality on the distribution of endowment of private inputs that are complementary in production with collective inputs (e.g., contribution to public goods such as irrigation and extraction from common-property resources) on efficiency in a simple class of collective-action problems. In an environment where transaction costs prevent the efficient allocation of private inputs across individuals, and the collective inputs are provided in a decentralized manner, we characterize the optimal second-best distribution of the private input. We show that while efficiency increases with greater equality *within* the group of contributors and noncontributors, in some situations there is an optimal degree of inequality *between* the groups.

The limitations of our model suggest several directions of potentially fruitful research. Our model is static. It is important to extend it to the case where both the wealth distribution and the efficiency of collective action are endogenous. For example, it is possible to have multiple equilibria with high (low) wealth inequality leading to low (high) incomes to the poor due to low (high) level of provision of public goods, which via low (high) mobility can sustain an unequal (equal) distribution of wealth. Also, in the dynamic case it will be interesting to analyze the effects of inequality on the sustainability of cooperation over repeated transactions. Second, technological nonconvexities and differential availability of exit options seriously affect collective action in the real world, and our model ignores them.[23] For example, the public good may not be generated if the total amount of contribution is below a certain threshold. This is the case for renewable resources like forests or fishery where a minimum stock is necessary for regeneration, or in the case of fencing a common pasture. Third, the empirical literature suggests that even when the link between inequality and collective action is consistent with the results in our model, the mechanisms involved may be quite different in some cases. For example, transaction costs in conflict management and costs of negotiation may be higher in situations of higher inequality. Fourth, following the public economics literature, in this chapter we focus mainly on the free-rider problem arising in a collective-action setup. Here, the issue is the sharing of the costs of collective action. But there is another problem, often called the bargaining problem, whereby collective action breaks down because the parties involved cannot agree on the sharing of the benefits.[24] Inequality matters in this problem as well. For example, bargaining can break down when one party feels that the other party is being unfair in sharing the benefits (there is ample evidence for this in the experimental literature on ultimatum games). More generally, social norms of cooperation and group identification may be difficult to achieve in highly unequal environments. Putnam (1993), in his well-known study of regional disparities of social capital in Italy, points out that "horizontal" social networks (i.e., those involving people of similar status and power) are more effective in generating trust and norms of reciprocity than "vertical" ones. Knack and Keefer (1997) also find that the level of social cohesion (which is an outcome of collective action) is strongly and negatively associated with economic inequality. Finally, we focus only on the voluntary provision of public goods and do not consider the possibility that the players might elect a decision-maker who can tax them and choose the level of provision of the collective good. The role of inequality in such a framework is an important topic for future research.[25]

NOTES

1. Evans and Jovanovic (1989) analyzed panel data from the National Longitudinal Survey of Young Men (NLS), which surveyed a sample of 4,000 men in the United States between the ages of 14 and 24 in 1966 almost every year between 1966 and 1981, and found that entrepreneurs are limited to a capital stock of no more than one and one-half times their wealth when starting a new venture.

2. See Ray (1998), chap. 12 for a review of this literature.

3. Indeed, the limited evidence that is available on the effect of land tenure reform suggests that the productivity gains can be large (Banerjee, Gertler, and Ghatak 2002).

4. In Olson this is the share of the total benefit to the group that accrues to an individual player.

5. An outcome Pareto-dominates another outcome if no one is worse off and some are strictly better off under the former compared to the latter.

6. Baland and Platteau (1997) provide some very interesting examples (there are similar examples cited by them in chapter 1) where richer agents tend to play a leading role in collective action in a decentralized setting. For example, in rural Mexico the richer members of the population take the initiative in mobilizing labor to manage common lands and undertake conservation measures such as erosion control.

7. Some of the contributions to the theoretical literature related to this result are Warr (1983), Cornes and Sandler (1984a and b), Bergstrom et al. (1986), Bernheim (1986), and Itaya et al. (1997).

8. Baland and Ray (1999) consider whether inequality in the shares of the benefit players receive from a public good is good or bad for efficiency might depend on whether the contributions of the players are substitutes or complements in the production function of the public good.

9. See also the technical version of this chapter (Bardhan et al. 2002), where we provide formal proofs of all our results.

10. The distribution neutrality literature is couched in the framework of a consumer choosing to allocate a given level of income between her private consumption and contribution to a pure public good. We adopt the framework of a firm using a private input and a public input to produce some good. While not exactly equivalent, formally these frameworks are very similar and what we call the private input is similar to the private consumption good in the distribution neutrality literature.

11. Agreeing upon such regulations is itself a collective-action problem.

12. The assumption that the market for the private input does not exist at all, while stark, is not crucial for our results. All that is needed is that the amount a person can borrow or the amount of land she can lease depends positively on how wealthy she is. Various models of market imperfections, such as adverse selection, moral hazard, costly state verification, or imperfect enforcement of contracts, will lead to this property.

13. We will refer to $\Pi = \sum_{i=1}^{n} \pi_i$ as joint surplus or joint profits later in the chapter.

14. In our companion paper to this chapter we also study extensively the case of constant returns to scale.

15. In particular we need the assumption that $b + cn \geq 0$ which implies that if a planner chooses the level of the collective input, she would choose a positive level of x_i for at least one player. This also ensures that the equilibrium is stable.

16. All technical details and formal proofs of the results in this chapter can be found in Bardhan et al. (2002).

17. For the technical conditions that ensure this property, see Bardhan et al. (2002).

18. For $|\varepsilon' - \varepsilon|$ small, we can think of that difference as a multiple of the derivative of g.

19. In the above formula for X, holding m constant a redistribution from noncontributors to contributors will increase w_i $(i = 1, 2, \ldots, m)$ with the increase being strict for some i.

20. Note however that a sufficiently large degree of inequality among contributors may reduce X below the first-best level in the $c < 0$ case.

21. Formally, this is because $\dfrac{m}{b + mc}$ is increasing in m. The intuition is, the new entrant to the group of contributors will contribute a positive amount, which would reduce the incentive of existing contributors to contribute due to diminishing returns. However, in the new equilibrium X must go up, as otherwise the original situation could not have been an equilibrium.

22. See Bardhan et al. (2002).

23. The model of Dayton-Johnson and Bardhan (2002) examines the effect of inequality on resource conservation with two periods and differential exit options for the rich and the poor in the case when technology is linear. In the preceding chapter, Baland and Platteau briefly discuss the effect of nonconvexities of technology in a static model.

24. See, e.g., Elster (1989).

25. Olszewski and Rosenthal (1999) address this question for pure public goods within the framework of the distribution neutrality literature.

References

Alesina, A., and E. La Ferrara. 2000. "Participation in heterogeneous communities." *Quarterly Journal of Economics* 115(3): 847–904.

Baland, J.-M., and J.-P. Platteau. 1997. "Wealth inequality and efficiency in the commons: I. The unregulated case." *Oxford Economic Papers* 49: 451–82.

Baland, J.-M., and D. Ray. 1999. "Inequality and efficiency in joint projects." Mimeo, Facultés Universitaires Notre-Dame de la Paix, Namur and New York University.

Banerjee, A., P. Gertler, and M. Ghatak. 2002. "Empowerment and efficiency: tenancy reform in West Bengal." *Journal of Political Economy* 110(2): 239–80.

Bardhan, P. 1984. *Land, Labor and Rural Poverty*, New York: Columbia University Press.

———. 2000. "Irrigation and cooperation: An empirical analysis of 48 irrigation communities in South India." *Economic Development and Cultural Change* 48(4): 847–65.

Bardhan, P., M. Ghatak, and A. Karaivanov. 2002. "Inequality, market imperfections, and the voluntary provision of collective goods." Mimeo, University of Chicago and University of California, Berkeley.

Bergstrom, T., L. Blume, and H. Varian. 1986. "On the private provision of public goods." *Journal of Public Economics* 29: 25–49.

Bernheim, B. D. 1986. "On the voluntary and involuntary provision of public goods." *American Economic Review* 76(4): 789–93.

Boyce, J. K. 1987. *Agrarian Impasse in Bengal—Institutional Constraints to Technological Change*. Oxford: Oxford University Press.

Cornes, R., and T. Sandler. 1984a. "The theory of public goods: Non-Nash behavior." *Journal of Public Economics* 23: 367–79.

———. 1984b. "Easy riders, joint production and public goods." *Economic Journal* 94: 580–98.

———. 1994. "The comparative static properties of the impure public good model." *Journal of Public Economics* 54: 403–21.

———. 1996. *The Theory of Externalities, Public Goods and Club Goods*. 2d ed. Cambridge, Mass.: Cambridge University Press.

Dayton-Johnson, J. 2000. "The determinants of collective action on the local commons: A model with evidence from Mexico." *Journal of Development Economics* 62(1): 181–208.

Dayton-Johnson, J., and P. Bardhan 2002. "Inequality and conservation on the local commons: A theoretical exercise." *Economic Journal* 112(481): 577–602.

Elster, J. 1989. *The Cement of Society*. Cambridge: Cambridge University Press.

Evans, D., and B. Jovanovic 1989. "An estimated model of entrepreneurial choice under liquidity constraints." *Journal of Political Economy* 97(4): 808–27.

Itaya, J., D. de Meza, and G. D. Myles. 1997. "In praise of inequality: Public good provision and income distribution." *Economics Letters* 57: 289–96.

Knack, S., and P. Keefer. 1997. "Does social capital have an economic payoff? A - cross-country investigation." *Quarterly Journal of Economics* 112(4): 1251–88.

Olson, M. 1965. *The Logic of Collective Action: Public Goods and the Theory of Groups*. Cambridge, Mass.: Harvard University Press.

Olszewski, W., and H. Rosenthal. 1999. "Politically determined income inequality and the provision of public goods." Mimeo, Northwestern University and Princeton University.

Putnam, R. 1993. *Making Democracy Work: Civic Traditions in Modern Italy*. Princeton, N.J.: Princeton University Press.

Ray, D. 1998. *Development Economics*. Princeton, N.J.: Princeton University Press.

Warr, P. G. 1983. "The private provision of a public good is independent of the distribution of income." *Economic Letters* 13: 207–11.

Chapter 4

ADOPTION OF A NEW REGULATION
FOR THE GOVERNANCE OF
COMMON-POOL RESOURCES BY
A HETEROGENEOUS POPULATION

Marco A. Janssen and Elinor Ostrom

The rich Lofoten cod fishery in northern Norway has been successfully self-governed and managed for more than one hundred years. The rules that regulate the use of this fishery—and make it likely that the fishery will be sustainable into the future—have been devised by the boat-owners themselves with minimal external assistance or coercion. Local regulatory committees are elected by the boat-owners, determine the rules for harvesting from the fishery, and effectively monitor this system (Princen 1998). Once their own rules are in place and monitored, and sanctions for noncompliance are regularly applied, it is relatively easy to understand why the boat-owners would comply with well-designed and enforced rules. How the users themselves developed their own rules and ways of monitoring and sanctioning noncompliance with these rules is much more difficult to understand given current accepted theories of collective action.

As discussed below, there are multiple examples of long-existing, self-governed systems for limiting resource use that increase the probability of sustainable resource systems (see Bromley et al. 1992; Ostrom et al. 2002). The design principles that characterize robust self-governed institutions have been identified and confirmed by multiple studies of successful and unsuccessful efforts at self-governance (see Ostrom 1990; Morrow and Hull 1996; Weinstein 2000). The evidence from the field, however, constitutes an anomaly. Existing theories of collective action

Thanks to Sam Bowles for his comments on an earlier version of this chapter. Also thanks to the participants of seminars at Indiana University, Universite Libre de Bruxelles, and the Annual Resilience Alliance Meeting 2001 in Chiang Mau. Support of the Resilience Alliance, the National Science Foundation (Grant application SES0083511) and the European Union (contract nr. IST-2000-26016) is gratefully acknowledged.

do not yet provide a full explanation for how the appropriators (harvesters) from a common-pool resource can solve three nested social dilemmas:

1. The first dilemma is that of multiple appropriators harvesting from a single common-pool resource. This is the "tragedy of the commons" dilemma (Hardin 1968). Most resource policy textbooks presume that appropriators will act individually and overharvest from a common-pool resource.

2. The second dilemma is that of spending time and effort to create a new set of rules that jointly benefit many of those who rely on a resource whether or not they contribute time and effort to the process of devising regulations. Since rules are themselves public goods, this is a public-good dilemma. The standard theoretical prediction is that rules will *not* emerge as the result of an endogenous process. Rather, those involved must have rules imposed upon them from the outside.

3. The third dilemma is that of monitoring a set of rules and imposing sanctions on those who break the rules. Monitoring and sanctioning are costly activities. They generate rule conformance—which benefits most appropriators whether or not they contribute to the activity. This is also a public-good dilemma. Most theories treat rule enforcement as an exogenous variable rather than something that the participants themselves undertake.

Given the extensive evidence that some local appropriators from common-pool resources do solve all three dilemmas, while others do not, a central question on our research agenda is: "How do rules emerge in complex common-pool resource systems used by multiple appropriators?" This chapter is our first effort to use agent-based computational modeling[1] to address this question. We will explore the factors that enhance or detract from the possibility that individuals appropriating (harvesting) from a common-pool resource will first, impose rules on themselves to limit their harvesting from a jointly used resource, and second, monitor and enforce their own rules. We will show that in order to adopt a rule to avoid a "tragedy of the commons," agents have to build up mutual trust relationships involving short-term costs. The degree of success of rule emergence depends, amongst other variables, on the heterogeneity within a population of agents and the type and frequency of interactions.

4.1. Why Use Agent-Based Computational Models

The use of agent-based computational models is still not widely accepted—especially by scholars using analytical theories, including game theory—as a foundation for doing institutional analysis. Thus, before discussing what agent-based computational modeling is, it is important to address why we choose this modeling approach. Game theory is a useful tool for conducting studies of the choice of strategies *within* a given set of rules. Given its usefulness, game theory will continue to be applied extensively to analyze many questions of relevance to the study of institutions and common-pool resources (Ostrom, Gardner, and Walker 1994; McGinnis 2000). To conduct a game theoretical analysis, however, one must assume that a fixed, commonly understood, and followed set of rules is already in place.

Evolutionary game theory is also an important tool for the institutional analyst, but strategies rather than rules are posited to evolve over time (for an excellent overview, see Gintis 2000). Further, to conduct a full analysis of a complex game usually requires that one assumes a homogeneous set of players facing a homogeneous biophysical world. While one can never model the full extent of the complexity that exists in regard to the governance of common-pool resources, introducing some degree of heterogeneity with regard to the attributes of participants and of the biophysical world they face is an important step in achieving a better theoretical understanding of these processes.

We are particularly interested in the resilience of institutional structures—the ability of a particular set of rules to absorb a disturbance. The resilience of an institutional structure, however, also depends on the heterogeneity of the biophysical environment and the participants. Thus, introducing heterogeneity is an essential aspect of our investigation. Further, we are not only interested in the possible existence of an equilibrium and what that equilibrium is, but also in the time-path toward an equilibrium state. Another aspect of analytical models in evolutionary game theory is the implicit assumption that each agent has an equal chance of interacting with every other agent. This implicit assumption results from the use of differential equations. Agent interactions, however, take place mainly within social networks. Recent investigations show that the structure of agents in a social network can have crucial consequences for social processes such as the evolution of cooperation (Ellison 1993; Cohen et al. 2001). Agent-based computational models are able to examine such social relationships.

Tournaments between strategies for playing repeated Prisoner's Dilemma games pioneered by Robert Axelrod (1984) can be considered as one of the first applications of agent-based computational models in social science. Agent-based computational models allow us to explore the impact of a variety of variables identified in the field as affecting the likelihood of successful self-organization including the size of the resource, the number of agents, the attributes that agents obviously carry (tags), and the presence or absence of trust. Using this modeling technique, it is possible to analyze how these important factors independently and interactively affect the likelihood of a rule being adopted and on the patterns of monitoring and sanctioning that may ensue. One can create an artificial, computational laboratory to examine how a more complex set of variables interacts than is possible with any fully analytical technique. Our approach in this chapter is novel even for agent-based computational models. Many of the important works in this tradition have examined the change of strategies over time rather than the change of rules over time (see, e.g., Axelrod 1997; Miller et al. 2002).

4.2. What Are Agent-Based Computational Models

During the last decade, an increasing number of scholars in social and natural science used multi-agent systems, which consist of a number of interacting agents (Epstein and Axtell 1996; Conte et al. 1997; Liebrand et al. 1998; Gilbert and Troitzsch 1999). Agents can represent animals, people, or organizations. Agents can be reactive, proactive, may sensor the environment, communicate with other agents, learn, remember, and move.

Within economics this field is called agent-based computational economics and studies economies modeled as evolving systems of autonomous interacting agents (Tesfatsion 2001). An important challenge of agent-based computational economics is studying how stylized facts at a macro level emerge from the bottom up. These approaches have been applied to financial markets, macroeconomics, innovation dynamics, economic districts, environmental management, labor economics, and other processes.

The two main components of agent-based computational systems are: (1) cellular automata (defined below) representing the relevant biophysical world; and (2) models of the agents representing how the agent is posited to process information, learn, and make decisions. Each agent is represented as a computerized independent entity capable of acting locally in response to stimuli or to communication with other agents. Therefore, the first task is to build an architecture for intelligent agents. The second task is to design a structure in which interacting agents may or may not accomplish a task.

John von Neumann and Stanislaw Ulam introduced the cellular automata (CA) approach at the end of the 1940s, mainly to give a reductionistic model of life and self-reproduction. The game of life, invented by John Conway in 1970, popularized the CA approach (Gardner 1970). This game consists of cells on a checkerboard which can have two states, "alive" and "dead." Time goes by discrete steps. According to some deterministic rules, which are the same for each cell, the state of a cell in the next time step depends on its own present state and the states of all its surrounding cells in the present period. The resulting surprisingly complex dynamics that evolved from this simple game attracted the attention of many people. Since the early 1970s, CAs have been used by many disciplines to study complex dynamic behavior of systems.

The basic features of a CA are (Hegselmann 1998):

- It includes a D-dimensional lattice.
- time advances in *discrete* steps.
- There exist a *finite* number of states. At each site of the lattice exists a cell, which is in one of the possible states.
- The cells change their states according to *local* rules, both in space and in time.
- The transition rules are usually deterministic, but nondeterministic rules are allowed as well.
- The system is *homogeneous* in the sense that the set of possible states is the same for each cell, and the same transition rule applies to each cell.
- The updating procedure can consist of applying the transition rule to all cells *synchronically* or *asynchronically*.

The architecture of agents in agent-based computational systems has been much influenced by work in Artificial Intelligence (AI). In this field a popular wave is the autonomous agents research or behavior-based AI, which studies the behavior of adaptive autonomous agents in the physical world (robots) or in cyberspace (software agents). This field in AI is strongly inspired by biology. The phenomena of interest are those traditionally covered by ethnology and ecology (in the case of animals) or psychology and sociology (in the case of humans). The agents often consist of sensors to derive information from the environment and intelligent functions such as perception, planning, and learning that react to that information. Behavior is defined as regularities observed in the interaction dynamics between characteristics and processes of a system and the characteristics and processes of an environment. Examples are: a theory at the behavior level that explains the formation of paths in an ant society in terms of a set of behavioral rules without reference to how they are neurophysiologically implemented. Another example is the study of behavioral rules implemented in robots who have to survive (they need to reload energy every now and then) in a physical environment with other robots as a way to explore emergent behavior in such a group. An overview of this field can be found in, for example, Steels (1995) and Maes (1995).

Distributed artificial intelligence is a relatively recent development of artificial intelligence studies (Bond and Gasser 1988). It concerns the properties of sets of intercommunicating agents coexisting in a common environment. The aim may be to study the properties of such systems in an abstract way, or to design systems of immediate practical use, or to use such a programmed agent-based computational system as a model of a human or other real-world system.

Agent-based computational systems often consist of interacting agents in a cellular automata environment. In this chapter we study the emergence of collective action from the bottom up. This is related to the studies on the evolution of cooperation (see Gintis 2000). This problem has been studied intensively during the last twenty years by agent-based computational models starting with the seminal work of Axelrod (1984). The original studies of iterated Prisoner's Dilemmas considered repeated interactions of two players. However, when a game consists of more than two players, it becomes more complicated to assess the consequences of possible behavior of the other players for any of the individual player's own strategy. The more agents involved in a common-pool resource, the more sophisticated procedures are necessary.

We will provide specific details about our model below in the section on "Model Description."

4.3. COMMON-POOL RESOURCES

Common-pool resources share two attributes of importance for economic activities: (1) it is costly to exclude individuals from using a common-pool resource either through physical barriers or legal instruments; and (2) the benefits consumed by one individual subtract from the benefits available to others (Ostrom and Ostrom 1977; Ostrom, Gardner, and Walker 1994). Recognizing this class of goods that share two important, theoretically relevant attributes enables scholars to identify the core problems facing individuals or groups who wish to utilize such resources for an extended period of time.

First, common-pool resources share with public goods the difficulty and cost of developing physical or institutional means of excluding beneficiaries. Second, the products or resource units from common-pool resources share with private goods the attribute that one person's consumption subtracts from the quantity available to others. Thus, common-pool resources are subject to problems of congestion, overuse, and potential destruction—unless harvesting or use limits are devised, implemented, and enforced. In addition to sharing these two attributes, particular common-pool resources differ on many other attributes that affect their economic usefulness, including their size, shape, and productivity and the value, timing, and regularity of the resource units produced.

Common-pool resources may be owned by national, regional, or local governments, by communal groups, by private individuals or corporations, or used as open access resources by whoever can gain access. Each of the broad types of property regimes has different sets of advantages and disadvantages (Feeny et al. 1990). Examples exist of both successful and unsuccessful efforts to govern and manage common-pool resources by governments, communal groups, cooperatives, voluntary associations, and private individuals or firms (Bromley et al. 1992; Berkes 1989; Singh 1994; Singh and Ballabh 1996).

In settings where a central authority has not already claimed and enforced ownership of a common-pool resource, an important theoretical question is how those who are appropriating resources from a common pool are able to develop their *own* rules limiting the quantity of resource units harvested. Since Hardin (1968) used the strong metaphor of "The tragedy of the commons," many scholars have accepted the view that local appropriators (fishermen, irrigators, pastoralists, or others appropriating resource units from a common-pool resource) are trapped in an inevitable and tragic destruction of the resource upon which they were dependent. Extensive studies of local common-property systems, however, demonstrate that the "tragedy" is not inevitable (Ostrom 1990; Bromley et al. 1992; Burger et al. 2001; Pathak and Korhari 2001). Successful self-organization is also not inevitable.

The core question is, how can a group of appropriators independently create their own rules, monitor each other's conformance with rules, and sanction one another when rule infractions are discovered. As Gallarotti (2001) points out, extensive empirical research documents the capabilities of individuals to organize themselves, establish new rules, monitor rule conformance, and sanction rule breaking, but little theoretical work has explored how rules emerge in the first place (for an initial sketch of a theory, see Ostrom 1990, chap. 6).

Thus, in this chapter we address the puzzle of why some groups form and establish their own rules to regulate their resources, and why other do not. Closely related is the question why some groups fail after making an initial start. Some communal systems fail or limp along at the margin of effectiveness just as private firms fail or barely hang on to profitability over long periods of time.

4.4. Factors Associated with Self-Organization

Scholars who have conducted extensive field research on locally self-organized institutions for managing common-pool resources have identified a set of attributes of appropriators that the researcher considers to be conducive to the evolution of norms, rules, and property rights that improve the probabilities of sustainability of common-pool resources. While there is some controversy about particular variables—such as the size of the group and the degree and kind of heterogeneity of the group—the following variables are frequently found in the list of factors considered by empirical researchers to be crucial foundations of self-governed resource use:

1. Accurate information about the condition of the resource and expected flow of benefits and costs are available at low cost to the participants leading to a common understanding of likely consequences of continuing the status quo (no regulation of use) as contrasted with feasible changes in rules (Blomquist 1992; Gilles and Jamtgaard 1981; Sethi and Somanathan 1996; Ostrom 1990).

2. Appropriators plan to live and work in the same area for a long time (and in some cases, expect their offspring to live there as well) and, thus, do not heavily discount the future (Grima and Berkes 1989).

3. Appropriators are highly dependent on the resource (Gibson 2001).

4. Appropriators use collective-choice rules that fall between the extremes of unanimity or control by a few (or even bare majority) and, thus, avoid high transaction or high deprivation costs (Ostrom 1990).

5. The group using the resource is relatively stable (Seabright 1993).

6. The size of the group is relatively small (Franzen 1994; Fujita, Hayami, and Kikuchi 1999; Wilson and Thompson 1993; Kirch 1997).

7. The group is relatively homogenous (Bardhan and Dayton-Johnson 2002, Bardhan 1993; Libecap 1995; Lam 1998; but see Varughese and Ostrom 2001).

8. Participants have developed generalized norms of reciprocity and trust that can be used as initial social capital (Bardhan 1993; Cordell and McKean 1992; Ostrom 1990).

9. Participants can develop relatively accurate and low-cost monitoring and sanctioning arrangements (Berkes 1992; Ostrom 1990).

In our agent-based computational model, described below, the first four factors are built into our model by assumption. We consider the eighth and ninth factors to be particularly important and we focus largely on the processes and consequences of establishing reciprocity and trust and on factors affecting monitoring and sanctioning arrangements. The fifth, sixth, and seventh factors are varied to some extent in the simulations described below.

4.5. ESTABLISHING TRUST

While many definitions of trust exist, all involve a trustor extending something of value to a trustee based on an assumption that the trustee will reciprocate the faith that the trustee has extended. A core aspect of most definitions of trust is the "intention to accept vulnerability based upon positive expectations of the intentions of the behavior of another"

(Rousseau et al. 1998). Using this conception of trust, one can recognize that almost all economic transactions other than immediate spot exchanges involve greater or lesser levels of trust (Arrow 1974). And, anyone willing to accept a rule restricting their actions in an economically important activity must trust that the others involved will follow that rule as well. If they do not trust others to cooperate and follow a rule, individuals are unlikely to follow risky strategies of cooperating with others. Once established, however, cooperation may almost be "habit-forming" based on the trust that others will continue to be trustworthy (Seabright 1993).

In noncooperative game theory, rational egoists do not trust other players voluntarily to perform a costly action unless either the other players expect greater benefits to occur than expected costs or unless some external agent enforces agreements. And yet, in many laboratory experiments of "The Trust Game," a large proportion of those individuals placed in the position of the trustor do make themselves vulnerable to others by investing resources in others that could be returned in a manner that makes all better off. And, a large proportion of those who are trusted are actually trustworthy and do reciprocate the trust (see Ostrom and Walker 2003 for an overview of these studies).

The degree of trusting behavior and trustworthiness, however, varies substantially in the experimental laboratory as well as in the field. Multiple contextual factors associated with the structure of experiments and field studies are posited to affect the variance in trusting and trustworthy behavior. The amount of information that individuals have about each other, the likelihood of repeated interactions, and the identity and homogeneity of the individuals involved all appear to affect the level of trust.

In the model simulations of the emergence and sustenance of a local rule, we thus place the development of trust as a key instrumental variable while examining how several other factors affect both the development of trust and the emergence and maintenance of a local rule. The model in this chapter is based on the agent-based computational models for the study of cooperation, but will add some new elements endogenously to introduce a new rule set, and to monitor and enforce these rules.

4.6. MODEL DESCRIPTION

A stylized simulation model is developed in which agents share a common resource. If no rule is implemented, the resource and the appropriators will experience serious collapses, and the feasible cooperative optimum situation will not be reached. A possible rule is known to the participants and could be implemented. Our aim with this model is to investigate the critical conditions under which a heterogeneous population will implement this rule, and how successfully it will be monitored and sanctions applied. The population of appropriators is heterogeneous in characteristics such as the intention to break rules, degree of monitoring, eating rates, and the symbols they wear.

Many possible rules could of course be implemented to avoid overharvesting, but only one particular set of rules is assumed to be a candidate in our model. Although we start this research avenue with the problem of adopting a candidate rule, our ambition is to understand how a variety of rules evolve. This requires, however, further conceptual developments on the evolution of rules (Janssen and Stow 2002). The choice to model only one candidate rule is caused by the fact that leaving open the possibility of more than one set of rules adds immense complexity that is not directly related to the questions at the core of our interests.

Our interest is to identify the critical assumptions that lead to a timely implementation of a rule set and an effective monitoring and sanctioning regime. As discussed above, the findings of field research and laboratory experiments show that the development of mutual trust is a crucial factor. Therefore, we are especially interested in how mutual trust development can be influenced.

To avoid overwhelming the reader with technicalities, we present only the basic equations of the model. The rest is explained verbally. The programming code of the model can be derived upon request. The model is implemented in CORMAS (Bousquet et al. 1998; http://cormas.cirad.fr), which is a shell around the object-oriented language Smalltalk. CORMAS[2] is especially designed to simulate agents in a cellular automata environment for the study of common-pool resources.

The model developed in this chapter differs from the standard models of a renewable resource since the resource is spatially explicit. This spatial element is included to restrict the knowledge of agents to available, local information. The resource is split up in $N \times N$ cells. To avoid edge effects, the corner cells are wrapped around to derive a torus, a donut shape system. Neighbors are defined by a so-called Moore neighborhood, which includes cells to the north, south, east, and west of the center cell as well as diagonal cells to the north east, north west, south east, and south west. These always form a square pattern. So a cell has eight neighbors, and a neighborhood contains nine cells.

Biomass on each cell grows according to the logistic function of equation (1). In this equation, a renewable resource (energy), x, is modeled according to the standard models in bioeconomics (Clark 1990) and develops according to a logistic growth equation,

$$x(t) = x(t-1) + r \cdot x(t-1) \cdot \left(1 - \frac{x(t-1)}{K}\right) - e_c \qquad (1)$$

where x is the biomass, K is the carrying capacity, r is the growth parameter, and e_c is the energy consumption of an agent.

Each cell has the same carrying capacity, but the initial values of the stocks are drawn randomly. In this spatial landscape a population of mobile agents exists. Only one agent can occupy a cell for any one time period. Agents can move each time step to another unoccupied neighboring cell with the highest biomass level. If there is no neighboring cell with a higher biomass level than the present cell, the agent does not move. The agents harvest a fixed percentage q of the cell biomass, with a maximum of $e_{c,max}$. The embodied energy e can be defined as the embodied energy in the previous time step minus the metabolic rate c, plus the energy consumption e_c.

If agents are not successful in harvesting energy, and the level of embodied energy depletes, the agent will die (i.e., leave the system). Agents can also reproduce, asexually, when their embodied energy level exceeds a certain threshold f. Above this energy level, the agent splits into two agents with an initial energy level equal to $f/2$. Genetic information is copied to the offspring, although genetic information mutates with a low probability p_m for each property.

Each agent has a number of properties that can differ among the population. These properties can be unobservable (krypta) or observable (manifesta) (Gambetta and Bacharach 2001). The unobservable properties are the fraction of biomass on a cell that is eaten by the agent (q), the intention to break the rule (λ), the probability that the agent will monitor and sanction others (p_s), and the weighting (w) assigned to the symbols. The observable features are the symbols (s). The agents have genetic symbols, which are unchangeable during the lifetime of the agent, and they have cultural symbols, which can be adapted by the agent. The evolution of the properties of the agents depends on genetic and cultural evolution as well as on learning.

The distribution of genetic information, the properties that remain fixed over the lifetime of an agent, may change over time as a consequence of mutation in the offspring. Cultural evolution influences the configuration of cultural symbols and depends on imitation processes (see Bowles 1998). Learning leads to adaptations of weighting the symbols to estimate trustworthiness.

The fitness of an agent varies related to its energy use during different activities. Agents with an initial very low eating fraction will not derive enough energy to survive, while other agents with higher levels derive more energy and are able to produce offspring. When a rule is implemented, the energy budget is also influenced by the energy spent when the agent breaks the rule and is caught. Consequently, a co-evolutionary process exists between the probabilities that agents break rules and that they monitor each other. If there are many agents breaking rules, it benefits to monitor, but then the benefits for breaking rules decline. The embodied energy can now be defined as:

$$e(t) = e(t-1) - c + e_c(t) - c_m - p + r \qquad (2)$$

where c_m is equal to the extra energy consumption for monitoring, p the penalty of being caught when breaking the rule, and r the reward for catching rule-breakers.[3]

4.6.1. Evolution of Mutual Trust

The agents start in a situation where there is no regulation. There is one candidate rule, namely, no harvesting is allowed when the energy level of the cell is below x_{min}.[4] Furthermore, if the rule is implemented an agreement exists on the sanction penalties, s_e, of rule-breakers, and how the collected penalties are allocated among the group. The question is under which conditions the candidate rule will be activated, and how successfully it will be monitored and sanctioned. Whether the rule will be implemented depends on the evolution of mutual trust.

The description of a mutual trust relationship is based on the work on indirect reciprocity (Nowak and Sigmund 1998). Within an indirect reciprocity approach agents keep track of image scores of individuals, where the image scores represent the degree of cooperative actions of the agent in the past. So, when an agent meets another agent it derives information about its past performance of cooperation. The drawback of such an image score is the assumption of perfect knowledge.

We propose another version of indirect reciprocity. All agents have symbols that are visible to each other. During interactions with others, agents learn to recognize those symbols and attach meaning to them to discriminate against people they think are trustworthy from those who are viewed as untrustworthy people. This can have important consequences. Although two agents may have a high image score, they may not trust each other. Another issue is whether symbols really represent discriminating factors. It is the belief of agents that they are able to recognize trustworthy others.

We assume that agents develop an expectation of the trustworthiness of others using observable information (the tags). Such an approach is in line with Macy and Skvoretz (1998). To update the relation between the tags and trustworthiness, agents interact with their neighbors. Each time step each agent interacts with a neighbor if this neighbor has an expected trust level, EY_{ij}, above a minimum, EY_{min}. During this interaction, agents exchange information. In formal terms, they play a basic trust game. One agent is the trustor and starts the interaction with another agent, the trustee. The probability that a trustor starts an interaction is stochastic and depends on the expected trust level EY_{ij}. When the trustor has started an interaction, C, representing cooperation, the trustee has to decide to perform action C or D. The probability of this decision depends on the expected trustworthiness of the trustor.

The relation between expected trustworthiness and the probability of choosing C or D differs for the trustor and the trustee. We assume that starting an interaction, which means a trustor chooses C, requires relatively more trust of the trustor in the trustee, than the trust that a trustee must have to respond to C with a choice of C. Starting the interaction involves more uncertainty, therefore a relative high level of expected trustworthiness is required. On the other hand, refusing to react positively to a proposed interaction is not very polite, and it reduces your perceived trustworthiness. The degree to which the probabilities to cooperate differ is represented by parameter $\varphi \geq 1$. If φ is equal to 1, the probabilities are equal for both trustee and trustor.

The payoff matrix of the trust game is constructed as follows. If an agent is starting an interaction or reacting to a proposed interaction, it will cost an amount of energy equal to α. The receiver will derive an amount of energy equal to β, where $\beta < \alpha$. Therefore, the net reward depends on the response.

trustee	C	D
trustor C	$(-\alpha + \beta, -\alpha + \beta)$	$(-\alpha, \beta)$
D	——	——

The relation between one's agent's assessment of the trustworthiness of the other agent with specific, observed tags is updated based on the actions of the other agent. For example, if a trustor chose C and the trustee reacts with D, the assessed trustworthiness is updated in such a way that agents with tags similar to the trustee are perceived as less trustworthy in the next round. If the trustee returns C, the perceived trustworthiness is reinforced. So, due to repeated interaction between agents, mutual trust can be developed or destroyed. Note that trust games have negative payoffs. The benefits of playing trust games are entirely indirect. By building up mutual trust relationships, the agents are more likely to benefit from other interactions in the future.

To calculate the expected trustworthiness of other agents, an agent makes an expectation based on observed symbols. This is implemented as a single-layer neural network:

$$EY_{t,i,j} = w_{t,i,0} + \sum_{k=1}^{ks} w_{t,i,k} \cdot y_{t,j,k} \qquad (3)$$

where $EY_{t,i,j}$ is the level of trust agent i has in agent j, $y_{t,j,k}$ are the inputs of the neural network, the observed symbols (-1 or 1) of the other agent j. Finally, the inputs are weighted by $w_{t,i,k}$.

A neural network is trained when new information about the input values is used to update the weights. The widely used Widrow-Hoff delta rule is used to train the neural network during the simulation (Mehrota et al. 1997).

$$\Delta w_{t,i,j} = \eta \cdot \delta_{t,i} \cdot \frac{\mathbf{y}_i}{\|\mathbf{y}_i\|} \qquad (4)$$

where

$$\delta_{t,i} = Y_{t,ij} - w_{t,i,0} - \sum_{k=1}^{ks} w_{t,ik} \cdot y_{t,j,k} \qquad (5)$$

where $\delta_{t,i}$ is the difference between the observed values and the expected value, and $Y_{t,ij}$ is the experienced trust during the interaction. The observed value is 1 in case of a positive interaction, and 0 in case of a negative interaction. The delta rule therefore updates the expectations according to the observed errors. The rate of updating depends on the value of η, which is suggested to lie between 0.1 and 1 (Gallant 1993).

4.7. MOTIVATION TO ADOPT THE RULE

The agents can become motivated to adopt the candidate rule. This motivation depends on the observed depletion of the resource, and on the mutual trust among agents. The general idea is that when an agent has sufficient trust in other agents, and the observed resource condition falls below a threshold, the motivation to implement the rule increases, otherwise the motivation decays each time step by a fraction υ. Reinforcement by observed depletion of the resource and trust in others can increase motivation.

The reinforcement of positive motivation can only be derived when certain conditions are met. First, the observed biomass level in the neighborhood, x_n, should be below a level $x_{n,min}$ (equal to $K/2$). Second, the expected regrowth of the biomass in the neighborhood should not be sufficient to satisfy the metabolism of the number of agents a_n in the neighborhood. Third, if the resource is not expected to satisfy the metabolism of the agents, a maximum life expectancy of the agent is calculated. If this expectancy is lower than minimum value T_y and the expected trust in the population $O(Y)$ exceeds a minimum level $O(Y)_{min}$, then the motivation will be reinforced. The value of T_y can be interpreted as the maximum number of time steps the agent wants to use for finding better opportunities. The expected trust in the population is defined as the moving average of expected trust in the last ($1/\theta$) neighbors. Thus, if θ is equal to 1, the trust in the population is equal to the trust in the most recent neighbor looked at while a θ of 0.05 leads to an average expected trust of the last twenty neighbors.

A possibility exists that the observed resource is depleted, but the population of agents has been decreased to such a low level that some agents do not meet others during a sequence of rounds. In such cases, it is not appropriate to reinforce motivation although the expected trust in the last $1/\theta$ neighbors meets the conditions. Therefore, when an agent has not met another agent for the past ten rounds, the motivation to implement a rule will not be reinforced.

An agent is motivated when m exceeds m_{min}. The regulation is implemented when a certain constitutional level of agents agrees with the adoption of the regulation. This could include several collective-choice rules, including: (1) 50 percent of the population plus one; (2) 50 percent of the weighted population plus one where the votes are weighted with the welfare level (embodied energy) of the voters; or (3) a decision by the leader of the group.[5] In the simulation experiments of this chapter we assume that the collective-choice rule is the first one, namely, 50 percent of the population plus one.

When a regulation is implemented agents can follow rules, break rules, and can monitor others. When an agent wants to harvest cell biomass below the tolerated level, it breaks the rule with a certain probability. If an agent has neighbors it monitors the neighborhood with a fixed chance to check whether a neighbor is breaking a rule. When the agent is caught it has to pay a penalty equal to the amount below the tolerated level and a percentage s_e of the embodied energy. The level of s_e increases with the number of times an agent has been caught breaking the rule.

The penalty is split up. A fraction $(1 - g)$ of the penalty goes to reward the monitoring agent, which derives a. The remaining fraction g of the penalty will be allocated among the whole population. Furthermore, when a rule-breaker is caught, the trust relationship is adjusted. The neural network of equation (5) is updated with an observation 0, a negative interaction with an agent.

Probability of breaking the rule is related to a fixed, genetic, habit to break rules λ, the level of trust in the population $O(Y)$, and the level of embodied energy. The higher the trust in the population, the lower the chance that the agent will break a rule. Furthermore, the higher the level of embodied energy, the lower the chance of breaking a rule.

4.8. THE COMPLETED COMPUTER EXPERIMENTS

The experiments focus on the determination of critical conditions that influence the ability of the agents to derive a cooperative solution to the sustainability of the resource system. The default setup is designed in such a way that, with plausible parameter values, a cooperative solution is likely to be derived. Additional sensitivity experiments test whether changes in the assumptions lead to structurally different solutions.

The experiments are performed using $N = 20$, thus 400 cells, and a Moore neighborhood, thus 8 neighbors for every cell. In table 4.1 the parameter values of the default case are listed. To stimulate cooperation, we assume in the default case no cost during the basic trust games and low monitoring costs.

In the first set of experiments all agents can use the whole lattice without limitations. We will test whether the type of neighborhood and the size of the lattice influence the outcomes of the default case. Furthermore, we will analyze the impact of the cost of monitoring, the sanction level, the share of the penalty allocated to the whole group, the costs of playing trust games, the chance of starting an interaction (parameter φ), the threshold values that influence motivation (T_y, m_{min}, and $O(Y)_{min}$), and the number of symbols. This set of experiments provides a comprehensive overview of the dynamics of the system.

In the second set of experiments, the torus is split up in two. When agents stay in their own region, they will build up their own set of cultural symbols. When agents can enter another region, for example in times of scarcity, they are strangers to the existing population. The first genetic symbol is here assumed to indicate the region of birth. For the sake of simplicity, we assume that offspring of an agent in a foreign region is born in the original region of its parent. Agents move probabilistically to the other region when their embodied energy is low and they observe scarcity in the neighborhood.

Four different cases are distinguished in the analyses of the two groups. First, the carrying capacities can be equal in each region ($K = 10$), or they can differ between the regions using $K = 5$ for one region and $K = 15$ for the other. Second, the agents can accept the rules in the foreign region, or they may not accept the foreign rules. Note that agents can only monitor and sanction when they are in their own region. Moreover, agents outside the region can vote for implementing the rule but they do not experience scarcity in their region of origin.

The theoretical cooperative optimum is equal to 100 agents and a biomass energy level of 2,000. This can be derived as follows. The maximum output of a cell occurs at $x = 5$. The regrowth is than equal to

TABLE 4.1
Parameter Values of the Model for the Default Case

Parameter	Value	Explanation
Resource		
r	0.20	Growth rate of the resource
K	10.0	Carrying capacity of a cell
Agent		
q	[0,1]	Fraction of a cell eaten by the agent
e_{max}	4.00	Maximum absolute level of energy consumption per time step
c	2.00	Energy metabolism per timestep
f	100.00	Embodied energy level above which the agent will derive offspring
#symbols (genetic)	5.00	Number of genetic symbols
#symbols (cultural)	5.00	Number of cultural symbols
λ	[0,1]	Habit to break rules
p_s	[0,1]	Probability of an agent to monitor and sanction
p_m	0.050	Probability of mutation of a "gene" during offspring generation
Trust		
φ	2.00	Parameter of skewness in starting to play basic trust games
α	0	Cost of starting an interaction
β	0	Reward of receiving an interaction signal
η	0.10	Updating rate neural network of trust expectations
Rule-definition		
x_{min}	4.00	Cell level of energy below which no harvesting is allowed
s_e	0.20	Initial sanction rate
g	0.70	Fraction of penalty allocated to the group
c_m	0.50	Energy cost per time step of monitoring a neighbor
Motivation		
T_y	10.00	Expected life without energy intake as a threshold level for motivation
υ	0.10	Decay rate of motivation
m_{min}	0.50	Minimum level of motivation before an agent is motivated to vote
θ	0.05	Decay rate of trust in neighbors
$O(Y)_{min}$	0.50	Minimum level of trust in neighbors before being motivated

0.2*5*0.5 = 0.5. Since each agent use 2 units of energy, and 400 cells produce 200 units of energy in the optimal case, 100 agents can be provided with energy. 400 cells of 5 units of energy equal 2,000 units of energy.

For each experiment 50 runs are performed for 3,000 time steps, which differ in the initial allocations of the agents, the initial level of energy at the cells, and the symbols and values of λ, q, p_m of the initial population. The initial number of agents is equal to 50 percent of the theoretical equilibrium, which is 50 agents in the default case.

4.9. RESULTS

To provide a basic understanding of the dynamics of the model, the default case will first be discussed in detail. Although fifty runs have been performed, we start with a discussion of a "typical" run.

The system experienced two crises before the candidate rule was adopted. The population size fluctuated between 10 and 100 during the first 400 time steps. After the rule adoption around time step 250, the population size gradually increased toward the theoretical equilibrium of 100 agents (figures 4.1 and 4.2). A similar development can be observed for the total amount of biomass energy on the torus (figures 4.1 and 4.2). Note that the population change follows the biomass energy figures with some delay. When the resource starts to recover after a crisis, still a large part of the lattice does not produce enough energy to sustain the population, and population continues to decrease for a while (figure 4.1).

Figure 4.3 shows that during the first period of scarcity, the fraction of agents agreeing with implementing the rule set did not surpass 50 percent. At that time, the system started to recover, and the motivation decreased. During the second crisis, the average trust level was higher than during the first crisis, leading to a larger proportion of motivated agents. The voting agents reach about 52 percent around time step 260.

The reason for the decrease of the trust in their neighbors after the two periods of crises is caused by two factors. First, agents have a trust level of 0.5 when they are born, and have to meet people to build up trust in their neighborhoods. Second, the fast increase of the population is likely to include agents with new combinations of symbols. In this case, new agents have to learn which agents (characterized by which set of symbols) they can trust. Since the average trust in the neighborhoods increases after the rule set has been implemented, the amount of rule-breaking decreased, as did the level of monitoring and the amount of energy harvesting, resulting in a steady increase of the population size (figures 4.1 and 4.2).

Interestingly, the eating fraction q increases during the period without the candidate rule in place. In a "cowboy" society (without any rules),

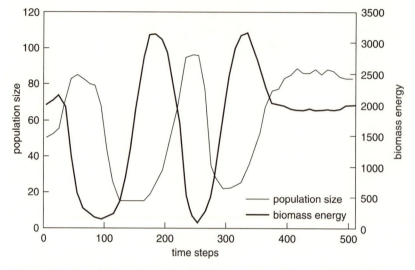

Figure 4.1. Population size and total biomass energy of a typical default run for the first 500 time steps.

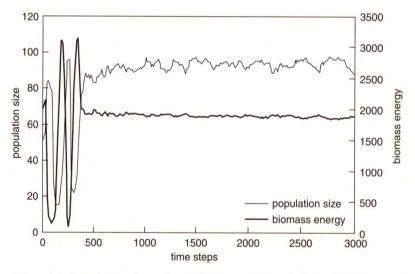

Figure 4.2. Population size and total biomass energy of a typical default run.

those who consume the most energy will get the highest number of offspring. Thus, evolutionary selection favors selfish agents. The higher eating rate causes a deeper collapse of the biomass energy during the period of scarcity. When the rule is implemented, the value of q decreases since it has lost its advantage in evolutionary selection.

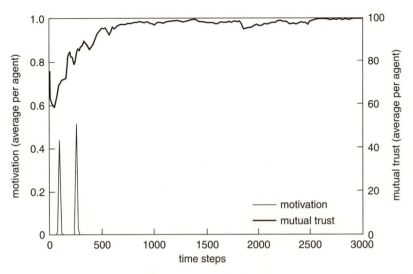

Figure 4.3. Motivation and mutual trust, both average per capita, of a typical default run.

The amount of monitoring is high during the period after rule adoption (figure 4.4). This high level is caused by the fact that agents have a genetic value for monitoring which is drawn from a uniform distribution in the initial population. Although the energy use of monitoring seems to be rather low, it prevents agents with a high probability of monitoring to produce many offspring. The individual benefits of monitoring do not compensate the cost of extra energy use during monitoring. Therefore, the fraction of monitoring decreases in time but monitoring as well as rule-breaking never disappear (see Weissing and Ostrom 1991 for a similar finding derived from a game theoretical model of monitoring and rule-breaking).

One of the main problems of agent-based computational models is the analysis and representation of the enormous amount of data from the simulation runs. In figure 4.5, the population size for the fifty runs is depicted. In most cases, the rule is adopted and the system converges toward a cooperative optimum. The timing of adopting the rule differs between the simulation runs (figure 4.6). In 15 percent of the cases, the rule is adopted in the first period of scarcity, while in about 75 percent of the cases, the rule is adopted in the second period of scarcity. In a few cases the system collapses entirely. Note from figures 4.1–4.4 that the second period of scarcity is more severe than the first one. During this period the agents may not be able to survive the crises, even after a rule is adopted. The cure can come too late to heal the system. The regularity in the timing of the collapses is caused by the fixed mutation level of the

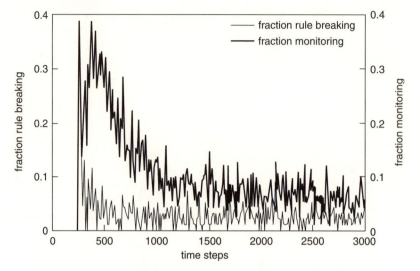

Figure 4.4. Fraction of the population breaking the rule, or monitoring the neighborhood of a typical default run.

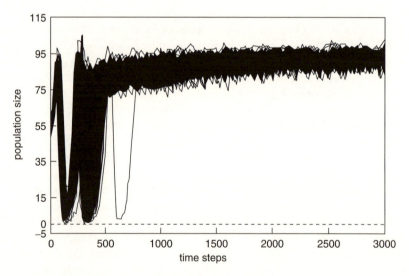

Figure 4.5. Population size for 50 different default runs.

agents and the logistic growth function of the resource. Whether a new collapse occurs depends on the implementation of the candidate rule restricting energy consumption and therefore population size.

For a number of conditions and assumptions, we have examined the consequences of introducing the candidate rule, as well as the monitor-

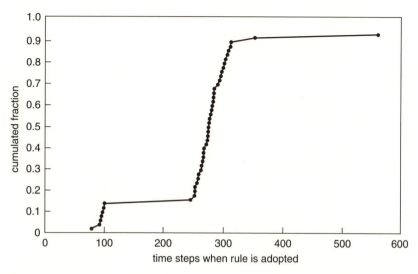

Figure 4.6. The time step at which the rule is adopted, starting with the fastest adoption.

ing and reinforcement. For each experiment fifty simulations have been performed. Statistics of the system at time step 3000, as well as of the time step of adoption of the rule, are the summary statistics characterizing an experiment and reported table 4.2.

4.9.1. Configurations of the Torus

The size of the lattice influences the vulnerability of the system and the timing of adopting the rule. A smaller lattice has a smaller number of initial agents and a lower population before the situation becomes critical. Due to the smaller reservoir of heterogeneity among the agents, the system becomes vulnerable to disturbances, such as resource scarcity. If the rule is not adopted after the first crisis, the system is more likely to collapse. A consequence of a small torus is the reduced probability that agents can survive due to little spots of biomass left over or because agents collected enough energy to survive a period of scarcity. When the rule is accepted, the monitoring rate decreases. Since monitoring rates are assumed to be fixed for an agent, a lower population size reduces the speed of evolution and thus of adjusting the monitoring rate. In case of a lattice with 900 cells, it may take a few crises before the rule is adopted. Due to the large initial variety of agents, agents are frequently meeting other agents with new combinations of symbols. Therefore, it takes longer to build up enough trust in other agents to support the proposed rule.

TABLE 4.2
Statistics of the Experiments when the Torus is One Region.

Experiment	Population Size	Energy Biomass	Trust	% Monitoring	% Breaking Rules	Time Step Adoption	% Collapse
Default	92.8 (3.7)	1915.1 (28.6)	98.4 (1.7)	9.2 (5.8)	2.7 (1.5)	257.8 (82.5)	6
100 cells	22.3 (1.9)	484.9 (21.4)	97.6 (5.3)	17.9 (14.4)	3.1 (4.3)	189.3 (269.4)	16
900 cells	210.6 (6.1)	4306.9 (39.3)	98.9 (0.7)	9.4 (6.3)	2.3 (1.1)	296.7 (57.4)	0
4 neighbors	39.6 (30.7)	1695.0 (1242.6)	74.6 (16.7)	0	0	0	70
25 neighbors	93.3 (3.7)	1910.6 (27.9)	99.7 (0.3)	3.7 (3.2)	2.0 (1.6)	63.7 (6.9)	0
$T_y = 8$	93.2 (3.8)	1918.0 (28.7)	98.7 (1.2)	11.2 (6.3)	2.2 (1.4)	303.7 (80.9)	28
$T_y = 6$	92.9 (3.1)	1917.2 (45.5)	98.0 (2.2)	9.5 (6.7)	3.1 (2.1)	434.7 (173.1)	64
$m_{min} = 0.6$	92.8 (3.5)	1921.0 (30.1)	98.5 (1.3)	12.2 (8.4)	2.3 (1.5)	335.0 105.8	16
$m_{min} = 0.7$	89.6 (12.0)	1985.5 (236.4)	98.1 (3.2)	9.7 (6.6)	2.7 (2.0)	478.6 (305.7)	64
$O(Y)_{min} = 0.6$	93.1 (3.9)	1914.5 (29.2)	98.5 (1.6)	9.7 (7.1)	2.3 (1.6)	311.7 (130.7)	18
$O(Y)_{min} = 0.7$	92.6 (4.0)	1913.1 (28.0)	97.2 (4.2)	10.7 (6.7)	2.9 (1.7)	330.8 (103.3)	34
$\alpha = 0.5; \beta = 0.25$	68.8 (2.2)	2094.6 (31.3)	98.1 (2.0)	12.6 (8.3)	2.5 (2.1)	393.0 (218.4)	18
$\alpha = 1; \beta = 0.5$	29.2 (22.7)	2316.8 (1348.7)	74.2 (10.8)	0	0	0	50
	51.0 (5.9)	2483.5 (263.0)	86.4 (10.7)	31.3 (15.7)	3.1 (2.5)	1822.8 953.2	10 rule adoption
$\varphi = 1$	93.7 (3.6)	1913.4 (23.8)	98.3 (1.5)	10.4 (7.9)	2.4 (1.7)	218.9 (90.6)	12
$\varphi = 4$	93.7 (3.5)	1914.4 (27.4)	98.9 (1.3)	9.9 (8.0)	2.5 (1.5)	265.2 (58.5)	10

Table 4.2 (*continued*)

Experiment	Population Size	Energy Biomass	Trust	% Monitoring	% Breaking Rules	Time Step Adoption	% Collapse
$s_c = 0$	92.5 (3.0)	1884.0 (37.2)	99.3 (0.8)	11.2 (7.2)	4.6 (2.8)	247.8 (86.8)	20
$c_m = 5$	84.8 (7.9)	1939.2 (92.0)	97.3 (5.9)	3.1 (3.2)	4.6 (5.1)	244.3 (79.4)	18
$g = 1$	94.0 (2.5)	1909.7 (22.0)	98.7 (1.4)	8.6 (4.6)	2.8 (1.7)	248.5 (95.9)	4
$g = 0$	84.3 (4.5)	1994.1 (37.5)	96.1 (2.7)	36.2 (13.0)	2.3 (1.8)	238.8 (84.4)	2
$K = 5$	19.2 (11.0)	593.6 (413.7)	73.3 (14.6)	0	0	0	12
$K = 15$	141.2 (4.1)	2664.7 (16.7)	99.2 (1.7)	6.5 (4.3)	2.2 (1.1)	80.9 (4.6)	0
2 symbols	94.6 (2.5)	1908.2 (18.0)	99.8 (0.3)	7.5 (5.2)	2.5 (1.4)	105.4 (53.5)	0

Note: The values are the average of noncollapsed runs in time step 3000. A run is collapsed when the population at time step 3000 is zero. The value between brackets is the standard deviation.

When agents only have four neighboring cells (south, north, east, and west), the system becomes vulnerable. In none of the simulations is a rule adopted. In 70 percent of the cases, the system collapses during the 3,000 time steps. The reason for this vulnerability is the reduced social space, which limits the number of social contacts and the ability to build up mutual trust. The opposite happens when the agents have twenty-four neighboring cells (a Moore neighborhood with radius 2). Agents have the opportunity to meet many agents each time step, which accelerates mutual trust relationships. The rule is adopted in all cases directly at the beginning of the first crisis. The monitoring rate is reduced since an agent can monitor more agents per time step due to the larger social space.

4.9.2. Motivation

When the threshold T_y is lowered, the agent will tolerate a lower level of resource scarcity before becoming motivated to vote for regulation. This delay in motivation causes a decrease in the performance of the system. The percentage of collapses increases, and when the rule is adopted, it will be later than in the default case. But when the rule is adopted, the performance in terms of monitoring and sanctioning is similar to the default case, as would be expected. An increased level of m_{min} will increase the time the agents have to build up motivation. This delays the moment of adopting the rule and increases the chance of collapse. Similar arguments hold for increasing the value of $O(Y)_{min}$, the minimum level of trust in neighbors.

4.9.3. Trust

In the default case, the interactions between agents in order to build up mutual trust was costless. One could think of the act of saying hi or waving one's hand as an example of this type of costless interaction. When positive costs are included ($\alpha > 0$; $\beta > 0$), agents who trust other agents lose energy in maintaining social contacts. One can think of this kind of interaction as involving the gift of small portions of "party" or "ritual" food that cost more than their energy benefit. Due to the extra energy use, the population growth is slower over time. Since trusting others reduces individual fitness, the average trust in others is lower than the default case. This slows down the introduction of the rule and increases the probability of a collapse. In case $\alpha = 1$ and $\beta = 0.5$, the probability of collapse is higher than 50 percent. When the system does not collapse, no rule is implemented in 40 percent of these cases, and the average population is low (around 30 agents). In 10 percent of these cases, a rule is implemented leading to a doubling of the population. The results do not significantly change for alternative values of φ.

4.9.4. Rule Definition

When the candidate rule does not include a provision that agents have to pay an extra fee when caught for breaking a rule, thus $s_c = 0$, the percentage of rule-breaking remains higher and the resource is more depleted than when these provisions are part of the rule. An increased percentage of the cases collapsed due to the high level of rule-breaking just after the introduction of the rule. The population level and the mutual trust level of the runs where the system did not collapse are high, which is caused by reduced probabilities of sanctioning rule-breakers and the lower rate of introducing new agents.

Increasing the costs of monitoring, c_m, reduces the level of monitoring and increases the level of rule-breaking. Due to higher monitoring costs, the average population size at the end of the simulations drops by 10 percent compared to the default case.

In the default case, 70 percent of the penalty is shared among the population, and the monitoring agent receives 30 percent of the penalty. When the monitoring agent does not derive any personal reward for monitoring, the monitoring level is lower. When a monitoring agent can keep all of the penalty earnings, it stimulates monitoring. But due to a high level of monitoring, the agents become aware of more rule-breaking than observed in the default case. This reduces mutual trust and increase the number of agents who do not survive after receiving a sanction (thus reducing the population size).

4.9.5. Carrying Capacity

A high carrying capacity ($K = 15$) increases the population size and the number of mutual interactions. The faster increase of mutual trust leads to a timely adoption of the rule in all cases. The lower monitoring rate is caused due to the higher population size and selection pressure to reduce monitoring costs. However, a lower carrying capacity ($K = 5$) reduces interactions between agents by such an amount that not enough mutual trust is built up to adopt the rule.

4.9.6. Number of Symbols

When agents have only one genetic and one cultural symbol instead of five of each type, the rule is adopted significantly faster. Due to less heterogeneity in the symbols the agents can learn faster who to trust.

4.9.7. Splitting the Torus

By splitting the torus into two, agents initially are allocated in two different regions and build up their own identity. This identity is the combination of cultural symbols that emerge in the two regions. When the agents from one region start to enter the other region, they are strangers and may not be trusted.

When the carrying capacities are equal in both regions, the rule is adopted in most cases (table 4.3). However, the population sizes are lower than the default case of one unified torus. The reason is the behavior of the agents is constrained by the boundaries of the area, which reduces the potential available energy. Since the carrying capacities in both regions are the same, and in most cases the rule is accepted, the number of agents moving to the other region after 3,000 time steps is low. There is a little difference between the cases where agents accept the rule in the other region or not. When agents do not accept a rule in another region, we found one case where the system collapses, compared with no collapse in the case of accepting the rule.

In some typical experiments we see that in periods of crises a lot of agents move to the other region. Not accepting the rule leads to sanction-

TABLE 4.3
Statistics of the Experiments When the Torus Is Split into Two Regions

Experiment	Population Size	Energy Biomass	Trust	% Monitoring	% Breaking Rules	% Collapse
K = 10 and accepting rules	84.8 (11.4)	1859.8 (193.0)	94.5 (2.5)	14.5 (10.3)	3.2 (2.4)	0 (10/6)
K = 10 and not accepting rules	90.9 (3.9)	1950.7 (71.1)	97.6 (1.4)	16.0 (8.8)	2.9 (1.6)	2
K = 5/15 and accepting rules	79.9 (6.6)	1652.1 (263.0)	94.9 (3.0)	7.8 (6.0)	3.6 (2.8)	0
K = 5/15 and not accepting rules	80.1 (6.2)	1701.0 (287.3)	95.0 (2.6)	8.7 (5.7)	4.1 (2.7)	0

Note: The values are average of noncollapsed runs of the whole torus in time step 3000. A run is collapsed when the population at time step 3000 is zero. The value between brackets is the standard deviation. In the last column, the values between brackets denote the additional percentage of cases where the system did not collapsed, but where one of the two regions was not able to introduce the rule.

ing and starvation of agents outside their own region (figures 4.7 and 4.8). But accepting the rule of the other region reduces the average mutual trust level, due to the higher level of strangers, and this increases the level of rule-breaking.

When the carrying capacities differ, the region with the highest carrying capacities rapidly introduces the candidate rule, and the region with the lower carrying capacities does not. This results in a significantly lower total population. This result can be explained by the different performance of the system for different carrying capacities (table 4.2). When a period of scarcity appears, the motivation grows rapidly, and the rule will be accepted. In the region with a low carrying capacity, the population grows slowly and thus remains low. Agents do not build much trust due to the low density and the few interactions. The period of scarcity starts later than in the neighboring region. Due to the low level of mutual trust, the motivation does not reach the threshold level. Many agents move to the other region. This improves the population size, but since they come in a region of strangers, their mutual trust relationship remains low. There is an important difference between accepting the rule of the foreign region or not (figures 4.9 and 4.10). Although the absolute population figures are the same for both cases, the distribution differs substantially between the two groups.

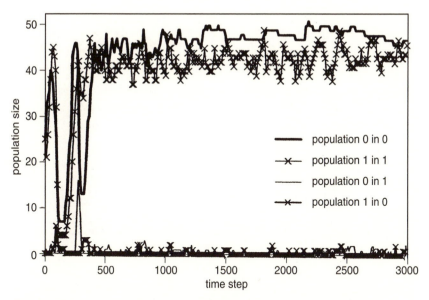

Figure 4.7. Population levels when torus is split in two regions with equal carrying capacities, and the agents accept the rules in the other region. The different lines refer to population size of agents born in region i and located in region.

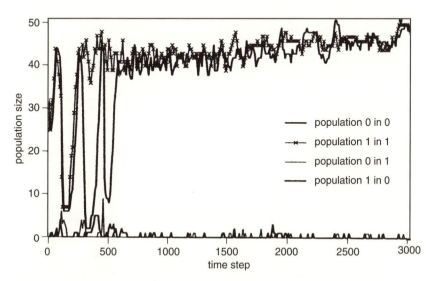

Figure 4.8. Population levels when torus is split in two regions with equal carrying capacities, and the agents do not accept the rules in the other region. The different lines refer to population size of agents born in region i and located in region j.

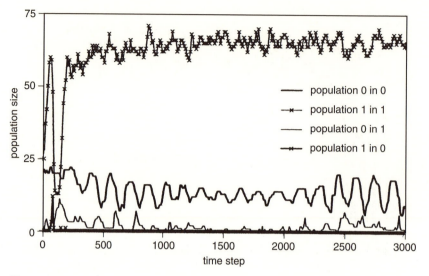

Figure 4.9. Population levels when torus is split in two regions with unequal carrying capacities (region 0: $K = 5$; region 1: $K = 15$), and the agents accept the rules in other regions. The different lines refer to population size of agents born in region i and located in region j.

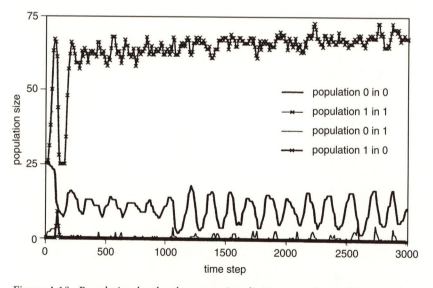

Figure 4.10. Population levels when torus is split in two regions with unequal carrying capacities (region 0: $K = 5$; region 1: $K = 15$), and the agents do not accept the rules in other regions. The different lines refer to population size of agents born in region i and located in region j.

4.10. DISCUSSION

As can be seen in reviewing tables 4.2 through 4.5, we are able to construct a large number of artificial worlds which vary in regard to important variables identified in the literature positing various explanations for why some groups of appropriators are able to design their own rules and govern a common-pool resource sustainably over a long period of time and others do not.

When examining real cases, the number of relatively comparable cases which differ in regard to only one or two potentially significant variables is limited in number and hard to find. The Pacific Islands Mangaia and Tikopia, for example, do share many attributes but yet had quite different histories. Mangaia collapsed in a typical overshoot and collapse, while the society at the much smaller Tikopia was able to develop a population control strategy that led to a sustainable development (although one may argue whether infanticide and expulsion are acceptable policies) (Kirch 1997).

Kirch (1997) argues that the differences in social and geographical scale of these two islands are an important factor for explaining the different histories of the islands. On Tikopia, everyone knew everyone on a face-to-face basis. Mangaia was big enough to develop social clusters, different identities (sets of tags), and a mentality of "us" versus "them." Kirch asserts that it was perhaps the inability of island residents to recognize that what happened in the next tribe's valley was also of concern for all tribes on the island. Kirch further recommends that the Pacific Islands are a wonderful "natural laboratory" for studying how various combinations of variables affect the likelihood of successful local initiatives to govern their own resource base successfully.

Use of agent-based computational models enables us to examine questions such as those raised by Kirch and others in environments that can be simulated multiple times so that one can assess the likely pattern of consequence of certain initial combination of variables in an evolutionary process over time. Our artificial worlds simulate different histories of agents living on an exotic torus. Like the Pacific Islands, there is no possible escape. We are aware of the limitations and the exploratory nature of the current version of the model. The encouraging experimental results, however, provide us further insights to complement findings from a much smaller set of field studies about the possible critical factors associated with self-organization of institutions.

Let us briefly return to the list of factors that have been identified by scholars doing extensive fieldwork as being associated with self-organization. As we indicated, we would build the first four factors listed into the basic structure of the model. In all of the runs summarized

TABLE 4.4
Statistics of the Experiments When the Torus Is Split into Two Regions

Experiment	Population Size	Population in Other Region	Energy Biomass	Trust	% Monitoring	% Breaking Rules	Time Step Adoption
K = 10 and accepting rules	42.9 (7.0)	0.8 (2.4)	922.6 (125.8)	94.2 (4.1)	12.8 (10.8)	2.8 (2.6)	412.9 (494.9)
K = 10 and not accepting rules	45.3 (2.8)	0.2 (0.5)	974.9 (38.8)	97.3 (1.8)	17.4 (14.9)	2.8 (2.2)	406.0 (450.6)
K = 5 and accepting rules	27.6 (18.2)	17.0 (15.8)	326.4 (253.3)	79.0 (2.7)	0	3.5 (3.9)	—
K = 5 and not accepting rules	11.9 (5.6)	1.2 (1.7)	377.7 (274.8)	70.2 (27.7)	0	9.7 (14.7)	—

Note: The values are average of noncollapsed runs of part A of the torus in time step 3000. A run is collapsed when the population at time step 3000 is zero. The value between brackets is the standard deviation.

TABLE 4.5
Statistics of the Experiments When the Torus Is Split into Two Regions

Experiment	Population Size	Population in Other Region	Energy Biomass	Trust	% Monitoring	% Breaking Rules	Time Step Adoption
K = 10 and accepting rules	41.9 (6.9)	0.9 (3.0)	937.2 (117.7)	94.5 (2.8)	15.9 (15.9)	3.9 (5.6)	349.4 (409.6)
K = 10 and not accepting rules	45.6 (2.8)	0.1 (0.4)	975.8 (48.8)	97.8 (1.8)	15.4 (13.2)	3.0 (2.7)	328.7 (428.5)
K = 15 and accepting rules	52.3 (14.9)	0	1325.8 (39.5)	97.9 (1.9)	10.6 (6.9)	3.8 (3.9)	77.5 (7.3)
K = 15 and not accepting rules	68.2 (2.5)	0	1323.3 (32.1)	97.5 (2.2)	10.1 (6.4)	3.1 (2.2)	78.1 (7.2)

Note: The values are average of noncollapsed runs of part B of the torus in time step 3000. A run is collapsed when the population at time step 3000 is zero. The value between brackets is the standard deviation.

in tables 4.2–4.5, agents had accurate information about the condition of the resource, they did not discount the future at all, they were highly dependent on the resource for survival, and they used a collective-choice rule (50 percent plus one) that falls between the extremes of unanimity or control by a few.

When these four factors are combined in the default condition with (1) a highly stable group, (2) zero costs of developing mutual trust, and (3) low monitoring and sanctioning costs, only 6 percent of the fifty artificial worlds collapsed and the average population size and energy biomass closely approached optimality. It did, however, take an average of 258 time steps before the agents on these artificial worlds voted on a rule to limit harvest levels on every cell. Further, most of these relatively "ideal" systems faced at least two resource crises before they implemented the candidate rule. If the relevant time step for a natural system is only a day, this is a relatively short time frame. But if the relevant time step is a year, that means that on average it take over 250 years before a group gets organized! The really good news is that once a group is organized they do not suffer further crises and trust levels tend to grow over time as the percent of rule-breakers falls over time.

We explored the fifth factor—the stability of the group—by splitting the torus in half and creating in essence two populations which could move back and forth. In this setting, we did find that subtle changes in key parameters made substantial differences in outcomes. Immigration of agents from another region decreases the performance of the system, even if the immigrants accept the rule of their new region. If strangers do not accept the rules, more rule-breaking happens, leading to higher monitoring costs. If strangers do accept the rules, the agents are confronted with a new type of agents with whom they have no experience, which will reduce the mutual trust level and increase rule-breaking and monitoring costs.

In examining the effect of the size of the resource and group—the sixth factor—our findings contradict some of the "conventional" wisdom. When a very small lattice is considered, the system is more vulnerable to collapse than when a larger lattice is assumed. If a rule is not adopted during the first resource crises, small systems are more likely to collapse than larger systems.

There are many forms of heterogeneity that can occur in regard to sets of agents using a common-pool resource. We constructed agents that varied in regard to the number of symbols they carried. We found that a high level of heterogeneity delays building up mutual trust relationships and the adoption of a rule regulating harvest. When agents carried only two symbols, none of the artificial worlds collapsed versus the range of collapse rates shown in the last column of table 4.2 for more heterogeneous agents. Heterogeneity does not have to be a bottleneck in adopting a rule, however, as long as mutual trust relationships can be created. For building up these mutual trust relationships it is important to meet many agents. The larger the social space (neighborhood definition), and the larger the total carrying capacity of the system (size of torus, carrying capacity of a cells), the faster mutual trust relationships are built up, and the faster the rule is adopted.

When the torus is split in two regions, "us" versus "them" can evolve. The performance decreases, especially when the ecosystem dynamics differ between the two regions, which is in line with the histories of Mangaia and Tikopia.

The bottom line of our analysis in regard to heterogeneity is that unlike often argued, heterogeneity within a population does not have to be the bottleneck for self-governance. Suitable conditions of the learning capacity of agents, and the structure and frequency of social interactions can stimulate creation of a trusting society. Within such trusting societies proposed regulations to solve common-pool resource dilemmas are more likely to be implemented and less costly to maintain.

Further, we find that levels of trust are important forms of social capital and groups that have made costly investments in building mutual trust are more likely to utilize their resource at close to optimal conditions over a long time frame. And, accurate and low-cost monitoring and sanctioning systems are also an important factor in the evolution of system performance over time.

NOTES

1. Throughout this chapter we refer to agent-based computational modeling, which is also known as agent-based modeling or multi-agent systems. A brief introduction is given in the sections on agent-based computational modeling. For a discussion on terminology we refer to Parker et al. (2003).

2. CORMAS stands for Common-Pool Resources and Multi-Agent Systems.

3. See Weissing and Ostrom (1991) for a game theoretic analysis of the costs and rewards of monitoring.

4. One can think of the candidate rule as being the rule used by a successful neighboring community in achievable a sustainable harvesting regime over time.

5. These three are only a small sample of the very large number of constitutional-level rules that could be used.

REFERENCES

Arrow, K. 1974. *The Limits of Organization*. New York: Norton Press.

Axelrod, R. 1984. *The Evolution of Cooperation*. New York: Basic Books.

————. 1997. *The Complexity of Cooperation. Agent-Based Models of Competition and Collaboration*. Princeton, N.J.: Princeton University Press.

Bardhan, P. 1993. "Rational fools and cooperation in a poor hydraulic economy." In *Development, Welfare and Ethics: A Festschrift for Amartya Sen*, ed. K. Basu. Oxford: Clarendon Press.

Bardhan, P., and J. Dayton-Johnson 2002. "Unequal irrigators: Heterogeneity and commons management in large-scale multivariate research." In *The Drama of the Commons*, ed. E. Ostrom et al., 87–112. Washington, D.C.: National Academy Press.

Berkes, F. (ed.) 1989. *Common Property Resources; Ecology and Community-Based Sustainable Development*. London: Belhaven.

———. 1992. "Success and failure in marine coastal fisheries of Turkey." In *Making the Common Work: Theory, Practice, and Policy*, ed. D. W. Bromley et al., 161–82. Oakland, Calif.: ICS Press.

Blomquist, W. 1992. *Dividing the Waters: Governing Groundwater in Southern California*. Oakland, Calif.: ICS Press.

Bond, A. H., and L. Gasser (eds.) 1988. *Readings in Distributed Artificial Intelligence*. San Mateo, Calif.: Morgan Kaufmann.

Bousquet, F., I. Bakam, H. Proton, and C. Le Page. 1998. "Cormas: Common-pool resources and multi-agent systems." *Lecture Notes in Artificial Intelligence* 1416: 826–37.

Bowles, S. 1998. "Endogenous preferences: The cultural consequences of markets and other economic institutions." *Journal of Economic Literature* 36: 75–111.

Bromley, D. W., D. Feeny, M. McKean, P. Peters, J. Gilles, R. Oakerson, C. F. Runge, and J. Thomson (eds.) 1992. *Making the Commons Work: Theory, Practice, and Policy*. Oakland, Calif.: ICS Press.

Burger, J., E. Ostrom, R. B. Norgaard, D. Policansky, and B. D. Goldstein (eds.) 2001. *Protecting the Commons*. Washington, D.C.: Island Press.

Clark, C. 1990. *Mathematical Bioeconomics: The Optimal Management of Renewable Resources*. New York: John Wiley & Sons.

Cohen, M. D., R. L. Riolo, and R. Axelrod. 2001. "The role of social structure in the maintenance of cooperative regimes." *Rationality and Society* 13: 5–32.

Conte, R. R. Hegselmann, and P. Terna (eds.) 1997. *Simulating Social Phenomena*. Lecture Notes in Economics and Mathematical Systems 456. Berlin: Springer.

Cordell, J. C., and M. A. McKean. 1992. "Sea tenure in Bahia, Brazil." In *Making the Commons Work: Theory, Practice, and Policy*, ed. D. W. Bromley et al., 183–205. Oakland, Calif.: ICS Press.

Ellison, G. 1993. "Learning, local interaction and coordination." *Econometrica* 61: 1047–71.

Epstein J., and R. Axtell 1996. *Growing Artificial Societies: Social Science from the Bottom Up*. Brookings, Mass.: MIT Press.

Feeny, D., F. Berkes, B. J. McCay, and J. M. Acheson. 1990. "The tragedy of the commons: Twenty-two years later," *Human Ecology* 18(1): 1–19.

Ferber, J. 1999. *Multi-Agent Systems: An Introduction to Distributed Artificial Intelligence*. Reading, Mass.: Addison-Wesley.

Franzen, A. 1994. "Group size effects in social dilemmas: A review of the experimental literature and some new results for one-shot N-PD games." In *Social Dilemmas and Cooperation*, ed. U. Schulz, W. Albers, and U. Mueller. Berlin: Springer-Verlag.

Fujita, M., Y. Hayami, and M. Kikuchi. 1999. The conditions of farmer participation in irrigation management: A Cross-section analysis for the Philippines. Paper prepared in the Social Science Division as part of the IRRI-Japan Shuttle Project, Tokyo.

Gallant, S. I. 1993. *Neural Network Learning and Expert Systems*. Cambridge, Mass.: MIT Press.

Gallarotti, G. M. 2001. "The rise of the classical gold standard: The role of focal points and synergistic effects of spontaneous order." *Humane Studies Review* 13(3):1–21.

Gambetta, D., and Bacharach, M. 2001. "Trust in Signs." In *Social Structure and Trust*, ed. K. Cook. New York: Russell Sage Foundation.

Gardner, M. 1970. "The Fantastic Combinations of John Conways New Solitaire Game Life." *Scientific American* 223: 120–3.

Gibson, C. C. 2001. "Forest resources: Institutions for local governance in Guatemala." In *Protecting the Commons: A Framework for Resource Management in the Americas*, ed. Joanna Burger et al., 71–89. Washington, D.C.: Island Press.

Gilbert, N., and K. G. Troitzsch. 1999. *Simulation for the Social Scientist*. London: Open University Press.

Gilles, J. L., and K. Jamtgaard. 1981. "Overgrazing in pastoral areas: The commons reconsidered." *Sociologia Ruralis* 2: 335–58.

Gintis, H. 2000. *Game Theory Evolving. A Problem-Centered Introduction to Modeling Strategic Interaction*. Princeton, N.J.: Princeton University Press.

Grima, A.P.L., and F. Berkes. 1989. "Natural resources: Access, rights to use and management." In *Common Property Resources; Ecology and Community-Based Sustainable Development*, ed. F. Berkes, 33–54. London: Belhaven.

Hardin, G. 1968. "The tragedy of the commons." *Science* 162: 1243–8.

Hegselmann, R. 1998. "Modeling social dynamics by cellular automata." In *Computer Modeling of Social Processes*, ed. W.B.G. Liebrand, A. Nowak, and R. Hegselmann, 37–64. London: SAGE Publications.

Janssen, M., and D. Stow. 2002. An application of immunocomputing to the evolution of rules for ecosystem management. In *Proceedings of the 2002 Congress on Evolutionary Computation*. Institute of Electrical and Electronics Engineers (IEEE), Piscataway, N.J.: 687–92.

Kirch, P. V. 1997. "Microcosmic histories: Island perspective on 'global' change." *American Anthropologist* 99(1): 30–42.

Lam, W. F. 1998. *Governing Irrigation Systems in Nepal: Institutions, Infrastructure, and Collective Action*. Oakland, Calif.: ICS Press.

Libecap, G. D. 1995. "The conditions for successful collective action." In *Local Commons and Global Interdependence. Heterogeneity and Cooperation in Two Domains*, ed. R. O. Keohane and E. Ostrom. London: Sage Publications.

Liebrand, W.B.G., A. Nowak, and R. Hegselmann (eds.) 1998. *Computer Modeling of Social Processes*. London: Sage Publications.

Macy, M., and J. Skvoretz. 1998. "Evolution of trust and cooperation between strangers: A computational model." *American Sociological Review* 63: 638–60.

Maes, P. 1995. *Modelling Adaptive Autonomous Agents*. In *Artificial Life: An Overview*, ed. C. G. Langton. Cambridge/London: MIT Press.

McGinnis, Michael (ed.) 2000. *Polycentric Games and Institutions: Readings from the Workshop in Political Theory and Policy Analysis*. Ann Arbor: University of Michigan Press.

Mehrota, K., C. K. Mohan, and S. Ranka. 1997. *Elements of Artificial Neural Networks*. Cambridge, Mass.: MIT Press.

Miller, J. H., C. T. Butts, and D. Rode. 2002. "Communication and cooperation." *Journal of Economic Behavior and Organization* 47, 2 (February): 179–96.

Morrow, C. E., and R. W. Hull. 1996. "Donor-initiated common pool resource institutions: The case of the Yanesha Forestry Cooperative." *World Development* 24(10): 1641–57.

Nowak, M. A., and K. Sigmund. 1998. "Evolution of indirect reciprocity by image scoring." *Nature* 393: 573–7.

Ostrom, E. 1990. *Governing the Commons: The Evolution of Institutions for Collective Action*, New York: Cambridge University Press.

Ostrom, E., T. Dietz, N. Dolsak, P. Stern, S. Stonich, and E. Weber (eds.) (Committee on the Human Dimensions of Global Change). 2002. *The Drama of the Commons*. Washington, D.C.: National Research Council, National Academy Press.

Ostrom, E., R. Gardner, and J. M. Walker. 1994. *Rules, Games, and Common-Pool Resources*. Ann Arbor: University of Michigan Press.

Ostrom, V., and E. Ostrom. 1977. "A theory for institutional analysis of common pool problems." In *Managing the Commons*, ed. G. Hardin and J. Baden, 157–72. San Francisco, W. H. Freeman.

Ostrom E., and J. Walker. 2003. "Introduction." In *Trust, Reciprocity, and Gains from Association: Interdisciplinary Lessons from Experimental Research*, ed. E. Ostrom and J. Walker. New York: Russell Sage Foundation.

Parker, D. C., S. M. Manson, M. A. Janssen, M. J. Hoffmann, and P. Deadman. 2003. "Multi-agent systems for the simulation of land-use and land-cover change: A review." Annals of the Association of American Geographers 93(2): 314–37.

Pathak, N., and A. Kothari. 2002. Communities and biodiversity: Lessons for governance from South Asia. Working Paper, International Institute of Environment and Development, Pune, India.

Princen, T. 1998. "From property regime to international regime: An ecosystems perspective." *Global Governance* 4: 395–413.

Riolo, R. L., M. D. Cohen, and R. Axelrod. 2001. "Evolution of cooperation without reciprocity." *Nature* 414: 441–3.

Rousseau, D. M., S. B. Sitkin, R. S. Burt, and C. Camerer. 1998. "Not so different after all: A cross-discipline view of trust." *Academy of Management Review* 23: 393–404.

Seabright, P. 1993. "Managing local commons: Theoretical issues in incentive design." *Journal of Economic Perspectives* 7(4): 113–34.

Sethi, R., and E. Somanathan. 1996. "The evolution of social norms in common property resource use." *The American Economic Review* 86(4): 766–88.

Singh, K. 1994. *Managing Common Pool Resources: Principles and Case Studies*. New Delhi: Oxford University Press.

Singh, K., and V. Ballabh. 1996. *Cooperative Management of Natural Resources*. New Delhi: Sage Publications.

Steels, L. 1995. "*The artifical life roots of artifical intelligence.*" In *Artificial Life: An Overview*, ed. C. G. Langton. Cambridge/London: MIT Press.

Tesfatsion, L. 2001. "Introduction to the special issue on agent-based computational economics." *Journal of Economic Dynamics and Control* 25: 281–93.

Varughese, G., and E. Ostrom. 2001. "The contested role of heterogeneity in collective action: Some evidence from community forestry in Nepal." *World Development* 29, 5 (May): 747–65.

Weinstein, M. S. 2000. "Pieces of the puzzle: Solutions for community-based fisheries management from native Canadians, Japanese cooperatives, and common property researchers." *Georgetown International Environmental Law Review* 12(2): 375–412.

Weissing, F., and E. Ostrom. 1991. "Irrigation institutions and the games irrigators play: Rule enforcement without guards." In *Game Equilibrium Models II: Methods, Morals, and Markets*, ed. Reinhard Selten, 188–262. Berlin: Springer-Verlag.

Wilson, P. N., and G. D. Thompson. 1993. "Common property and uncertainty: Compensating coalitions by Mexico's pastoral *Ejidatorios*." *Economic Development and Cultural Change* 41(2): 299–318.

Chapter 5

INEQUALITY AND THE GOVERNANCE
OF WATER RESOURCES IN MEXICO
AND SOUTH INDIA

Pranab Bardhan and Jeff Dayton-Johnson

In recent years, policy-makers and researchers have acknowledged that a critical dimension of environmental sustainability is the local one: the success with which communities husband collectively managed natural resource systems (Baland and Platteau 1996). It is furthermore by now a commonplace observation that the "Tragedy of the Commons" framework is not always appropriate for analyzing the use of local commons (Ostrom 1990). Nevertheless, some communities successfully manage local resource systems, while others fail to do so and suffer the consequent effects of resource degradation and poverty. The task for researchers and policy-makers today is to identify the factors and mechanisms that lead some communities to be successful and others to fail. This chapter focuses on a particular factor—inequality—from the perspective of a particular kind of local natural resource system, and a particular kind of research. We describe and analyze a pair of field studies of relatively large numbers of community irrigation systems, one in South India, the other in Central Mexico.

For the South Indian field study, Nirmal Sengupta at the Madras Institute of Development Studies helped in the design of the survey and supervised the data collection process; R. Manimohan, A. Raman, and J. Jeyaranjan provided invaluable assistance in the data collection and coding process. Data analysis for the South Indian study was conducted jointly by Pranab Bardhan and Laura Giuliano. For the Mexican data-collection exercise, Sam Johnson III and his colleagues at the International Irrigation Management Institute (IIMI) Mexico Country Program provided warmly appreciated guidance and assistance, as did Juan Pablo Flores Pérez of the Celaya office of the Secretaría de Agricultura, Ganadería y Desarrollo Rural. Thanks are due to Samuel Bowles, Peter Richerson, and Lore Ruttan for detailed comments on this chapter, and to participants in a workshop held at the Santa Fe Institute. Both field studies reported in this chapter were supported financially by the MacArthur Foundation; the writing of this chapter was supported financially by the Russell Sage Foundation. We are grateful to both organizations.

A controlled supply of water is a matter of life and death for poor farmers in the arid and semi-arid regions of the developing world, including South India and Central Mexico. For many such farmers, irrigation control at the local level is largely provided by community organizations, formal or informal (mostly the latter). In South Asia, for example, while main canals are often publicly managed, water distribution and allocation are managed by local organizations at the level of secondary canals, tanks or reservoirs, and field channels. In Mexico, at least half of the country's irrigated area is served by local irrigation organizations entirely autonomous of public irrigation authorities. Community irrigation institutions attempt to solve a broad range of collective-action problems. They pool efforts and resources for the construction and maintenance of canals and field channels. They regulate water distribution and allocation and monitor violations of local rules. In cases of tank or reservoir irrigation, they mobilize resources to desilt, weed, and stop encroachments on reservoir beds. They repair, maintain, and control water allocation from public and community tubewells. Indeed, water reform, in the sense of building or promoting such community institutions of cooperation, is at least as important as land reform in rural development.

What factors distinguish successful from unsuccessful community irrigation systems? It is in this context that the study of inequality among users of the commons is important. Two questions in particular will be explored in this chapter. How does inequality among the members of an irrigating community affect the success with which that community undertakes the collective tasks enumerated above? Second, how does inequality affect the crafting and evolution of local institutions for running irrigation systems?

Contextual analysis of field data collected from such community-based irrigation systems will be an important contributor to our knowledge about these issues. Game theoretic models of cooperation among self-interested agents in repeated situations of strategic interdependence provide some useful insights.[1] But, in view of their admissibility of multiplicity of equilibria, many of the comparative-static questions cannot be satisfactorily resolved without recourse to empirical research. Until recently, most empirical studies of community-based irrigation (like most studies of common-pool resource systems generally) focused on one or two systems per study.[2] We have learned a great deal from these case studies, but they do not have the degrees of freedom necessary to discern relationships among the institutions of governance, various dimensions of performance, and the structural characteristics of resource-using communities. What is needed are field studies of relatively large numbers of irrigating communities, to test hypotheses regarding institutions and group characteristics.

The relative paucity of such large-scale studies is not difficult to understand. In the last two decades, development economists have enjoyed the availability of high-quality micro-datasets, but comparable datasets regarding communities are less plentiful. Large numbers of observations for household surveys can be collected in a single village; for the kind of irrigation study we describe herein, the unit of analysis is the village itself, and collecting a single observation can take days or weeks. Moreover, variables indicating cooperation or its absence are difficult to quantify. Despite these obstacles, several studies of relatively large numbers of resource-using communities in developing countries have been carried out recently.[3]

5.1. INEQUALITY AND WATER GOVERNANCE

Irrigators, or users of some other common-pool resource, may be heterogeneous in economic, social, cultural, or other dimensions. There are many relevant types of economic inequality alone. These variants of economic heterogeneity include inequality in wealth or income among the members of a resource-using group, inequalities in the sacrifices community members make in cooperating with commons-management regimes, inequalities in the benefits they derive from such regimes, and inequalities in outside earnings opportunities ("exit options"). There are other kinds of disparities that may have economic consequences, and those in turn affect cooperation. For example, locational differences, to the extent that they are not already reflected in landholding or wealth differences, might not be adequately taken into account if one considers only wealth inequality. Head-end and tail-end farmers in irrigation systems face different incentives to cooperate (Bardhan 1984: 215; Ostrom 1994). Long-run locational advantages and disadvantages will be capitalized into land values if land markets work reasonably well. Thus, the head-end/tail-end inequality is another version of wealth inequality. Of course, in many parts of the world, land markets notoriously do not work well. Even if head-end/tail-end differences are perfectly captured in land values, such locational differences provide strategic opportunities that are not normally available simply as a result of wealth differences. Head-end farmers, poor or not, get the water first. Similarly, differences in ability or efficiency in resource extraction will affect cooperative behavior (Johnson and Libecap 1982). These differences in many cases will be closely correlated with wealth. Differences in rates of time preference (Ostrom 1990: passim) will lead to differential impatience among commons users in making short-run sacrifices for resource conservation.

Ethnic heterogeneity such as differences in language, caste, or tribes among irrigators will also affect cooperative behavior. An irrigating community may be socially heterogeneous if its users come from various villages. Of course, in many cases, ethnic or social heterogeneity will be correlated with economic heterogeneity, as certain castes or ethnic groups are also more likely to be richer or poorer than other groups. Nevertheless, these noneconomic types of heterogeneity potentially have effects independent of the economic heterogeneity with which they are correlated.

Other types of inequality or heterogeneity are measured by state variables like trust or social cohesion—the absence of which Baland and Platteau (1995) called "cultural heterogeneity." Generally, shared values or interpretations of social problems—cultural homogeneity—can facilitate cooperation in the use of the commons. It is even conceivable that cultural homogeneity and pronounced economic heterogeneity coexist in a stable relationship. For example, highly unequal agrarian societies might sometimes exhibit widespread adherence to a hierarchical ideology that facilitates monitoring and enforcement of cooperative agreements. Cultural heterogeneity exists, then, when there is more than one community of interpretation or community of shared values, among the members of a group. This can overlap with ethnic or social or locational heterogeneity, but need not.

Indeed, there may be at least three major dimensions to heterogeneity in this setting. The first is inequality of wealth and power within a community. This type of heterogeneity might have positive or negative effects on cooperation; it may damage trust, or it might promote unilateral provision of collective goods by the larger agents (the so-called "Olson effect" described below). A second heterogeneity may be observed in the division of labor. Thus, some community members specialize in political leadership, which facilitates community projects. This second dimension of heterogeneity might have no direct effect on trust or solidarity per se, but by custom or via the exercise of power, leadership positions may fall to individuals who inspire distrust or envy. These first two dimensions of inequality are likely to be correlated; if they are, the net effect of heterogeneity on cooperation may be difficult to predict. Finally, a third dimension of inequality is the social (between-community) or ethnic variant discussed above.[4]

How does heterogeneity affect commons outcomes? Broadly, theoretical and case-study research has tended to diverge into two camps: those studies that find a positive role for heterogeneity, and those that point out a negative role. (Much of the theoretical work is assessed in greater detail in other chapters of this volume.) That inequality may favor provision of collective goods can justifiably be called an "Olson effect." Mancur Olson (1965: 34), in a classic hypothesis, explained the effect this way:

> In smaller groups marked by considerable degrees of inequality—that is, in groups of members of unequal "size" or extent of interest in the collective good—there is the greatest likelihood that a collective good will be provided; for the greater the interest in the collective good of any single member, the greater the likelihood that that member will get such a significant proportion of the total benefit from the collective good that he will gain from seeing that the good is provided, even if he has to pay all of the cost himself.

Restraint in groundwater extraction, for example, and cooperation with canal-cleaning efforts are approximately public goods, or at the very least generate substantive externalities: one villager's actions provide benefits to most or all other members of the community. In such settings a dominant player might internalize a sufficiently large share of the collective good he provides. Thus, Olson's hypothesis suggests that inequality is beneficial to successful irrigation management, as large landowners—through whose landholdings significant portions of the canal network pass—will clean most or all of the canals even if all others free-ride on their efforts.[5]

Olson effects are also likely if there are large fixed costs involved in setting up a commons-management regime. These costs might be material, such as the building of fences around pasturelands, or the construction of irrigation canals. Such start-up costs also involve the organizational effort to collectively mobilize a community of resource users. Vaidyanathan (1986) illustrates the historical importance of local elites in promoting the emergence of irrigation-management regimes in India, China, and Japan. Powerful elites in Vaidyanathan's history are successful in part because they centralize decision-making power as much as they command material wealth. Large start-up costs of this type are an example of increasing returns in the production technology.[6] Irrigation provides no benefit until the expense of building a dam or a canal (or both), or drilling a tubewell, has been undertaken; but thereafter, added effort systematically increases crop yields. In this setting, wealthier farmers may be able to mobilize the capital necessary to build the dam or install the tubewell. Increasing returns also exist if there is a threshold stock of the resource (as in the case of aquifers) below which regeneration is impossible. Baland and Platteau (1997) confirm the theoretical possibility of this Olson effect when there are such increasing returns. Widening inequality in this setting can lead to discrete jumps in cooperative actions (e.g., maintenance effort or restraint in resource use) by the wealthier players. But they show that this result depends critically on assumptions about the characteristics of the resource-using technology.

Not everyone agrees, of course, that inequality is good for successful management of the commons. The case-study literature in particular is replete with examples of the harmful effects of inequality. Consider a handful of Indian irrigation examples. Jayaraman's (1981) study of surface-water irrigation projects in Gujarat notes the importance of a relatively egalitarian structure to farmers' coming together to form a water users' association. Similarly, Easter and Palanisami's (1986) study of ten tank irrigation groups in Tamil Nadu shows that the smaller the variation in farm size among farmers, the more likely that water users' associations will form. Aggarwal (2000) shows with data from group-owned wells in two Indian villages that, in contrast to routine maintenance activities, there is far less cooperation in matters of long-term group investment; her data furthermore demonstrate that the standard deviation in land ownership has a negative effect on cooperation in such group investments.

This ambiguous relationship between inequality and successful commons management calls for more careful theoretical work, and larger-scale empirical work that permits careful testing of hypotheses. While this chapter is largely devoted to looking at the latter kind of research, we will return to the theoretical literature (considered at various points throughout this volume) below.

5.2. The Field Studies

The Indian and Mexican studies summarized below were conceived and designed together in order to permit a modicum of comparative analysis. Naturally, differences between the study regions preclude perfect comparability of all concepts and measures. Nevertheless, in both cases the unit of analysis is the irrigating community (rather than, for example, the household or the individual); in both cases information was collected on the institutions of local resource management (including, notably, the rules in place), structural characteristics of the resource-using group (e.g., number of users, pattern of landholding, physical specifications of the system), and measures of cooperation; in both cases, approximately fifty communities were surveyed. Finally, in both studies, we attempt to use the structural variables to explain both the rules and the level of cooperation.

A potential problem in discerning the effect of inequality on cooperation and institutional evolution is that inequality might be endogenous. That is, cooperation or the institutions of governance might affect inequality. Certainly if we used inequality of income (which is indeed endogenous) as our indicator of inequality, this would be a serious problem. In both studies, however, wealth inequality—specifically, landholding inequality—is used rather than income as an explanatory variable. Conceptually, landholding inequality could also be endogenous, if, for example, cooperation in irrigation affected land transactions. In both South India and Central Mexico, however, the distribution of landholding can effectively be treated as exogenous. The land market in South India is so inactive that landholding inequality is probably given more by history and demography than by endogenous land transactions. In Central Mexico, meanwhile, the agrarian reform of the 1920s and 1930s essentially froze the distribution of landholding in each irrigation system. Liberalization of the land market since the early 1990s has not resulted in an increase in land transactions as the process of individual titling has proved complex and laborious.

A second potential shortcoming of the design of the Indian and Mexican studies is that, by using the irrigation community as the unit of analysis, we ignore cases where there is no cooperative community whatsoever. Strictly speaking, this criticism is correct: our results should be interpreted as exploring the effect of inequality in communities where some minimum threshold of cooperation is already present. In practice, however, this minimum threshold is quite low: in both studies, pains were taken (at times over the objections of local agricultural officials) to include communities with low levels of cooperation. Moreover, one could argue that this potential source of selection bias would tend to mute the measured effects of inequality on cooperation. If indeed inequality thwarts cooperation, then some unequal villages will have failed to form irrigation institutions, and thus will be excluded from our sample; those that remain in the sample, all else equal, must be at least marginally better at overcoming the obstacles to collective action, inequality among them. Thus, the generally negative effect of inequality on cooperative effort that we detect might have been larger in absolute value had the sample been extended to include villages without irrigation organizations.

5.3. SOUTH INDIA

Consider a pair of observations—irrigation communities—from South India. The irrigation system A6,[7] in Tiruchi district, is an isolated "chain tank" system—that is, it is a small reservoir that is not part of a larger government-run canal system. The degree of inequality among the thirty-seven farmers in A6 is quite high; the Gini coefficient, based on irrigated land ownership, is 0.729. The water rules at A6 are traditional, and have been handed down over the course of several generations. Opening and closing of sluice gates and field irrigation can only be performed by system guards, known in A6 and much of the study area as *neerani*. Each irrigating household must contribute one man-day of labor per year for maintenance. Quality of maintenance of field channels and distributaries is poor. Although the system is under the general administration of the government (in the guise of the Public Works Department or PWD), farmers have traditionally made independent regulation arrangements, meeting twice yearly to plan water distribution. Villagers do not report substantial violation of water-allocation rules.

In contrast to the high-inequality, low-maintenance A6, village G4, in Coimbatore district, has a Gini coefficient of only 0.201 and very good maintenance of its infrastructure. The twenty-one farmers of G4 are part of a larger government system, a large-scale inter-river basin water transfer scheme known as the Parambikulam Aliyar Project (PAP). Because of G4's location in PAP, the PWD has a prominent role in day-to-day decision-making, more so even than in other irrigation communities that are part of other large government systems. PWD officials operate the canals and sluices, but farmers can irrigate their fields at any time while water is in the canals.[8] There is no formal mobilization of labor for maintenance in G4; contributions are restricted to "gift-giving"—groundnuts and coconuts, for example—to pay for maintenance. Despite high levels of maintenance, villagers in G4 report that water-allocation rules are violated frequently.

5.3.1. The Data

Data were collected from forty-eight villages like A6 and G4, spread over six districts in the South Indian state of Tamil Nadu.[9] The unit of analysis is the *ayacut*, a selected part of the irrigation system in each village corresponding either to a tank or a branch of canal with roughly 50 hectares of command area. Half of the selected irrigation units belong to canal systems (like G4 above), and the other half to more traditional tank systems. ("Tanks," in the parlance of South Asian irrigation, refer to ponds, lakes, or other reservoirs.) Among tank systems, half of the surveyed ayacuts belong to what are called isolated or chain tank systems (like A6 above), and the other half to system tanks, where the tanks are, unlike in the former case, linked to larger irrigation units. Within each system the villages were randomly chosen; within each village a sample of ten farmers (stratified by land-size classes) was chosen. Most of the analysis reported here is based on data for the irrigation unit or ayacut as a whole; in some cases we have derived data from the individual farmers' responses. In general, on matters of cooperation differences across villages are much more prominent than intra-village differences among the ten farmers.

5.3.2. Irrigation Organization

The majority of the water users' organizations surveyed are traditional and informal community organizations that have been in existence for some time; twenty-seven of the forty-eight surveyed are either "traditional" (as in A6) or at least twenty years old. Nevertheless, only thirteen of these units have formal associations (and ten of these have formal associations not at the village or sluice levels, but at the supra-village zonal level). The organization in twelve of the (canal-based) irrigation units surveyed has been set up relatively recently and is run directly by the PWD. In another twelve canal-based irrigation units, although the PWD is the official management authority, the traditional village committee manages irrigation matters at the local level.

Institutions for managing irrigation—including appointment of guards as monitors and enforcers, the frequency of meetings, mobilization of collective labor, mobilization of funds, method of cost-sharing, and involvement in non-irrigation activities—vary greatly among ayacuts. One function of the water users' organization is to mobilize community labor for the purpose of maintaining and repairing the field channels. Generally, it appears that community labor is most common in those organizations that are traditional or have existed for over forty years. While most of these units mobilize community labor both for regular maintenance and for emergency repairs, several units report mobilizing community labor only in the event of emergency repairs. Community labor does not appear to be used systematically in any of those units where the PWD directly runs the organizations.

About three-quarters (37 in number) of the units surveyed have some formal system of fundraising. Of these, twenty-eight units have a system of dues, fines, and/or taxes. Such a system is most prevalent in canal-based units. In the tank-based systems, an alternate system of fundraising is possible: the sale of collective resources such as fish and trees (or, in the case of G4, "gifts" of coconuts and groundnuts). Nineteen of the tank-based units have collective funds mobilized this way; ten of these supplement the collective fund with a system of dues and/or tax collection. About half of the water users' organizations report participating in other, usually villagewide, activities. In A6, farmers cooperate to stage the temple festival, for example. This does not appear to be true of any PWD-run organizations.

5.3.3. Measuring Cooperation

Important dependent and independent variables from the South Indian study are summarized in table 5.1. Three alternative variables can be

TABLE 5.1
Summary of Variables, South India

Variable Name	Obs.	Mean	St. Dev.	Minimum	Maximum
Measures of Cooperation					
Index of quality of maintenance of distributaries and field channels	45	1.31	0.92	0	2
No conflict over water within village in the last 5 years	48	0.67	0.48	0	1
Water allocation rules frequently violated by at least one group	48	0.52	0.50	0	1
Explanatory Variables					
No. of beneficiary households using this irrigation source	48	52.67	54.29	11.00	279.00
Gini coefficient of landholding of beneficiary households in ayacut	48	0.41	0.11	0.15	0.73
At least 75% of sampled farmers are members of the same caste group	48	0.69	0.47	0	1.00
Number of Months there is Access to Irrigation	48	3.65	1.20	2.00	7.00
No equal access to water because of topographical nature of the ayacut	48	0.46	0.50	0	1.00
System is partially or fully lined	48	1.96	0.82	1.00	3.00
Ayacut is in a canal system	48	0.50	0.51	0	1.00
PWD takes all decisions on water allocation	48	0.25	0.44	0	1.00
Village is situated at tail end of the irrigation system	48	0.75	0.44	0	1.00
No conflict with other villages over water	48	0.44	0.50	0	1.00
Index of connection with urban areas	48	2.46	0.74	1.00	3.00
Measure of extent to which farmers are market oriented	48	2.39	0.70	1.00	3.00
Estimated fraction of total irrigated land held by sampled farmers outside the Ayacut	48	0.26	0.18	0	0.66
Irrigation organization has been there for 20 or more years	48	0.56	0.50	0	1.00
There exists at least one guard in the Ayacut	48	0.38	0.49	0	1.00
Cost-sharing proportional to landholding	48	0.19	0.39	0	1.00
Formal water rights exist, as opposed to customary rights	48	0.33	0.48	0	1.00

interpreted as indicators of cooperation within the community on matters of irrigation: (a) quality of maintenance of distributaries and field channels; (b) absence of conflict in water allocation in the ayacut in the last five years; and (c) extent of violations of water-allocation rules.

5.3.4. *Explanatory Variables*

For the purposes of this chapter, the most important explanatory variable is heterogeneity, both social and economic. Social homogeneity or heterogeneity is captured by a dichotomous variable that takes a value of 1 in villages where at least 75 percent of the sampled farmers in the village are members of the same generic caste group (in most cases a "backward" caste group). By this admittedly crude measure, 69 percent of the ayacuts in our dataset are relatively socially homogeneous. Economic heterogeneity is measured by the Gini coefficient of inequality of landholding of farmers in the ayacut area: the mean value of the Gini in our dataset is 0.41. Another obvious explanatory variable to consider is group size: the number of households using the particular irrigation source varies between 11 and 279, with a mean of 53. The usual presumption in the literature on local commons, stemming from the early work of Olson (1965), is that cooperation works better in small groups. In small irrigation communities peer monitoring is easier, the common-knowledge assumption of models of strategic decisions is likely to be more valid, shared norms and patterns of reciprocity are more common, social sanctions may be easier to implement through reputation mechanisms and multiplex relationships, and hydrologic needs of farmers may even be relatively similar. On the other hand, there may be some positive economies of scale in larger groups, particularly in matters of pooling resources, appointing guards, lobbying with officials, and so on.

Another factor that affects cooperation in water management is the physical condition of water availability. In conditions of extreme scarcity, arrangements of cooperation often break down. When there is greater access to water, it pays the irrigators to cooperate in maintaining field channels and in obeying allocation rules. In our dataset, the villages with acute water scarcity in general exhibit less cooperation, but (probably for historical reasons) the water-scarce villages are also more likely to have canal-based irrigation. Thus, the effect of water scarcity must be disentangled from that of possible bureaucratic inefficiencies in the release of canal water. We measure water availability by the number of months in a year that the farmers in the ayacut have access to water: this varies from 2 to 7 months, with a mean of 3.7 months overall, and 2.8 for the canal areas. Other variables related to physical conditions include whether the topographical nature of the ayacut precludes equal access to water for all the farmers, and whether the irrigation channel is lined.

Government involvement is indicated in two ways. First, half of the villages are part of government-administered canal systems. Second, we have an indicator equal to 1 if the PWD makes all the decisions about water allocation and distribution even at the local level. In the canal-area villages there is not merely lower water availability, water is also more inequitably distributed: in 19 of 24 canal-area villages in our dataset (as opposed to only 2 of the 24 villages served by tank systems), there is evidence of such inequity of water supply or access. In general, the water-release cycles may be more unreliable from the farmers' point of view when they are administered by PWD officials. Of course, these associations may stem from a problem of endogeneity: is PWD involvement more likely where irrigators' cooperation has failed? Some background checking revealed that the villages where PWD takes all the decisions are all located in Coimbatore district and are precisely those where, for primarily physical reasons of long-term water scarcity, a large-scale system of inter-river basin water transfer scheme had been undertaken by the government. The problem of endogeneity is thus not that serious here.

A few variables relate to the locational context of the ayacut in question. In our dataset, 75 percent of the villages are at the tail end of their respective system. Other things remaining the same, being at the tail end may unite the farmers of the village in their struggle to get more water away from the more favorably located villages. We have also used a variable to indicate those villages where no water conflict is reported with other villages. Only 44 percent of villages report that there is no such conflict with other villages. The locational context is also important in the matter of the exit options open to the villagers. We measure this with an indicator variable for the connection of the village to urban areas or transport and communication modes (like bus and telephone). A somewhat different kind of exit-option variable may be indicated by how much access an ayacut member has to water sources outside the ayacut. Thus, we include the estimated fraction of the total irrigated land (of the sampled farmers in the ayacut) that is outside the ayacut. For all of these exit option–like variables, our prior expectation is a negative effect on cooperation.

History of cooperation in a village may matter, as cooperation may be self-reinforcing, or, "habit-forming," as Seabright (1997) explains in a theoretical model. We therefore control for villages where the water users' organization has existed for twenty years or more. These villages are characterized by more use of community labor in maintenance works and emergencies, are more likely to hire guards for monitoring and enforcement, and are more likely to use cost-sharing proportional to landholding.

TABLE 5.2
A Logit Model of the Choice of Cost-Sharing Rule, South India

Variable	Estimated Coefficient	t-ratio
No. of beneficiary households using this irrigation source	0.0265	2.0
Gini coefficient of landholding of beneficiary households in Ayacut	9.8831	1.9
Ayacut is in a canal system	4.1930	2.5
Irrigation organization has been there for 20 or more years	2.6285	2.0
Formal water rights exist, as opposed to customary rights	2.0355	1.6
Observations	48	
Log Likelihood	−13.7212	
Pseudo R-sq.	0.4076	

We also asked questions about the farmers' perception of the process of rule crafting. For example, we have an indicator for villages where at least four out of ten sampled farmers believe that the water rules were crafted by the elite. We also had a variable for villages where the rules are generally perceived as fair, but we dropped this variable as it almost exactly coincides with cases of cooperative behavior.

5.3.5. Analysis Results: Institutional Choice

The rules in place are expected to be an important determinant of cooperation; at the same time, the rules are likely to be explained by structural characteristics of the community and the irrigation system. Therefore, we estimate the likelihood of observing proportional cost-sharing as a function of inequality and other variables; table 5.2 reports the results of a logit model of the likelihood that the ayacut shares costs proportionally to landholding size. Proportional cost-sharing is observed in 19 percent of ayacuts. Attention should be paid, in the first instance, to the sign and statistical significance of the estimated coefficients reported in table 5.2. A positive and significant coefficient indicates that the variable in question increases the probability of observing proportional cost-sharing, controlling for other factors. In particular, the estimated coefficient on the Gini term is positive and significant: ayacuts with more unequally distributed wealth are more likely to share canal-maintenance costs proportionally to wealth. Note that equal division of costs would be effectively regressive in the presence of inequality. Therefore, greater inequality increases the likelihood of a progressive tax to finance maintenance and repairs.[10]

5.3.6. Analysis Results: Determinants of Cooperation

Table 5.3 reports the results of three logit models, each with a different dependent variable measuring the degree of cooperation in surveyed villages.[11] Columns 2 and 3 show the results of an ordered-logit model of the index of quality of maintenance of distributaries and field channels. A positive and significant ordered-logit coefficient can be interpreted as increasing the probability that the (three-level) index in question rises one level. The maintenance-quality index is uniformly lower in ayacuts with higher inequality in landholding: the coefficient for the Gini coefficient is negative and significant. Moreover, maintenance is also lower, and significantly so, in villages where rules are perceived to be crafted by the village elite. This "elite-rule" variable is an index equal to 1 if at least 40 percent of the respondent farmers in the village—sometimes including members of the elite—said that the rules were crafted by the elite. It does not necessarily indicate that the rules are perceived to be unfair. Incidentally, "elite" refers not just to the dominant caste (which in this area is a pretty low caste), but to the richer farmers. The urban-linkage variable likewise has a significant and negative effect on maintenance. This demonstrates that exit options hamper cooperation, but it might also indicate a negative effect of inequality if the rich are better able to exercise those exit options. All three results point to a negative effect of inequality on canal maintenance.

The channel-maintenance results also demonstrate the positive (but not always significant) effect of the proportional cost-sharing rule on maintenance. Proportional cost-sharing could be perceived as more fair than, for example, cases where all farmers have to bear the same cost even though the larger farmers get more of the benefit, or where there is no cost-sharing rule whatsoever. The presence of proportional cost-sharing was estimated in table 5.2, and the estimated probability is used as an explanatory variable in the table 5.3 models. The Gini coefficient has a positive effect on the presence of proportional cost-sharing (possibly indicating social pressure for a redistributive adjustment of the cost-sharing rule to take account of wealth disparities). The estimated probability of proportional cost-sharing, meanwhile, has a somewhat significant positive effect on channel maintenance. Thus, the effect of inequality of land distribution on the quality of field-channel maintenance is twofold: on the one hand, the direct effect is negative, but the indirect effect, working through the cost-sharing rule, is positive.

Columns 4 and 5 of table 5.3 report the results of a logit model estimating the probability that there has been no intra-village conflict over

TABLE 5.3
Logit Models of Cooperation, South India

| | Dependent Variable | | | | | |
| | Index of Quality of Maintenance of Distributaries and Field Channels (0–1–2) | | No Intra-village Water Conflict, Last 5 years (0–1) | | Water Allocation Rules Frequently Violated by at Least One Group (0–1) | |
Variable	Coefficient	t-ratio	Coefficient	t-ratio	Coefficient	t-ratio
No. of beneficiary households using this irrigation source	−0.0339	−1.8	−0.0868	−1.6	0.0350	2.3
Gini coefficient of landholding of beneficiary households in ayacut	−23.2620	−2.1	−106.6778	−1.9	25.3600	0.7
Gini squared			76.2725	1.7	−34.9862	−0.7
At least 75% of sampled farmers are members of the same caste group			2.9169	1.7	−0.8536	−0.6
Number of months there is access to irrigation	4.5637	1.7	1.4893	1.3	−0.8960	−1.6
No equal access to water because of topographical nature of the ayacut					1.1632	0.9
PWD takes all decisions on water allocation	4.8454	2.0				
Village is situated at tail end of the irrigation system	1.5790	1.0				
No conflict with other villages over water	−2.2385	−1.0				

TABLE 5.3 (continued)

| | Dependent Variable | | | | | |
| | Index of Quality of Maintenance of Distributaries and Field Channels (0-1-2) | | No Intra-village Water Conflict, Last 5 years (0-1) | | Water Allocation Rules Frequently Violated by at Least One Group (0-1) | |
Variable	Coefficient	t-ratio	Coefficient	t-ratio	Coefficient	t-ratio
Index of connection with urban areas	-4.2900	-3.1	-3.2398	-1.3	2.1425	2.4
Estimated fraction of total irrigated land held by sampled farmers outside the Ayacut					5.8283	1.5
There exists at least one guard in the Ayacut (estimated probability)	10.3531	2.4	22.4376	1.6	-7.5257	-2.8
Cost-sharing proportional to landholding	9.6847	1.7				
At least 40% of farmers feel rules were crafted by the elite	-7.9717	3.2				
Observations	45		48		48	
Log likelihood	-16.5396		-10.3061		-15.7310	
Pseudo R-sq.	0.5619		0.6627		0.5266	

water in the previous five years. (Thus, negative estimated coefficients indicate a higher probability that an ayacut has witnessed internal water-related conflict.) Once again, the Gini coefficient has a significantly negative effect, but the square of the Gini term is significantly positive, indicating that the negative impact of inequality on intra-village water-related conflict is diminishing in inequality.[12] The coefficient for within-village caste homogeneity (75 percent or more of the farmers belonging to the same caste group) is positive and significant, confirming that social homogeneity promotes cooperation.[13]

Finally, columns 6 and 7 of table 5.3 report the results of a logit model of the probability that water-allocation rules are frequently violated by at least one group. Both for the ayacut as a whole and for the sampled farmers our data definitely suggest that the rule violations are more often by the better-off farmers; one presumes they can get away with such violations more easily. Here the signs of the coefficients for the Gini coefficient, the square of the Gini, caste homogeneity, tail-end location, and ownership of irrigated land outside the ayacut are as expected from the other statistical models in the table, but they are not significant. The effect of group size is positive—that is, group size promotes rule violation—and highly significant, indicating the difficulty of preserving cooperative behavior in large groups. As in the maintenance models, the urban-linkage index has a positive and significant effect; this is an indication of the negative effect of exit options on cooperation, and potentially also of inequality, if it is the rich who are better positioned to exploit exit options.

From the list of independent variables explaining rule violation, we had to drop the dummies indicating PWD decision-making and the perception that the rules were crafted by the elite, because in both cases their values perfectly predicted the value of the dependent variable. This means in all the villages where PWD decides on water allocation and distribution, frequent rule violations are reported: this may be because the rules are typically rigid and insensitive to local needs, farmers are less normatively committed, officials are bribed to look the other way, and so on.[14] In contrast, in the villages where the village elite, rather than government officials, craft the rules, there is no violation of rules reported. Since, as we have noted before, the better off are usually the more frequent violators of rules, this result means that they tend not to violate the rules they crafted.

In all twelve PWD-run units there are rotational water-allocation rules by which the farmers are allotted a certain number of hours of water access per acre or are allowed access to water only in alternate weeks. In all of these units these rotational rules are frequently violated and particularly the rich farmers appropriate more water than is their due. And yet in half of these units (particularly where the inequality in land distribution among the farmers is low), as we have seen before, field channels are well maintained and there was no incidence of water conflicts within the village in the last five years. This means inflexible rules of the government (enforced by corruptible agents) are frequently violated without necessarily damaging intra-village cooperation, suggesting again that when rules do not enjoy the backing of community norms, rule obedience is not necessarily an indicator of cooperation among farmers.

5.4. CENTRAL MEXICO

Consider, as above, two observations from the Mexican dataset. The small irrigation group Nuestra Señora del Rosario[15] in the impoverished *municipio* of Ocampo illustrates the breakdown of collective management. There are five water users at Rosario, all private landowners, who formed the water users' association in 1983. The farmers have not irrigated for several years, but not because of water scarcity: the farmer on whose land the levee sits, Don Leonardo, will not release water for irrigation.[16] As a consequence, water-allocation and canal-cleaning arrangements have disappeared, and the system's infrastructure is in disrepair. The degree of inequality, as measured by the Gini coefficient on irrigated landholding, is 0.57. Rosario, like the other irrigation systems in the Mexican sample, is formally autonomous of all state control; nevertheless, intervention by the National Water Commission to reestablish the legal common-property regime and renew irrigation service would be especially fruitful.

San Sergio, poorer than Rosario, and likewise located in the hilly and arid Mesa del Centro of the study area (in the *municipio* of San Felipe), has achieved superior collective action. Its eighty-four farming households belong to a water users' association formed during Mexico's agrarian reform, in 1936. There are three water sources at San Sergio, and a sophisticated system of rotation of irrigation. Each member household has 1.25-hectare landholdings in each of three irrigation zones, and a 1-hectare rainfed plot. By design, then, the Gini coefficient in San Sergio is zero. The modern San Sergio dam irrigates two zones, and two colonial-era levees irrigate the third. Such scattering of plots explicitly compensates for irregularities in the distribution of water.[17] Irrigation at San Sergio is based on a crudely volumetric scheme known as *caños*, based on the number of turns of the valve at the headgates of the dam: each turn of the valve releases four to six *caños*, more if the dam is full. The state of repair of infrastructure at San Sergio is generally good, although the earthen field-intakes are in poor condition. Farmers here manage six or seven irrigations per year, contrasted to an average of just over one in most of the studied systems. The greater frequency of application of water makes possible the cultivation of slightly higher-valued crops, like the *mulato* chile, which require more careful water management.[18]

5.4.1. The Data

The Mexican study was limited to reservoir-based, or surface-water, irrigation systems. (These would be called "tank" systems in South Asia.) In Mexico, several thousand *unidades de riego*, or irrigation units, autonomous from public control, irrigate approximately half of the country's irrigated area; the remainder is served by public irrigation districts. Data were collected in the central state of Guanajuato by means of a survey of the governing councils (*mesas directivas*) and inspection of the canals of fifty-four randomly chosen unidades in Guanajuato.[19]

5.4.2. Irrigation Organization

Table 5.4a presents summary characteristics of the sample systems. Among the characteristics of the water users' association noted in the table are the number of *ejidos*—quasi-communal farming groups created during Mexico's agrarian reform—represented among the members of the association; the presence of more than one ejido among the association members indicates social heterogeneity.

Table 5.4b summarizes the complex of rules chosen by the water users in forty-nine of the irrigation communities (in most of the five communities left out of the table, years of inactivity have led to the disappearance of rules altogether): the water-allocation and cost-sharing arrangements, the labor-mobilization regime, and the presence or absence of a water master. Water is allocated, in each unidad, either (a) proportionally to each household's landholding, or (b) in equal shares to all households. Similarly, maintenance and repair costs are shared either (a) proportionally to landholding, or (b) equally among all.[20] Ostrom (1990: 92 and passim) argues that successful institutions to manage local commons frequently exhibit *congruence* between cost-sharing and allocation rules: "appropriation rules restricting time, place, technology and/or quantity of resource units are related to local conditions and to provision rules requiring labor, material, and/or money." This "congruence hypothesis"—namely, that governance regimes for the commons with equivalent rules for cost-sharing and benefit allocation perform better and endure longer—is echoed in field studies of irrigation. Chambers (1980: 41), drawing on his experience in South Asia, asserts that "communal labor is most likely to be effective . . . where labor obligations are proportional to expected benefits." Siy (1987) shows that under the *atar* distributive rule in the

TABLE 5.4a
Characteristics of the Sample, Central Mexico

Variable	Units	Mean	St. Dev.	Minimum	Maximum
System characteristics					
Reservoir capacity	1,000 m³	3,431	9,665	30	50,000
Command area	ha	449	931	16	6,014
Canal network	km	11.2	12.1	0.5	54.6
Lined canals	proportion	0.23	0.32	0	1
Government-constructed	(0,1)	0.60		0	1
Characteristics of the water users' association					
Households	no.	123	140	15	676
Ejidos	no.	1.8	1.6	0	8
Mean landholding	ha	3.3	2.3	0.3	10.0
Gini coefficient		0.267	0.246	0.000	0.747
Year of formation		1953	22	1883	1992
Performance, 1994/95					
Irrigation supply	1,000 m³	1,636	5,393	0	37,500
Irrigated area	ha	405	1,118	0	6,014
Output per unit water	pesos/1,000 m³	933	1,357	0	7,517
Output per unit land	pesos/ha	3,796	4,853	0	25,000
Economic characteristics, 1994/95					
Wage	pesos/day	27	6	14	45
Output price	pesos/ton	1,115	1,170	0	5,141

successful Philippine *zanjeras* (irrigation societies), the ratio of individual benefits to labor contributions is roughly equal for all members of a given organization. Dayton-Johnson (2000a) develops a simple game theoretic model formalizing the congruence hypothesis: in that model, full compliance with the rules of the system is a noncooperative equilibrium outcome when there is congruence between the cost-sharing and allocation rules. In table 5.4b, the eight unidades with proportional water allocation and proportional cost-sharing and the seventeen with equal division of both water and costs exhibit congruence in their distributive rules. From the perspective of the congruence hypothesis, the puzzle to be explained is the presence of twenty-four irrigation systems—a nonnegligible fraction of the sample—with incongruent rules. Other institutional characteristics summarized in table 5.4b include the mode of canal-cleaning: collective canal-cleaning is carried out by all households working side by side on predetermined days; household canal-cleaning assigns a stretch of the canal network to each household for cleaning.

5.4.3. Measuring Cooperation

Unlike the South Indian study, which considered a range of measures of cooperation, the Mexican study looks at one particular dimension—infrastructure maintenance—in greater detail. Thus, table 5.4c summa-

TABLE 5.4b
Joint Distribution of Institutional Characteristics, Central Mexico

	Cost-sharing		Water Master		Canal-Cleaning	
	Proportional	Equal-division	Present	Absent	Collective	Household
Water allocation						
Proportional	8	23	25	6	11	18
Equal-division	1	17	10	8	9	8
Cost sharing						
Proportional			8	1	0	8
Equal-division			27	13	20	18
Water master						
Present					12	21
Absent					8	5

Note: Three systems have different canal-cleaning regimes; therefore the numbers in columns 5 and 6 sum only to 46.

TABLE 5.4c
Infrastructure Maintenance, Central Mexico

Condition of . . .	N	Good (%)	Fair (%)	Poor (%)
Lining of primary canals	26	50.0	38.5	11.5
Lining of secondary canals	13	53.8	46.2	0.0
Water gates	40	20.0	62.5	17.5
Field intakes	46	13.0	54.3	32.6
Grubbing (control of brush and growth around canals)	54	24.1	33.4	42.6
Canal side-slopes	54	51.9	35.2	13.0

Condition of . . .	N	None (%)	Some (%)	General (%)
Damage by animals and vehicles crossing the canals	46	65.2	26.1	8.7
Filtration of water around canals and channels	49	44.9	40.8	14.3

rizes the distribution of several indicators of the quality of infrastructure maintenance from the Mexican survey. These measures were collected during a canal inspection at each of the sampled systems. We assume that the observed quality of maintenance in each case increases with the level of cooperation in cost-sharing. For each indicator, each irrigation system was given a score of "good," "fair," or "poor." For the indicators of filtration and animals trampling the canals, the meaning of the scores is slightly different, indicating that the problem is "general," "present but not generalized," or "absent." Three of these indicators are used below in ordered-logit models of the quality of maintenance: the state of repair of field intakes, the small and simple structures that regulate the flow of irrigation water into individual parcels; the degree of definition of canal side-slopes (important since almost all are earthen canals, unlined with cement or concrete); the degree of filtration (leakage) of water around the canals.

5.4.4. Explanatory Variables

Table 5.4a reports that the average Gini coefficient, calculated on the basis of irrigated landholding, is 0.27, lower than in the South Indian sample; the maximum Gini is 0.76, the minimum 0.00 (fifteen cases). The average group size is 123 households. The average age of the water users' association is 43 years, although the oldest such organization in the sample was founded in 1883, and the newest was only four years old at the time of the survey. The statistical model in table 5.5 includes the share of the canal network lined with concrete or cement; the larger this share, the lower the overall amount of cooperative effort needed to maintain the infrastructure.[21] Water depth is a measure of relative scarcity of irrigation water in the unidad; it is measured in millimeters, according to the formula 1 mm = 10 cubic meters per hectare.

5.4.5. Analysis: Institutional Choice

What structural community characteristics are associated with particular irrigation institutions? As in the South Indian study, we estimate a model of institutional choice: table 5.5 reports the results of a logit model predicting the presence of a proportional water-allocation rule.[22] Note that table 5.2 reports a similar model for the South Indian data, but one that estimates the probability of proportional *cost-sharing* rather than water allocation. To ease interpretation of the results, the explanatory variables have been normalized so that each has a mean value equal to 0 and a standard deviation equal to 1. The table shows that the impact of inequality is large, positive, and significant: a 1-standard-deviation increase in the Gini coefficient increases the probability of observing proportional water allocation. Social heterogeneity, as measured by the number of ejidos represented among the irrigation-group members, has no significant effect on the choice of rules.

The prevalence of unidades that combine proportional water allocation with equal division of costs appears to counter the congruence

TABLE 5.5
A Logit Model of the Choice of Proportional Water Allocation,
Central Mexico

Variable	Estimated Coefficient	t-ratio
Gini coefficient	2.8839	2.65
Number of households in the irrigation system	2.1657	0.84
Number of ejidos represented among irrigation-system members	−0.1890	0.14
Age of water users' association	1.6156	1.79
Water depth (Reservoir capacity relative to command area of the reservoir)	−1.0819	−1.23
Ratio of smallest parcel size to local wage	0.2344	0.13
Proportion of canal network that is lined	0.8775	1.39
Constant	1.7708	1.48
Observations	48	
Log likelihood	−11.83	
Pseudo R-sq	0.62	

Note: Each of the explanatory variables is normalized with mean zero and standard deviation equal to one.

hypothesis of Ostrom and others, but it is consistent with an interpretation of unequal bargaining power and institutional evolution. Compare the gains from proportional water allocation mixed with equal division of costs, relative to equal division of both water and costs (the congruent rule). For households with landholding wealth above the mean level, those gains rise with inequality in the landholding distribution: the higher a household's landholding lies above the mean, the larger the difference between its water share and its maintenance-labor share. For those group members with wealth below the mean, however, the attractiveness of this incongruent rule is decreasing in inequality: as a household's landholding size drops, its share of water benefits drops, while its labor contribution remains constant. How the actual rule choice reflects these different preferences toward adoption of the proportional or proportional-allocation rule depends on the mechanism that aggregates households' preferences. Assume for the moment that, as is plausible in a hierarchical agrarian social order, the will of the larger landholders is more highly weighted by this mechanism. Then increased inequality will be associated with a higher probability of observing the incongruent rule that we witnessed in half of the Mexican irrigation groups. This outcome could emerge even if this incongruent proportional-allocation rule performs miserably in terms both of mobilizing maintenance effort and minimizing transaction costs, if the wealthier households can impose their preference for that relatively nonegalitarian rule on the group. This process is consistent with Ostrom's (1996) interpretation of evidence regarding bargaining over rules in a group of irrigation systems in Nepal. (This raises the question of why the poorer households cannot pay off the wealthy to switch to a better-performing rule.)

5.4.6. Analysis: Determinants of Cooperation

Table 5.6 summarizes results of three logit models of collective effort in the Mexican irrigation systems, as measured by the state of repair of the infrastructure.[23] While there are important differences across the three models, the following generalizations can be made. First, social heterogeneity lowers cooperative effort. In all three cooperation models, social heterogeneity—the number of ejidos represented in the unidad—is associated with lower maintenance levels. Controlling for other factors, costs associated with organizing irrigation across ejido boundaries lower aggregate cooperative effort. Moreover, the quantitative importance of this form of social inequality is larger than that of economic inequality. Second, and nevertheless, economic inequality lowers cooperative effort. In all three models, a Gini-squared term is included and inequality is interacted with (the predicted probability of) the presence of proportional water allocation. Therefore, the full effect of inequality is not limited to the estimated coefficient on the Gini term; the marginal effect of an increase in inequality on maintenance effort is a function also of the level of the Gini coefficient, and the presence of a proportional water-allocation rule. Once calculated, the full effect of the Gini coefficient is negative in each of the three maintenance models. (The effect is evaluated at the mean value of the independent variables.) The full effect of inequality, thus computed, on side-slope definition is −0.1238 percent; that is, a one-unit increase in the Gini coefficient starting at its mean level reduces side-slope definition by −0.12 percent. The full effect of inequality on field-intake condition is −1.03 percent, and the full effect on filtration control is −0.02 percent. The components of this full effect, however, do not all have negative signs. The estimated coefficient on the square of the Gini term is positive in all cases, suggesting a positive effect of inequality on canal maintenance that is higher at higher levels of inequality. The estimated coefficient on the interaction between (predicted) proportional water allocation and the Gini term is negative: conditional

TABLE 5.6
Logit Models of Infrastructure Maintenance, Central Mexico

	Dependent Variable					
	Definition of Side Slopes		Condition of Field Intakes		Control of Filtration Around Canals	
Variable	Coefficient	t-ratio	Coefficient	t-ratio	Coefficient	t-ratio
Number of households	-0.0107	-0.7	0.0112	0.7	0.0125	0.8
Gini coefficient	0.0087	0.1	0.1305	0.9	-0.0314	-0.2
Gini squared	0.0014	1.2	0.0051	2.7	0.0040	2.4
Number of ejidos	-0.6916	-2.3	-0.7392	-2.0	-0.6795	-2.3
Command area	0.0023	1.1	0.0023	1.1	0.0047	2.5
Wage	-0.1123	-1.3	-0.0688	-0.8	-0.2392	-2.4
Irrigation supply	-0.0004	-1.5	-0.0004	-1.3	-0.0003	-0.7
Dummy for government construction	1.4298	1.8	-0.2095	-0.2	-0.0992	-0.1
Interaction: proportional water allocation (estimated probability) and number of households	0.0133	0.8	-0.0121	-0.7	-0.0187	-1.1
Interaction: proportional water allocation (estimated probability) and Gini	-0.1016	-0.7	-0.4814	-2.5	-0.1968	-1.2
Proportional water allocation (estimated probability)	0.8587	0.5	7.0442	2.6	2.2328	1.0
Observations	48		40		43	
Log likelihood	-42.4		-28.3		-36.2	
Pseudo R-sq.	0.1228		0.2577		0.1784	

TABLE 5.7
Calculating the Total Effect of Inequality on Cooperative Effort, Central Mexico

	A	B	C	D	E
	Effect of Gini on Choice of Proportional Water Allocation	Effect of Proportional Water Allocation on Maintenance	Indirect Effect of Inequality via Rule Choice	Direct Effect of Inequality on Maintenance	Total Effect
Maintenance Indicator			(A times B)		(C plus D)
Side slope definition	0.3585	−1.56	−0.56	−3.04	−3.60
Condition of field intakes	0.3585	−186.12	−66.71	−25.31	−92.02
Filtration	0.3585	−2.16	−0.77	−0.48	−1.26

Note: The magnitudes reported in columns A, B, and C are percentages, caused by a one-standard-deviation in inequality (as measured by the Gini coefficient). The percentages, in turn, reflect increases or decreases in the probability of observing a proportional water-allocation rule (A) or a one-point increase in maintenance (B and D).

on having chosen proportional water allocation, increasing inequality reduces the level of cooperative effort.

This full effect of inequality on cooperation, however, does not fully exhaust the effect of inequality on cooperative effort. This is because the quantitatively most important determinant of cooperative effort in all three models is the presence of proportional water allocation, which is in turn partly a function of the level of inequality. Thus, table 5.7 adds the indirect effect of inequality on canal maintenance (via the effect of inequality on the choice of rules) to the direct effect for each of the three models. Column A shows that an increase in the Gini coefficient of one standard deviation increases the probability of observing proportional water allocation (controlling for the other explanatory variables in table 5.5) by 35.85 percent.[24] Column B shows the effect of proportional water allocation on each of the three indicators of collective-maintenance effort. Thus, for example, a one-unit increase in the estimated probability of adopting proportional water allocation reduces the probability of a one-unit increase in observed filtration maintenance by 2.16 percent. Column C multiplies these two effects to give the indirect effect of a one-standard-deviation increase in inequality on observed maintenance. Therefore, the indirect effect of inequality on the control of filtration is 0.3585 times −2.16, or a −0.77 percent reduction in the probability that filtration maintenance will rise one level. Column D gives the direct effect; this is the marginal effect of a one-standard-deviation increase in inequality (properly accounting for interaction and squared terms) on observed maintenance, computed on the basis of the estimated coefficients reported in table 5.6. Thus, an increase in the Gini coefficient of one standard deviation reduces the probability of a one-unit increase in observed filtration maintenance directly by −0.48 percent. The total effect of inequality (Column E) simply adds the direct and indirect effect. For filtration, inequality reduces the probability that maintenance rises one grade by −0.77 − 0.48 = −1.26 percent.

5.5. Interpretation

What can we deduce about the relationship between inequality and community irrigation from our review of the Indian and Mexican evidence? First, there is a generally negative association between inequality and cooperative outcomes. An increase in the Gini coefficient of landholding inequality is associated with lower maintenance and greater incidence of water-related conflict in South India. The full effect of the Gini coefficient on various indicators of maintenance (properly accounting for interaction terms and quadratic terms) is negative in the Mexican data as well. This suggests that Olson effects are not as prevalent in these irrigation systems as the negative effect of inequality on conservation found in Dayton-Johnson and Bardhan (2002). In that model (which is couched in terms of a fishery), conditional conservation is a best response for each fisher to conditional conservation by the other, under conditions of perfect equality of fishing capacity. ("Conditional conservation" means simply conserving when one's counterpart conserves.) As inequality increases, however, some fishers' capacity is reduced to the point where their claim on the future benefits of conservation is too small to induce them to conserve today.[25]

The results of the field studies also clearly underscore the importance of institutions, the local rules for managing irrigation resources and infrastructure. In the first instance, both studies provide evidence that the rules in place affect the level of cooperation. The presence of proportional cost-sharing is associated with higher field-channel maintenance in South India, while the presence of proportional water allocation is associated with higher field-intake maintenance in Mexico. At the same time, economic inequality has a close relationship with these rules. Inequality is strongly associated with the presence of proportional cost-sharing in South India, indicating pressure for progressive redistribution. Conversely, inequality is strongly associated with proportional water allocation in Mexico; given that most of these systems have equal division of costs, this is evidence of pressure for regressive redistribution. Also relevant in this connection is that maintenance is lower in South India in systems where a substantial fraction of farmers believe that the rules were crafted by the local elite. Thus, in South India, water-allocation rules are less likely to be broken when they are crafted by the elite, but maintenance arrangements are *more* likely to be violated in these cases.[26]

These interpretations of the relationship between inequality, rules, and performance are broadly consistent with a number of game theoretic models of cooperation (as in Dayton-Johnson and Bardhan 2002). Nevertheless, the empirical results suggest that a critical impact of inequality on cooperation on the commons is mediated by social norms. Thus, social heterogeneity often has a negative impact on cooperative outcomes. Caste homogeneity reduces the incidence of intra-village water conflict in South India. Social heterogeneity—the number of ejidos from which irrigation-group members are drawn—has a uniformly negative and significant effect on maintenance in all of the Mexican results. Certain types of community—caste groups or ejidos—have at their disposal means of monitoring and enforcing cooperative agreements; the efficacy of those means diminishes as they cross community boundaries. This is indirect evidence that some kinds of group-based resources—social norms or social sanctions—are critical to the successful management of irrigation resources. (Baland and Platteau 1995 refer to this as "cultural homogeneity.")

That economic outcomes might be affected by these community-level resources has been suggested by Akerlof's (1997) analysis of "social distance," for example, and indeed by the burgeoning social-science research on "social capital" (e.g., Putnam 1993; Knack and Keefer 1997; Narayan and Pritchett 1999). Part of the disutility suffered by community members who break rules is the pecuniary loss that is imposed on them by the explicit rules: if you don't clean your stretch of the canal, you don't get any water. But certainly there is some nonpecuniary disutility from rule-breaking, and arguably, people experience more of this when the others they've cheated are more socially proximate. By extension, the internal or psychic disutility of rule-breaking is lessened the greater the social distance among players.

Results of experimental economics support, or are at least broadly consistent with, this type of finding. Indeed, one of the most active areas of experimental research in economics has to do with explaining the apparently anomalous results of the "Ultimatum Game" (Thaler 1988; Roth 1995), in which players inefficiently reject offers they perceive as unfair. Rabin (1997) provides a general theory of bargaining structures that suggests that fairer environments, in which asymmetries in bargaining power are relatively low, may lead to more efficient outcomes. Sally (2001) suggests that sympathy is a key factor in determining willingness to cooperate (by changing payoffs as suggested above); sympathy, in

turn, is an inverse function of physical and psychological distance between a person and others. Other experimental results confirm that
power asymmetries and social distance affect the outcome of games in
ways not necessarily consistent with conventional economic modeling.
Lawler and Yoon (1996) report results of exchange experiments in which
equality of power significantly increases the probability of mutual agreements, which in turn generate feelings of cohesion between the players.
(Many of these issues are considered at greater length in the context of
commons games by Cardenas and Ostrom 2001.)

An intriguing question raised by these results is whether cultural or social heterogeneity is itself fostered by economic inequality. Thus, for example, Cardenas (this volume) reports the results of laboratory commons
games played by experimental subjects who are themselves farmers and
commons users in rural Colombia. He finds that farmer-players with a
greater wealth distance from the other players seem less willing to cooperate. (The novelty of Cardenas's research is that he measures players' actual wealth levels, not wealth measured in terms of tokens given them to
play the laboratory game.)

While our review of the Indian and Mexican evidence cannot provide
sufficiently refined data to discern among these varied hypotheses about
norms, bargaining power, and perceptions of fairness, our results nevertheless indicate that these issues should be at the forefront of future theoretical and empirical research on local commons.

NOTES

1. Seabright (1993) provides a useful overview.

2. Surveys of the case-study literature for irrigation communities include
Chambers (1980); Coward and Levine (1987); Kähkönen (1999); Tang (1992,
1994); and Yoder (1994). Vaidyanathan (1986) provides a historical survey of
irrigation organization in Asia. Dayton-Johnson (1999b) updates these surveys
in an explicitly economic framework.

3. These include Agrawal and Goyal (1999); Edmonds (2002); Fujita,
Hayami, and Kikuchi (2000); Khwaja (2000); Lam (1998); and Tang (1992); we
survey this literature more generally in Bardhan and Dayton-Johnson (2002).

4. We are grateful to Peter Richerson for the observations made in this paragraph.

5. Aspects of Olson's hypothesis are formalized by Bergstrom, Blume, and
Varian (1986), and by Itaya, de Meza, and Myles (1997).

6. Such increasing returns are referred to by many authors as "nonconvexities." This is a potentially confusing terminology, given that returns are convex in
the size of the system—even though this generates a nonconvex production set.

7. The names of irrigation systems and people given in this section are fictitious.

8. Thus, G4 employs a "continuous-flow" water-distribution regime, associated in the case-study literature with the *karanhakota* regime of Sri Lanka; this contrasts with the *warabandi*, or turn-taking, water-distribution rule for surface-water irrigation. See Dayton-Johnson (1999b).

9. The full results of the data analysis for the South Indian study are reported in Bardhan (2000).

10. First-stage logit estimates of the presence of guards were also estimated. The Gini coefficient was included in that estimation, but was not statistically significant. Therefore, the indirect impact of inequality does not act through its effect on the decision to hire guards. The only significant variables for predicting the presence of a guard were (with their signs indicated in parentheses) urban linkage (+), traditional organization (+), and whether the ayacut is part of a larger canal system (−). The interested reader is referred to Bardhan (2000, table 5).

11. Alternative specifications of all three models are reported in Bardhan (2000, tables 2, 3, and 4); the interested reader will also find more extended discussion of the effect of variables other than inequality on cooperation.

12. The statistically significant estimated coefficient on the square of the Gini term does not imply a U-shaped relationship between inequality and cooperation in the South Indian sample. Given the estimates in table 5.3, the effect of the Gini coefficient on intra-village conflict is negative up to a Gini value of about 0.7, which is about 3 standard deviations above the mean.

13. Caste homogeneity is important primarily because sanctioning against violations might be more difficult across castes. Caste homogeneity, however, is not necessarily a good indicator of whether some individuals are willing or able to be Olsonian entrepreneurs.

14. Lam (1998) reports from his study of irrigation systems in Nepal that in nearly half of the government agency–managed systems the extent of rule-breaking is medium or high, whereas the corresponding percentage in farmer-managed systems is only about 12 percent.

15. As in the South Indian section, all proper names used here are fictitious.

16. The week before Rosario was surveyed for this study, the four irrigators other than Don Leonardo sought out the survey team with a litany of complaints against Don Leonardo. Not only did he refuse to let anyone near the water, he allegedly stole some of their sheep, too.

17. Scattering of plots to reduce inequities in the access to irrigation water is widely observed in the field-study literature; the *panguva* share system in Sri Lanka and described by Leach (1961), for example, serves this purpose. See also Dayton-Johnson (1999b).

18. At another nearby community, villagers reported that they did not grow chiles because they are "too much work."

19. The Mexican data-collection exercise is described in greater detail in Dayton-Johnson (1999a).

20. Other water-allocation and cost-sharing rules from the field-study literature are assessed in Dayton-Johnson (1999b).

21. In all but one of the surveyed systems, lining was carried out at the time of system construction or rehabilitation, by some agent other than the water users. Thus, it is effectively exogenous. The lined-share variable, accordingly, is defined

as the percentage of the canal network that is lined times an indicator variable equal to zero if the government undertook any canal-lining at the system subsequent to the original construction of the system, and one otherwise. This correction is meant to ensure that the measured lined share is indeed exogenous to the choice of distributive rule.

22. A more extensive discussion of the statistical model and the explanatory variables is provided in Dayton-Johnson (2000a).

23. Further details regarding these statistical models, and a more extensive discussion of the explanatory variables, is provided in Dayton-Johnson (2000b).

24. This number is the marginal effect of inequality evaluated at the vector of mean values of the variables in table 5.5, properly accounting for interaction and squared terms; see Dayton-Johnson (2000a, table 8) for further details.

25. A more general discussion of inequality and collective-good provision with concave production functions and capital-market imperfections is discussed in the chapter in this volume by Bardhan and Ghatak.

26. Lore Ruttan has suggested that when lower castes feel disenfranchised, they dare not violate water-allocation rules, but they neglect canal maintenance. Because they have smaller plots, they also have less to lose by this strategy. The elites, in contrast, maintain canals but break water-allocation rules when they feel disenfranchised—when these rules are crafted by PWD agents.

References

Aggarwal, R. M. 2000. "Possibilities and limitations to cooperation in small groups: The case of group-owned wells in Southern India." *World Development* 28: 1481–97.

Agrawal, A., and S. Goyal. 1999. Group size and collective action: Third-party monitoring in common-pool resources. Leitner Working Paper No. 1999–09. New Haven, CT: The Leitner Program in International Political Economy, Yale University.

Akerlof, G. A. 1997. "Social distance and social decisions." *Econometrica* 65: 1005–27.

Baland, J.-M., and J.-P. Platteau. 1995. "Does heterogeneity hinder collective action?" Cahiers de la Faculté des sciences économiques et sociales de Namur, Serie Recherche No. 146, Collection "Développement."

———. 1996. *Halting Degradation of Natural Resources: Is there a Role for Rural Communities?* Oxford: Clarendon Press.

———. 1997. "Wealth inequality and efficiency in the commons, i: The unregulated case." *Oxford Economic Papers* 49: 451–82.

———. 1998. "Wealth inequality and efficiency in the commons, ii: The regulated case." *Oxford Economic Papers* 50: 1–22.

Bardhan, P. K. 1984. *Land, Labor and Rural Poverty: Essays in Development Economics.* New York: Columbia University Press.

———. 1993. "Symposium on management of local commons." *Journal of Economic Perspectives* 7: 87–92.

————. 1995. "Rational fools and cooperation in a poor hydraulic economy." In *Choice, Welfare, and Development: A Festschrift in Honour of Amartya K. Sen*, ed. K. Basu, P. Pattanaik, and K. Suzumura. Oxford: Clarendon Press.

————. 2000. "Irrigation and cooperation: An empirical analysis of 48 irrigation communities in South India." *Economic Development and Cultural Change* 48: 847–65.

Bardhan, P. K., and J. Dayton-Johnson. 2002. "Unequal irrigators: Heterogeneity and commons management in large-scale multivariate research." In National Research Council, *The drama of the commons*. Washington, D.C.: National Academy Press.

Bergstrom, T. C., L. Blume, and H. Varian. 1986. "On the private provision of public goods." *Journal of Public Economics* 29: 25–49.

Cardenas, J. C., and E. Ostrom. 2001. What do people bring into the game? How norms help people overcome the tragedy of the commons. Unpublished manuscript, Workshop on Political Theory and Policy Analysis, Indiana University.

Chambers, R. 1980. "Basic concepts in the organization of irrigation." In *Irrigation and Agricultural Development in Asia: Perspectives from the Social Sciences*, ed. E. Walter Coward, Jr. Ithaca and London: Cornell University Press.

Coward, E. Walter, Jr., and G. Levine. 1987. "Studies of farmer-managed irrigation systems: Ten years of cumulative knowledge and changing research priorities." In *Public Intervention in Farmer-Managed Irrigation Systems*, ed. IIMI / WECS. Kathmandu, Nepal: International Irrigation Management Institute (IIMI), Colombo, Sri Lanka, and Water and Energy Commission Secretariat (WECS).

Dayton-Johnson, J. 1999a. "Irrigation organization in Mexican *unidades de riego*." *Irrigation and Drainage Systems* 13: 55–74.

————. 1999b. Peasants and water: A review essay on the economics of farmer-managed irrigation. Unpublished manuscript, Dalhousie University.

————. 2000a. "Choosing rules to govern the commons: A model with evidence from Mexico." *Journal of Economic Behavior and Organization* 42: 19–41.

————. 2000b. "Determinants of collective action on the local commons: A model with evidence from Mexico." *Journal of Development Economics* 62: 181–208.

Dayton-Johnson, J., and P. K. Bardhan. 2002. "Inequality and conservation on the local commons: A theoretical exercise." *Economic Journal* 112(481): 577–602.

Easter, K.W., and K. Palanisami. 1986. Tank irrigation in India and Thailand: An example of common property resource management. Staff paper, Department of Agricultural and Applied Economics, University of Minnesota.

Edmonds, E. 2002. "Government-initiated community resource management and local resource extraction from Nepal's forests." *Journal of Development Economics* 68(1): 89–115.

Fujita, M., Y. Hayami, and M. Kikuchi. 1999. The conditions of collective action for local commons management: The case of irrigation in the Philippines. Unpublished manuscript, Takushoku University, Foundation for Advanced Studies on International Development, and Chiba University.

Itaya, J., D. de Meza, and G. D. Myles. 1997. "In praise of inequality: Public good provision and income distribution." *Economics Letters* 57: 289–96.

Jarayaman, T. K. 1981. "Farmers' organizations in surface irrigation project: Two empirical studies from Gujarat." *Economic and Political Weekly* 16: A89–A98.

Johnson, R. N., and G. D. Libecap. 1982. "Contracting problems and regulation: The case of the fishery." *American Economic Review* 72: 1005–22.

Kähkönen, S. 1999. Does social capital matter in rural water delivery? A review of literature. SCI Working Paper No. 9, Social Capital Initiative, World Bank.

Khwaja, A. 2000. Can good projects succeed in bad communities? Collective action in the Himalayas. Unpublished manuscript, Harvard University.

Knack, S., and P. Keefer. 1997. "Does social capital have an economic payoff? A cross-country investigation." *Quarterly Journal of Economics* 112: 1251–88.

Lam, W. F. 1998. *Governing Irrigation Systems in Nepal. Institutions, Infrastructure, and Collective Action.* Oakland, Calif.: ICS Press.

Lawler, E. J., and J. Yoon. 1996. "Commitment in exchange relations: Test of a theory of relational cohesion." *American Sociological Review* 61: 89–108.

Leach, Edmund R. 1961. *Pul Eliya: A Village in Ceylon.* Cambridge: Cambridge University Press.

Narayan, D., and L. Pritchett. 1999. "Cents and sociability: Household income and social capital in rural Tanzania." *Economic Development and Cultural Change* 47: 873–97.

Olson, M. 1965. *The Logic of Collective Action.* Cambridge, Mass.: Harvard University Press.

Ostrom, E. 1990. *Governing the Commons: The Evolution of Institutions for Collective Action.* New York: Cambridge University Press.

———. 1994. "Constituting social capital and collective action." *Journal of Theoretical Politics* 6: 527–62.

———. 1996. Incentives, rules of the game, and development. In *Proceedings of the Annual Bank Conference on Development Economics 1995.* Washington, D.C.: World Bank, 207–34.

Putnam, R. D., with R. Leonardi and R. Y. Nanetti. 1993. *Making Democracy Work: Civic Traditions in Modern Italy.* Princeton, N.J.: Princeton University Press.

Rabin, M. 1997. Bargaining structure, fairness, and efficiency. Unpublished manuscript, University of California, Berkeley.

Roth, A. E. 1995. "Bargaining experiments." In *Handbook of Experimental Economics*, ed. J. Kagel and A. Roth, 253–348. Princeton, N.J.: Princeton University Press.

Sally, D. 2001. "On sympathy and games." *Journal of Economic Behavior and Organization* 44: 1–30.

Seabright, P. 1993. "Managing local commons: Theoretical issues in incentive design." *Journal of Economic Perspectives* 7: 113–34.

———. 1997. "Is cooperation habit-forming?" In *The Environment and Emerging Development Issues*, vol. 2, ed. Partha Dasgupta and Karl-Goran Mäler. Oxford: Clarendon Press.

Siy, R. Y. Jr. 1987. "Averting the bureaucratization of a community-managed resource: The case of the zanjeras." In *Public Intervention in Farmer-Managed Irrigation Systems*, ed. International Irrigation Management Institute and Water and Energy Commission Secretariat, Nepal, 35–47. Colombo, Sri Lanka: IIMI.

Tang, S. Y. 1992. *Institutions and Collective Action: Self-Governance in Irrigation*. San Francisco: Institute for Contemporary Studies.

———. 1994. "Institutions and performance in irrigation systems." In *Rules, Games, and Common-pool Resources*, ed. E. Ostrom, R. Gardner, and J. Walker. Ann Arbor: University of Michigan Press.

Thaler, R. H. 1988. "Anomalies: The ultimatum game." *Journal of Economic Perspectives* 2: 195–206.

Vaidyanathan, A. 1986. "Water control institutions and agriculture: A comparative perspective." *Indian Economic Review* 20: 25–83.

Yoder, R. 1994. *Locally Managed Irrigation Systems: Essential Tasks and Implications for Assistance, Management Transfer and Turnover Programs*. Colombo, Sri Lanka: International Irrigation Management Institute.

Chapter 6

MANAGING PACIFIC SALMON: THE ROLE
OF DISTRIBUTIONAL CONFLICTS
IN COASTAL SALISH FISHERIES

Sara Singleton

Not all failures to manage natural resource systems sustainably stem from inequality or an inability to solve distributional conflicts. Resolving such conflicts or overcoming other barriers to collective action may in fact *facilitate* the overexploitation of natural resources if members of a group are generally agreed that such overexploitation constitutes the best means to a more highly valued end. In other situations, inequality in resource holdings many increase the likelihood of conservation (Baland and Platteau 1999). But inequality and distributive conflicts do cause or contribute to many such failures. All the many institutions governing the use of environmental resources—property rights in various bundles, formal regulations, informal conventions or practices, as well as written and unwritten contracts—have distributional implications that are in practice critical to their success. Distributional effects often determine whether institutions will be able to function without prohibitively expensive implementation costs or even whether they will be established at all. Thus, they highlight the shortcomings of simple models of exchange or government regulation that ignore the facts that control over others is always too costly and difficult to be complete; that asymmetries of information are typical, rather than exceptional; that success in many activities requires the exercise of significant initiative on the part of agents; and that government employees rarely have either the resources or the incentives to fully monitor and enforce regulations. All of these factors are present

The author would like to thank Jean-Marie Baland, Michael Taylor, Lore Ruttan, and Peter Richerson for helpful comments on earlier versions of this chapter, as well as Samuel Bowles, Pranab Bardhan, and the Sante Fe Institute for organizing and supporting the workshop in which it was originally presented. I also wish to thank Lee Hoines at the Washington State Department of Fish and Wildlife, who provided tribal catch data, and a reviewer who wishes to remain anonymous, who provided helpful corrections on various points in the text. Such errors as remain are solely my responsibility.

in large, complex common-pool resource systems (CPRs) because: (i) it is difficult to observe, let alone control, the actions of users; (ii) resource systems cross boundaries and resource stocks migrate, making accountability problematic and decreasing the likelihood that anyone will contribute voluntarily, even conditionally;[1] (iii) public and private goods are generally present simultaneously within the same resource system, which results in the costs of conservation being borne disproportionately by local groups, or, conversely, in the underprovision of public goods; (iv) users of CPRs are diverse constituencies with different preferences as to various management institutions, goals, and the appropriate mix of public and private goods. The complex web of relationships surrounding large common-pool resources gives rise to a correspondingly large scope for contestation among various participants. Inequality and distributional conflicts are obviously at the heart of this process.

This chapter looks at how a group of users of one such CPR—a large, transboundary salmon fishery in the Pacific Northwest region of the United States—have grappled with these issues and both succeeded and failed in creating management institutions that combine elements of equity and efficiency. While this CPR system is particularly complex—legally, politically, and ecologically—there is nothing unique in the underlying issues surrounding this case or the distributional struggles resulting from them. In fact, it is precisely because such conflicts are both ubiquitous and pivotal to the design of management institutions that a close examination of how the participants themselves view these issues—the arguments they advance and the larger principles that these represent, the process through which they deliberate and structure of agreements they eventually settle on—serves to illuminate larger questions about institutional design and environmental sustainability.

To provide a somewhat broader, historical perspective on how inequality and distributional conflict shape management institutions, the chapter begins with a "snapshot" of the institutions in place during the period just prior to Western contact, approximately two centuries ago. The management institutions of aboriginal people quite strikingly align individual incentives so as to encourage efficiency in a variety of situations involving both predictable and unpredictable resource flows, uneven spatial distribution of resources, joint production with some degree of specialization and trade. The fact that such institutions, while *efficiency-enhancing*, did not always provide equal shares or otherwise generate egalitarian results in the short term creates an interesting puzzle, especially given the fact that such societies were highly decentralized and thus lacked the coercive capacities of a centralized state (Singleton 1998, 1999).

The main section of the chapter looks at Pacific Northwest salmon fishing as it is today co-managed by seventeen Native American tribes (descendants of the tribes discussed in section 6.1) along with state and federal management agencies and an international regulatory body that promulgates regulations that govern fishing on transboundary stocks. It focuses particularly on intertribal allocation conflicts and how present-day institutions governing intertribal allocation both succeed and fail to resolve them, the implications of these successes and failures for our understanding of how distributive conflicts affect the ability of groups to overcome collective-action problems associated with their use of a shared resource system and how that, in turn, affects the prospects for environmentally sustainable management institutions.

6.1. Prologue: The Political Economy of Early Coastal Salish Societies

Perhaps best known for their beautifully carved masks and totem poles, the aboriginal peoples of the Northwest coast of North America (see figure 6.1) were among the most affluent of hunter-gathering tribes, and the region supported one of the densest nonagricultural populations known to anthropologists (Donald 1997; Suttles 1987). The material basis of these rich and sophisticated societies was the presence of abundant marine resources such as clams, oysters, halibut, seals, whales, and particularly salmon. Yet the Pacific Northwest was hardly a Garden of Eden, and cooperation—among individuals, within kinship groups, between villages and even across tribal boundaries—was essential if its inhabitants were to survive and prosper. Different food resources were abundant at particular times and in particular places, but taking advantage of these often narrow windows of opportunity required the skillful organization of labor and technology (Onats 1984; Suttles 1987; Richardson 1982; Suttles 1987; Boyd 1999; White 1999).

The physical environment of the region can be divided into three different resource zones: coastal; saltwater bays, estuaries, and river mouths; and the inland, upriver areas. Each was the source for different sorts of resources, but even within the same zone, availability varied with topography, the proximity of salt or fresh water, and the effects of different microclimates. And, of course, few food resources were available throughout the year. By far the most important food resources for the Coastal Salish tribe were seven species of Pacific salmon, which at particular points in the year may be caught in great abundance. The challenge facing aboriginal people, then, was to develop the capacity to harvest temporarily abundant food resources with a limited supply of resident labor, to insure themselves against the risks posed by occasional resource failures and to gain access to a wider variety of resources than what was

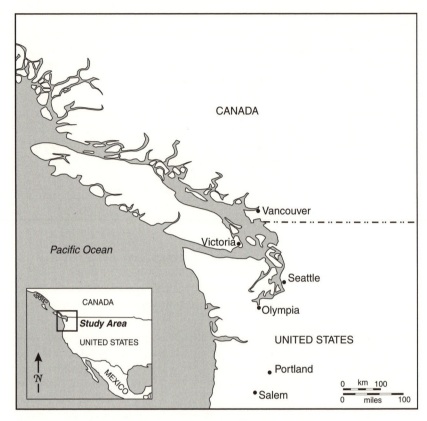

Figure 6.1. Location of the case area within North America.

available in their own, fairly small resource territories (Suttles 1987; Lane 1973; Ferguson 1983).

6.1.1. Social Organization and Marriage Institutions

During the winter, the Coastal Salish lived in permanent villages comprised of large, cedar-planked longhouses occupied by one or more extended families, while in the summer, families migrated to a series of temporary gathering sites. Extensive kinship networks conveyed secondary usufructuary rights to the territories of relatives (Suttles 1987; Onats 1984; Barsh 1982). Coastal Salish marriages created and maintained networks that made it possible for individual families to harvest food and other raw materials from various resource zones, while avoiding the high transaction costs that would have been associated with trade of finished goods, especially trade in the absence of centralized state authority.

It also minimized shirking problems since each family produced for its own use and family members could easily monitor each other. Not surprisingly, the parents of children from wealthy families sought marriage partners from distant resource zones or those whose resource territories complemented their own. Poorer families had to be content with mates from their own or nearby villages. Once established, the constellation of relationships created by marriage might continue even after the death of one of the partners, as in the apparently common situation of men marrying the sister of a deceased spouse. Kinship networks facilitated the movement of people to and from resource territories and by so doing, allowed families to insure themselves against the risk of resource failure and to ensure smooth seasonal fluctuations in food resources.

6.1.2. Property Rights

The Coastal Salish had a variety of well-maintained property rights expressing different degrees of exclusivity, and held by individuals, house groups, families linked by marriage, and members of villages. Individuals or groups could possess rights to particular tools and to spiritual or professional knowledge, such as the right to perform particular ceremonies or sing particular songs, and primary or secondary rights to particular natural resources such as rights to dig clams or gather berries at particular spots. Property rights among the Coastal Salish were largely context-dependent—they varied according to the type of available harvesting technology and how production was organized as well as to the type of resource present, the level of concentration or productivity of the resource, and the types of variability to which it was subject. This sophisticated, fine-grained understanding of property rights and division rules allowed for the creation of institutions in which incentives were closely aligned with the requirements of allocative efficiency.

Where resources were thinly distributed and thus relatively costly to defend, where there were few economies of scale in either labor or equipment, or where long-term sources of variability were not subject to control by the individuals utilizing the resource, the property institutions were those of either open access or, more commonly, communal property open to members of the group, who were bound to extend usufructuary rights to kin. The efficiency-enhancing dimensions of these arrangements are apparent once we consider that in all of these sorts of productive activities, variability in output was due either to natural forces (in which case, no particular set of institutional arrangement was any better than another) or the amount of effort or skill employed by the individual hunter-gatherer. And since individual families kept whatever they produced, incentives to shirk were attenuated.

Property rights were quite different where resources were highly concentrated or where there were potential efficiency gains from large-scale cooperation. For example, the construction of weirs—barriers made of sticks or logs that trapped salmon returning upstream to spawn—is a large-scale enterprise, requiring perhaps a month-long effort by one or more villages. Owners of the site functioned as entrepreneurs, directing the weir's construction. Once completed, the weir itself was considered to be the property of the whole village and any resident could fish from the narrow walkway running across it. But both the fishing site itself and the platforms extending from the basic structure and the smokehouses built along the bank in which to dry the fish were the property of individual families. Other types of fishing practiced by aboriginal groups involved complex share contracts in which owner-captains supplied the initial start-up costs for six or eight husband-and-wife teams, and all shared in the profits (Stern 1934).

6.1.3. Distributional Issues and the Creation of Efficient Institutions

Precontact tribal societies were able to create a highly efficient set of institutions that allowed people to solve a variety of collective-action problems associated with the organization of labor in joint production and efficient use of available natural resources. One reason for this is that these were close-knit communities, who were able to call upon the social resources afforded by multidimensional relations, shared beliefs and preferences, and stable membership to solve problems related to potential free-riding. The explanation for one surprising aspect of these institutions—the fact that people appear to have been willing to go along with rules that distributed rewards unequally—is, I argue, that such rules were embedded in broader social institutions that allowed all, or nearly all, to benefit when aggregate wealth increased. By solving distributional conflicts, precontact societies were able to utilize a larger set of potential institutions, some of which clearly enhanced efficiency, than do groups facing similar collective-action problems today.[2] I have not argued that such institutions were intended to maintain environmental sustainability—that they were responsible for the robust salmon populations that existed at the time of Western contact or that they reflected conservation concerns or a conservation ethic. Although I do not reject such arguments, they appear to me to be inconclusive. What *is* apparent is that the Coastal Salish were successful in resolving distributional conflicts and in solving various sorts of collective-action problems and that by so doing, they met at least one of the requirements for any durable solution to environmental problems.

6.2. THE SOCIAL AND BIOLOGICAL CHALLENGES OF MANAGING PACIFIC SALMON TODAY

Widespread non-Indian settlement of the area began in the nineteenth century, and the superior military forces at the disposal of the settlers easily overcame such resistance as was offered by the native inhabitants. During the 1850s, Coastal Salish bands were forced to sign treaties giving up their lands in exchange for certain guaranteed rights, including the right to fish. After members of these many small, kinship-based bands had been assembled somewhat haphazardly onto a few "tribal" reservations, they were more or less forgotten, along with their treaty rights. Initially, some Indians were able to compete successfully with non-Indian fishers as the fishery rapidly expanded to supply the canneries, but as the interception of one gear-type by another drove the fishery farther into the marine waters, lack of access to capital for larger boats and more efficient equipment sharply curtailed Native participation in what was an important sector of the regional economy for nearly a century.[3]

Throughout this period the state of Washington essentially refused to recognize Native fishing rights extending beyond what other state residents possessed. Nor would it allow tribal authorities to regulate their own fisheries. After many years of both overt and covert resistance, the tribes achieved a stunning legal victory in 1974, when a federal district court ruled that the treaties signed in the mid-1850s entitled tribes to one-half of all harvestable salmon bound for the waters where they had traditionally fished (*U.S. v. Washington* 1974). In addition, tribes were given the authority to regulate the activities of their own fishermen and to share equally in management responsibility for the entire fishery with state and federal authorities. The decision precipitated an enormous amount of conflict throughout the region and the legal decision was appealed all the way to the U.S. Supreme Court, where it was affirmed in 1979 (*State of Washington v. Washington State Commercial Passenger Fishing Vessel Association et al.*, 443 U.S. 658 1977; Cohen 1986). Eventually, state and tribal leaders were able to look beyond their tumultuous, conflict-ridden history and create a set of functional institutions that attempt to balance conservation requirements with the social, economic, and recreational needs of a large number of widely separated and heterogeneous groups of fishermen (Singleton 1998). Yet in the 1980s, as the Indian commercial salmon fishery expanded and competition among tribes increased, what remained were a set of potentially devastating intertribal conflicts over how tribes were to solve a variety of collective-action problems accompanying their reinstated property rights and newly acquired management responsibilities.

6.2.1. The Complexity of Salmon Ecology and Management Practices

The intrinsic complexity of managing Pacific salmon means that fisheries managers from widely separated areas must coordinate information-gathering and decision-making over an extended period of time, while balancing a variety of competing values. Nearly all of the myriad decisions that must be made in the course of the fishing season have allocational consequences and thus provide sites or forums for distributive conflict. The sheer difficulty of designing institutions that encourage cooperation in the pursuit of environmental sustainability among a large number of semi-autonomous actors in a highly competitive environment can best be illustrated through a brief overview of salmon ecology and management practices.

While once so plentiful that their spawning runs were reported to have choked the area's many rivers and tributaries, many stocks of Pacific salmon are today in serious decline (National Research Council 1996). Salmon are an anadromous fish—hatched in small, freshwater streams, they migrate to the ocean and spend several years feeding before returning to natal streams to spawn. During their return migration they swim thousands of miles and cross both national and state boundaries, encountering a succession of fishermen and other predators, habitat alternations, dams and other obstacles. Seven species of salmon return to the rivers and tributaries of Puget Sound and the Washington coast: *Oncorhynchus tshawytscha* (chinook or king); *Oncorhynchus nerka* (sockeye or red); *Oncorhynchus gorbuscha* (pink, which only appear in alternate years); *Oncorhynchus kisutch* (coho or silver); *Oncorhynchus keta* (chum or dog); *Oncorhynchus Salmo* (steelhead or anadromous rainbow trout); and *Oncorhynchus clarki* (sea-run cutthroat trout). Within each species are a number of stocks—genetically distinct populations that return to a particular river or tributary. For management purposes, these small stocks are lumped together by river system or in some cases by combining several small rivers or tributaries in a region. Escapement goals (the quantity of fish that must be allowed to pass through to spawning areas in order to perpetuate the stock) are established for each group of closely related natural stocks and set the parameters for harvest decisions. Taken together, all stocks of a particular species comprise a run.

Different runs pass through different areas in successive but overlapping waves. Chinook begin entering Puget Sound in early spring, followed by sockeye and pinks in the summer months, and coho and chum in the autumn and early winter. The fishing season is divided into management periods, which correspond to the intervals during which the majority of a run is expected to pass through a given area. Time and gear requirements are keyed to the escapement goals of particular stocks present and change throughout the season, according to which runs are present in a particular area at a particular time. For all species, fisheries managers attempt to spread the catch throughout the run, in order to avoid altering the genetic pool by artificially selecting the early or late segment of the run (Clark 1985).

Preliminary run estimates are used to divide the harvestable fish equally between the Indian and non-Indian fishermen and to create an annual management plan that will allow both sides to take their share at pre-ferred times and places. Once the fishing season actually begins, the esti-mates are updated with information generated through test fisheries and by way of the tickets detailing catch information that fish buyers must submit daily. By comparing these estimated catch figures with the prior predictions of run sizes, managers can determine whether their earlier predictions were accurate. Many tribal fisheries are locally bounded, and the court has ruled that ensuring that each tribe has the opportunity to exercise its treaty rights requires that tribal/nontribal shares be calculated on a species-by-species, region-by-region basis. There is no such ruling with respect to sharing between tribes. The tribes and the state use the same models and accounting system to see whether escapement goals are going to be met and to keep track of how many fish have been caught and by whom, in order to calculate each side's remaining allocational share. Toward the end of the season, catch data are generated daily, as each side tries to catch its remaining share without fishing into the escapement.

All areas are closed to fishing unless specifically opened by either the state (for the non-Indian fishermen) or the tribes (for the Indian fisher-men). While jointly authored, annual management plans set the manage-ment periods for the different stocks and specify the overall catch figures for each run, the actual fishing times and gear requirements are set for the non-Indian fishermen by the state and for the Indian fishermen by the reg-ulatory agencies of each tribe. The state and the tribes (collectively or indi-vidually) may challenge each other's regulations on the basis of conserva-tion (if one party believes that further fishing will compromise escapement goals) or allocation (if one side suspects the other side has already taken its allocational share). Where the tribes share fishing areas (and this is the rule, rather than the exception), each tribe has the authority to draft regulations for its own members, although the tribes make an effort to coordinate their regulations in shared areas. All regulations are updated weekly, guided by current run-size estimates and by how much of the two sides' allocational shares remain. Thus, in any one of thirty-four designated fishing areas, there could conceivably be fishermen from as many as eight different tribes, plus the nontreaty fleet, all fishing under separate regulations that change every week.

A number of biological factors complicate the management process. First, runs overlap, which results in conflicts between the requirements of stocks of various species. The preservation of natural runs and the diverse genetic material they embody is a high priority for fisheries managers, so when the run of a weak, natural stock overlaps with a strong stock from another species, this creates difficulties. To fully protect the weak run, fisheries managers would have to delay an opening on the stronger stocks because it is impossible to catch one without catching the other. Delaying the opening means that fishermen will be prevented from catching otherwise harvestable fish, an outcome that fisheries managers are understandably reluctant to produce, particularly on many tribal reservations, where alternative employment opportunities are limited and the human dimensions to management decisions are immediate and transparent. The same overlap problem is created when hatchery and wild stock are present simultaneously, since hatchery stocks can be fished much more intensively than wild stocks. Similarly, when stocks are mixed in the marine areas, the decision to protect a wild, weak stock may result in drastic curtailment in opportunities to catch healthy stocks in the ocean fisheries.

Finally, fisheries management is an imprecise science, and that imprecision creates space for competing interpretations of the same set of facts. Different fisheries models or different interpretations of the same model have consequences for the timing and duration of the fisheries of different groups. If fish run-size projections are interpreted conservatively, strict limits will be imposed on the early fisheries. If these estimates later turn out to be overly pessimistic, fisheries that take place later in the season will be allowed more fishing opportunities. The converse is, of course, also true. If forecasting models are interpreted in such a way as to allow longer openings in the early part of the season, those fishing later could have their fishing ended prematurely. Since different tribal and nontribal user groups fish in spatially fixed locations, all of these decisions have clear distributional consequences and occasion much strategic posturing in both the state/tribal and intertribal annual management negotiations. Such conflicts continue through the fishing season. While the state/tribal conflicts that all but paralyzed the system in its early years have more or less been solved—or at least shelved—intertribal disputes have now taken precedence. Flurries of last-minute crisis negotiation, litigation between tribes, and emergency court orders are a regular part of each season's management of fisheries. Directly or indirectly, such conflicts are about distributive issues.

6.2.2. The Problem of Intertribal Allocation

The underlying logic of the problem facing the tribes is simple, although the details of particular conflicts are often exceedingly complex. Tribes

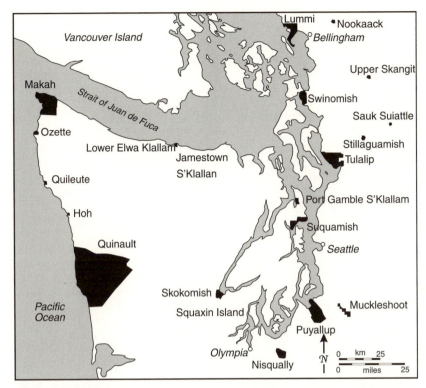

Figure 6.2. Locations of tribes in Puget Sound. Salmon enter the system where the Strait of Juan de Fuca joins the Pacific Ocean and first head east and then north, to rivers and streams in Canada and Northwest Washington, or east and then south, to spawning grounds in the mid- and south-Puget Sound. Some salmon also migrate in through Johnstone Strait, which is in Canadian waters to the north of the area depicted in the map. (Map by Blake Feist.)

must compete among themselves for portions of what is an increasingly scarce resource. Under the terms of the legal decision, each tribe is limited to fishing in its "usual and accustomed places" (UAPs), which correspond to the areas where their ancestors fished. In many areas, tribal UAPs overlap, which encourages overcapitalization and destructive competition and further complicates the challenge of maintaining weak stocks while targeting stronger ones. And while some tribes have extensive UAPs that include the marine waters through which all stocks pass on their way to natal spawning streams, others are limited to fairly small areas, usually in the immediate vicinity of their reservations (see figure 6.2). In the precontact era, tribes fished almost exclusively in the rivers and streams close to their own territories. Today, large, highly efficient boats have made it possible for the fishermen of some tribes to intercept stocks headed for the UAPs of other tribes, in a pattern strongly reminiscent of the displacement of native fishermen by nonnative immigrants at the turn of the century. Although the court established *where* different tribes could fish, it did not determine *how much* each tribe could catch or enforce claims made by some tribes to particular salmon stocks originating in rivers and tributaries on their reservations. For several of the tribes in the southern region, who were particularly active in the long battle to regain fishing rights and who are now near the end of a gauntlet of fisheries, the resulting allocational patterns have been perceived as especially unfair. As is evident in table 6.1, while all tribes in the case area have relatively low median incomes, gross per capita incomes from fishing differ markedly from tribe to tribe. The general pattern, from highest incomes to lowest, more or less follows the migratory path of the fish as they enter the Strait of Juan de Fuca from the ocean and attempt to make their way to spawning grounds in North or South Puget Sound.

Intertribal conflict over allocational shares is time-consuming, inefficient, and destructive to both resource stocks and intertribal relationships. The fact that different groups of tribes fish in succession means that fishermen are encouraged to fish as hard as they can before fish pass out of their areas, which frustrates management goals of spreading the catch throughout the duration of the run. Large, overcapitalized fleets make it that much more difficult to predict the impact on stocks of particular time, place, and gear regulations. In areas where such uncertainties have been reduced, tribes have had greater success in overcoming such problems. For example, in one area that four tribes share exclusively, they have been able to reach an agreement banning purse-seiners, the largest, least cost-effective boats.[4] In areas shared with other tribes, they have been unable to do so, because this would put them at risk of losing the majority of the catch to tribes without such restrictions. Regulations governing internal tribal allocation are similarly imperiled. If a tribe were to impose limits on new entrants, it would increase efficiency, but at the cost of losing a share of fish to other tribes without such regulations. So far, the only tribe in Washington State that has such limits is on the Pacific Coast, where fish are more dispersed and the regulatory and distributive issues quite different.

Intertribal conflicts also have the potential to spill over into a variety of areas of *shared* interests. These include the need to adopt a unified bargaining position in the face of external challenges and the need to maintain intertribal organizations to take advantage of economies of scale in scientific and technical expertise. And until recently, when fish hatcheries fell into disfavor among fisheries biologists, it was assumed that all tribes shared an interest in encouraging each other to maintain hatcheries, since

TABLE 6.1
Characteristics of Tribes with Fishing Rights in Western Washington (excludes tribes who fish only in Pacific Ocean and coastal streams)

Tribe	Number of Members in WA State (1989)[a]	Median Income per Household (1989)[a]	Fishing Areas (UAPs)	Percentage of Tribal Share; All Species and Stocks (lb.)(1982–88)	Gross Mean Income per Active Fishermen 1982–88[d]
Makah	1,418	$17,037	Mixed stock marine	7.3	>$60,000
Lower Elwha Kallam	213	$24,583[b]	Mixed stock marine and in-shore or terminal area marine	2.3	$20,000–$30,000
Port Gamble S'Klallam	394	See above	Mixed stock marine and in-shore marine	4.1	$30,000–$40,000
Jamestown S'Klallam	91	See above	Mixed stock marine and in-shore marine	1.3	$30,000–$52,000
Skokomish	671	$15,982	In-shore marine and river	8.7	$10,000–$25,000
Lummi	2,713	$21,326	Mixed stock marine, in-shore marine, and river	28.8	$14,000–$18,000
Nooksack	766	$12,768	In-shore marine and river	3.3	$8,000–$16,000
Swinomish	622	$16,563	Mixed stock marine, in-shore marine, and river	8.6	$10,000–$22,000
Upper Skagit	309	Not reported[c]	River only	1.5	$2,000–$5,000
Sauk-Suiattle	135	Not reported	River only	<1	$3,000–$10,000
Tulalip	1,899	$24,261	Mixed stock marine, in-shore marine, and river	12	$14,000–$36,000
Stillaguamish	127	Not reported	River only	<1	$1,000–$10,000

TABLE 6.1 *(continued)*

Tribe	Number of Members in WA State (1989)[a]	Median Income per Household (1989)[a]	Fishing Areas (UAPs)	Percentage of Tribal Share; All Species and Stocks (lb.)(1982–88)	Gross Mean Income per Active Fishermen 1982–88[d]
Suquamish	548	$18,977	Mixed stock marine, in-shore marine, and river	4	$10,000–$26,000
Muckleshoot	969	$15,172	In-shore marine	4.9	$2,000–$22,000
Puyallup	865	$24,615	Mainly river	3.5	$1,000–$10,000
Nisqually	379	Not reported	River and in-shore only	3.3	$9,000–$15,000
Squaxin Island	409	$28,616	River and in-shore only	6	$1,000–$20,000

[a]*Source* of figures is 1990 U.S. Census.
[b]U.S. Census figures combine all three S'Klallam Tribes in reporting figures.
[c]The 1990 U.S. Census did not report this information for tribes of fewer than 400 persons.
[d]Nearly all tribal fisheries declined during this period, thus higher figures represent earlier years.

once hatchery fish are released into the wild, they increase the number of available fish to all. In addition, there is the need for an orderly, predictable, and jointly coordinated fishing season, without which the fishing season is disrupted with last-minute court challenges and crisis negotiation. The fact that each of the seventeen tribes is a semi-sovereign political body and thus has the legal authority to open and close fisheries or promulgate gear restrictions independently introduces the nightmarish possibility of fishermen from perhaps eight different tribes fishing in the same area under different regulations regarding gear, fishing times, and so on, along with a very large nontreaty fleet, fishing under much more restrictive regulations set by the Washington State Department of Fish and Wildlife. The possibilities for conflict are nearly limitless. This is not a scenario any of the managers would like to see played out on the fishing grounds.

Tribes have been aware from the outset of the desirability of agreeing on a set of institutions or intertribal allocation principles that would allow them to overcome such problems. Discussions have proceeded along two basic tracks. The first concerned general, overarching principles that could be used as the basis for solving particular conflicts. Both the principles themselves and the discussions surrounding them illustrate a range of perspectives on equity, efficiency, and the cultural dimensions of fishing. Yet despite many years of informal negotiation, which culminated in an eighteen-month formal mediation process during 1987–9, the tribes have been unable to agree on any of these, for reasons that are discussed in the following section. The second track along which this institution-building process has proceeded reflects the far more mundane, incremental process through which tribes have found partial solutions to the day-to-day problems they encountered in attempting to coordinate their fishing efforts and their collective-bargaining efforts in negotiations with the state. Out of this incremental process grew a messy patchwork of formal and informal, written and unwritten understandings that eventually became the allocational framework that structures the tribes' annual fishing agreements.

I discuss both the meta-principles and the institutions that were finally adopted in some detail below. While there is little that is unique about them or about the eventual outcome to the tribes' negotiations, they highlight with unusual clarity the complicated process by which groups summon both equity and efficiency in wrestling with a difficult, but by no means uncommon, set of problems.

6.3. Intertribal Allocation Principles: What They Discussed

During the protracted discussions between tribes over meta-principles for intertribal allocation, different tribes have argued for radically different criteria that could act as general, underlying principles guiding the resolution of particular disputes. Some of the proposed principles reflect one or another conception of equity, while others seem to favor efficiency. Agreement on *any* of the principles would of course increase predictability and reduce litigation and related transactions costs. Principles 1–7 in the following list have been proposed by one or more tribes (*U.S. v. Washington* 1991). No tribe has suggested principles 8 or 9, even though these are the two principles used most often in fisheries around the world or most often proposed by fisheries economists. Their omission from tribal discussions is not due to ignorance, but rather to widely shared beliefs that such principles are either politically untenable, or undesirable for other reasons.

6.3.1. *Principles Considered by the Tribes*

1. *Shares proportionate to a tribes's size.* This is a strongly redistributive principle that is proposed or supported by some of the larger tribes. Unless it were implemented as a one-time-only allocation, it would encourage growth in tribal membership either through higher birthrates or changes in rules governing tribal enrollment. It does not reward skill, effort, conservation, or investment in habitat restoration or hatcheries.

2. *Shares proportionate to the number of fishermen per tribe.* This a slightly less redistributive principle, as *ceteris paribus* there will be more fishermen among the tribes with better fishing opportunities (e.g., the intercepting tribes) than among those without. Since what was proposed was a one-time allocation, after which time tribal shares would have been set, adopting such a principle would not encourage overcapitalization or new entrants. The fact that many individuals fish part-time or largely for subsistence purposes would have made the definition of who was or was not a fisherman controversial. Tribes with large fleets supported this principle; others did not.

3. *Shares based on recent historical catch and/or dependency on fishery.* This principle could be defended under some versions of equity, although some might object that current investments are at least partly a reflection of previous (perhaps inequitable) allocations. And while this principle avoids the definitional problems of principle 2, it provides even more encouragement for overcapitalization and thus undermines efficiency. The Lummi Tribe, which caught the largest proportion of the tribal share during this period, was a strong proponent of this principle.

4. *One tribe/one share within each region where a tribe has UAPs.* This principle discourages overcapitalization and overcrowding because shares would not be sensitive to increases in the size of the tribe or the size of the fishing fleet. It would give tribes a better opportunity to adopt internal conservation regulations. On the other hand, it violates at least some conceptions of equity, particularly since there are very large differences in size between tribes, both in terms of total membership and in terms of fishing fleet. Implementing such a principle would require considerable disruption to current distribution patterns. Not surprisingly, small tribes favor this principle, while larger tribes, or those with historically larger shares, are opposed to it.

5. *Shares based on investment in hatcheries or protection of fish habitat.* Tying allocational shares to investments in hatcheries or habitat protection is an efficiency-enhancing principle because it enlarges the resource base, but only up to the point where investment ceases to be productive. With respect to hatcheries, there is considerable debate among fisheries experts currently as to where that point is, and whether hatcheries produce net

benefits at all, as opposed to merely displacing wild stocks. Nonetheless, at the time it was being proposed, this principle was seen as efficiency-enhancing in that it increased the amount of fish available to all tribes.

6. *Shares proportionate to efforts/investments by each tribe in pursuing litigation and other means to increase the overall tribal share.* Partly in response to principle 5, several tribes proposed including resources expended in pursuing political and legal channels to increase the collective tribal share as "productive investment."[5] Obviously there are definitional problems in terms of what would or would not count under this category.

7. *Shares proportionate to the relative quantities of fish taken at treaty time.* This principle resonates with strongly felt convictions among tribal members as to the importance of culture and tradition, which are particularly prominent in fishing issues because of the close connection between fishing rights and treaties signed in the 1850s. It would be difficult to establish what the distributional pattern was at the time treaties were signed unless fishing was sharply limited in the marine waters and fish were caught closer to their places of origin. To do so would allocate more fish to the South Sound tribes but might also decrease the commercial value of the fish, which is higher earlier in the season. It would also sharply limit mixed-stock fisheries, which are among the most lucrative for the North Sound tribes. Tribes with a large stake in the current distributional pattern obviously opposed this principle. Some tribes have argued that principle 1—shares proportionate to the size of tribes—would be a reasonable approximation of the sharing arrangements that existed at the time the treaties were signed.

6.3.2. Omitted Principles

8. *Individual Transferable Quotas (ITQs).* Under this method, quotas based on predicted run sizes would be established, distributed according to a previously agreed-upon criterion such as catch in previous years, and thereafter exchanged through a market. (In the case of tribal fishing rights, there could well be legal restrictions to prevent those rights from being transferred to individuals outside of the tribe.) The standard assumption is that ITQs will gravitate to the most efficient fishermen. No tribe has endorsed this principle for salmon fishing and several have specifically rejected it.

9. *Open Competition.* Tribes are currently limited to fishing within their respective UAPs, but nothing prevents them from issuing mutual invitations and thereby allowing open competition between fishermen from all tribes throughout the case area. This is how the nontreaty fishery and many other fisheries around the world are organized. Doing so would encourage overcapitalization and a variety of other "commons"

problems. With the partial exception of the four coastal tribes, who fish under quite different environmental conditions, no tribe has endorsed this method.

Tribes have adopted different positions during negotiations and articulated different arguments in support or opposition to one or another of these principles. The most obvious sources of division are a tribe's spatial location and adjudicated fishing rights and how these affect a tribe's ability to intercept fish along the migratory path. The four South Sound tribes (Muckleshoot, Nisqually, Puyallup, and Squaxin Island) who brought the matter to court in 1986 demanded that 90 percent of South Sound–origin fish be allowed to return to their areas.[6] They have made a number of arguments in support of this claim. With respect to equity, they contend that each tribe is entitled to a "fair share" of the fish returning to their usual and accustomed fishing areas, which is defined as the amount necessary to assure them a "moderate income" or reasonable livelihood from the fishery.[7] In addition, they argue that as the original litigants in *U.S. v. Washington* and as leaders of the long campaign of popular protest and civil disobedience that preceded that decision, equity requires that they receive a "fair" share of current benefits. They further contend that the considerable investments that South Sound tribes have made in habitat rehabilitation and fish hatcheries have gone unrewarded, and in fact, their catches have declined steadily in the years since the legal ruling in 1974 (*U.S. v. Washington* 1986).[8] And finally, all the South Sound tribes argue that their asymmetric bargaining position relative to the North Sound tribes—North Sound tribes can catch both "their own" fish plus intercept those headed for South Sound, while the South Sound tribes are entirely dependent on South Sound stocks and have no means to issue credible threats to North Sound tribes—requires that they seek redress from the court, rather than settling the issue amongst themselves. Thus, the South Sound tribes, by asking the court to settle not just the sort of in-season disputes that it had up until this time adjudicated, but to establish overall sharing principles, sought to alter both the decision rules and the forum within which intertribal allocational issues would be decided. Political actors frequently attempt to alter the scope of conflict as a way of changing the outcome, so neither the initial claim nor the reaction to it by other tribes should be particularly surprising.

The response of the Makah tribe, which is first on the interception path and whose fleet was at the time expanding, was to attempt to deny such a move by claiming that tribal sovereignty precluded the court's jurisdiction. While that claim failed, throughout the entire period under discussion, the Makah tribe consistently sought to absent themselves from both formal and informal negotiations. Given their spatial location, it is not surprising that they would resist any change in the status quo. For the Makah tribe, intertribal allocation issues were simply much less of a problem, at least not in terms of their economic interests. The fact that they are geographically isolated and historically have had only limited ties to the other tribes—the members of the Makah tribe are descended not from the Coastal Salish, but from Nootkan language-speaking bands—may have contributed to the difficulty other tribes have had in eliciting their cooperation.

The Lummi tribe was one of the few tribes that had been able to maintain a commercial fishery prior to the 1974 legal decision. Its fishermen were thus ideally positioned to take advantage of the new fishing opportunities presented by the legal decision in 1974 and the federal loans available to tribal fishermen in the years right after the decision. They also have extensive UAPs in both North and mid- Puget Sound. They have by far the largest fleet—dwarfing any other tribe by at least a factor of three and in the case of some tribes, many times that—and throughout the 1980s, harvested the largest share of the overall treaty share. Thus, the Lummi could credibly claim that any fundamental alteration of the status quo arrangements would come at a very high cost to their members, nearly all of whom were directly or indirectly dependent on the fishery. Given the investments their fishers had made in boats, equipment, and the development of fishing skills, both before and after the legal decision in 1974, the Lummi tribe argued that a fundamental reallocation by the court would violate basic principles of equity. This claim was strengthened by the fact that, as is evident from table 6.1, the per capita share for Lummi fishermen is in the middle to low range for all tribes, and thus they could scarcely be seen as reaping large profits at the expense of other tribes.

While never specifically denying the legitimacy of the court's role in adjudicating intertribal allocation conflicts, the Lummi tribe's initial response to the South Sound tribes' demands was to seek to expand the scope of issues and the number of parties. In so doing, they sought to *redefine* the issue from that of a zero-sum conflict between tribes, to one between Indians and non-Indians in which the objective was, or should be, an expansion of the supply of the fisheries resource available to all the case-area tribes. Among the issues the Lummi tribe sought to include were: spousal fishing—whether nonmember spouses could participate in tribal fisheries; the definition of tribal membership—whether all tribes should be required to maintain a consistent requirement as to tribal blood quantum level; and whether tribal members should be allowed to lease boats from non-Indians for some share of the catch, in effect transferring some of the financial benefits of the fishery to non-Indians. They also sought to expand the number of parties to the dispute to include the state of Washington and the state of Alaska, which intercepts fish headed for Puget Sound, as well as the Coastal tribes from Washington, Canadian fishermen, and several other groups indirectly involved with tribal fishing. Other tribes argued that it was not necessary to reach agreement on these issues in order to proceed on the more immediate questions of intertribal allocation, and it was the latter view that prevailed in court. Then, at a much later point in the negotiations, when the Lummi Tribe's favored principle—historical catch and historical dependency on fishery—failed to gain the assent of the other tribes, the Lummis argued for what came to be known as the "doomsday rule" or the "nuclear option." Under this rule, no tribes would fish until all issues were agreed upon. Clearly, the Lummi tribe was seeking to bring pressure on the Makah tribe and the three S'Klallam tribes, all of whom fish before the Lummis and several of whose fleets were expanding at this time.

The Jamestown S'Klallam, the Port Gamble S'Klallam, and the Lower Elwha S'Klallam are all fairly small tribes and are relative newcomers to the fishery. The Jamestown S'Klallam tribe was not federally recognized until 1981 and thus did not have fishing rights until that time. Nonetheless, the favorable location of all these tribes along the Strait had given them significant potential to expand their fisheries and this prospect alarmed other tribes. In opposing principles based on historical catch or fleet size, these tribes brought a quite different set of arguments to bear on the question of equity. All three S'Klallam tribes and the Skokomish tribe argued that the "historical injustices" (e.g., obstacles created by the state and federal governments) that had prevented them from developing their fisheries earlier should not now be used as a basis to deny them their "rightful fishing heritage" (*U.S. v. Washington* 1989). Instead, they argued for the establishment of equal shares for tribes sharing UAPs in each region and for fleet size limitations on all tribes *except* small tribes such as themselves, who need "the time and opportunity to establish their rightful share in tribal fisheries" (*U.S. v. Washington* 1989).

The Nooksack tribe also invoked history, culture, and equity in arguing against principles that would preserve status quo arrangements. Given that the Nooksack fishermen fish upriver from the very large Lummi tribal fleet, it is not surprising that this tribe would be sympathetic to those who sought a guaranteed return of 90 percent of each run to its river of origin. In addition, however, the Nooksack tribe claimed that the basis of the treaty rights of tribes (and the principle on which intertribal allocation should rest) should follow from "the accurate determination and faithful reconstruction, within the contemporary reality, of the pre-treaty relationship between the Indians and the fisheries which sustained their culture and economy" (*U.S. v. Washington*

1989). The Nooksack tribe thus sought a more expansive framing of the question of equity, which would include the *process* or historical sequence of events leading up to current distributional patterns. The Nooksack tribe argued that the present configuration of tribes, and even the notion of *tribe* itself, has its origins in the native pacification and containment strategy undertaken by the Washington territorial government at the time the treaties were signed. Thus, it has no particular claim to legitimacy as the basis for allocating a scarce resource. And since, at the time the treaties were written, all individuals had access to enough salmon to more than meet their needs, the substantive principle that would best replicate the relationship between individuals of Coastal Salish descent would be "equal access among tribes possessing [equal rights], with specific allocation to be made on the basis of tribal enrollment" (*U.S. v. Washington* 1989).

Despite the wide range of claims made for or against various principles, there were some points on which all or nearly all tribes could agree. At the minimum, all tribes express support for the idea that no tribe could be entirely denied a fishery. Nearly all tribes agree that tribes have a special claim to fish whose places of origin are within their UAPs and home areas.[9] Endorsing such a principle requires a difficult balancing act for many tribes, however, since nearly all of the tribes that have "their" fish intercepted by other tribes also intercept fish headed for others. In addition, all the tribes are internally heterogeneous, with both small and large boat fishermen. To the extent that they want to protect the opportunities for their own small-boat fishermen, they must argue for principles that reserve a high percentage of a particular stock to the tribes whose UAPs include its river of origin. Yet, in order to maximize their tribe's share, and at the same time offer greater opportunities to fishermen with larger boats (and consequently larger operating expenses), they need to assert that mixed stock or marine fisheries are equally valid expressions of treaty rights. And finally, all tribes agree on the desirability of having "home waters" where their own members fish exclusively.

6.4. Why the Search for General Principles Failed and What the Tribes Created Instead

The end result of more than a dozen years of formal and informal negotiations is that no general principle for intertribal allocation has been discovered that is acceptable to all tribes. This is true despite the fact that it would appear that several of these principles could result in greater allocative efficiency, that is, that the adoption of one or another of these principles would result in a larger total output from a given set of inputs. For example, permanently fixing each tribe's allocation share according to *any* of the preceding principles (preferably on the basis of a principle that encouraged efficiency) would allow tribes greater security and thus create greater opportunities for regulations that would reward conservation and discourage overcapitalization. Nonetheless, all of these principles have been rejected by the tribes for the simple reason that none can be established without potentially making at least one tribe worse off, that is, none can be reached through a succession of *pareto superior* moves. Although one or more of these principles could satisfy a *pareto optimality* standard in which winners could compensate losers and still be better off, without a set of broader institutions in place that would assure losers that they would, in fact, be compensated, such arrangements are ruled out.[10] This situation is not unusual, but in fact is replicated all over the world when broader social and political institutions fail to redress the inequalities that may result from shifts to more *efficient* arrangements or those that are more *environmentally sustainable* (Johnson and Libecap 1982; Acheson 1988). And although the specific questions facing tribes today are very different from those their ancestors faced, it is hard to escape the conclusion that the range of institutions to which they may look for solutions is narrower today because such institutions are no longer embedded in a broader framework of redistributive institutions.

Yet, despite their inability to resolve allocational issues at the level of overarching principles, the tribes have been able to proceed some distance toward solving intertribal conflicts. They have also been able to cooperate in areas where they share interests such as creating and maintaining a highly effective intertribal fisheries organization and in orchestrating their participation in annual negotiations with state and international regulatory agencies so as to achieve common objectives. In fact, one of the most striking aspects of the intertribal allocational conflicts of the 1980s is the degree to which tribes were able to divorce themselves from these conflicts when faced with an external threat.[11]

The framework agreement that emerged from the eighteen-month mediation process in 1987–9 was an extension and codification of the network of formal and informal, written and unwritten agreements between different subsets of tribes and governing different stocks and different species. It essentially preserves historical catch patterns between tribes. Thus, of the seven principles the tribes considered, the agreement comes closest to principle 3—shares based on historical catch and historical dependency of tribal members on fishery—but with some modifications to assure South Sound tribes of a slightly larger share than they had been receiving. Although tribes agreed to most of its provisions, there were enough unresolved issues to prevent formal acceptance of the plan.

Nonetheless, perhaps 80 percent of the agreement is replicated during negotiations over annual fishing plans, and thus at least partially achieves one of the initial goals—to bring about greater stability and predictability in tribal fisheries and reduce the need for costly, in-season litigation.

Two types of institutions govern allocation. The first involves a more refined definition of *property rights* than the UAPs created by the court. Among these are *primary or exclusive rights,* which allow tribes to exercise exclusive regulatory and fishing rights in areas recognized as their "home waters," for example, a bay or river mouth on a tribe's reservation. Tribes have at least some incentives to limit overcapitalization within their own fleets in these areas and they have greater freedom to create opportunities for their own small-boat fishermen. All tribes embraced the "home waters" concept very soon after the initial legal decision and the only remaining sources of disagreement stem from occasional boundary disputes. Primary exclusive rights govern only a small area of the case area, however. Tribes may also have *secondary rights* to a somewhat larger area in which they must allow other tribes to fish, but where they may set fishery regulations. This reduces destructive conflict among tribes and eliminates the possibility that different tribes sharing UAPs will establish inconsistent or incompatible regulations over the same fishing grounds. Where a number of tribes share UAPs, regulations are arrived at through negotiations between all tribes sharing *in-common rights.*

Another category of institutions is bilateral and multilateral *allocation share agreements* over different species and different stocks. These generally contain the following three-tiered sharing formula, which is triggered by different levels of abundance in different years, as established through run-size predictions made at the beginning of the season.

Level I. At the level of lowest abundance, 85 percent of a shared fish stock is allocated to the tribe or tribes whose reservations or UAPs encompass the stock's place of origin, and intercepting tribes are capped at 15 percent. This is a "basic-needs" principle. While less than what the South Sound tribes originally demanded, it is a slight improvement upon what they had been receiving.

Level II. At the next level of abundance, additional fish (above and beyond those that would have been allocated under the *Level I* allocation) are shared equally between intercepting and terminal area tribes. Although the claim has been made that increasing the share of the earlier, intercepting fishers increases efficiency, the most compelling explanation is that the intercepting tribes would not have accepted any less, given what they were already catching at the time of the negotiations and what they might have hoped to continue to catch without a formal agreement.

Level III.   At the highest level of abundance, the additional fish are harvested according to the *Level I* sharing formula—85 percent to the tribes at or near streams of origin; 15 percent to the intercepting tribes. The intention is to provide rewards to tribes who have invested in hatchery production or habitat restoration and to encourage future efforts to expand the supply of fish available to all fishers.

6.5. CONCLUSIONS

Shared history, a sense of solidarity, and the prospect of ongoing interactions have allowed tribes to control or eliminate the worst problems resulting from conflicts over intertribal allocation. Many of the institutions with which the Coastal Salish tribes manage their fisheries at the beginning of the twenty-first century offer greater potential for overcoming collective-action problems associated with large-scale CPR management than those of their counterparts in the nontribal fisheries, who face their own set of distributional and overcapitalization problems and whose institutional choices are much narrower. Nontribal fishermen also have even fewer incentives to conserve fish stocks or to invest in habitat rehabilitation than do tribal members, given that they have even less control over competing users. Yet the remaining unsolved allocational problems in fisheries clearly make it more difficult for tribes to adopt tough conservation measures. For example, managers are quite conscious of the fact that limiting entry or imposing additional harvest restrictions to fisheries in any of the shared areas would be irrational (as well as untenable politically) since it would allow other tribes to absorb the surplus. In the (few) situations where entry limitations are in place, they are in areas where a tribe has exclusive rights or is at the very end of fisheries. In the absence of broader institutions that would allow for side payments or other means of redressing the distributive effects of change, incentives to overcapitalization and overexploitation of fisheries continue to exist. This is despite the fact that even ten years ago, at least one tribal fisheries manager was willing to admit privately that environmental conditions warranted shutting down all salmon fisheries. Since that time, many wild stocks have continued to weaken to the extent that two species within the Puget Sound region are currently listed as "threatened" with extinction under the federal Endangered Species Act.[12] For tribes perhaps most of all, the permanent loss of the genetic diversity of wild fish upon which all the stocks ultimately depend would truly be a tragedy.

Managing large-scale, complex CPRs is, at best, a matter of choosing between imperfect alternatives. The potential to create and maintain institutions for the sustainable use of any environmental resource system, but particularly that of a large-scale CPR, is inevitably conditioned, constrained, and at times, even precluded by the failure to solve distributional conflicts. While states can impose such institutions and (perhaps) keep them in place through coercive hierarchies, such efforts have often proved to be unworkable because of prohibitively high transaction costs.[13] Yet the range of institutions that groups can draw upon to solve environmental collective-action problems themselves is today significantly narrowed by the lack of broadly inclusive social and economic institutions or social networks—what some have termed either social capital or simply *community* (Bowles 1999; Putnam 2000; Taylor 1982). Many recent policy initiatives in both industrialized and industrializing countries try to replicate the beneficial effects of such social structures, but the potential of such efforts is sharply limited by failures to resolve (or even sometimes to acknowledge) distributional conflicts and the effects of inequality.

NOTES

1. A strategy for action based on *conditional cooperation* would be one in which a party makes contributions to a public good contingent on the others making similar contributions. Without some sort of formal or informal institutions with which to verify performance or make credible commitments, contributions stemming from this type of motivation are unlikely.

2. The two groups obviously face different sorts of issues in resource management. I would argue, however, that the basic structure of problems, especially with respect to distributional implications, is similar.

3. Even in 1988, by which time the fishery had significantly declined, sport and commercial salmon fishing generated more than $1.25 billion for the regional economy (including northern California, Oregon, and Washington) (Dandeisk and Buck 1999).

4. Although purse-seine boats are more expensive to operate and represent large, financially risky investments for tribal fishermen, they outcompete other gear-types due to their size.

5. "Productive" investment is obviously a subjective term since at any given point, the amount of harvestable fish is fixed—what goes to the tribal share must come out of either the Canadian share or the nontreaty domestic share. But for the collectivity defined as these twenty tribes, investments in litigation or lobbying clearly do have the potential of increasing the overall amount of harvestable fish.

6. Since the South Sound tribes are only demanding a larger share of stocks that home to their regions, even if they were to received everything they asked for, tribal shares in the overall numbers of fish taken would not be equalized.

7. This is the same principle that the courts have used regarding the rights of tribes relative to the State (*U.S v. Washington* 1974).

8. The Nisqually Tribe further argues that it has a right to catch its share of Nisqually River stocks at the times and places it chooses—such as in the river, with small boats, in a manner that comes closer to the traditional fisheries than many other tribes. Realizing that goal would, of course, require that interceptions be sharply curtailed.

9. The Makah, who have no significant salmon streams and fish almost entirely on stocks heading to other regions, are an exception.

10. There are clearly other reasons why tribes would reject an agreement that limited their rights to fish that are unrelated to instrumental rationality.

11. Whether this is due to instrumental rationality or a predisposition to cooperate with members of one's symbolically marked group is difficult to determine.

12. Many factors contribute to salmon decline in addition to overfishing. They include habitat loss, hydroelectric dams that block passage to salmon, and hatchery production through the displacement of wild stocks by hatchery stocks (NRC 1996).

13. Even without such costs, the problem remains of how or why state managers would necessarily be sufficiently motivated to create optimal management institutions.

REFERENCES

Acheson, James. 1988. *Lobster Gangs of Maine*. Hanover, N.H.: University Press of New England.

Baland, Jean-Marie, and Jean-Philippe Plateau. 1999. "The ambiguous impact of inequality on local resource management." *World Development* 27(5): 773–88.

Barsh, Russel L. 1982. "The economics of a traditional coastal Indian salmon fishery." *Human Organization* 41: 170–76.

Bowles, Samuel. 1999. " 'Social capital' and Community Governance," with Herbert Gintis. Sante Fe Institute Working Paper 2001, Dec. 2000.

Boxberger, Daniel L. 1989. *To Fish in Common: The Ethnohistory of Lummi Indian Salmon Fishing*. Lincoln: University of Nebraska Press.

Boyd, Robert, ed. 1999. *Indians, Fire, and the Land in the Pacific Northwest*. Corvallis: Oregon State University Press.

Clark, William G. 1985. "Fishing in a sea of court orders: Puget Sound salmon management ten years after the Boldt decision." *North American Journal of Fisheries Management* 5: 21–34.

Cohen, Fay G. 1986. *Treaties on Trial: The Continuing Controversy over Northwest Indian Fishing Rights*. Seattle: University of Washington Press.

Dandeisk, John, and Eugene Buck. 1999. "Pacific salmon and anadromous trout: management under the Endangered Species Act." Congressional Research Service Report No. 98-666, http://cnie.org/NLE/crsreports/biodiversity/biodv-22cfm.

Donald, Leland. 1997. *Aboriginal Slavery on the Northwest Coast of North America*. Berkeley: University of California Press.

Ferguson, R. Brian. 1983. "Warfare and redistributive exchange on the Northwest Coast." In *The Development of Political Organization in Native North America,* ed. Elizabeth Tooker, 133–47. Philadelphia: American Ethnological Society.

Johnsen, Bruce. 1986. "The formation and protection of property rights among the Southern Kwakiutl Indians." *Journal of Legal Studies* 15: 41–67.

Johnson, Ronald N., and Gary D. Libecap. 1982. "Contracting problems and regulation: the case of the fishery." *American Economic Review* 72: 1005–20.

Lane, Barbara. 1973. "Political and economic aspects of Indian-white culture contact in Western Washington in mid-19th century." *United States Exhibits 20–30, U.S. v. Washington*, 384 F. Supp. 312.

National Research Council. 1996. *Upstream: Salmon and Society in the Pacific Northwest*. Washington, D.C.: National Academy Press.

Onats, Astida R. Blukis. 1984. *Northwest Anthropological Research Notes* 18: 86–106.

Putnam, Robert. 2000. *Bowling Alone: The Collapse and Revival of American Community*. New York: Simmon & Schuster.

Richardson, Allan. 1981. "The control of productive resources on the Northwest coast of North America." In *Resource Managers: North American and Australian Hunter-Gatherers,* ed. Nancy M. Williams and Eugene S. Hunn, 93–112. Boulder, Colo.: Westview Press.

Singleton, Sara. 1998. *Constructing Cooperation: The Evolution of Institutions of Comanagement*. Ann Arbor: University of Michigan Press.

———. 1999. "Commons problems, collective action and efficiency: past and present institutions of governance in Pacific Northwest salmon fisheries." *Journal of Theoretical Politics* 11(3): 367–91.

State of Washington v. Washington State Commercial Passenger Fishing Vessel Association and Washington Kelpers Association, 89Wn. 2d 276, 571 P 2d 1373 (1977).

Stern, Bernhard J. 1934. *The Lummi Indians of Northwest Washington*. New York: Columbia University Press.

Suttles, Wayne. 1987. *Coast Salish Essays*. Seattle: University of Washington Press.

Taylor, Michael. 1982. *Community, Anarchy and Liberty*. New York: Cambridge University Press.

U.S. Department of Commerce, U.S. Census Bureau. 1990. *Characteristics of American Indians by Tribe and Location, Table 1.*

U.S. v. Washington, 384 F. Supp. 312 (1974).

U.S. v. Washington, Subproceeding no. 86–5, 1991. "Report and Recommendation on 1991 Area 10 Chum Fishery." Magistrate John Weinberg.

Response of Jamestown Lower Elwah and Port Gamble Bands of Klallams and Skokomish Tribe to Mediator's Report. 1989.

Response of Nooksack Tribe to Mediator's Report. 1989.

Transcript of Proceeding, Subproceeding No. 86-5. Sept. 6, 1986.

White, Richard. 1999. "Indian land use and environmental change: Island County, Washington, a case study." In *Indians, Fire, and the Land in the Pacific Northwest,* ed. Robert Boyd. Covallis: Oregon State University Press.

World Resources Institute. 2000. "Diminishing Returns: World Fisheries Under Pressure." *World Resources 1998–1999*. Oxford: Oxford University Press.

Chapter 7

HETEROGENEITY AND COLLECTIVE ACTION FOR EFFORT REGULATION: LESSONS FROM THE SENEGALESE SMALL-SCALE FISHERIES

Frederic Gaspart and Jean-Philippe Platteau

Much attention has recently been paid to the potential influence of inequality or heterogeneity on people's ability to organize collectively, particularly with respect to management of local-level natural resources. Speaking generally about this issue makes little sense insofar as heterogeneity or inequality is obviously a multidimensional phenomenon, the different facets of which may carry varying implications for collective-action capacities. Important among these different facets are: income or wealth (or productive capital) inequality, inequality in access to alternative income opportunities, social stratification or differential positions in the local power structure, skill disparity, ethnic and cultural heterogeneity, and diversity in techniques employed or in patterns of resource use.

This study would not have been possible without the financial support of the Fondation Universitaire pour la Coopération Internationale au Développement (FUCID) and the Centre de Recherche en Economie du Développement (CRED), both at the university of Namur. This support is gratefully acknowledged as well as the collaboration of partner institutions in Senegal, the Centre de Recherche et de Développement de Technologies Intermédiaires pour la Pêche (CREDETIP) and the Collectif National des Pêcheurs Sénégalais (CNPS). The latter played a major role to facilitate our preliminary contacts with the surveyed fishing communities and demonstrated great willingness to exchange views with us. Ousseynou Dieng, researcher at the CREDETIP, was a key performer at the level of data collection and coding. He was responsible for the direct supervision of the team of field investigators during the household survey and was continuously present on the field sites from the beginning of the data collection process. François Migeotte and Catherine Mélard, both from CRED, were the direct collaborators of Ousseynou Dieng and made an important contribution at the level of collection, coding, and processing of the data as well as in the writing of insightful field notes and preliminary reports. As director of CREDETIP, Aliou Sall assumed on-the-spot responsibility for the administration of the project. Finally, the Centre de Recherche Océanographique de Dakar-Thiaroye (CRODT) provided us with price and output series for a number of fish species.

The existing literature tends to suggest that all these dimensions except the first one have an unambiguously negative effect on collective action. As for income or wealth inequality, economic analysis can be harnessed to show that in certain circumstances or at certain levels collective action is encouraged rather than hindered by inequality. In particular, inequality is more likely to prompt collective action when it facilitates the establishment of a regulatory authority, and, in appropriation problems, when it places constraints on the individual harvesting efforts of the smaller users. In contrast, if regulatory instruments are limited in a way that emphasizes uniform treatment of all participants, inequality between them tends to make collective agreement and effective enforcement of such instruments more difficult. When a decentralized setup of voluntary contributions to a common good is considered, the impact of wealth or income inequality is again ambiguous. This is because larger participants are inclined to contribute more whereas the reduced stake of the smaller ones has the effect of dampening their incentives to contribute (see Baland and Platteau, chapter 2 of this book, for a most recent survey of this issue).

Our purpose in this chapter is to examine the rather unique experience of Senegalese small-scale fishermen with effort regulation during the 1990s in order to assess the potential role of various sources of heterogeneity. Indeed, an interesting feature of the Senegalese material under concern is that many of the aforementioned types of heterogeneity are present in the fishing centers where effort regulation has been attempted. Interestingly, not only have effort-restraining schemes been tried in some locations and not in others, and for some fish species and not others, but also they have been discontinued after some time in certain cases while enduring for a rather long time in other cases.

Section 7.1 provides background information about attempts at effort limitation by artisanal, maritime fishermen of Senegal. In section 7.2, details about the sample and the data are presented. Section 7.3 proposes an econometric test to decide in which case (which location and which species) effort limitation is likely to have an effective impact on producer prices, the most important objective apparently pursued by the fishermen when setting their effort restrictions. This will allow us to see whether there is a convergence between potentially and actually successful schemes. In other words, do we find that effort regulation occurs and persists where objective conditions (i.e., the market structure) for its success are comparatively good while it fails where those conditions are comparatively bad? If convergence is found, one can hypothesize that rules tend to be violated where a sufficient number of people have come to realize that they are not very profitable, thereby ultimately causing the collapse of the regulatory scheme. Section 7.4 forms the central part of the chapter. The influence of heterogeneous characteristics of resource users on their assessments of effectiveness of collective action (in the form of effort limitation) is measured and discussed. Since an appropriate market structure is a necessary but not sufficient condition for successful effort limitation, such a question is fully warranted. Section 7.5 summarizes the main findings of the study.

Essentially, we show that the adverse effect of technical heterogeneity on collective regulation has been overcome to a large yet not complete extent through deliberate efforts to adapt catch limitations to the specific conditions of each fishery, that is, through the devising of differentiated regulation methods. Wealth inequality seems to promote rather than block collective action while the presence of migrant groups is a hindrance only insofar as it is accompanied by polarization into conflicting fishing techniques or patterns of resource use in a sort of interrelated game. As for skill differentials, one of the potentially most problematic dimensions of heterogeneity, they do not create difficulties for effort regulation if skilled fishermen happen to target more valuable species since catch limitations are specified in quantity terms.

7.1. A Historical Sketch of Effort-Limiting Schemes along the Senegalese Coastline

7.1.1. A First Attempt to Regulate Access to the Resource

In Kayar, one of the main fishing centers along the Senegalese coastline (located on the so-called Petite Côte, north of the Dakar Peninsula), competition for access to in-shore waters has been a constant source of tensions between migrant fishermen (from Saint-Louis in the extreme north of the country) operating bottom-set nets and resident fishermen. Such tensions may easily erupt into acts of physical violence, as evidenced by the occurrence of several deaths following a violent confrontation in 1985. The conflict is especially severe because it takes on an ethnic dimension. Indeed, it opposes fishermen using passive gears (like bottom-set nets) to those using active gears (such as lines and purse seines), and it turns out that resident fishermen are entirely specialized in active fishing techniques while a category of fishermen from Saint-Louis operate bottom-set nets to the exclusion of any other technique.[1]

Note that fishermen from Saint-Louis have a long tradition of mobility along the West African coast, a result of the fact that the fishing zone of Saint-Louis (Guet Ndar) is not sheltered from the strong winds of the Atlantic Ocean and is therefore accessible only during a limited part of the year. As a consequence of deep-rooted migration habits, the Saint-Louisiens tend to consider the sea as an open-access resource that does not belong to any community in particular. People from Kayar have an almost opposite conception of sea tenure: being originally an agricultural community with lands located not far from the sea, they are inclined to view the adjacent water space as their own territory, in much the same way as they see their agricultural lands.

In February 1986, the government of Senegal set up a special commission charged with the task of defining and monitoring an exclusive fishing zone, marked by buoys, in which bottom-set nets were to be prohibited from operating.[2] Unfortunately, conflicts between bottom-set net operators and other fishermen remained pervasive as illegal encroachments upon the exclusive zone were quite frequent. In most cases, the commission did not deal with them partly due to a lack of monitoring equipment.[3]

In 1990, leaders of the fishermen in both communities decided to take more initiative and, with the support of some outstanding public authorities (such as the governors of Saint-Louis and Thies, and the General Khalife of the Muslim brotherhood of the *Layènes* in Yoff), they created the *Comité de solidarité Kayar-Guet Ndar* with a view to assuming more responsibilities in the monitoring operations and conflict resolution mechanisms. Results, however, remained quite below the expectations generated by this intercommunity solidarity movement.

All this happened during a period of growing pressure on fish resources both because of increased activity of foreign and national industrial vessels in the in-shore waters and a rapid expansion of the artisanal fleet itself. The pressure even accelerated during the 1990s: between 1994 and 1997, for example, the number of pirogues operating in the different sites of artisanal fishing increased by as much as 42 percent![4] Furthermore, the artisanal fishing sector underwent rapid transformation, particularly under the impact of significant technical innovations, including the shift from cotton to nylon nets, the motorization of traditional canoes (and their adjustment to permit the repair of an outboard engine), the introduction of large purse seines capable of collecting large schools of pelagic fishes, the fitting of ice boxes to the pirogues designed for hook-and-line fishing, and so on.[5] As a result, the productivity of boats and fishing gears in the small-scale sector has increased enormously, compounding the effect of their sheer multiplication on fish landings.

7.1.2. *Effort-Restraining Schemes*

The first attempt by small-scale fishermen to regulate their harvesting efforts was made in 1992 in the village of Kayar. Interestingly, this initiative was launched by the *Comité de solidarité Kayar-Guet Ndar* which was initially created with another purpose in mind (see supra). The intent was to reduce the market power wielded by local fishmerchants (known as *mareyeurs* in Senegal) and, more specifically, to increase producer prices for the pelagic species targeted by purse seines. It was decided that canoes equipped with purse seines would be allowed to make a single trip per day during the season suitable for this type of fishing. A special committee named *comité des sennes tournantes* (committee for purse seines) was established to ensure proper enforcement of the rule. The scheme has persisted to this date.

Two years later (1994), the so-called *comité des pêches* (committee of the fisheries) was set up by the fishermen of Kayar to extend the experience of purse seines to the domain of line fishing which targets demersal species destined for export markets. This step was taken soon after the devaluation of the CFA, when fishermen started fearing a severe decline of their profit margins owing to a rapid rise of their production costs (especially, the costs of fuel and the prices of imported fishing equipment). Output prices did not rise significantly either because the species concerned were not of an exportable variety or because fish intermediaries succeeded in preempting a large share of the gains from devaluation.

The existence of the latter phenomenon was actually confirmed in the course of interviews conducted with some management staff of fish-processing factories in Dakar. According to them, indeed, commission agents in charge of purchasing raw fish on the landing sites on behalf of export companies did not hesitate to collude with the purpose of preventing prices paid to the producer from increasing after devaluation. The system of payment applied by these companies actually encouraged trade malpractices since they used to pay a predetermined price per unit weight (based on world market prices) to their commission agents, leaving them free to appropriate any residual gain obtained by underpaying fishermen. In other words, fishmerchants were able to deprive fishermen of the beneficial effects of devaluation. It is in reaction to this glaring manipulation of market prices that the fishermen started to demonstrate, first in Yoff (near Dakar) and soon thereafter in Kayar where the protest movement took on the form of a strike stretching over three consecutive days during which fishmerchants were starved of fish. Fishermen from Kayar demanded prices five to ten times higher than those offered them by the *mareyeurs*!

Since merchants refused to raise their prices substantially after fishermen returned to fishing, the latter decided to sell the fish themselves to the factories by renting refrigerated vans and transporting the raw product to Dakar. This was nevertheless a temporary solution soon succeeded by a systematic attempt to limit catches of demersal species through the fixing of a maximum number of boxes of fish that a canoe is allowed to unload on the beach for disposal. Most of the time, the number of boxes is set at three, yet the *comité des pêches* can increase or decrease the quota depending on prevailing demand and supply conditions. In actual practice, the quota per canoe never falls below two boxes of fish because fishermen consider that line fishing cannot be profitable if catches are smaller than this quantity.

Clearly, such a scheme proved more sustainable than lock-out movements—which are hard to maintain given the lack of intertemporal markets to smooth temporary disruptions of economic activity—and direct sales of fish to export companies—which confront fishermen with considerable costs due to their lack of experience and skills in marketing.

Migrant fishermen from Saint-Louis operating in Kayar during part of the year have played a critical role in diffusing in their native area the institutional innovation adopted by purse-seine operators in Kayar. To regulate fishing trips by canoes operating purse seines as well as to achieve some other collective ends (particularly, to encourage mutual help groups for sea rescue operations and insurance against damages to nets, engines, and canoes), a special organization known as the *Union des Profession-nels de la Pêche Artisanale de Guet-Ndar* (U.P.P.A.G.) had been created as early as November 1992. A first attempt to limit trips by purse seines was made in October 1993 when fifty-five canoes operating this gear participated in a scheme allowing for only one trip every two days. In order to implement the rotating scheme, the canoes concerned were divided into two groups (one of 22 and the other of 23 units) according to the quarter of residence of their owners. During the year 1994, the experience was repeated with a total of fifty-eight participating canoes, and again in 1995. Yet, around the middle of December 1995, the scheme was brought to an end due to internal tensions leading to a large incidence of violations. On the other hand, no regulation of fishing effort among line fishermen has ever been attempted in Saint-Louis.

Yoff (in the Dakar area), as we pointed out earlier, was actually the place where the idea of fixing quotas of fish landings for line-fishing canoes was initially attempted before being emulated in Kayar. Unlike what is observed in the latter fishing site, however, regulation in Yoff is implemented only during the period running from January to May when landings are particularly abundant. A special committee composed of twelve members chosen among the seven quarters (called *penthies*) of the village is in charge of monitoring the regulatory measure during the above period. In due time, however, serious tensions broke out in the village that led to the discontinuance of the scheme (in February 1997). Opposition to the measures by an important leader eager to recoup considerable investment expenditures in fishing assets (purchase of three canoes equipped with echo-sounders) has been frequently mentioned as the trigger of the crisis. Yet, at the same time, there seems to be a widespread belief that the members of the committee are not up to their task and should be replaced by more dynamic leaders.

In trying to emulate their colleagues from Yoff, fishermen of Soumbedioune (also in the Dakar area) have been much less successful than those of Kayar. In August 1994, they decided to enforce a scheme limiting to three boxes the quantity of valuable demersal export species (the sea bream and the dentex) that line fishermen were allowed to land per day. Toward that purpose, they set up a special committee made up of six members. After a short period of barely three months, the experience had to be ended amidst a lot of disillusionment.

7.2. The Sample Data

As is evident from the above historical sketch, Saint-Louis, Yoff, and, above all, Kayar are places where important experiments in effort regulation have been made. In these sites, as well as in two control sites—Soumbedioune (in the Dakar area) where a short-lived experience of effort regulation has been attempted, and Hann (also in the Dakar area) where no such experience has ever taken place—household questionnaires were addressed to fishermen. The purpose of the household survey, conducted during the year 1997 (between April and July), was essentially to determine the level of support of regulatory schemes (whether existing in the location surveyed or not) among the fishermen as well as to examine whether some categories are more supportive than others and why.

The stratified random sampling method has been applied so as to have adequate representation of different fishing techniques in use in each site as well as to distinguish between owners and crew within each technique and, when the need arises, between residents and immigrants within the owners' stratum. Table 7.1 gives the characteristics of the sample for each of the five aforementioned fishing sites.

The sample contains data about attitudes of two categories of fishermen—those who have gone themselves through a (sustained) experience of effort control and those who have not. The latter either belong to a location where effort control has been carried out with respect to some fishing technique (not the one which they themselves use), or not. While in Kayar purse seines and lines are regulated (bottom-set nets are subject to loosely applied access rules), this is true only of purse seines in Saint-Louis and of lines in Yoff. Adding the fishermen, both owners and crew laborers, belonging to these three locational-technical configurations, we have a sample of 127 units in the category of fishermen having experienced effort regulation (see the figures in bold characters). The re-

TABLE 7.1
The Structure of the Sample as Per Fishing site, Technique, and Ownership Status

Fishing Site	Purse Seine		Line Fishing		Line with Ice		Bottom-Set Nets		Beach Seine		Total	
	own	crew	own	crew	own	crew	own	crew	own	crew	own	crew
Kayar	**19**[a]	**17**	**15**[c]	**12**	—	—	**11**[d]	**6**	—	—	45	35
Saint-Louis	**19**	**21**	14	8	—	—	10	7	—	—	43	36
Soumbedio.	—	—	13	12	11	14	—	—	—	—	24	26
Yoff	**11**[b]	**11**	10	14	1	0	—	—	5	10	27	35
Hann	7	8	6	8	10	10	—	—	—	—	23	26
Total	56	57	58	54	22	24	21	13	5	10	162	158

Notes: Numbers referring to cases where regulation has taken place are indicated in bold types.
[a]Among whom are 11 residents, 6 immigrants native of Saint-Louis and 2 immigrants from Fass Boye.
[b]Among whom 7 are residents and 4 are immigrants from Saint-Louis.
[c]Among whom 8 are residents and 7 are from Saint-Louis.
[d]All of them are actually native of Saint-Louis.

maining category comprises 193 fishermen. In our analysis (see section 7.4), we will use mainly the complete sample of all fishermen (320 units).

Random selection of households within each subsample was made by choosing a central physical point in the fishing site and letting enumerators move in different directions and pick up every house out of a fixed number (which varied according to the site concerned) until the predetermined size of each subsample was eventually reached (the so-called random walk technique). Unfortunately, difficulties in meeting household heads for a long enough time to have the questionnaire filled up were much more serious than foreseen, as a consequence of which the actual sample size was significantly smaller than initially envisaged. Reduction of sample is especially noticeable with respect to crew laborers due not only to pressure on their limited time available for leisurely talks during the fishing season but also to reluctance of their owner-employer to let them speak outside their control. Eventually, crew laborers came to form about half the total sample of 320 households whom we could interview in good conditions.[6]

7.3. THE EFFECTIVENESS OF EFFORT-LIMITING SCHEMES

From our historical overview in section 7.1, it is patent that the main motive behind the efforts of Senegalese small-scale fishermen to limit their landings has been their desire to curb the market power of local fishmerchants and obtain higher prices for their fish rather than to manage and conserve the resource.[7] The question then arises as to whether

TABLE 7.2

Econometric Estimates of Inverse Demand Functions for Sardines (based on price and output data pertaining to the years 1991–93)

Site	Sub-species (sardines)	β (inverse Demand Elasticity)	γ (Substitution Effect)	δ (Speculation Effect)
Inverse Demand Estimations : $\ln P_t = \alpha + \beta \ln Q_t + \gamma \ln P_{subst} + \delta \ln P_{t+1}^e$				
Kayar	Round	−0.01	0.46**	—
	Flat	−0.20**	0.97**	—
St.-Louis	Round	−0.07	−0.00	—
	Flat	−0.11**	1.20**	—
Hann	Round	−0.03	0.36*	.60*
	Flat	−0.08	0.40*	.19

Note: **indicates significance at the 95 percent confidence level while * indicates significance at the 90 percent level.

effort regulation actually can be effective in achieving its economic objective of increasing producer prices. In order to assess the fishermen's ability to exert market power in a sustainable way, we must establish whether demand elasticity is greater or lower than −1 for every regulated product. A value below −1 for demand elasticity would insure that a monopoly can find one positive level of output that maximizes profit and, therefore, that the fishermen's cartel can precisely define the target level of aggregate output.

Unfortunately, due to difficult logistical problems, we could only obtain from the CRODT (Centre de Recherches Océanographique de Dakar-Thiaroye) monthly price and landing data pertaining to the years prior to devaluation (in 1994). Moreover, as many price series are incomplete, we have to confine our attention to three fishing sites (Kayar, Hann, and Saint-Louis) and to a restricted number of seven fish species (the flat sardine; the round sardine; the white grouper known locally as thiof; a thread fin called capitaine in the Francophone and cassava fish in the Anglophone part of West Africa; and three fish species belonging to the sea bream family—the rose sea bream, and the so-called pagre and dentex). The conclusions must therefore be interpreted with the appropriate caution.

Details about the econometric model used to estimate (inverse) demand elasticities are provided in appendix 7.1. In table 7.2, we present the results obtained for the above two types of sardines, the only pelagic species for which data are available. The inverse demand equation has the following form:

$$\ln P_t = \alpha + \beta \ln Q_t + \gamma \ln P_{subst} + \delta \ln P_{t+1}^e,$$

where P_t is the current estimated price of the fish species concerned, Q_t is the current quantity produced, P_{subst} is the price of a close substitute, and P_{t+1}^e is the anticipated price of the species (estimated on the basis of past-observed prices using autoregressive processes of order one).

It is evident from the table that it is only for flat sardines in Kayar and Saint-Louis that inverse demand elasticities are significantly different from zero.[8] Demand elasticities (the inverse of the βs shown in the table), are lower than -1, which conforms to theory. For round sardines in the three fishing sites and for flat sardines in Hann, one cannot reject the hypothesis of a perfectly elastic demand, which should preclude any regulation effort from causing an increase in prices. These results are not really surprising in light of the following circumstances. First, in Kayar and Saint-Louis, sardines are not refrigerated but are sold immediately to artisanal fish processors who condition fish for local consumption. Second, Hann is a suburb of the capital Dakar and freezing sardines for other markets (such as cities in the hinterland) is much more common there. Moreover, the area of Dakar forms a large integrated market strongly articulated with export outlets, contrary to Kayar and Saint-Louis which are more isolated physically.

It is probably not coincidental that purse seines, which target only pelagic species among which flat sardines are important, are regulated in Kayar and Saint-Louis but not in Hann and Yoff (bearing in mind that, like Hann, Yoff is located in the suburb of Dakar). Finally, it may be noted that, as expected, all substitution effects are positive, indicating actual substitutability (rather than complementarity) between fish species.

As far as demersal species caught by hooks and lines (or bottom-set nets) are concerned, estimations of inverse demand functions yield complicated results (not shown here) from which Kayar emerges as the most suitable location for effective attempts at effort regulation. It is indeed apparent that demersal species for which demand is not perfectly elastic are the thiof in Kayar (but not in Saint-Louis and Hann); the capitaine in Kayar; the rose sea bream in Kayar; and the pagre in Saint-Louis and Hann.

To sum up, the hypothesis that regulation of fishing effort should be observed only where inverse demand is strongly elastic (or demand is rather inelastic) is broadly confirmed by our econometric testing procedure. Kayar, the place where the most successful experiments took root, appears as the location where, at least before the devaluation, market conditions were clearly favorable to a producer cartel. Operators of purse seines in Saint-Louis also seem to wield potential market power.

Finally, it must be reckoned that, as discussions with fishermen leaders (particularly when presenting our results to a selection of them in the late nineties) have persuaded us, they tend not to have a good or quick grasp of the critical role of the market environment for effort-limiting efforts.[9]

Conceivably, they might thus embark upon such efforts even though they are not sustainable. This is one reason why it is important to have a complementary look at other factors—particularly, the various dimensions of heterogeneity which are the focus of this study—susceptible to influencing support for effort regulation. The other reason is more evident: a conducive market structure is a necessary but not sufficient condition for successful regulation (as witnessed by the eventual failure of the attempt to regulate effort among purse-seine fishermen in Saint-Louis).

7.4. The Impact of Heterogeneity on the Perceived Success of Effort-Limiting Schemes

7.4.1. Regulation Methods in Light of Various Types of Heterogeneity

TECHNICAL HETEROGENEITY AND DIFFERENTIATION
OF EFFORT-LIMITING SCHEMES

Specific characteristics of the fishing techniques used make it difficult to work out a single formula for implementing effort limitation. Disagreement is therefore bound to arise if uniform treatment of fishermen employing differing techniques is sought. Differentiation of the regulation methods applied appears as the only way out of this type of heterogeneity. In Kayar, revealingly, as pointed out in section 7.1, methods of effort limitation differ between purse-seine and line fishermen.

First consider the case of canoes operating purse seines. Regulation of fishing effort through catch quotas is hardly feasible. In this type of fishing, indeed, huge quantities of schooling fishes may be caught with a single sweep of the net handled from one or two motorized canoes. There are two distinct reasons why purse-seine fishermen would resist the idea of having to throw excess produce back to the sea after a successful haul. The first reason lies in the fact that forgoing a catch that has actually been hauled in entails a much higher subjective cost than forgoing a potential catch that is not yet in the net. This is an interesting application of the prospect theory of Kahneman and Tversky (1979) according to which subjects tend to evaluate prospects in terms of gains and losses relative to some reference point, rather than hypothetical final states (wealth positions) as assumed by expected utility theory. The so-called value function depicted by these authors captures the idea of loss aversion that is critical in the aforementioned fishermen's attitude (the function is steeper for losses than gains).

The second reason has to do with insurance considerations. Since catches may vary widely from one day to the other, imposing a system of catch ceilings means that fishermen would have to forgo a windfall catch on a "lucky" trip while under poor natural conditions their catches may fall well short of the authorized maximum. In other words, a system of catch quotas would prevent fishermen from smoothing bad and good catches as effectively as they can do under a system of free landings. In the case of purse-seine fishing, therefore, limitation of fishing trips unaccompanied by catch quotas appears as a second-best solution imposed by technological (a discrete process of fish harvesting) and ecological (ample and largely unpredictable catch variations) constraints.[10]

Since catching fish with hooks and lines is a continuous process that can be interrupted almost at will (quantities of fish caught can be "finely tuned" by the fishermen), fixing catch quotas per trip is a practical proposition for line-fishing canoes. Furthermore, imposing limits on the number of fishing trips per day does not appear to be necessary because (i) the average length of a sea trip for these canoes is close to nine hours (average computed over a sample of eighty fishermen) due to the long distances traveled to reach the fishing grounds; and (ii) landing sites are not lighted, forcing markets to close at 6:00 p.m. and boats to return before that time. In actual practice, therefore, the system of catch quotas applied to line fishing conforms with the prescription of economic theory.

As for canoes equipped with ice boxes made of polystherene (a rather recent innovation used in small-scale fisheries to help conserve fish on board), they undertake much longer voyages. They travel up to several hundred kilometers, northward to Mauritania and southward to Casamance and Guinea Bissau. Their voyages extend over several days and, increasingly, they come to exceed a week's time. For operators of such canoes, catch quotas have not been a feasible proposition so far. This is true even allowing for the fact that quotas could be adjusted upward to take account of the length of each fishing trip: for example, the landing per canoe could be fixed on a daily basis so as to make the total allowable quota proportional to the length of the voyage. The fact of the matter is that fishermen who go far out at sea for long periods of time are willing to support the cost and duress of prolonged fishing trips only because they expect high catches at the destination point. Therefore, a constraint on allowed catches, even though proportional to the number of days spent out at sea, would entail more sacrifice for them than for the fishermen who undertake short sea trips.

HETEROGENEITY IN PHYSICAL CAPITAL AND THE IMPOSITION OF EFFORT LIMITS ON A PER UNIT BASIS

If a uniform limitation, whether in terms of fishing trips or fish boxes landed, would be imposed on all fishermen irrespective of the number of fishing units owned, comparatively big owners would immediately op-pose it. Inequality in capital endowments would thus stand in the way of a workable regulation of fishing effort. In the communities of small-scale Senegalese fishermen concerned, however, effort limits are typically set on a per unit basis. Each purse seine is permitted to operate once every day in Kayar and once every two days in Saint-Louis, while each line-fishing canoe is allowed a fixed quota in Kayar and Yoff.

It is remarkable that, as revealed by our household survey, there appar-ently exists a complete consensus about such a manner of sharing the burden of effort reduction. Indeed, all the fishermen interviewed hold the opinion that it would be unfair to impose identical quotas (whether in terms of landings or fishing trips allowed) on all equipment owners, re-gardless of the size of their capital stock. With identical aggregate quotas, so it is felt, large owners would be suddenly deprived of the possibility of maintaining the profitability of part of their fishing assets. In addition, crew laborers working on units prohibited from operating would become unemployed unless some employment-sharing mechanism is agreed upon within the fishing community. Even small capital owners insist that these consequences ought to be avoided.

Heterogeneity in ownership of physical capital obviously takes on an added dimension when the situation of crew laborers who do not own any fishing asset is being considered. Nonetheless, a peculiar feature of la-bor contracts in small-scale fisheries not only in Senegal but all over the world is that workers are given a sort of fixed wage component, usually paid in kind, plus a predetermined share of the net proceeds accruing from the sale of the catches (Platteau and Nugent 1992). In these so-called mixed share-cum-fixed wage contracts which answer the need for both in-surance and incentive motives, it must be emphasized that the share com-ponent usually represents by far the largest portion of total labor remu-neration. The immediate implication for our purpose is the following: if the aim of effort-limitation and catch restrictions is to obtain better prices for fish so that the total value of the landings is increased, then crew workers should naturally support such schemes because they meet their own interests. Consequently, we ought not to observe more opposition to them among crew workers than among owners of fishing assets.

HETEROGENEITY IN SKILLS AND THE PRINCIPLE
OF SKILL-NEUTRAL QUOTAS

Heterogeneity in skills is more difficult to handle than heterogeneity in techniques and inequality in capital endowments. This is essentially be-cause skill levels are not easily observable. It is revealing that Senegalese small-scale fishermen believe it would be unfair to award larger quotas to better-skilled operators. In the interviews, many of them actually denied that significant skill differentials exist in their community and they took pains to explain that better performances on the part of some fishermen are only transient phenomena likely to be reversed as soon as luck turns its back on them to favor other fishing units. The prevalence of this standpoint has no doubt influenced the selection of effort-reducing methods in the villages surveyed: quotas or rules regarding fishing trips are uniform or skill-neutral, meaning that they are set independently of the skill levels of the fishing teams subject to regulation.

As the aforementioned interviews indicate, it would be practically impossible for fishermen to reach an agreement about their respective skill levels. It is not only that skill differentials are difficult to measure in an objective manner. Indeed, we do not doubt that fishermen have some clues about skill rankings within their community, at least regarding the best and worst performers. Yet, the interesting fact is that they do not want to disclose them in public because officializing them would give rise to unbearable tensions. Low performers would feel ashamed to admit their insufficiency while good ones are wary of self-declaring their superiority, which could be interpreted as misplaced boasting. Community life encompasses many spheres of human interactions, and tensions or frustrations in one sphere, say in meetings where regulatory schemes are discussed, can easily spill over into other walks of social life, including the domain of interpersonal relations and private affairs. This is especially true when fishermen belong to the same family or lineage.

From economic theory, however, we know that uniform quotas are bound to hurt the interests of the better-skilled agents—in this case, captains leading fishing teams—who may lose or gain little from effort regulation (Johnson and Libecap 1982; Libecap and Wiggins 1984; Libecap 1990; Baland and Platteau 1998, 1999). It is therefore to be feared that these agents will be prompted to abstain from supporting and perhaps even to violate or circumvent the rules prescribing uniform treatment for all operators regardless of their skill levels. Unfortunately, we are unable to test that hypothesis to the desirable extent since we do not have at hand a comprehensive reliable yardstick of the relative skill levels of sample fishermen. This said, we will see later that we have available to us two satisfactory indicators of at least who are among the most dynamic, progressive, venturesome, and skilled line fishermen (no equivalent indicator is available for operators of purse seines). By using them, we will be able to show that the aforementioned hypothesis is partly borne out and partly rejected for reasons that are perfectly understandable on the basis of economic analysis.

Clearly, to the extent that uniform quotas are hurting the interests of at least a fraction of comparatively skilled fishermen (whether purse-seine or some category of line operators), it would be surprising if they were universally followed by all fishermen. In fact, violation of quotas can be considered as an adaptive device used by this category of fishermen to correct their unfair treatment under such a system. Insofar as they harvest relatively big catches and fines are lump-sum amounts (so that their expected net income is higher than the expected cost of being caught bringing excess fish ashore), skilled fishermen may even be willing to pay the fines in the event that their violation is detected. It is therefore useful to pause for a while at this stage to ask what we do know about the incidence of rule-breaking.

Unfortunately, data about actually observed actions were not made available to us. Fishermen leaders sitting on the executive committees in charge of implementing the schemes argued indeed that there was no such thing as a diary reporting the known cases of rule violation. This was not thought to be an important shortcoming since, according to them, there had been only a few cases of clear infringement of the set regulations concerning effort restrictions. When asked again to describe cases of sanctioning by the committee in charge, they typically argued that punishing is rarely meted out because there are few rule-breakers. Following their account, only once had a fisherman been threatened with confiscation of his equipment and the threat did not have to be executed because the culprit paid the fine on the eve of the announced seizure.[11]

The leaders' claim that the incidence of rule infractions is very low is however not congruent with the reported fact that, in the case of line fishermen, the fine imposable in the event of rule-breaking has been gradually revised upward (from 15,000 to 30,000 and then to 50,000 CFA) when it appeared that it was not dissuasive enough. On the other hand, our household questionnaire contains a question that allowed fishermen to express in the privacy of their homes their personal opinions about whether the effort-limiting schemes are effectively implemented. The general pattern of their answers turns out to be largely at odds with the optimistic assessment of the relevant committee's members. As a matter of fact, more than 40 percent of the sample fishermen believe that rule violations are frequent.[12]

Moreover, as further probing revealed, those fishermen who perceive the rate of infractions to be high also think that proper sanctions are not applied to violators: enforcement of the rules is low with the attendant consequence that other participants are demotivated. Some interviewees actually expressed a good deal of aggressiveness when addressing that issue. In the light of such findings, it seems highly unlikely that the prevailing extent of rule-breaking is an equilibrium position vindicated by the negative discrimination against comparatively skilled fishermen that results from the setting of uniform effort-restricting measures. Rather, it

TABLE 7.3
Extent of Rule-Breaking as Measured by Frequencies of Fishermen Considering
that Rule Violations Are Common (as per location and fishing technique)

Technique/Site	Low Incidence of Rule Violations	High Incidence of Rule Violations	Total
Line fishing Kayar	12 (44.44%)	15 (55.56%)	27 (100%)
Line fishing Yoff	11 (45.83%)	13 (54.17%)	24 (100%)
Purse seine Kayar	27 (75.00%)	9 (25.00%)	36 (100%)
Purse seine Saint-Louis	24 (60.00%)	16 (40.00%)	40 (100%)
Total	74 (58.27%)	53 (41.73%)	127 (100%)

appears to be a destabilizing force that could eventually cause the collapse of the schemes.

It bears emphasis that the subjective assessment of rule violations varies significantly between fishing techniques and locations. This is evident from table 7.3. The perceived incidence of rule-breaking is noticeably large among line fishermen (around 55 percent of them believe that there are many rule violations), whether in Kayar or in Yoff, and it is significantly larger than that obtaining for purse-seine fishermen (in Saint-Louis and especially in Kayar).[13] The fact that cheating is easier with lines than with purse seines largely accounts for this statistically significant difference. It is indeed obviously easier to conceal a box of fish that has been caught in excess of the prescribed quota, and to dispose of it in a secret manner, than to make an additional, illegal sea trip without being noticed (thanks to mutual monitoring, violations are easily detected in this case). The fact that sale transactions may take place out at sea or on the beach itself but amidst crowds of people gathering at peak landing times greatly facilitates the discreet disposal of excess catches under a system of catch quotas.

In addition, the perceived rate of infractions among purse-seine fishermen is much larger in Saint-Louis than in Kayar. A crucial difference between the schemes implemented in these two locations seems to largely explain the poorer achievements of the former compared with the latter in terms of effectiveness of enforcement. To recall, while purse seines may be operated one time per day in Kayar, they are allowed to work only once every two days in Saint-Louis. The more stringent limitation imposed in Saint-Louis determines a comparatively strong reluctance of local operators to abide by the rule. In fact, fishermen are eager to work every day because ecological conditions may vary appreciably from day to day. They always worry that they might miss a bumper catch that will not happen again, or they are deeply frustrated if the day they are allowed to operate turns out to be a bad one that they will not be able to make up for till after two days or more. Frustration is especially great when the sea is too rough to ride on their fishing day since they then feel that they have been robbed of effective fishing time.

Moreover, well-to-do fishermen from Saint-Louis lend their fishing equipment to poorer relatives or friends when they themselves want to rest or take a break. Following the effort-limiting regulation, however, such loans of equipment may only take place on days during which the fishing unit concerned is allowed to operate. This solution is deemed unfair by both donors and donees because the custom is interpreted as a way to assist the poor who should not be subject to the regulation. Being permitted to go out at sea only once every two days, well-to-do fishermen are discouraged from helping poorer fellow fishermen who resent the new situation.

Finally, there is in Saint-Louis a strong tradition of so-called special sea trips (*ndiaylou*) whereby different members of an extended family join together to earn incomes required for a collective purpose, say, financing a wedding, a baptism, or helping a relative who has suffered from an accident or illness. Insofar as these sea trips are meant to serve the interests of a limited fraction of the community, they were supposed to fall under the scope of the effort-limiting scheme. Fishermen nevertheless find it hard to comply with such a requirement since they do not privately benefit from the income thus earned, hence the frequent practice of eschewing the commission's approval for these special sea trips and the consequent suspicion that some fishermen use the pretext of a *ndiaylou* to increase their allowed time of fishing. The problem is less acute in Kayar, where the practice of special sea trips has practically vanished.

For all these reasons, it is not surprising that limitations of sea trips for purse-seine canoes were discontinued in Saint-Louis by the end of 1995 while they persisted in Kayar.

SOCIOCULTURAL HETEROGENEITY ALONG THE NATIVE-MIGRANT DIVIDE

We have already pointed out that in Kayar there is a deep antagonism between operators of passive gears (bottom-set nets) and operators of active gears (purse seines and lines) with the former all being migrant fishermen from Saint-Louis (see section 7.1). In other words, what we witness here is an area of conflict between two different types of fishing techniques that arises from different patterns of use of the resource available in the in-shore waters. In a nutshell, there is heterogeneity of objectives regarding the resource and such heterogeneity can usually be overcome only through intergroup agreements about sharing the claimed territory. Yet, such agreements about regulation of access to the waters are hard to come by or unlikely to be effectively implemented, especially when heterogeneity in use patterns is compounded by a social or cultural heterogeneity.[14] (Think of the difficulty of resolving conflicts between farmers and herders in many parts of SubSaharan Africa.) The latter type of heterogeneity, indeed, helps define a "common foe" which can be easily vilified and made responsible for the problems encountered by the native resource users.[15]

Unlike bottom-set net operators, fishermen handling purse seines or hooks and lines under their respective effort-restraining schemes are culturally heterogeneous. The presumption is that the deep-seated conflict that has long opposed native and migrant fishermen about the use of bottom-set nets is likely to rebound on the effectiveness of these other regulatory attempts that involve both groups of people. Our econometric estimates presented later in this section will enable us to test this hypothesis. Note furthermore that migrant fishermen from Saint-Louis are also present in significant numbers in Soumbedioune and that a fraction of them have even settled there permanently. It will be interesting to know whether opinions about the usefulness of regulatory schemes differ among these various categories of fishermen, bearing in mind that attempts at effort regulation have been short-lived in this location (see section 7.1).

HETEROGENEITY IN BARGAINING POWER VIS-À-VIS FISHMERCHANTS

It is a common feature of many small-scale fisheries in the Third World that boat owners are sometimes involved in exclusive relationships with a particular fishmerchant through sales-tying debts (see Platteau and Abraham 1987; Platteau and Nugent 1992). Productive loans are thus given to fishermen on the explicit condition that their catches will be disposed of through the lender-merchant and interest payments typically will be subtracted from the sale proceeds, possibly in the form of reduced purchase prices. In this manner, merchants try to secure a sufficient supply of raw material to keep their business running. If effort-limiting schemes devised by Senegalese fishermen are aimed at countering the bargaining power of fishmerchants, as we have documented in section 7.1, we naturally expect that fishermen entangled in sales-tying debts will not readily participate in such schemes. The threat of lender-merchants asking for immediate re-

TABLE 7.4

Proportions of Fishermen Engaged in Exclusive Sale Relationships with Merchants, According to Fishing Techniques and Sites

Technique/Site	Kayar (%)	St-Louis (%)	Yoff (%)	Hann (%)	Soumbedi (%)	Total (%)
Line	22.2	40.9	16.7	71.4	24.0	31.2
Line + ice box	—	—	0.0	15.0	24.0	19.6
Purse seine	13.9	15.0	0.0	26.7	—	13.3
Beach seine	—	—	0.0	—	—	0.0
Bottom-set net	58.8	76.5	—	—	—	67.6
Total	26.3	35.4	6.4	34.7	24.0	25.6

payment of their loans would surely act as a powerful deterrent discouraging any action susceptible of antagonizing them. Moreover, if it is the case that credit-cum-marketing relationships are pervasive in some fisheries, we would predict that catch limitations would be impossible to enforce for lack of a critical mass of operators ready to abide by the rules.

Table 7.4 shows precisely that there are significant variations across fishing techniques in the incidence of such interlinked relationships: it actually varies from a zero proportion of fishermen with exclusive sales arrangements in the case of line and purse-seine fishing in Yoff to more than three-fourths of fishermen in this category for bottom-set net fishing in Saint-Louis. On an average, about a quarter of all the sample fishermen have special credit links with fishmerchants.

The most interesting finding emerging from the table is no doubt the existence of a significant, negative relationship between the incidence of sales-tying debts, on the one hand, and the presence of an effort-limiting scheme, on the other hand. Thus, these debts are especially pervasive for operators of bottom-set nets (close to 59 percent in Kayar and 76.5 percent in Saint-Louis), and for line fishermen in Hann (more than 71 percent) and Saint-Louis (close to 41 percent), all fisheries for which effort-limiting schemes are conspicuously absent. By contrast, the most active location for such schemes, Kayar, exhibits comparatively low proportions of fishermen tied to fishmerchants through credit links (about 22 percent for line fishermen and barely 14 percent for purse-seine operators). Low proportions are also observed for purse-seine operators in Saint-Louis (15 percent) and line fishermen in Yoff (less than 17 percent), two other fisheries which have attempted to limit fishing effort.

Note that the presence of an endogeneity bias—credit-cum-marketing relationships tend to disappear when effort regulation is adopted—is rather unlikely insofar as owners of fishing assets cannot easily terminate

TABLE 7.5
Logit Estimate of the Determinants of Fishermen's Beliefs Regarding the Extent of Rule-Breaking

Rulebreaking	Coef.	Std. Err.	z	P > |z|	[95% Conf. Interval]	
Migrantkayar	−.3441515	.6098426	−0.564	0.573	−1.5394210	.8511181
Education	.5771422	.4131097	1.397	0.162	−.2325380	1.3868220
Leaderkayar	−1.8969440	1.1061750	−1.715	0.086	−4.0650070	.2711190
Youngmarrkay	−1.6990020	.8667965	−1.960	0.050	−3.3978920	−.0001124
Purseseine	−.9869905	.4222457	−2.337	0.019	−1.8145770	−.1594042
Exclusive	.9430304	.5326338	1.771	0.077	−.1009126	1.9869730
Constant	.0151894	.3768604	0.040	0.968	−.7234434	.7538221

Log Likelihood = −75.822999

Number of obs = 127
chi2(6) = 20.92
Prob > chi2 = 0.0019
Pseudo R2 = 0.1213

such agreements owing to the obligation to repay their debts in a short period of time. For another thing, indebtedness to fishmerchants does not appear to be systematically related to wealth: as is evident from the above, its prevalence is essentially explained by characteristics pertaining to location and targeted fish species.

7.4.2. Econometric Results: Characteristics of Fishermen with an Optimistic Assessment of Enforcement Performance

Judging by what has been said thus far, we expect the perceived rate of rule violations to be relatively high among line fishermen and fishermen involved in exclusive sale relationships with particular merchants, and to be relatively low among purse-seine operators and the local leadership (as already pointed out, in public or in group interviews they made a very positive assessment of the scheme's success). These predictions are all confirmed in the logit model that we used to estimate the determinants of fishermen's beliefs regarding the extent of rule-breaking in the effort-limiting scheme that concerns them. The econometric results are presented in table 7.5 based on the restricted sample of fishermen who have been actually involved in effort-limiting experiments, whether sustained to the time of interview or not. The dependent variable, denoted rulebreaking, is a dummy that takes on the value 1 when the incidence of violations is deemed to be large and 0 when it is deemed to be low by the fisherman concerned.

Four explanatory variables turn out to be statistically significant. First, the dummy *exclusive*, which has unit value when the fisherman is committed to a particular merchant through a credit link and zero value when he is free to sell his catches to whomever he wants, comes out with a positive coefficient (significant at 90 percent confidence level). As expected, "free" fishermen are more positive than "tied" fishermen regarding the extent of rule-breaking. Second, the dummy *purseseine*, with unit value when the fisherman is a purse-seine operator and zero value when he works with hooks and lines, has a negative coefficient (significant at 95 percent confidence level), indicating that purse-seine operators have a more optimistic assessment of the effectiveness of the schemes' enforcement than line fishermen.[16]

Third, we have the dummy *leaderkayar*, which is intended to identify fishermen leaders in Kayar. It takes on value 1 when the fisherman is relatively old (more than 47 years old) and has three wives (no fisherman has more than three wives in the locations surveyed), and value 0 otherwise. These two criteria, indeed, are important indicators of high social status in fishermen communities. Seniority still remains an important basis for exercising authority and wielding prestige while the number of wives is a good proxy for wealth and is actually strongly correlated with the number of fishing units owned. The coefficient of *leaderkayar* has the expected negative sign that confirms the public statements made by the members of the Kayar's elite, that is, well-to-do and influential persons who play a leadership role not only in the effort-limiting scheme but in many other collective initiatives as well (cleaning of the beach, construction and maintenance of the village mosque, assistance in the event of sea accidents, etc.). Understandably, they may have special difficulties in seeing the dysfunctionings of an undertaking with which they are strongly identified. Or, it may be that they are more confident in its eventual success in spite of what they perceive as minor problems which they are therefore prone to downplay.

It must be pointed out that, if the coefficient of *leaderkayar* is significant only at the 90 percent confidence level, it is entirely due to strong multicollinearity: indeed, this variable is highly correlated with *education* (leaders tend to have comparatively high levels of education as measured in the way explained below) and, above all, with *purseseine* (only 10 percent of Kayar's leaders do not own at least a purse seine).[17] It is obviously impossible to remove the latter variable from the regression owing to the critical influence of fishing technique on the assessment of rule-breaking. Revealingly, the proportion of comparatively old fishermen with three wives who stated a low incidence of rule infractions in Kayar is as high as 90 percent compared with only 57 percent for all other categories taken together, a phenomenon that is observed neither in Saint-Louis nor Yoff (where interaction of age and marriage position has no impact on the perception of rule-breaking). This probably reflects the fact that in Kayar more than in any other fishing village on the Senegalese coast there exists a well-established power structure based on traditional ascriptive criteria (social status is critically dependent on lineage and seniority under a strongly patriarchal system) combined with high wealth achievements (translated in fishing assets and wives).

The agricultural origin of the village where even today cultivation (of vegetables) remains an important activity for many fishermen's families especially during the lean fishing season largely accounts for the specific social structure of Kayar. It stands in stark contrast to Saint-Louis, for example, where fishermen are completely specialized in fishing activities and therefore migrate to other fishing grounds when fish disappear from the local waters or when the sea is too rough (see section 7.4.1). Apparently, fishing communities are traditionally less cohesive but also less hierarchically structured than peasant societies. Two reasons at least may account for this difference. For one thing, there are probably fewer needs for coordination in fishing societies because of a smaller range of externalities that are obvious for the people—external effects are much more complex in fishing than in agriculture so that people do not easily grasp them (see Baland and Platteau 1996: chap. 10; and Baland and Platteau 2005). And, for another thing, agricultural villages are typically founded by particular families or lineages that were first to "clear the bush" and delimit the corresponding land territory. As a consequence, they retain a dominant sociopolitical position because of their role as first settlers (see, e.g., Gruenais 1986: 290–91). Such is not the case in maritime fishing areas where the water space is not easily appropriable or delimitable by a particular lineage. Access is therefore more open and relationships between resource users more horizontal and decentralized.

Fourth, the dummy *youngmarrkay* represents another specific combination of age and marriage characteristics. It is equal to 1 when the fisherman is a relatively young person (between 24 and 35 years of age) who has one or several wives and is working in Kayar, while it is equal to 0 when he does not fall into that age category or does, yet is still a bachelor.[18] The significantly negative coefficient of *youngmarrkay* means that this category of presumably prosperous and dynamic young fishermen tends to have an optimistic appreciation of the fishermen's ability to enforce their regulatory measures (see appendix 7.2 for a more detailed tentative explanation).

On the other hand, the migrant-native divide in Kayar does not appear to influence the subjective perceptions of rule-breaking: the coefficient of the variable *migrantkayar*—a dummy with unit value when the fisherman is a (temporary) migrant from Saint-Louis operating in Kayar, and with zero value otherwise—is nonsignificant. The same holds true of education, here measured by another dummy variable called *education*, which takes on value 1 when the fisherman has more than either six years of koranic schooling or six years of primary school in French language, and 0 value otherwise.

7.4.3. Econometric Results: Impact of Heterogeneity on the Assessment of Effectiveness of Effort Regulation

Since attempts at effort regulation in Senegalese maritime communities were historically motivated by the objective of countering the fishmerchants' market power, fishermen were explicitly asked whether they believed that objective had been effectively attained, that is, whether catch limitations actually resulted in higher purchase prices. In addition, because there is increasing talk, at least in public meetings of various fishermen's organizations (such as the Collectif National des Pêcheurs Sénégalais and the Fédération des Groupements d'Intérêt Economique), about the need to reduce pressure on fish resources thought to be threatened with over-exploitation, we have also asked fishermen whether they believed that their effort restrictions were ecologically useful. The underlying idea is that opinions about the likely effects of such restrictions either have an important influence on the actual behavior of fishermen vis-à-vis the rules (provided, of course, that they are not otherwise constrained in their actions), or serve to rationalize their actions so as to prevent cognitive dissonance.

Of course, we are aware that the relationship may go in the reverse direction as well: not only do the above sort of opinions influence whether the fishermen who hold them act in support of, or try to circumvent, effort-limiting measures, but also past or ongoing experiences with effort regulation that are themselves shaped by such actions help determine opinions or beliefs regarding their potential impact. Unfortunately, to decipher fully the reciprocal causation network between opinions or beliefs, on the one hand, and actual experiences, on the other hand, is not a feasible operation because we have no way of imposing identifying restrictions on the determinants of either endogenous variable. As a consequence, we must be content with predicting opinions on the basis of predetermined individual characteristics of resource users, be it through direct or indirect effects. The effect is indirect insofar as opinions bear upon the actual outcome of an effort-limiting scheme which, in turn, influences those opinions.

In order to determine whether the various dimensions of heterogeneity discussed in section 7.4.1 bear upon fishermen's opinions regarding the two aforementioned effects, we have chosen to estimate a multinomial logit model in which three dummies appear as dependent variables in three successive regressions: *econly*, which is equal to 1 when the fisherman professed a belief in the economic but not in the biological effect, and which is equal to 0 otherwise; *bionly*, equal to 1 when the fisherman mentioned the biological but not the economic effect, and equal to 0 otherwise; and *ecobio*, equal to 1 when the fisherman pointed to the two effects simultaneously, and equal to 0 otherwise. The comparison group is composed of those fishermen who expressed clear skepticism about both the biological and economic effects of the regulatory measures. The objective pursued is therefore to identify factors susceptible to explaining adherence to the three other groups.

Eight dimensions of heterogeneity, most of which have been discussed in section 7.4.1, are tested for their possible influence on fishermen's subjective perceptions of the effectiveness of effort-limiting schemes and hence, presumably, on their willingness to abide by the rules set toward such a purpose. These are: heterogeneity in terms of fishing techniques; ownership of physical capital, skills, education, alternative income opportunities, bargaining power vis-à-vis fishmerchants, social status, and leadership; and feeling of identity with the fishing location (whether a permanent resident or a temporary migrant and, in the former case, whether born in the village or not). If not yet done, the way to measure these multiple facets of heterogeneity is explained while commenting on the results.

Two final methodological remarks are in order. To begin with, we have opted for estimating the model on the basis of the whole sample because, even in locations where no effort-limiting scheme has been attempted or where such attempts have been short-lived, fishermen are usually well-informed about experiences occurring in Kayar and Saint-Louis. Yet, fishermen operating beachseines are dropped on account of their small number so that the total sample size is 305 units. In the second place, in choosing the estimation method, we have allowed for the sequential nature of our sampling procedure (in a first step, a few villages were selected within which a number of households were thereafter randomly drawn). With such a procedure, observations drawn within the same village are not independent and standard errors of estimators must be corrected. The effect of the correction for clustered sampling is to increase confidence intervals of estimated coefficients. The results obtained are displayed in table 7.6.

Technical Heterogeneity

Two binary variables allow us to distinguish between the three dominant fishing techniques used (bear in mind that beachseines have been dropped): *purseseine* is a dummy equal to 1 when the technique operated by the fisherman is a purse seine, while *bottomset* is equal to 1

TABLE 7.6

Multinomial logit estimates of the determinants of fishermen's beliefs in economic and biological effects of effort regulation (all locations and all fisheries)

	Coef.	Std. Err.	t	P > |z|	[95% Conf. Interval]	
1. Econly						
Education	.0079904	.3044872	0.03	0.980	−.8374015	.8533824
Migrantkayar	−.4527731	.5477613	−0.83	0.455	−1.9736020	1.0680560
Migrantsoumb	(dropped)					
Purseseine	−.7285102	.7610674	−0.96	0.393	−2.8415720	1.3845520
Bottomset	−.3142599	.3761463	−0.84	0.450	−1.3586090	.7300896
Icebox	−1.3552940	.2750748	−4.93	0.008	−2.1190240	−.5915639
Longdistance	2.3719090	.8669874	2.74	0.052	−.0352338	4.7790520
Otherincome	−1.4565010	1.2206140	−1.19	0.299	−4.8454690	1.9324660
Assetowner	−.0738367	.2467887	−0.30	0.780	−.7590320	.6113586
Leaderkayar	(dropped)					
Exclusive	.3149284	.3351381	0.94	0.401	−.6155642	1.2454210
Constant	.5080996	.1935205	2.63	0.058	−.0291994	1.0453990
2. Bionly						
Education	.8538310	.3094064	2.76	0.051	−.0052188	1.7128810
Migrantkayar	−1.4352770	.3819341	−3.76	0.020	−2.4956960	−.3748577
Migrantsoumb	(dropped)					
Purseseine	−.2928476	1.5490180	−0.19	0.859	−4.5936110	4.0079160
Bottomset	−2.1752960	1.2614020	−1.72	0.160	−5.6775100	1.3269190
Icebox	−1.8451350	.3824510	−4.82	0.008	−2.9069890	−.7832806
Longdistance	2.1387670	1.3789450	1.55	0.196	−1.6897980	5.9673310
Otherincome	−.3215491	.5396202	−0.60	0.583	−1.8197750	1.1766770
Assetowner	−.2404457	.4711482	−0.51	0.637	−1.5485630	1.0676710
Leaderkayar	2.0204240	.6144186	3.29	0.030	.3145245	3.7263240
Exclusive	−.0444406	.1515883	−0.29	0.784	−.4653171	.3764360
Constant	−.4191433	.8593979	−0.49	0.651	−2.8052140	1.9669280
3. Ecobio						
Education	.4394644	.1218645	3.61	0.023	.1011143	.7778145
Migrantkayar	−2.1644220	.8367702	−2.59	0.061	−4.4876690	.1588241
Migrantsoumb	1.4591620	.5733784	2.54	0.064	−.1327919	3.0511150
Purseseine	−1.2903560	.9325765	−1.38	0.239	−3.8796030	1.2988910
Bottomset	−2.5690950	.5751594	−4.47	0.011	−4.1659940	−.9721969
Icebox	−2.9117620	.5207717	−5.59	0.005	−4.3576560	−1.4658680
Longdistance	2.5864510	.8455979	3.06	0.038	.2386951	4.9342070
Otherincome	.6416442	.3906145	1.64	0.176	−.4428755	1.7261640
Assetowner	−.1731293	.4025492	−0.43	0.689	−1.2907850	.9445266
Leaderkayar	1.8692700	.5683632	3.29	0.030	.2912410	3.4472990
Exclusive	−.3278897	.4289497	−0.76	0.487	−1.5188450	.8630656
Constant	1.2472330	.7166773	1.74	0.157	−.7425818	3.2370490

Number of obs   = 305
Number of strata = 1
Number of PSUs = 5
Population size   = 05
$F(1, 4)$ = 2.97
Prob > F   = 0.1597

when the technique concerned is the bottom-set net. Line fishing is therefore the reference category. From table 7.6, it is evident that the coefficient of *purseseine* is nonsignificant in all three regressions, indicating that, whether they fish with a purse seine or with hooks and lines, fishermen do not differ significantly in their appreciation of the effects of effort-restricting schemes. A straightforward reason for this lies in the above-explained fact that fishermen have succeeded in tailoring the measures adopted to the specific characteristics of these two techniques (see section 7.4.1).

On the other hand, not only is the coefficient of *bottomset* negative and significant (at the 99 percent confidence level) in the third regression, but it is also a rather large coefficient. Here again, we can easily account for such a result. As a matter of fact, bottom-set net operators are in direct conflict with purse seiners and line fishermen about the use of inshore waters, and this gear conflict has caused such a deep antagonism between the two categories of fishermen (in Kayar) that the former look with suspicion at all attempts made by the latter to regulate fishing effort (see section 7.4.1). It is therefore not surprising that they tend to hold negative views about the usefulness of such attempts.

Heterogeneity in Skills

We have available to us two proxies to measure heterogeneity in skills or, more precisely, to identify categories of comparatively dynamic fishermen. There is actually an overlap between such proxies and technical variables. First, we have the line fishermen who operate canoes equipped with ice boxes and are therefore able to undertake distant fishing voyages spanning several days. The corresponding variable is the dummy *icebox*, which is equal to 1 when the fisherman operates lines from a canoe equipped with an ice box, and to 0 otherwise. As can be seen from the table, the coefficient of this variable is negative and highly significant in all three regressions. Moreover, it has the largest value, close to −3.0, in the third regression. In other words, this category of particularly dynamic line fishermen are comparatively reluctant to admit to the advantages of effort limitation, whether economic or biological. This result no doubt reflects the aforementioned fact that these fishermen operate in conditions that make collective schemes of effort regulation especially hard to accept (see section 7.4.1). It therefore confirms the hypothesis of Johnson and Libecap according to which comparatively skilled or industrious and adventurous resource users tend to oppose a uniform quota system insofar as it hurts their specific interests.

Second, we have those fishermen who stated that they go farther and farther into the sea in order to target valuable species of exportable value (such as the rose sea bream known as the dentex). These fishermen can be considered to belong to the most dynamic and progressive sections of their fishing communities because they have responded to the 50 percent devaluation of the CFA (in 1994) by shifting to exportable species of fish, thereby showing their eagerness to seize upon new economic opportunities and their quick adaptability to changing circumstances. To isolate those fishermen, we have created a dummy variable called *longdistance*, which takes on unit value when the fisherman explicitly mentioned having made such a shift. The coefficient of *dist* turns out to be positive and significant in the first and third regressions, implying that profit-seeking and flexible fishermen have a marked tendency to stress the economic impact of catch limitations. The tendency is marked because the value of the coefficient is by far the largest in the first regression while being the second largest in the third one (hovering around 2.5).

Here is therefore a case where, contrary to expectations, progressive fishermen seem to strongly support uniform regulation of fishing effort. A plausible explanation behind this apparently puzzling finding is that the profitability of restrictive measures that result in a rise of unit producer prices is likely to increase with the initial level of these prices. Since this initial level is comparatively high in the case of exportable varieties, and since the uniform quotas applied to all line fishermen are specified in quantity rather than value terms, the interests of fishermen who target these varieties are not hurt by such quotas, as hypothesized by Johnson and Libecap. Economic analysis thus enables us to account for the different attitudes of two categories of dynamic fishermen vis-à-vis catch limitations: while fishermen undertaking long fishing voyages are reluctant to support catch quotas because of the considerable fixed costs involved by their mode of operation, those who target exportable varieties clearly support them because they stand to gain from measures that raise unit prices.

It bears emphasis that the majority of progressive fishermen targeting exportable varieties are line fishermen operating from Hann and Soumbedioune, that is, two locations with no real experience in effort limitation.[19] This may seem surprising since they could have conceivably acted as determined leaders in initiating and devising regulatory measures. However, one should not lose sight of the fact that Hann and Soumbedioune are both located in the Dakar area, with the consequence that they are strongly integrated into the most important fish market center (see section 7.3). Unless quota restrictions are tightly coordinated between the various fish landing sites in and around Dakar, no doubt a most difficult task, they have no chance of succeeding. Moreover, the presence in these two locations of long-distance line fishermen who are strongly opposed to effort regulation considerably complicates the problem of designing and enforcing catch limitations.[20] Here, heterogeneity of resource users therefore appears to form a serious impediment to collective action.

It bears noting that the two aforementioned dimensions of skill heterogeneity do not appear to be correlated with wealth inequality (the chisquare tests are not significant even at the 90 percent confidence level). In other words, if skilled fishermen presumably earn comparatively high incomes, being rather young, they did not yet have the time to accumulate enough assets to make them rich.

HETEROGENEITY IN OWNERSHIP STATUS

The coefficient of *assetowner*—a dummy equal to 1 when the fisherman is an owner of fishing assets and to 0 when he is a simple crew laborer— is nonsignificant in all three regressions, meaning that owners and crew laborers do not assess differently the impact of effort regulation. This result is entirely according to our expectation: the share system of labor remuneration in small-scale fisheries ensures that crew laborers participate in the benefits of any scheme that has the effect of raising fish prices.

HETEROGENEITY IN EDUCATIONAL ASSETS

The coefficient of *education* is significant and positive in the second and third regressions, meaning that more educated fishermen (with at least six years of French or Koranic school) are more inclined to signal the biological advantages of effort-restraining schemes, together with the economic advantages or not. This finding probably reflects the fact that people with a longer schooling experience have been more sensitized to the importance of environmental problems. Furthermore, a general effect of education is to combat fatalistic attitudes and to instill confidence in people's ability to influence their living conditions through various forms of purposeful collective action. This applies not only to environmental but also to social, political, and economic problems. In particular, educated people may better learn that producers can sometimes change market conditions through organizing collectively in order to reduce the power of merchants.

HETEROGENEITY IN TERMS OF ACCESS TO ALTERNATIVE INCOME OPPORTUNITIES

The variable *otherincome* is a binary variable with unit value if at least one member of the household earns income from an activity other than fishing (and this includes activities centered on the marketing of fish, or organizational activities that bring incomes), and/or when the household owns some agricultural land or more than one house (from which rental incomes can possibly be earned), and with zero value otherwise. Its coefficient is nonsignificant in all three regressions. However, it is worth noting that in the first regression the coefficient of *otherincome* is large and negative. Furthermore, it becomes statistically significant if the estimation is made without the correction for clustered sampling.[21] If that result is to be taken seriously, it would mean that fishermen with more alternative income possibilities are comparatively reluctant to admit the economic impact of regulatory schemes.

The prediction for such an impact is admittedly ambiguous. On the one hand, when they can rely on complementary sources of income, fishermen are expected to be more supportive of effort regulation because they are better able to endure the loss of fishing incomes in the short or medium term so as to benefit from higher incomes in the long term.[22] Yet, on the other hand, fishermen with greater alternative income opportunities may pay less attention to their fishing incomes and feel less ready to incur sacrifices in order to increase them. This is all the more so if alternative incomes originate in fish marketing (usually by the fishermen's wives), since gains accruing to fishermen under the form of increased unit prices must then be weighed against the losses suffered by fishmongers within the household.

HETEROGENEITY IN TERMS OF BARGAINING POWER VIS-À-VIS FISHMERCHANTS

The coefficient of *exclusive* is nonsignificant in all three regressions, indicating that the beliefs of fishermen involved in sales-tying debts with merchants do not differ from those of other fishermen regarding the effectiveness of catch limitations.

HETEROGENEITY IN TERMS OF SOCIAL STATUS AND LEADERSHIP

The coefficient of *leaderkayar* is positive (exhibiting a relatively large value of about 2.0) and significant in the second and third regressions, meaning that the Kayar elite have a marked tendency to acknowledge the economic and the biological effects.[23] Such a result is not surprising in the light of what has been already said about their critical role in the initiation and implementation of the effort-limiting schemes. What deserves to be added here is that the Olsonian argument cannot be reasonably invoked to explain the leadership role played by comparatively wealthy fishermen. As a matter of fact, because of the large number of fishermen concerned by the regulatory measures in Kayar as well as the relatively low degree of concentration of asset ownership in the hands of the individual members of the local elite (who are heavily represented among purse-seine own-ers),[24] there is no way the benefits internalized by the latter can realistically cover the costs of initiating collective regulation, unless, of course, they could form a kind of coalition. The involvement of the elite in a variety of other activities suggests that political dividends as well as gains in terms of social recognition and prestige are important benefits that comparatively wealthy fishermen hopefully derive from their leadership role. Equally im-portant is their ability to assert their standing beyond the village commu-nity and to improve their profile in wider spheres of interaction and in-fluence. Various sorts of perks distributed by foreign funding agencies (whether private or public) or their local partner institutions (such as Non-Governmental Organizations), and sometimes also by their own gov-ernment, constitute an attractive reward for village leaders (see Abraham and Platteau 2002; in the same vein, see Johnson 2001: 968–9).[25]

HETEROGENEITY IN TERMS OF SOCIAL IDENTITY

Finally, let us look at the influence of the native-migrant divide on the beliefs and assumed behavior of Senegalese fishermen vis-à-vis regula-tory measures, whether they actually exist or not in their village. There are two results here. For one thing, we find that temporary migrant fish-ermen (from Saint-Louis) operating in Kayar tend to have a more pes-simistic appraisal of the effectiveness of these measures than resident fishermen, as evidenced by the negative and significant signs of the coef-ficients of *migrantkayar* in the second and third regressions (the coeffi-cient has a rather high value in the last regression).

It is interesting to note that the beliefs of fishermen native of Saint-Louis but permanently settled in Kayar do not differ from those of fishermen na-tive of Kayar. In this case, therefore, the true source of heterogeneity is nei-ther the ethnic origin (both Kayar and Saint-Louis are inhabited by Wolof people) nor the native location of the operating fishermen, but the tran-sient or permanent character of the residence of migrant fishermen in Ka-yar. While stranger fishermen permanently settled in the latter location seem to identify themselves with the host community (they share the same opinions and beliefs), those who return every year to Saint-Louis once the fishing season starts there appear to distinguish themselves from the per-manent residents of Kayar, whether native of Kayar or Saint-Louis.

For another thing, temporary migrant fishermen (again from Saint-Louis) operating in Soumbedioune have a marked proclivity to stress both the economic and biological effects of catch restrictions compared with residents. Indeed, the coefficient of *migrantsoumb*—a dummy equal to 1 when the fisherman has this characteristic, and equal to 0 otherwise—is significant and positive in the third regression.[26] It is thus remarkable that migrant fishermen originating from the same fishing site have a different assessment of the usefulness of regulatory schemes according to whether they operate in Kayar or in Soumbedioune.

Such a difference presumably reflects the deep antagonism between migrant and resident fishermen born of the protracted conflict around the use of bottom-set nets in the former area. Owing to the absence of bottom-set nets, such a conflict could not occur in the latter area. Clearly, divergent opinions and conflicting behaviors between migrant and resident fishermen in Kayar arise from economic considerations all the more important as livelihoods of both groups are at stake. That permanent residents native of Saint-Louis align themselves with local fishermen despite the fact that some of them use bottom-set nets is indicative of their willingness to be fully integrated in the host community. Their long-term economic security indeed depends on successful integration and guaranteed access to local fishing waters and housing sites. As for the fact that migrants in Soumbedioune are even more supportive of effort restrictions than residents, it is probably due to their having been exposed to the experience of such restrictions in Saint-Louis where market conditions are more conducive to effective regulation than in landing sites in and around Dakar (see section 7.4.1). Note again that migrants permanently settled in Soumbedioune tend to hold the same beliefs as native fishermen.

7.4.4. Econometric Results: Characteristics of Fishermen with a Positive Attitude Vis-à-Vis a Centralized Sales Organization

Fishermen were not only asked what they think about the effects of the effort-limiting schemes attempted in some of their communities, but also whether they believe they could personally benefit from the setting up in their village of a centralized organization handling the sale of all the fish catches (in the way it is done in Joal for the octopus). A logit model identifying the characteristics of fishermen who support or do not support the creation of such an organization yields unexpectedly good results. Those results are reported in table 7.7 in which the dependent variable, labeled *cooperative*, is a binary variable set to 1 when the fisherman expresses support, and to 0 when he does not. All explanatory variables, except *experience* (a dummy equal to 1 when the fisherman resides in a location where catch limitations have been attempted, and to 0 otherwise), have already been defined.

The most striking finding is that, unlike what we observed in the case of catch limitations, crew workers do not share the same view as the owners of fishing assets. Indeed, they appear to be more skeptical than the latter about the improvement that a centralized sale organization could bring to them: the coefficient of *assetowner* is positive and statis-

TABLE 7.7
Logit Estimates of the Determinants of Fishermen's Support for a Centralized Marketing
Organization (all locations and all fisheries)

Cooperative	Coef.	Std. Err.	t	P > |z|	[95% Conf. Interval]	
Experience	.3756765	.2247917	1.67	0.170	−.2484455	.9997984
Education	.3618228	.1769650	2.04	0.110	−.1295109	.8531566
Migrantkayar	−.9268388	.1519190	−6.10	0.004	−1.3486340	−.5050440
Migrantsoumb	−1.3760290	.1755403	−7.84	0.001	−1.8634070	−.8886508
Rulebreaking	.4981396	.1770018	2.81	0.048	.0067037	.9895755
Purseseine	−.7546134	.3625698	−2.08	0.106	−1.7612680	.2520417
Icebox	.2883149	.4934009	0.58	0.590	−1.0815860	1.6582150
Bottomset	.5885141	.2960060	1.99	0.118	−.2333303	1.4103590
Otherincome	−.4628535	.4659469	−0.99	0.377	−1.7565290	.8308225
Longdistance	−.9130836	.4372171	−2.09	0.105	−2.1269930	.3008257
Leaderkayar	1.7936540	.3540416	5.07	0.007	.8106766	2.7766310
Youngmarrkay	−.8992853	.3008078	−2.99	0.040	−1.7344620	−.0641090
Assetowner	.6599143	.2203570	2.99	0.040	.0481051	1.2717240
Exclusive	−.1906008	.3657172	−0.52	0.630	−1.2059950	.8247929
Constant	.5159037	.4925212	1.05	0.354	−.8515544	1.8833620

Number of obs   = 305
Number of strata = 1
Number of PSUs = 5
Population size   = 305
F(3, 2)   =
Prob > F   =

tically significant. A plausible explanation behind this skepticism lies in the fact that a sales organization, so they believe, is likely to create opportunities for asset owners, in collusion with managers, to underreport prices to their crew laborers and thereby rob them of part of their due share of the catch proceeds. Open, competitive sales carried out on the beach are much more transparent than those that would be run through a centralized organization. In other words, the widespread fear among simple crew workers of collusive practices between owners and fishmerchants creates a collective-action failure in the field of fish marketing.

Other interesting findings emerge from table 7.7. In particular, progressive fishermen bent on catching valuable species in distant fishing grounds (those for whom *longdistance* = 1) tend to oppose a marketing organization (yet the level of statistical significance is only 90 percent). This contrasts with their positive attitude toward catch quotas. There is, of course, no contradiction here since the two methods to achieve higher producer prices are entirely different and there are solid reasons to believe that implementing an effort-restraining scheme is a much less arduous task than building up and managing a viable sales organization. The same negative attitude regarding the impact of such an organization is shared by comparatively young and prosperous fishermen (for whom *youngmarrkay* takes on a unit value).

On the other hand, leaders from Kayar show a strong support for centralized marketing of fish landings (note the high value of the coefficient of *leaderkayar* which is significant at the 99 percent confidence level) that they were actually trying at the time of the survey and strongly defended in public meetings (which we attended) in spite of the serious problems that we pointed out to them.[27] Their attitude seems to be one of indiscriminate support for any sort of collective action that unites fishermen. Just the opposite is the attitude of (temporary) migrants from Saint-Louis operating in Kayar who tend to resist any idea of collective action whether it concerns catch limitations or centralized selling of the landings. This time, however, we find migrants operating from Soumbedioune also skeptical about the likely benefits of a centralized sale organization. In both cases, the level of statistical significance is high (99 percent) and the values of the coefficients are the second and third largest in the regression behind that of *leaderkayar*.

An additional result is the positive influence of the *rulebreaking* variable. The fact that fishermen who have a pessimistic stance about enforcement of catch quotas tend to have a positive attitude toward the establishment of a marketing organization is not really surprising. For them, it seems, the latter provides an alternative organizational form which would hopefully raise fishermen's incomes more effectively than quotas. Finally, fishermen operating purse seines tend to have a negative opinion about the role of a sales organization compared to other fishermen. The explanation lies in the characteristics of the produce. Indeed, the demersal species caught by fishermen operating lines and bottom-set nets are luxury products that can be sold directly by a fishermen's organization to specialized export companies. The same cannot be said of the pelagic species harvested by purse seines which are mainly destined for domestic markets (and other African countries) and necessitate a complex and decentralized network of fishmerchants operating at wholesale and retail levels.

7.5. SUMMARY OF FINDINGS AND CONCLUSION

Given that attempts at effort limitation in Senegalese small-scale fisheries have been clearly motivated by economic rather than by ecological considerations (for a similar conclusion regarding a Thai fishery, see Johnson 2001: 956, 972), and by output price rather than input price considerations, it is evident that such attempts cannot yield satisfactory effects if demand is perfectly elastic with respect to prices, such as happens under well-integrated markets approximating perfect competition. It is revealing that effort restrictions tend to have been longer sustained precisely in the areas and the fisheries in which negative price-effort elasticities have been observed. It is nevertheless useful to inquire into the complementary role of various dimensions of group heterogeneity that are likely to shape fishermen's attitudes toward effort regulation. This is so not only because a conducive market structure is a necessary but not sufficient condition of successful regulation, but also because fishermen, at least in the short run, do not arguably have a good understanding of the critical role of the prevailing market structure (they might thus embark upon nonsustainable effort-limiting efforts).

What then are the main lessons to be drawn from our inquiry, bearing in mind that our results are based on opinions privately expressed by fishermen in a sample of locations and fisheries that may or may not have succeeded in laying down and implementing effort-restricting rules during a significant period of time?

To begin with, *wealth inequality* does not appear to have been a serious impediment to collective action. In the most successful case, that of Kayar, the evidence actually points to the positive role of the wealthy local elite made of prosperous polygamous elders who often enjoyed high positions in the traditional social structure. Such a finding, however, does not bear out the Olsonian hypothesis according to which wealthier resource users may be more willing to initiate and organize collective action because they internalize a comparatively large share of the expected benefits. (Bear in mind that effort restrictions under all existing schemes are strictly proportional to the asset base.) Political dividends, social prestige, and various economic perks seem to be the real motive prompting Kayar's elite to bear the costs of initiating collective regulation.

Moreover, the division between owners of fishing assets and simple crew workers does not hamper the effectiveness of effort limitations: other things being equal, the latter are as supportive as the former of attempts in that direction. This is not surprising at all since a large part of labor remuneration is calculated as a proportion of the proceeds from the sale of the catches. Interestingly, crew laborers distrust a centralized sales organization which they fear could be run at their expense due to malpractices of fishmerchants acting in concert with asset owners.

Insofar as inequality in asset ownership is reflected in the fact that poorer owners are indebted to fishmerchants to whom they have committed their landings while more well-to-do owners remain free from such sales-tying debts, it is bound to hamper collective action. The evidence here is compelling: in fisheries or locations where the proportion of fishermen entangled in credit-cum-marketing relationships is quite large, no regulatory measures have been attempted. Yet, it is noticeable that there is no correlation between indebtedness to fishmerchants and wealth. On the other hand, wealth inequality appears to have aroused opposition to effort regulation when, as was observed in Saint-Louis, it was organized in such a way as to undermine customary insurance mechanisms operating through work-sharing practices.

Technical heterogeneity is potentially an important obstacle to collective organization. This is most vividly illustrated by the failing attempts to share the fishing space of Kayar's in-shore waters between operators of passive gears and those of active gears. As far as catch-restricting schemes are concerned, however, the problem of technical heterogeneity has been generally well overcome by devising measures specific to each fishery or technique so that peculiar characteristics could be taken into account (the case of Kayar again comes to mind here). A major problem nevertheless remains with long-distance line fishermen (all found near Dakar) who are opposed to effort restrictions out of fixed-cost considerations. Their attitude is at variance with that of other line fishermen who are involved in one-day fishing trips and essentially target the same species. Here, as attested by the absence of schemes in the area of Dakar, heterogeneity appears to be a major stumbling block in the way of collective regulation of fishing effort. Note moreover that the effort-limiting scheme applied to line fishing involves more monitoring problems than that applied to purse-seine fishing (hence the larger incidence of rule-breaking in the former fishery), an unavoidable result arising from different technical conditions. The fact that Kayar's leadership is almost entirely made of purse-seine fishermen explains why effort-limiting measures were started among this category of fishermen, thereafter to be extended to line fishing, where conditions are less suitable for effective enforcement of these measures in spite of their potentially higher benefits.

The native-migrant divide has proven a rather intractable problem in the otherwise successful case of Kayar. Nonetheless, it bears noting that the difficulties encountered within regulatory schemes enforced for operators of lines and purse seines among whom there are both native and migrant fishermen—the latter being much less supportive of the schemes than the former—are largely an upshot of a deep antagonism originating elsewhere. This is the acute and prolonged conflict that has always opposed these two categories of fishermen around the use of passive gears (bottom-set nets) which are exclusively operated by fishermen from Saint-Louis against the will of native people. In other words, the problematic factor here is the polarization that has been caused by the total specialization of migrant fishermen in the debatable technique. Confirmation of this interpretation is provided by the available evidence for a fishing village located near Dakar (Soumbedioune) where, as a matter of principle, migrant operators did not show less support for regulatory measures than native operators. In this instance, indeed, no polarization process has been created by the use of passive gears that are not suitable in this area. Lastly, migrants from Saint-Louis who have permanently settled in Kayar seem to have identified themselves with the local people rather than with temporary migrants from their native area, which makes good sense in terms of long-term considerations of economic security.

Skill heterogeneity is potentially the most serious hurdle standing in the way of effective collective regulation. It is also a dimension of heterogeneity that is not easy to observe or measure because people are not willing to disclose their assessment of relative rankings in terms of competence or skills. This said, we are fortunate enough to have available to us two good (partial) proxies of skills: (line) fishermen who have quickly adapted to a substantial devaluation of the CFA money (in 1994) by shifting to exportable species, and long-distance (line) fishermen. The former category of fishermen are strong supporters of effort-restricting measures. In fact, the standard argument that comparatively skilled resource users are susceptible to losing most from uniform catch quotas and should therefore oppose them does not apply in the case under study. The reason is straightforward: since they target the most valuable (exportable) species and since quotas are set in quantity terms, they are actually the most likely to gain from unit price increases possibly resulting from collusive practices among producers.

As for long-distance fishermen, opposition rather than support regarding catch quotas is the rule. Such a difference between the two categories of relatively progressive and skilled line fishermen is perfectly explainable in terms of economic analysis: indeed, while the interests of adaptive fishermen are not hurt by uniform quotas (specified in quantity rather than value terms), those of long-distance fishermen are especially hurt owing to the presence of sizable fixed costs. In terms of cost structure, there is indeed a considerable difference between, on the one hand, the one-day fishing trips undertaken by dynamic fishermen eager to capture new profit opportunities even if that involves going far out at sea and, on the other hand, the one-week trips undertaken by those who operate canoes equipped with ice boxes.

Finally, *heterogeneity in terms of access to alternative income sources and in terms of educational achievements* does not appear to bear upon the attitudes of the fishermen toward effort regulation. In the case of the former, this result is not really surprising. If alternative income opportunities take on the form of fish marketing occupations, indeed, divergence of interests is likely to arise within households regarding the desirability of fish supply restrictions.

To conclude, heterogeneity of resource users is not as damaging for collective action, effort regulation in particular, as one could have anticipated. First, specific characteristics or circumstances may neutralize the potentially negative effects of heterogeneity, such as observed in the case of dynamic line fishermen who started to target comparatively valuable species in response to money devaluation. Second, the adverse impact of heterogeneity may be partly overcome or circumvented through deliberate efforts to adapt catch limitations to the specific conditions of each category of users, that is, to devise differentiated regulation methods. That such a strategy encounters limits is nevertheless attested by the difficulty to take account of the peculiar interests of long-distance operators within the category of line fishermen. Third, the native-migrant divide is a source of problems only when native and migrant fishermen are polarized into conflicting fishing techniques or patterns of resource use. Moreover, conflicts opposing native and migrant fishermen in a problematic arena tend to create a negative externality that undermines the reaching of consensus regarding regulatory schemes in other domains of resource use. Fourth, inequality of wealth does not necessarily make collective action more difficult if the wealthier users provide the required leadership. Fifth, class differentiation between asset owners and crew laborers does not constitute an obstacle to effort regulation because the prevailing remuneration system causes the interests of both categories to actually converge.

Appendix 7.1. Estimating Inverse Demand Functions for Various Species of Fish and Various Locations

Estimating demand elasticity is usually a tricky operation because prices and quantities are simultaneously determined by supply and demand. Fishing is nevertheless a special activity in this regard: when sellers meet buyers on the shore, it is too late to adjust the quantity. On the other hand, the possibility of conserving fish in freezing facilities enables speculation although it does not leave the quality of the product unaffected. Expected future prices must clearly enter the determinants of demand if this effect is to be taken seriously. This reintroduces a simultaneity problem in the demand curve, insofar as future prices may be a function of current prices. Fortunately, past prices and seasonal dummies provide good exogenous variables to instrument for expected future prices. Besides quantity and expected future prices, prices of substitute goods also affect demand. These are of course endogenous (since a good is a substitute of its substitutes) and can be instrumented for on the basis of past values and seasonal dummies as well.

On the basis of these considerations, we assume that market data are generated by a three-step process. First, fishermen form an expectation of the day-price on the basis of past prices and of the season. Second, quantities are determined by the joint effect of the fishermen's willingness to sell at the expected price and of a random shock. And, third, actual prices are fixed by the demand curve. Two points deserve to be made at the present stage. On the one hand, we have no special hypothesis to test about step 2 in this process. Indeed, supply curves may well be positively sloped or backward bending since they involve choices between labor and leisure that are known to exhibit a wide variety of possible patterns. On the other hand, besides our main hypothesis that demand curves have an elasticity below −1, we want to test whether expectations may be formed with a high degree of accuracy in step 1. This is actually a condition for an efficient computation of the target level of aggregate output: if prices are not correctly anticipated, a cartel is bound to fail because day-to-day losses are not likely to be compensated by gains on the average if fishermen are not perfectly patient.

Mathematically speaking, we are estimating the following system of equations:

(expectations) $P_t = \alpha + \beta^* s + \gamma^* B(P) + u_t$,   with $P_t^e = P_t - u_t$

(supply) $\log Q_t = \delta + \varepsilon^* \log P_t^e + v_t$

(inverse demand) $\log P_t = \phi + \rho^* \log Q_t + \sigma^* \log P_{t+1}^e$
$$+ \theta^* \log P_t^{\text{subst}} + w_t$$

where P_t is the price at time t; s is a vector of eleven dummy variables representing the month of the year; $B(P)$ is a vector of lagged prices (the number of lags is chosen through a standard ARIMA procedure, i.e., by inspecting correlograms; typically, 0 or 1 lag is used); Q_t is the quantity at time t; u, v, and w are normally distributed residuals (with seasonal heteroscedasticity); parameters to be estimated include β and γ, which are real vectors, and α, δ, ε, ϕ, and p, which are real numbers.

An inverse demand curve is estimated because observation errors occur frequently in prices and rather infrequently in quantities; it is safer to let those errors appear in the residuals of an inverse demand function than to estimate a demand curve with a stochastic regressor (remember that expected future prices and prices of substitute goods are replaced by an instrumental variable in this equation).

APPENDIX 7.2. IDENTIFICATION OF FISHERMEN ACCORDING TO THEIR ASSESSMENT OF ENFORCEMENT PERFORMANCES

In order to determine the characteristics of the fishermen who believe that the incidence of rule-breaking is large, we started by estimating a logit model in which explanatory variables include an indicator of wealth;

TABLE A7.2.1
Logit Estimate of the Determinants of Fishermen's Beliefs Regarding the Extent of Rule-Breaking

Rulebreaking	Coef.	Std. Err.	z	P > |z|	[95% Conf. Interval]	
Assetowner	−.1421856	.5423711	−0.262	0.793	−1.205213	.9208421
Migrantkayar	−.4854577	.6086912	−0.798	0.425	−1.678470	.7075551
Education	.7311907	.4189728	1.745	0.081	−.0899809	1.5523620
Age	.0269207	.0195801	1.375	0.169	−.0114556	.0652971
Wives	−.6393262	.3257245	−1.963	0.050	−1.2777350	−.0009178
Purseseine	−.8468396	.4076245	−2.077	0.038	−1.6457690	−.0479103
Exclusive	.9533989	.5235918	1.821	0.069	−.0728222	1.9796200
Constant	−.5938881	.6224267	−0.954	0.340	−1.8138220	.6260458

Log Likelihood = −76.883164

Number of obs = 127
chi2(7)   = 18.80
Prob > chi2 =   0.0088
Pseudo R2   =   0.1090

the continuous variable *wives*, which measures the number of wives of the fisherman; an indicator of the age of the fisherman; another continuous variable, *age*, measured in years; and the variables *assetowner, exclusive, purseseine, migrantkayar,* and *education*, which have already been defined in the text. Note incidentally that there is not much meaning in introducing location variables because there is perfect correlation between technique and fishing site in two of the three villages (only purse seines are regulated in Saint-Louis and only lines in Yoff). The results of this first attempt are shown in table A7.2.1.

A striking finding is that, controlling for age, fishermen with more wives, that is, comparatively rich fishermen, tend to be relatively optimistic regarding rule violations. Yet, when the age variable is dropped, the coefficient of the wealth variable ceases to be statistically significant. A close look at the data brings out the statistical clue behind this puzzle. There are indeed two specific ways in which age and number of wives interact to produce an effect on the assessment of rule-breaking. (i) For one thing, such assessment is comparatively low among rather old fishermen (more than 47 years) who have three wives: only 21 percent of them believe that there are many rule violations compared with a proportion of 44 percent for all other categories taken together. It bears emphasizing that the above-noted difference of attitude is perceptible only in the village of Kayar: when Yoff and Saint-Louis are considered separately from Kayar, there is no remaining effect of age and number of wives. In other words, the leadership phenomenon is even more marked in Kayar than what the above figures indicate.

TABLE A7.2.2
Assessment of Extent of Rule-Breaking According to Certain Age and
Marriage Characteristics, All Villages (Kayar, Yoff, Saint-Louis) and
Kayar Only (figures in parenthesis)

Age and Marriage Characteristics	Proportion of Fishermen Stating a Large Incidence of Rule-Breaking
a. Aged 24–35 years and unmarried	57% (64%)
b. Aged 24–35 years and married	32% (15%)
c. More than 35 years old and married but excluding people of category (e) below	50% (44%)
d. More than 35 years old and married	43% (31%)
e. More than 47 years old and three wives	21% (10%)
f. Total average	42% (38%)

(ii) For another thing, it appears that fishermen who have one or several wives before reaching 36 years of age have a lower propensity to state high rates of rule-breaking than unmarried fishermen belonging to the same age class or than older married fishermen. Thus, 32 percent of married fishermen aged between 24 and 35 years (marriages before 24 years are exceptional) have deemed violations of effort-limiting prescriptions to be pervasive as against 57 percent of those unmarried in the same age bracket and against 50 percent of married fishermen older than 36 years but excluding those older than 47 years with three wives (bear in mind that unmarried fishermen older than 36 years are very few). Again, this relationship vanishes as soon as Kayar is left out of the picture. When this village is considered separately, differences in the above proportions are quite pronounced: the proportions of Kayar's fishermen reporting a large extent of rule-breaking are 15 percent for those married in the 24–35 age category, 64 percent for those unmarried in the same category, and 44 percent for married fishermen older than 36 years but excluding the presumed leaders (more than 47 years with three wives).[28]

Table A7.2.2 summarizes these findings in the light of which it is now possible to improve upon the initial econometric model. Toward that purpose, we give up the rather rough explanatory variables measuring the fishermen's age and number of wives and replace them by the *leaderkayar* and *youngmarrkayar* dummies (see the main text for definition). The new results are displayed in table A7.2.3.

One of the expected effects is borne out by the new estimate: the coefficient of the *youngmarrkay* variable is significant at a 95 percent level of confidence. This is not true of the *leaderkayar* variable, which is not significant at the 90 percent level of confidence. There is, however, a straight-

TABLE A7.2.3

A New Logit Estimate of the Determinants of Fishermen's Beliefs Regarding the Extent of Rule-Breaking

Rulebreaking	Coef.	Std. Err.	z	P > |z|	[95% Conf. Interval]	
Assetowner	−.4069745	.4145090	−0.982	0.326	−1.2193970	.4054481
Migrantkayar	−.3085531	.6094500	−0.506	0.613	−1.5030530	.8859469
Education	.6617543	.4264266	1.552	0.121	−.1740264	1.4975350
Leaderkayar	−1.6861250	1.1313190	−1.490	0.136	−3.9034700	.5312191
Youngmarrkayar	−1.6960000	.8687579	−1.952	0.051	−3.3987340	.0067345
Purseseine	−1.0256980	.4266358	−2.404	0.016	−1.8618890	−.1895070
Exclusive	1.0024790	.5381882	1.863	0.063	−.0523505	2.0573090
Constant	.1627518	.4070024	0.400	0.689	−.6349582	.9604618

Log Likelihood = −75.335438

Number of obs = 127
chi2(7)   =   21.90
Prob > chi2   =   0.0026
Pseudo R2   =   0.1269

TABLE A7.2.4

A New Logit Estimate of the Determinants of Fishermen's Beliefs Regarding the Extent of Rule-Breaking (ownership variable omitted)

Rulebreaking	Coef.	Std. Err.	z	P > |z|	[95% Conf. Interval]	
Migrantkayar	−.3441515	.6098426	−0.564	0.573	−1.5394210	.8511181
Education	.5771422	.4131097	1.397	0.162	−.2325380	1.3868220
Leaderkayar	−1.8969440	1.1061750	−1.715	0.086	−4.0650070	.2711190
Youngmarrkayar	−1.6990020	.8667965	−1.960	0.050	−3.3978920	−.0001124
Purseseine	−.9869905	.4222457	−2.337	0.019	−1.8145770	−.1594042
Exclusive	.9430304	.5326338	1.771	0.077	−.1009126	1.9869730
Constant	.0151894	.3768604	0.040	0.968	−.7234434	.7538221

Log Likelihood = −75.822999

Number of obs = 127
chi2(6)   =   20.92
Prob > chi2   =   0.0019
Pseudo R2   =   0.1213

forward statistical explanation for this disappointing result, namely that the leadership variable is strongly correlated with all the other variables present in the equation, except, of course, the *youngmarrkay* variable. It is therefore easy to make the *leaderkayar* variable become statistically significant by removing some correlated variable(s). This is done in table A7.2.4 where the *assetowner* variable has been left out, which is sufficient to cause the coefficient of *leaderkayar* to become significant. On the other hand, while the coefficient of *education* was significant in table A7.2.1, it is no more so in tables A7.2.3 and A7.2.4.

NOTES

1. A purse seine is a net characterized by the use of a purse line at the bottom of the net. The purse line allows the net to be closed like a purse and to thus retain all the fish caught. The purse seines, which can be very large, are operated by one or two boats. A bottom-set net is a gillnet, that is, a type of gear that serves to gill, entangle, or enmesh the fish. Gillnets may be used to catch fish on the surface, in midwater, or on the bottom. In the latter case, one speaks of bottom-set nets.

2. This commission is composed of four members, namely the chief of the local fisheries administration, the head of the local gendarmerie squad, and one representative of each fishing community (resident and migrant fishermen).

3. The commission had received a canoe equipped with an outboard engine for surveillance operations, yet the boat could not be operated because of a lack of working capital for fuel expenses and maintenance of the equipment.

4. Although smaller than the average, the expansion of the artisanal fishing fleet in the most important ports remains quite impressive: 33 percent in the Cap Vert (Dakar) area, 31 percent in the Grande Côte, and 8 percent in the Petite Côte (CRODT 1998: table 38; CRODT and DOPM 1998: table 11).

5. Pelagic fishes spend most of their life swimming in the water column and have little contact with or dependency on the bottom. Pelagic fishes are often species that have reached their adult stage. By contrast, demersal fishes live in close relation with the bottom and depend on it.

6. In Kayar, for example, we could interview only seventeen crew laborers operating purse seines while the initial intent was to include as many as thirty of them in the sample. In Saint-Louis, the sample of crew laborers fishing with lines is only eight people instead of the fifteen initially scheduled. The worst case is that of the crew operating bottom-set nets in the same site (seven fishermen interviewed instead of the twenty operators planned in the study sample scheme).

7. This is in spite of the well-documented fact that pressure on fish resources has increased significantly during the last decades, particularly on bottom-dwelling species living in coastal waters which are considered to be overexploited (Barry-Gérard, Kebe, and Thiam 1992; Barry-Gerard, Fonteneau, and Diouf 1992). As for coastal pelagic species, biologists of the Centre de Recherche Oceanographique de Dakar-Thiaroye (CRODT) believe that they are rapidly nearing optimum exploitation. Public authorities are increasingly aware of the threat on fish resources as evidenced by the fact that the notion of "biological rest" has been recently introduced in the fishing agreement struck with the European Community for the period 1997–2001.

8. Note that values smaller than -1 for inverse demand elasticities would imply that equilibrium catches are equal to zero.

9. Thus, at least some fishermen leaders from Soumbedioune wanted to emulate the experience of Kayar without realizing the differences in the market environment between the two areas. And fishermen leaders from Kayar complained about recent trends of diminishing fish prices in spite of their effort restrictions. Still, the measures were not called into question.

10. It is a second-best method because fishermen are encouraged to circumvent the limitation by lengthening the fishing time and increasing the productivity of each permitted trip, say through the use of more performing nets.

11. Enforcement of regulatory measures is supported by sanction systems that are essentially similar between the fishing sites. In Kayar, when a canoe equipped with a purse seine is found exceeding the limit of one fishing trip per day, the rule provides that a fine of 100,000 CFA is imposed on the owner. If he refuses to comply, the canoe and the net are confiscated till he pays the fine, and they can be sold in case of prolonged default. However, grace delays to pay the fine are extendable to 10–15 days when the rule-breaker is a well-known fisherman with solvency problems. The same system applies to canoes equipped with lines: concealment of fish boxes exceeding the allowed quota is punished by a fine amounting to 50,000 CFA. In Saint-Louis, the amount of the fine imposed on rule-violators is 50,000 CFA and, as a matter of principle, the owner of the purse seine at fault is not permitted to go back to sea unless he has paid the fine. In Yoff, the amount of the fine is 30,000 CFA for line fishermen exceeding their quota (compared to 50,000 CFA in Kayar).

12. Note that we have also asked fishermen whether they have themselves violated the rules, yet the answers are unreliable and will therefore be ignored (only 9 out of 127 fishermen in the restricted sample confessed to having done so).

13. According to the Fisher test, the difference between line- and purse-seine fishermen is statistically significant at a 2 percent level of confidence.

14. Note that fishermen from Kayar are essentially from the same ethnic background (Wolof people) as those of Saint-Louis.

15. Thus, in his study of a small-scale fishery in Thailand, Johnson (2001) points out that "when talking about the declining catch, for instance, villagers would almost universally associate blame with the push nets and trawlers that operated in the area." The idea largely prevailed that "the fishing problem was the work of a capitalist, predominantly Sino-Thai constituency on Phuket. . . . By framing the resistance in this way, villagers were able to direct the movement against a non-Muslim, predominantly non-rural constituency. In so doing, they could both improve group cohesion and construct a political project in which the costs of change were allocated *outside* the village community" (p. 968). In a similar vein, see Baland and Platteau 1996: chap. 10; Platteau 2000: chap. 3.

16. Since only these two techniques have been submitted to an effort-limiting scheme, a single binary variable is sufficient to measure technical heterogeneity.

17. If we would add another dummy variable to determine whether the fisherman is an equipment owner or a simple crew laborer, the coefficient of *leaderkayar* would just stop being significant (more precisely, it would be significant at an 86 percent level of confidence only). This is again due to multicollinearity since all leaders in Kayar are equipment owners. It is worth emphasizing that, when this new dummy variable is introduced in the regression, the value of the coefficient of *leaderkayar* remains quite stable.

18. To arrive at the specific combinations of age and marriage characteristics represented by the *leaderkayar* and the *youngmarrkayar* variables, we have actually followed a progressive procedure that is more fully described in appendix 7.2.

19. More exactly, while their overall proportion is 11 percent in the whole sample, they form more than one-third of line fishermen operating canoes equipped with ice boxes in Hann and Soumbedioune; about one-fifth of line fishermen operating simple canoes in Kayar, Hann, and Soumbedioune; and one-fifth of purse-seine fishermen in Hann.

20. Fishermen operating canoes equipped with ice boxes are present in Hann and Soumbedioune but not in Kayar and Saint-Louis.

21. Interestingly, this is the only result that differs between the two econometric estimates—the one with and the one without the correction for clustered sampling.

22. Larger incomes may accrue in the medium or long term to the fishermen because of increased market power or better conservation of fish resources.

23. The *leaderkayar* variable is dropped in the first regression because no leader has signaled the economic effect only.

24. It is noteworthy that the average number of purse-seine fishing units owned by members of the elite (as defined by our *leaderkayar* variable) works out to 3.111 to be compared with 1.873 for the other owners. In addition, 45 percent of the purse-seine owners belong to Kayar's elite according to our definition (statistic inferred from our sample data).

25. Thus, leaders belonging to fishermen's organizations do sometimes travel abroad upon the invitation of various nongovernmental organizations in the Northern Hemisphere and international agencies such as the European Community. They also gain privileged access to logistical means (e.g., vehicles, telephones) put at the disposal of their organization by foreign funding agencies. They can even benefit from handouts coming from the government if the latter is willing to "buy" their cooperation and avoid political spillover effects resulting from the formation of independent grassroots organizations.

26. Note incidentally that migrant fishermen from Saint-Louis operating in Soumbedioune never mentioned the economic or the biological effect alone (*migrsou* is perfectly predicted in the first two regressions).

27. In actual fact, they acquired a second-hand truck (donated by a fishermen's organization from Brittany, France) in order to transport the collected fish to Dakar and sell it directly to fish-processing factories. The experience was far from successful since the leaders concerned were eventually obliged to rent the truck to local fishmerchants in order to repay the debts incurred.

28. It is certainly not easy to explain why married fishermen (with either one or two wives) who are relatively young (less than 36 years) tend to be optimistic in their statements about rule-breaking, and why this phenomenon is observed in Kayar and not in Saint-Louis or Yoff. A plausible hypothesis rests on the following scenario. Before reaching their thirties, fishermen are typically bachelors (only 18 percent of the sample fishermen who are less than 29 years old are married),[28] working and living with their father whose opinions about the effectiveness of the effort-limiting scheme shape their own perceptions to a large extent; hence the high proportion of them (62 percent in Kayar) who consider the rate of infractions to be high. When they enter the 29–35 age category, they usually get married (the marriage rate in this category is 82 percent), which implies that they form their own household and become more independent of their father (even though they may well continue to operate his boat and nets). At that stage, they are inclined to

play an active role in a profusion of organizations such as the *Comité Villageois de Développement*, the local branch of the CNPS (*Collectif National des Pêcheurs Sénégalais*), and the Federation of the GIE (*Groupements d'Interêt Economique*) which are particularly active in Kayar and have been jointly involved in initiating and monitoring the effort-limiting scheme. Participation in these collective ventures has the effect of arousing hope among them that organizational dysfunctionings can be put under control. Thus, only 9 percent of married fishermen between 29 and 35 years old in Kayar have expressed pessimistic beliefs about enforcement of the effort-limiting scheme in particular. After a few years of experience, however, fishermen begin to realize that collective regulations are plagued with the opportunistic acts of a significant number of them and they come to a more realistic assessment of the effectiveness of their enforcement. In this, they exhibit more flexibility than the old elite whose identification with the regulatory measures is stronger. In Yoff and Saint-Louis, such a turnaround in beliefs is not observed presumably because there are fewer local organizations through which young married people can make their own direct experience of collective action.

References

Abraham, A., and J. P. Platteau. 2002. "Participatory development in the presence of endogenous community imperfections." *Journal of Development Studies* 39(2): 104–36.

Baland, J. M., and J. P. Platteau. 1996. *Halting Degradation of Natural Resources—Is There a Role for Rural Communities?* Oxford: Clarendon Press.

———. 1998. "Wealth inequality and efficiency on the commons—Part II: the Regulated Case." *Oxford Economic Papers* 50(1): 1–22.

———. 1999. "The ambiguous impact of inequality on local resource management." *World Development* 27(5): 773–88.

———. 2005. "Economics of common property management regimes." In *Handbook of Environmental Economics*, chap. 18, K.G. Mähler, and J. Vincent. Amsterdam: North-Holland.

Barry-Gérard, M., A. Fonteneau, and T. Diouf. 1992. *Evaluation des ressources exploitables par la pêche artisanale*, Rapport d'une séminaire tenu au CRODT (Dakar), 2 tomes. Paris: Editions de l'Orstom.

———. 1992. "Exploitation des ressources halieutiques côtières dans les eaux sous juridiction sénégalaise." In A. T. Diaw, A. Ba, P. Bouland, P. S. Diouf, L.A. Lake, M.A. Mbow, P. Ndiaye, and M.D. Thiam (eds.), *Programmes zones humides de l'UICN. Actes de l'atelier de Gorée*, 27–29 juillet 1992, pp. 291–310.

CRODT (Centre de Recherches Océanographiques de Dakar-Thiaroye). 1998. *Archives scientifiques* 205 (February).

CRODT (Centre de Recherches Océanographiques de Dakar-Thiaroye) and DOPM (Direction de l'Océanographie et de la Pêche Maritime). 1998. *Recensement national du parc piroguier et des infrastructures liées à la pêche.* Ministère de la Pêche et des Transports Maritimes, Observatoire Economique de la Pêche au Sénégal, Dakar.

Gruenais, M.-E. 1986. "Territoires autochtones et mise en valeur des terres." In *Espaces disputés en Afrique noire*, ed. B. E. Crousse, E. Le Bris, and E. Le Roy, pp. 283–98. Paris: Karthala.

Johnson, C. 2001. "Community formation and fisheries conservation in Southern Thailand." *Development and Change* 32(5): 951–74.

Johnson, R. N., and G. D. Libecap. 1982. "Contracting problems and regulation: The case of the fishery." *American Economic Review* 72: 1005–22.

Kahneman, D., and A. Tversky. 1979. "Prospect theory: An analysis of decision under risk." *Econometrica* 47(1): 263–91.

Libecap, G. D. 1990. *Contracting for Property Rights*. New York: Cambridge University Press.

Libecap, G. D., and S. N. Wiggins. 1984. "Contracting responses to the common pool: Prorationing of crude oil production." *American Economic Review* 74(1): 87–98.

Parlement Européen. 1996. *Document de travail sur les accords internationaux de pêche*. Commission de pêche (written by P. Crampton), Brussels.

Platteau, J. P. 2000. *Institutions, Social Norms, and Economic Development*. Amsterdam: Harwood Academic Publishers.

Platteau, J. P., and A. Abraham. 1987. "An inquiry into quasi-credit contracts: The role of reciprocal credit and interlinked deals in small-scale fishermen communities." *Journal of Development Studies* 23(4): 461–90.

Platteau, J. P., and J. Nugent. 1992. "Share contracts and their rationale: Lessons from marine fishing." *Journal of Development Studies* 28(3): 386–422.

Chapter 8

WEALTH INEQUALITY AND OVEREXPLOITATION OF THE COMMONS: FIELD EXPERIMENTS IN COLOMBIA

Juan-Camilo Cardenas

This chapter is aimed at illustrating, through the use of experimental methods applied in the field, how wealth and wealth heterogeneity can affect the possibilities of self-governed solutions to commons dilemmas in the use of natural resources. Various arguments, empirical and theoretical, have been offered in this volume on how inequality might play a role in the solution or worsening of collective-action dilemmas. The use of economic experiments, in the field or the campus labs, makes it possible to control for different forms of inequalities and their effect over individual decisions and aggregate outcomes. The results reported here are one example of such application of the method by showing how social distance, created from differences of wealth in a group, can affect the emergence of self-regulatory mechanisms that solve the collective-action dilemma.

From the theoretical chapters by Baland and Platteau, and by Bardhan, Ghatak, and Karaivanov in this volume, we learned the many different ways in which inequalities of wealth and income can affect the production function of the public good, or the relative position of the players in the game and the asymmetric costs and benefits that emerge from such heterogeneities. Since there is more than one dimension in which inequality can foster or constrain cooperation and sustainable use of the environment, and in some cases the directions can go in opposite ways, it is important to understand and separate these, and also to explore empirically the relative importance they play. From Baland and Platteau's two types of models some arguments come into play in the discussion that follows. In their first model of the common good they explore how

Much of the research that generated these ideas and results is because of the enthusiasm of Sam Bowles, who made the proposal to bring the lab to the field years ago. Jean-Marie Baland and Pranab Bardhan as co-editors, and Pete Richardson and Lore Ruttan as discussants, contributed greatly to enrich the last version. Thanks also to Maria Claudia Lopez for her assistance in the analysis of the video and audio data.

wealth determines the level of benefits that each resource user perceives depending on their relative share of the public good provided from the collective action. In their second model, the authors study how wealth affects the relative level of appropriation of the common-pool resource. In both models the heterogeneity is introduced into the production technology or in the distribution of gains according to choices. However, it can be the case that both technology of production and individual capacity of appropriation of the resource are symmetric and yet the group faces other types of heterogeneity that create distance among the players affecting, for instance, the frequency of interactions that can occur for solving the collective-action problem. As the chapter by Janssen and Ostrom has suggested, such frequency affects directly the possibilities of building trusting relationships that help adopt rules that promote cooperation. In the absence of enforceable mechanisms to coordinate actions, inequality can make cooperation more difficult to achieve. I will come back to this argument in the analysis based on the empirical evidence that follows here, when showing how at the micro and group levels wealth inequality can restrict the possibilities of self-governed solutions to these group dilemmas.

Based on an experimental design emulating a group externality associated with the extraction of a natural resource, eighty villagers from three rural communities participated in ten group sessions of a decision-making exercise, involving actual monetary incentives, with two stages of several rounds each. In the first stage the participants made decisions with no possibilities to coordinate actions with their group members, while in the second stage they were allowed to have, before each round, three to five minutes of open and nonbinding discussions with the other players in their group.

Besides replicating the same findings that the experimental labs have shown systematically on the effectiveness of face-to-face communication reducing free-riding in common-pool resource experiments, and against the tragedy of the commons prediction, the results presented here provide further insights into the role that wealth and inequality may play in solving the tragedy. Because the subject pool is composed of a more heterogeneous population than that of students as used in the university labs, and because our subjects were actual users of natural resources who face daily the dilemma designed in the experiment, we took advantage of this extra information and studied how these variables about their context could be related to the decisions they made in the field lab we designed.

At the end of the experimental sessions in each of the three villages we held a community workshop to discuss the preliminary data on the experiments with the purpose of discussing with the participants plausible explanations for the results, and relations between the experiments and the decision-making and outcomes in their reality. This exercise in fact originated some of the ideas presented here.

Beginning with an anecdotic event, a set of hypotheses emerged which provided the research questions for this chapter. During a workshop, one of the participants upon discussion of the social optimum solution to the experiment claimed that he had tried with only partial success to convince the rest of the people in his group to make decisions that would increase the group earnings. The discussion at the workshop then turned to others from that group, one of which hinted that she did not trust much of his advice and therefore did not follow it. Trust and reciprocity are key triggers of cooperation in groups facing social dilemmas, and this seemed to be a case where, despite being people who knew each other and lived in the same village, there were factors that restricted trust and therefore cooperative decisions. Given that the experimental incentives and rules were exactly the same for all groups, there might be other factors involved in the decision-making that became apparent from the experimental environment. Further exploration of the experimental data and of the participants' information collected about their economic and social contexts suggests in fact that the individual and group wealth composition could explain a good portion of variation not only for the decisions in this group, but for the entire sample of groups.

In this chapter I will argue that the wealth composition of the participants has at least two ways of affecting their decisions in this experimental design. First, wealth determines the way a household allocates effort between private and collective alternatives of income, and therefore determines the dependence of households on the commons. Second, wealth determines the relative social and economic position of a household with respect to others in the group sharing the commons, and therefore can affect the attitudes of others in the group regarding trust and willingness to cooperate when opportunistic incentives might induce players not to.

After describing the experimental design and the subjects' pool, I will present the general findings of the experiment. Then I will focus on the problem of explaining the variation in cooperative decisions through the actual socioeconomic characteristics of the participants. Some implications will be drawn on the different ways that wealth and inequality may affect the way groups solve commons dilemmas through self-governed or community mechanisms.

8.1. ON COOPERATION, GROUP IDENTITY, TRUST, AND WEALTH-BASED DISTANCE

This volume covers many aspects of how inequality and heterogeneity can affect the possibilities of collective action, in particular with respect to the possibilities of a sustainable use of natural resources. The theoretical grounds and the relevant literature on how heterogeneity and inequality may affect collective action are well documented in other chapters with no need to cover them again here, and which go back to seminal works by Olson (1965), Bergstrom, Blume, and Varian (1986), and Baland and Platteau (1996) among others. I will only mention a few sources that are relevant to the arguments and findings emerging from the results about to be presented, and given that this is the only chapter that uses experimental methods.

The study of how groups solve these dilemmas has a wide and long empirical base from the social psychology and economic experimental literature as well as from several other social sciences, most of which support the idea that groups can endogenously devise ways of inducing and sustaining cooperative decisions by their members through a variety of self-governed mechanisms such as social norms based on group identity, pecuniary and nonpecuniary sanctions and rewards, mutual monitoring, among others, all these with experimental support (Kramer and Brewer 1984; Orbell, van de Kragt, and Dawes 1988; Ostrom, Gardner, and Walker 1994; Ledyard 1995; Kollock 1998; Ostrom 2000). Much of this literature shows how face-to-face communication among group members in general proves to be very effective in reducing free-riding, as Sally (1995) showed in his meta-analysis of three decades of experiments involving face-to-face communication.

Furthermore, the experimental literature has explored in various ways how asymmetries among players may affect the choices of games where there are conflicts between individual and collective interests and outcomes. Since group identity has been a recurring element in the literature as a powerful factor explaining self-governed cooperation, any factor associated with heterogeneities that may impede group identity should be of interest here. Kollock (1998), for instance, provides evidence from a set of Prisoner's Dilemma experiments where the behavior of college students changed, for the same payoff structure, depending on the information they received about the affiliation of the other player (being from the same fraternity, from any other fraternity, from the same campus, from another campus, or from the campus police department). Lawler and Yoon (1996), for instance, show in a series of experiments how the level and equality of power among players increased the frequency of mutual agreements. Hoffman, McCabe, and Smith (1996) also explore how social distance can affect cooperative behavior, and for the particular case of common-pool resources, Hackett, Schlager, and Walker (1994) show how communication can still produce strong results despite heterogeneities introduced in the payoff structure. Ledyard (1995) includes "heterogeneity" as a rather weak but important factor in explaining contributions in public goods experiments, and his survey suggests that it might be one of the factors decreasing cooperation although the literature does not seem conclusive.

Sally (2001) proposes a formal model to introduce the concept of sympathy as a key determinant of the player's willingness to cooperate, defining sympathy as the "fellow-feeling person i has for person j" and models it as a function of both the physical and psychological distances between i and j. Arguing a reciprocity effect, he suggests that persons will reduce their fellow-feeling for another when they feel they are being manipulated and taken advantage of. Further, in a related but not experimental study, Alesina and La Ferrara (2000) showed from a General Social Survey (1974–94) sample from U.S. citizens that the participation in social activities as contributions to their neighborhoods decreased for more unequal and more racially or ethnically heterogeneous groups.

In brief, there is support for the argument that the context in which the members of a group attempt to solve endogenously a dilemma may play an important role, apart from asymmetries in the material incentives that differentiate best response strategies across players. The context can be at the individual level where each player may regard the others in the group differently due to social positions, status, or sense of belonging to the group, or at the group level because of agreed norms that affect the members as a whole. The experiments conducted in the field, and the data gathered about these issues, in fact support these arguments.

8.2. Bringing the Lab to the Field: An Experimental Design

In order to test some of the alternative theories on cooperation and the use of the commons, we can make use of experimental methods where human subjects participate in a series of decision-making exercises where there is an environment of real economic incentives, and institutional and technological environments that emulate the type of dilemma of interest. By introducing changes in some of the experimental factors (e.g., the payoffs structures, or the rules that govern the individual decisions), we can observe variations in behavior and outcomes and derive causal relations, in this case regarding the role of wealth and heterogeneity in cooperation. The experimental design that follows is inspired by the conventional experimental literature on common-pool resources and group externalities (Ostrom, Gardner, and Walker 1994; Ledyard 1995). However, what is new here is that the experimental lab was brought to the field so that the human subjects were people who in their daily life made decisions and faced dilemmas similar to those in the experiment. For this purpose, the model that follows was designed to emulate the situation these communities face and to create the environment of incentives for the experiment.

8.2.1. A Simple Model of the Individual Use of the Commons

Assume a group of households surrounding an area (the commons[1]) with a certain set of attributes that provide ecological goods and services to society. Some of these households may have private control over certain assets such as livestock or land. Some may extract resources from the commons such as firewood or water from it, but they might also be affected like the rest of the village by the level of erosion, sedimentation, water pollution, or biodiversity levels directly related to the aggregate extraction of resources from the natural area being exploited by these households. Thus, the model proposed here will be applicable to many settings in which household income is a combination of private and collective options, and would hold for settings where not even common property exists, but where there is joint access to a local ecosystem.

THE HOUSEHOLD'S UTILITY FUNCTION

Define $U_i(x_i, \Sigma x_j)$ as the level of utility for user i, with $i, j \in (1, n)$, where well-being is derived from the allocation of total effort e_i (e.g., total household labor) between private alternatives $(e_i - x_i)$ and the individual extraction (x_i) of resources from the commons. Individual extraction x_i generates direct benefits to the household, but on the other hand individual allocation of effort into private alternatives $(e_i - x_i)$ will also increase i's well-being. Third, aggregate allocation (Σx_j) of effort by the group of households into extracting the commons will generate a negative externality to i and the rest of the households. If benefits to i are increasing in i's effort to extract the commons as well as in i's effort into her own private alternatives, and decreasing in aggregate extraction, we can define:

$$U_i = U_i(x_i, \Sigma x_j) = U_i[f(x_i), b(\Sigma x_j), w_i(e - x_i)] \tag{1}$$

where $f(x_i) = \gamma x_i - \frac{1}{2}\varphi(x_i)^2$, where γ and φ are strictly positive and are chosen in part to guarantee $f(x_i) > 0$, for $x_i \in [0, e]$. The strict concavity of $f(x_i)$ indicates diminishing marginal private returns to effort extracting resources; $b(\Sigma x_j) = q^0 - \frac{1}{2}(\Sigma x_j)^2$, where b is a quadratic function of the aggregate amount of time individuals in the community spend collecting firewood; q^0 is interpreted to be the maximum level of nonuse benefits when the natural area is in its ecological climax. The concavity of b is based on the assumption that at low levels of aggregate extraction the ecosystem is able to provide most of its ecological benefits, but after a certain level of extraction these capabilities begin to diminish at increasing rates.

And last, we can assume that the marginal return on the private alternative is a linear function, at a constant rate of w_i times the amount of effort not allocated into extracting resources from the commons. Therefore, we can express the utility function as:

$$U_i(x_i, \Sigma x_j) = U_i[(q^0 - \tfrac{1}{2}\Sigma x_j)^2 + (\gamma x_i - \tfrac{1}{2}\varphi(x_i)^2) + w_i \times (e_i - x_i)] \quad (2)$$

for each individual i, and for all j users of the commons.

SOCIAL VERSUS INDIVIDUAL EFFICIENCY IN THE USE OF THE COMMONS

A simple case is when all households face the same utility function and have the same marginal returns from their private and collective alternatives. From (2) we can therefore express the joint welfare function as

$$W(x) = n[(q^0 - \tfrac{1}{2}(nx)^2) + (\gamma x - \tfrac{1}{2}\varphi(x)^2) + w \times (e - x)]. \quad (3)$$

The first-order condition for the maximization of $W(x)$ requires that $-xn^2 + \gamma - \varphi x - w = 0$. Solving for x, the optimal individual level of extraction should be $x^{so} = (\gamma - w)/(\varphi + n^2)$, which basically equates the marginal rate of gains from the private alternative to the sum of the marginal gains from extracting the commons and perceiving the other nonconsumptive goods and services from extraction.

However, achieving such a socially efficient outcome will require certain institutions if the individuals do not coordinate their actions. Due to the structure of the payoffs function, there is a group externality and a conflict between individual and collective use of the commons. Each individual benefits from increasing its extraction, but suffers the costs of aggregate extraction for which it has only partial control, in the baseline case where we assume the absence of institutions correcting the externalities. If for the moment we again assume symmetry in the payoffs structures of the n individuals, and symmetry in the assumptions about behavior of the individuals, we can derive the optimizing decision x^* by each player as a best response function of the others' expected behavior, and of the parameters in equation (1). The symmetric Nash equilibrium where each individual, by choosing x, maximizes the utility function shown in (1), requires that:

$$x^{nash} = (\gamma - w)/(\varphi + n). \quad (4)$$

Clearly, $x^{nash} = (\gamma - w)/(\varphi + n) > (\gamma - w)/(\varphi + n^2/) > x^{so}$ as long as $\gamma > w$ which we will assume for purposes of simplicity.[2] Given that the individual payoffs function is increasing in x_i, at equilibrium, these n individuals will find themselves in a commons dilemma where individual and group interests are in conflict. For any specified number of households, n, and for any level q^0 of ecological services for an unexploited commons, the distance in aggregate payoffs between the two benchmarks depends on the marginal returns from extracting resources (determined by γ and φ), and on the marginal rate on the private alternatives, w.

In the particular case of the private alternative, w, clearly higher exit options should under this model induce a reduction in the individual extraction of the commons and—at equilibrium—a socially superior outcome given that the reduction in gains for less resource extracted is more than compensated by the increase in the outside option, and also by the increase in ecological benefits from a lower aggregate extraction. This would clearly suggest, for policy purposes and under the assumptions given here for the rationality and incompleteness of the contracts among the individuals, that improving the private alternatives of the commons users such as higher returns on land or labor, better crops prices, subsidies for education, and the like, should reduce the pressure over natural resources over which there is joint access and lack of institutions.[3]

However, recall that the symmetric Nash equilibrium that supports these conclusions assumes that the individuals are not devising any institution to correct the failures generated by the group externality. Rather, they are following their Nash best responses given the assumption that everyone else in the users' group will do so, in a noncooperative game. Once external agents or self-governance institutions emerge that attempt to align the individual and collective goals, these predictions would just provide a set of benchmarks but not necessarily a prediction of actual behavior.

On the other hand, the theoretical analysis is based on the assumption of symmetry in both outcomes and behavior across decision-makers. In reality, groups of commons users usually show various types of asymmetries, the central theme of this chapter and volume. In general, these asymmetries can be related to the different components of the individual payoffs function shown above. For instance, there might be heterogeneities in the exit private options the players face because of education or assets, or in the marginal returns from extracting the commons due to better technologies for harvesting the resources. Later I will mention how this was introduced in another set of experiments we conducted in the same three villages, but reported elsewhere (Cardenas et al. 2002).

The economic experiment designed for the field uses the model above to create a set of incentives and decision-making space under different rules. The particular design and definition of parameters, and the benchmarks used to analyze the data from the different sessions conducted in the field, are given in the following sections.

8.2.2. The Experimental Design and Its Application in the Field

Through a simple decision-making exercise, eight people in a group had to make repeated individual decisions that had salient economic incentives (in kind and cash) and with the kind of externalities common to these commons dilemmas. The average earnings, about two minimum wage days of work, at the end of the sessions compensated for the time they spent participating in the experiment and in a community workshop held at the end in each village to discuss preliminary results and hypotheses. The instructions read to the participants and the forms used for running the experiment can be obtained from the author.

During a typical session, each participant had to decide in each round of the game the number of months (from 0 to 8) she would allocate to extract resources from a jointly used forest. The net earnings from such decision, which she could view in a payoff table, based exactly on the payoffs function in equation (2), which increases with individual extraction, but decreases with total group's extraction, giving rise to the commons dilemma.[4] To complete the earnings structure, any month not allocated to extract from the forest would yield a constant marginal private return equal to all players.

In the case reported here of symmetric payoffs for all eight participants, we chose the parameters of the payoffs structure such that if every player chose one month in the forest, for a maximum of eight, the group would achieve the social optimum solution where group earnings would be maximized. And if each player chose six months, they would find themselves in the Nash suboptimal equilibrium at about 24 percent of social efficiency.[5] During the first stage of all sessions the participants had to make a series of decisions (rounds) under no possibility of interaction among themselves, and then, depending on the subsample, they would face a different institution—either face-to-face communication among the players, or an external regulator that would enforce a certain social norm aimed at improving social efficiency.[6]

In another variation of the same experimental design, we introduced a payoff structure to emulate the case of asymmetric incentives where two of the players had a much better opportunity cost of time not allocated extracting the forest, while the other six had a much worse than the baseline symmetric case. This asymmetry was generated by assigning two different values for w in equation (3) ($W_H = 60$ for two players randomly chosen,

TABLE 8.1
Benchmarks for Social Optimum and Nash Equilibria

Two Benchmarks for Equilibria in the Commons Game		Symmetric Choices and Outcomes (for all 8 players)
Social optimal solution (GroupMax strategy)	Individual decision (X^{opt})	$X_S^{opt} = 1$
	Yields ($) per round per player	$Y_S^{opt} = \$645$
	Group yields	$SUMY_S^{opt} = \$5,160$
Nash solution (IndivMax strategy)	Individual decision (X^{nash})	$X_S^{nash} = 6$
	Yields ($) per round per player	$Y_S^{nash} = \$155$
	Group yields	$SUMY_S^{nash} = \$1,240$

and $W_L = 20$ for the other six, thus maintaining the same average marginal return on the private option equal in both cases to 30 as in the symmetric case). The results of these experiments, reported in Cardenas et al. (2002), suggest that such asymmetry did in fact increase efficiency and cooperation, but contrary to the Nash theoretical prediction. It resulted from the higher cooperation by the six players with lower exit options, while the two "wealthier" ones remained close to their Nash strategy.

For the symmetric case, the design had two benchmarks described earlier: the social optimal solution when each player chooses one month (i.e., 8 months group total) and social efficiency is at 100 percent, and the Nash solution where each player chooses six months (i.e., 48 months group total) where efficiency for the group is only at 24 percent. Cases for the asymmetric groups were similar. The summary of the predicted benchmarks for the Nash outcome and the social optimum case are included in table 8.1.

8.2.3. Subjects Pool: Three Rural Villages in Colombia

To conduct the experiments, three locations (see map in figure 8.1) were selected where the community faced the kind of dilemma being modeled. In all three cases an ecosystem provided multiple goods and services to the villagers in terms of direct and indirect use values. In all three cases there are extractive activities for self-consumption or for the market, but such extraction creates a negative group externality because of reduction of the ecosystem's capacity to provide other services.

In the village of Encino (Santander), located in the eastern Andean region, residents enter local tropical cloud forests to extract firewood, log

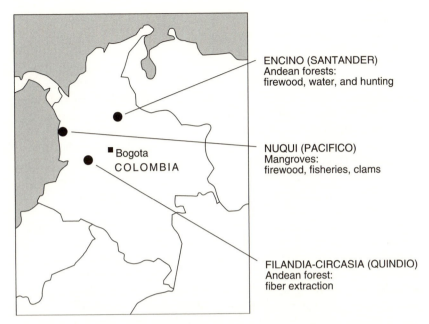

ENCINO (SANTANDER)
Andean forests:
firewood, water, and hunting

NUQUI (PACIFICO)
Mangroves:
firewood, fisheries, clams

FILANDIA-CIRCASIA (QUINDIO)
Andean forest:
fiber extraction

■Bogota
COLOMBIA

Figure 8.1. Location of the three rural villages where experiments were conducted.

timber on a small scale, and to hunt. Like all of the sites we visited, water for consumption and irrigation comes nearly untreated from local rivers that flow from nearby forests. The second location is in the Quindio coffee region in the mid-Andes, where water quality degradation is also caused by forest cover losses near the villages of Circasia and Filandia. In Quindio, subjects for our experiments were drawn specifically from a group of families whose livelihood is related to the extraction and processing of natural fibers from local forests for handcrafting baskets for local and regional markets. As in Encino, water is drawn from local rivers and residents are aware that extracting forest products can lead to lower water quality. In Nuquí (Chocó), located on the Pacific coast, villagers harvest coastal mangroves for firewood and other wood products, as well as for fishing and gathering fish, shrimp, and mollusks, but their water comes from farther inland; hence, they do not experience a direct link between their exploitation of local sources of wood and water quality. However, they face a similar dilemma because their exploitation of the mangroves for wood adversely affects coastal fish populations upon which they also depend.

To sum up, the population from which the subjects for these experiments were drawn is of rural households that live in areas that depend heavily on extracting products from local forests. In each location, exploitation of local forests affects another aspect of their livelihoods adversely: water quality in Encino and Quindio, and fish populations in Nuquí. Hence, the subjects face social dilemmas in their daily lives that are similar to the one we created for them in the experiments. For recruitment, we invited all people over fifteen years old who had the ability to write and do some basic numbers, and avoided having more than one individual per household participate in the same session. As participants arrived, they were assigned to different sessions according to their available schedule. Also, we randomly assigned people at the same scheduled time in different groups of the session to avoid pregame agreements among people showing up or signing for the same session. It is clear that the eighty people recruited for the experiments cannot be considered a random sample of the population in the villages they come from and that the results have to be evaluated within this context. On the other hand, and differently from experiments with university students, in each of the three villages our participants generally knew each other well, having lived in the same village for most of their lives. This is rather crucial for the type of question addressed, namely, the search for self-governed solutions to the tragedy of the commons within communities that share a set of natural resources.

Schooling, age, and income levels varied significantly for the participants within each group. Most participants had fewer than six years of schooling, roughly half were between thirty and fifty years old, and all were sixteen or older. The fraction of income from extractive activities and the labor allocated to it varied widely across the participants, which also provided us with individual-level data key for the analysis.

During the summer of 1998, we spent about ten days in each of the villages, including the first day randomly inviting people to sign up for the experiments, four to five days conducting the experiments, a day processing the most important data of decisions and outcomes, and a final day for a workshop with all participants and others interested to discuss the preliminary analysis we made of the experimental data.

About 180 people participated in more than twenty sessions in all three villages under three major experimental treatments already mentioned, an external regulation aimed at reducing extraction not discussed here, and two subsets of groups that were allowed, after the first noncooperative stage of the game, to have face-to-face communication periods between decisions in each round. For fifteen of these groups (10 under the symmetric payoffs table and 5 under the asymmetric ones), we introduced in the second stage a new rule that allowed a five-minute conversation before each round decision. Such conversation would be free but would not permit any threat or promise of transferring earnings after the session. They would make choices for another set of around nine or ten rounds under this new treatment.

TABLE 8.2
Average Choices (Extraction Levels) and Earnings at the End of
Noncommunication and Communication Stages

| | Average Last 3 Rounds in Each Stage | | | |
| | End Stage 1 (rounds 6–8) (No Communication) | | End Stage 2 (rounds 17–19) (Communication) | |
Group	X Choice	Y$ Earnings	X Choice	Y$ Earnings
CQS11	5,13	274,42	2,17	603,00
CQW41	3,04	527,75	2,88	547,17
CEW42	3,75	456,96	3,42	497,67
CES12	4,79	320,33	3,46	491,46
CNW41	5,42	244,67	3,42	490,50
CES11	3,88	441,08	3,67	467,50
CNS12	4,21	394,46	3,92	403,13
CNW42	4,79	319,58	4,33	383,88
CNS11	4,63	342,96	4,58	347,79
CEW41	4,19	402,13	5,75	187,63
Average 10 Symmetric Groups	4,38	372,43	3,76	441,97

8.3. BASIC RESULTS ON COOPERATION AND COMMUNICATION

From the set of ten groups under the No Communication and Communication stages, several conclusions emerge. As in most experimental evidence, people do not behave according to the conventional model prediction and groups do not end up at the Nash equilibrium based on material outcomes and self-regarding behavior. Communication proved to be effective on average but with wide variations. But further, people seemed to use information from their actual context with respect to themselves and the others in the group to adjust their experimental behavior. Table 8.2 summarizes the behavior and outcomes for the ten groups at the end of both stages of the experiment.

8.3.1. Unexplained Variation and the Role of Social Heterogeneity

As in most studies, face-to-face communication proved to be an effective mechanism for inducing more cooperative behavior. The results reject in general the "cheap talk" argument that when agents make promises with no enforceable consequences, such promises remain as such, and moves toward cooperative choices do not happen. Our results showed that the ten groups improved social efficiency and therefore earnings by about 10 percent on average, after communication was allowed. Although the result may seem small, it should be noted that this is the resulting social efficiency at the end of stage 2, and that during some rounds the average was above that. Some groups were able to increase social efficiency by 50 percent between the last rounds of the first stage and the last rounds of the second. Some of the groups achieved levels of almost maximum social efficiency, while others achieved almost no improvement despite all groups facing the exact same material payoffs and the same laboratory environment and rules. Such variation seems wider than in experiments conducted with students and deserves further discussion.

The variation of behavior and outcomes across and within the groups is very much consistent with the rest of the evidence in the literature (Ledyard 1995; Ostrom et al. 1994). In our case it cannot be explained by changes in the lab institutions and other environment variables in the experimental design, such as framing, since they were all equal across groups. It might be explained by the individual data and the specific conditions in each round in terms of reciprocity and learning effects determined choices in one round as a function of choices by each player and the others in previous rounds. If we eliminate the assumption of homogenous rationalities across players and consider the case for types, for example, rational egoists and reciprocators (Ostrom 2000) within the group, each group might have a different composition of players' preferences determining their actions. Further, the possibility of communication as a space for transforming the set of norms allows each group in particular, and each individual, to construct a new image of the game, that is, a new set of internal payoffs now in terms of utility and not necessarily of monetary values. Guilt, respect, spite, or emotions in general now could be affecting the choice after a few minutes of debate over what should be a better choice to make in the next round, and based on experience from previous ones. The next section attempts to explore these arguments empirically.

8.3.2. Postgame Workshops: The Role of Group Composition

As mentioned in the beginning of the chapter, an anecdotic event caught our attention during one of the community workshops where we were exploring possible explanations for the only partial success of communication in a particular group where at least one of the participants was calling for everyone else in the group to lower their extraction level. During the followup workshops, and after the Nash and social optimum equilibria were discussed from the model, one of the participants from this group eloquently mentioned that he was trying during several rounds to get the others to reduce their "months in the forest" to increase group and individual earnings. Since we had a poster with average choices over rounds for each group, we asked the rest of the group why they thought that such advice was not followed. Another participant from the same group responded:

"I did hear Don _____ (name omitted) saying that, but usually I don't see him face to face, so I did not really believe him." This was followed by laughter from the rest of the assistants.

Notice that in this particular case we had several conditions that usually promote cooperation in experiments of this kind. Face-to-face communication, the emergence of an explicit norm that called for reducing the level of extraction, and all eight players knew each other and belonged to the same village. And yet the increase in cooperation was not as significant as in other groups. We went back to the audio and video data first and explored plausible explanations for why such clearly effective advice by one player was not followed.

In fact, the dialogue for the first round after communication was allowed shows that this particular person used phrases like the following regarding the number of "months in the forest" as the key decision in the experiment:

"But it is better not to go to the forest so often."
"But it is better to go for just a short time."
"That's why it is better not to go to the forest so often."

Interestingly, the conversation for this group over rounds was also mixed with references to the actual levels and frequency of extraction from water and firewood sources in that village. By the second round under communication his call was even more explicit:

"Do not mark 5, 6, or 7 and you will see that you can earn way more money."

In the next round this same person reinforces his call:

"The game is going very well, just play 2 or 3 and you will see how well you do."

Later in other rounds the same person reinforced to the others his suggestion that choosing levels 1, 2, or 3 will bring earnings up significantly, and also that if they chose levels 5, 6, or 7 and look at the bottom of the table they will see the poor results.

If such a message was so prevalent, why did the average choice for that group not go down as expected? Moreover, how were the decisions distributed across the eight players, and in particular the decision of this player acting as a leader? Since we had demographic and socioeconomic information about each participant and could match the information with the videotapes, we were able to observe choices individually and associate them with characteristics of the actual context of each player. This exercise turned out to be very interesting. The group was composed of six women and two males, one of whom was the one trying to influence the decisions of the others, as mentioned before. These two males, we later learned from informal interviews, belonged to one of the wealthiest families in the village, which we could confirm with our survey data. While the average of the reported household wealth in terms of land, livestock, and equipment for the six women was $1.98 million Colombian pesos, the two male players reported $5.86 million pesos.[7] Further, when asked in the survey to which and how many community organizations they belonged, the two males reported none, while the six other people averaged 1.67 organizations.

Matching these data with the experimental decisions was also interesting. For the entire set of decisions before and after communication, we separated the individual choices of the wealthy players (players 2 and 7) from the less wealthy ones, as shown in figure 8.2.

Recall that the social optimum solution requires every player to choose $x = 1$, while the Nash equilibrium requires that $x = 6$ for every player. In the two panels of figure 8.2 we can observe the distribution of choices for both stages (before and with communication) for the poorer players in the upper panel and for the wealthier ones in the lower panel. Notice (lower panel) how the two players did not change their strategy toward a more cooperative behavior in the second stage, but rather reinforced their strategy to be close to the Nash prediction. Meanwhile, the other six players (upper panel) were in fact following the new "norm" of playing low numbers, with a median of two, and significantly less attempts to make decisions close to the Nash best response, that is, $X_i = 6$. Notice that from the transcripts mentioned before, it was one of the two players 2 or 7 who was calling for a reduction of extraction during the second stage, clearly a strategy he did not follow. The rather poor social efficiency outcome can be explained then by a mix of types that on average reduced the commons extraction only partially. The average earnings for all eight players at the end of the first stage was $457, while at the end of the second stage it increased to only $498, as shown in table 8.2 earlier. Recall that at the social optimum levels earnings can be $645. Both earnings and choices are statistically different for these two types, but being only one case in the sample, we should examine the entire set of sessions.

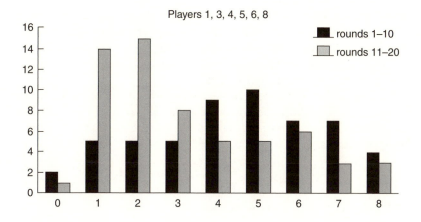

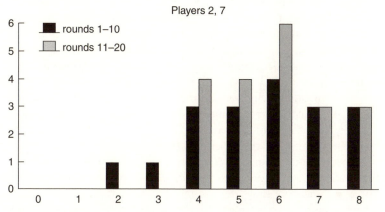

Figure 8.2. Distribution of extraction levels during stages 1 (rounds 1–10, NoCommun) and 2 (rounds 11–20, Communication). Upper panel: six poorer players. Lower panel: two wealthier players.

One could argue that gender may explain the differentiation in strategies by the two males as compared to the six females, for instance by a women's group identity that fostered cooperation, while the males, by feeling excluded, could deviate from such norm. Agarwal (this volume) discusses how gender inequalities can then introduce asymmetric ways in which forests are used by both genders and how rules can be broken and kept differently. In the data for this particular experimental session, however, this does not seem to be the case for the type of mechanisms discussed by Agarwal. Neither the tapes, nor the demographic data, seem to support that the lack of cooperation during the second stage was based on gender differences. It was one of the males who promoted the strategy of reducing the number of months in the forest, but the females followed it more closely, and further, there were no special dialogues against or in favor of a certain strategy during the group discussion that could support the argument of the women building the cooperative strategy based on their gender identity.

The alternative hypothesis suggested here is that wealth differences within a group can affect cooperation, particularly under self-governed institutions such as face-to-face communication. Such testing follows in the next sections.

8.4. GENERALIZING TO THE TEN GROUP SAMPLE: THE ROLE OF REAL CONTEXTS AND WEALTH

The analysis of the particular group mentioned before provided one possible hypothesis that wealth and wealth differences within a group can affect cooperation. In that particular case one could argue that the two males, having better private alternatives such as land, would be less familiar with collective-action solutions with actual neighbors as could be the case with the other six women, usually engaged in more cooperative activities with other neighbors in the village (e.g., firewood gathering, water management, livestock husbandry, unpaid labor exchange among farms). Second, the distance generated by wealth could also create problems in the building of reciprocity as there could be a less frequent history of interactions among distant players, needed to build trust.

If these arguments hold, first, wealthier players would cooperate less in the experiment as they are less familiar with the types of dilemmas created through the experiment and less familiar with solving them with the actual neighbors they are playing with. Second, greater distances in terms of wealth within a group would imply smaller levels of aggregate cooperation as there is less trust or reputation history on which to build cooperation.

Since all other material incentives and rules of the game were held constant across the ten groups, we could study how observable variables gathered through the exit survey about their socioeconomic characteristics and demographics might explain behavior during the experiment.

To analyze wealth across players, we gathered information about their household ownership of land, livestock, and equipment. Using local market prices for these items, we could construct a proxy for the household wealth of the participants. With these data, we then constructed different measures of wealth heterogeneity within groups and compared across groups. On the other hand, the information gathered about the economic

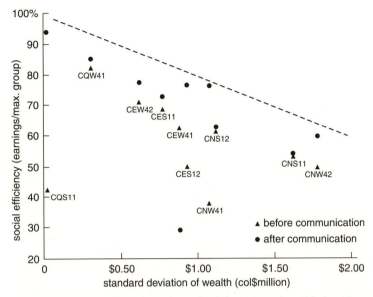

Figure 8.3. Social efficiency and standard deviation of wealth for 10 groups (before and after communication). The dotted line does not represent a fitted line from a regression but a type of "ceiling" that could be imposed to limit the social efficency depending on the level of wealth heterogeneity.

activity of the participant, whether the household depended mostly on land, livestock, wage labor, or extractive activities, was a significant predictor of the level of individual cooperation in the experiment.

Figures 8.3 and 8.4 illustrate these points by plotting the social efficiency achieved by each of the ten groups at the end of the communication rounds, and two measures related to wealth composition. Figure 8.3 plots in the horizontal axis the standard deviation of wealth for the eight participants in each group, showing a downward trend in social efficiency as the variance of wealth among participants in a group increases.[8] Thus, a kind of "inequality ceiling" could be suggested where, no matter what the start point was at the beginning of the second stage, cooperation and social efficiency would be constrained by the wealth composition of the group.

The argument for such possible relation can be complemented by the data in figure 8.4, where the same ten groups' efficiency is plotted against the fraction of players in the group that reported resource extraction as their main activity for income source.[9] It seems from the results that groups composed of players who in their daily activity are more familiar with resource extraction activities and whose income thus depends on

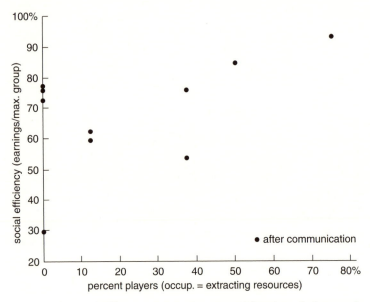

Figure 8.4 Social efficiency in experiments and fraction of players whose actual main income source is from extractive activities.

less private wealth, found it less difficult to overcome the tragedy by constructing an agreement through face-to-face communication and implementing it for higher levels of group and individual earnings. Many of the dialogues of the groups included constant references to how familiar the game was to their daily extraction of water, firewood, fish, or mollusks. Table 8.3 complements these data and shows the average of the ten groups (Avg 10) compared to the individual groups data. Notice also that the change in social efficiency from the end of the first stage to the end of the second stage is correlated with the fraction of players whose main occupation is extraction of resources, and also the fraction of players whose reported main source of income is land for agriculture or livestock.

8.5. WEALTH, INEQUALITY, AND COOPERATION: AN ECONOMETRIC EXERCISE

So far the argument for the variation in the success of the self-governed mechanism in the experiment, that is, nonbinding face-to-face communication, is that the experience, wealth, and occupation of the experiment participants seemed to be correlated with the social efficiency achieved during the experiment at the end of the second stage.[10] In the next step

TABLE 8.3
Experimental Outcomes and Actual Occupation of Participants

Group	Social Efficiency (End of Stage I) (%)	Social Efficiency (End of Stage II) (%)	Change in Social Efficiency (%)	% of Players with Extraction of Resources as Main Occupation	% of Players with Land as Main Income Source
CEW41	62.35	29.09	−33.26	0.00	87.50
CEW42	70.85	77.16	6.31	0.00	75.00
CES12	49.66	76.20	26.53	0.00	25.00
CES11	68.39	72.48	4.10	0.00	50.00
CNW42	49.55	59.52	9.97	12.50	25.00
CNS12	61.16	62.50	1.34	12.50	37.50
Avg 10	57.74	68.52	10.78	22.50	37.50
CNW41	37.93	76.05	38.11	37.50	25.00
CNS11	53.17	53.92	0.75	37.50	50.00
CQW41	81.82	84.83	3.01	50.00	0.00
CQS11	42.55	93.49	50.94	75.00	0.00
Coefficients of correlation with % change in social efficiency (without Avg. 10):				0.5732	−0.71560
(Pearson correlation test) p-value:				0.0830	0.02000

of the analysis I will come back to the original anecdote where a participant did not trust the agreement that the wealthier person was suggesting for the experiment, to explore more on the microfoundations of cooperation at the player level.

The hypothesis of social distance proposed here is that within a group an explicit agreement during the group discussion might not be followed by a player who perceives a social distance toward the rest of players in the group. In a sense, social distance here is considered as the opposite of Sally's (2001) concept of sympathy (i.e., the fellow-feeling person i has for person j). Many of the arguments on why communication is so powerful in increasing cooperation in social dilemmas is that it allows creation of a group identity, reinforces group goals and their benefits, or creates nonpecuniary social costs to free-riders. Further, the key to cooperation once an agreement has emerged in a discussion is trust in the next decision, which is still private and confidential for most of these experiments, including this one. For less sympathy, or wider social distance between a player and the rest of the group, one could expect less trust on the others honoring the agreement. To explore this econometrically with the experimental data, we can lower the level to the individual decision level and explore whether i's behavior can be explained as a function of i's occupation or wealth (as discussed earlier), but also as a function of the wealth composition of the group. Since we can explore dynamic effects at the decision level in each round, the model will be complemented with exploring the possibility of reciprocity effects over rounds. Table 8.4 summarizes the econometric results for three different estimators, a simple ordinary least squares regressor, and a fixed effects model with fixed effects for groups and for individuals.[11] The dependent variable we want to explain is the number of months in the forest in a certain round, during the communication rounds.

Consistent with the arguments on how wealth and wealth differences can explain the variation in cooperation within and across groups, we observe that wealthier players, and players with a wider wealth distance to the other seven players, were more likely to increase their extraction, that is, to behave closer to the Nash strategy. The cross effect of wealth*wealth distance, with a negative and significant coefficient suggests that the negative effect of social distance on cooperation is much stronger for those with lower wealth levels. However, since the mean for wealth in the eighty participants is 0.8542, with a standard deviation of 1.0913, the positive relation between extraction and wealth or wealth distance holds for most of the range in the sample.

Finally, the reciprocity effect is confirmed by the data, although the size of the coefficient is rather small although significant. Notice that the variable $\Delta \text{sum}X$ measures the reduction in the aggregate extraction level by the other seven players between the last two rounds. The negative

TABLE 8.4
Individual Round Choices as a Function of Reciprocity, Wealth, and Social
Distance (t_data). (simple, fixed groups, fixed individual models)

Dependent Variable: X Choice (Months in the Forest) During all Communication Rounds			
Indep Variables (p-values below):	Simple OLS	Fixed Effects (Groups)	Fixed Effects (Individuals)
Intercept	2.3967	1.6539	0.7749
	(0.0001)	(0.0001)	(0.0670)
ΔsumX (reduction) by other 7 players between $(t-1)$ and t^*	−0.0235	−0.0244	−0.0271
	(0.0379)	(0.0308)	(0.0026)
Wealth$_i$	0.8601	1.1560	8.5718
	(0.0001)	(0.0001)	(0.0001)
Wealth distance to other 7 players**	1.2299	1.8223	0.9197
	(0.0001)	(0.0001)	(0.1373)
Wealth * wealth distance	−0.4094	−0.5760	−3.2542
	(0.0001)	(0.0001)	(0.0001)
Fixed effects: Number of dummies not reported	0	9	72
N (including all 10 groups)	688	688	688
Adj.R2	.0949	0.1054	0.4342
F-test (p-value)	0.0001	0.0001	0.0001

*Defined as DELTSUM7 = [lag(SUMX7) − SUMX7] ⇒ If DELTSUM7 > 0 then the other 7 players reduced their months in the forest from the previous round. Thus, if the estimated coefficient is negative, a reduction by the others is accompanied by a reduction by player i, implying a reciprocity effect.
**WLTHD2SA = abs(Wealth$_i$ − 3wealth$_j$/7), j i.

and significant coefficient suggests then that if the others decreased their sum of months in previous rounds, the average player reduced her months in the forest in the next round, rather than increased them as the Nash strategy would suggest.

8.6. Conclusions: On Methods, Tools, and the Microfoundations of Cooperation

Most studies on inequality and collective-action or cooperation dilemmas, both theoretical and empirical, have focused on asymmetries of the material payoff structures of the public good and the private options of the players of the game. In the case of experimental studies this approach has allowed us to study how asymmetries in the payoff structures affect cooperation. On the other hand, most experimental evidence on studies of economic and social phenomena is based on university labs and with students as subjects. Enriching the evidence with participants, who daily face the dilemmas being modeled and studied, seems to be a promising path. The experimental design and results here show how within a group other types of asymmetries different from material incentives, such as experience and social distance, may affect the solution of collective action, at least through a self-governed device.

From these results one could infer that poverty in itself is not a limitation to cooperation in the commons. Further, poorer but homogenous groups seem to be willing to cooperate in order to increase their collectively generated individual benefits, even if at personal short-run costs. This however does not invalidate the necessity of addressing problems of poverty and lack of opportunities which affect other issues of well-being, eventually including the use and management of natural resources. The only claim from these results is that blaming the poor and not other institutions that create poverty and mismanagement of commons might deviate the attention away from structural problems, such as inequality.

In chapter 7 in this volume, Platteau and Gaspart explore some of these arguments using survey data from small fisheries in Senegal. In general they find no severe impediment to build collective action from wealth inequality. Their data suggest arguments of the Olsonian type, where wealthier individuals may play a role in favor of achieving the collective action for socially efficient regulations on effort. The ambiguous effect in the estimation results, they argue, is related to the fact that there are confounded effects in the role that leadership plays in the wealthier. One of the features of the results here presented is that there are fewer possibilities of these confounded effects playing a role when using controlled experiments with the actual resource users. For instance, the effect of leadership to promote cooperation within the lab may have no effect but within the lab only, given the confidentiality of the experimental data toward other members of the community.

Inequality does seem to affect negatively the possibility of collective action when it creates social distance within a production technology of symmetric endowments, appropriation, and distribution of material benefits of the common pool. Heterogeneous groups may find it more difficult to cooperate if, for instance, there are wealth distances in the group that limit the possibility of getting group communication to be effective for building trust, cooperation, and a commonly shared goal. Even if all agents depend equally on the commons, inequality and wealth distance within a group can limit cooperation, at least for the case when groups were allowed to communicate and devise a self-governance solution. This brings us back to the discussion begun by Bardhan, Ghatak and Karaivanov at the end chapter 3 (this volume), on the bargaining problem of achieving collective action. Ultimately, wealth inequality might be creating more difficult conditions for the group to decide over the individual choices and shares of the outcome, if compared to a more homogenous group.

Janssen and Ostrom discuss how a nested system of dilemmas needs to be solved when common-pool appropriators need to devise self-governing institutions. Aside from the problem of free-riding that generates the overexploitation, two more dilemmas need to be solved, one of devising the rules to solve the first tragedy, and another one when the players need to invest energy into enforcing the rules. In all three cases there is an incentive problem, that individual effort to conserve the resource, or to construct the rules or enforce them, is privately costly and one's benefits from such three efforts depend on cooperation by others. In the evidence shown here, I have argued that wealth differences among the players may restrict the solution to the second and third type of dilemmas.

Janssen and Ostrom (this volume) introduce trust and trustworthiness in their agent-based model and explore how agents may choose to adopt among possible rules to solve the tragedy of the commons. Their simulations do not necessarily prove that the heterogeneity among artificial agents is a constraint for the emergence of socially efficient rules, but the building of mutual trust was the critical explanatory factor of good rules being adopted. The adoption of desirable rules was strongly dependent on creating institutional environments where social interactions were sufficiently frequent to build the trust required. The experimental results discussed in this chapter suggest that the lack of trust among the players impeded players 2 and 7 in particular to create the level of cooperation that would decrease individual extraction and increase payoffs. This would be coherent with Janssen and Ostrom in that the greater distance in terms of wealth among the participants in the experiment is probably inversely correlated with the frequency of interactions they have had in the past, as the wealthier, for instance, are more likely to focus on their own private assets while the poorer would probably be more likely to interact with other poor when fishing or gathering firewood.[12]

Public policy regarding the rural sector in much of the developing world has reduced its attempts to directly change the distribution of wealth toward more equal institutions. Greater attention is being paid to progressive policies focused on the poorest, and on the creation of safety nets. Such strategy surely can change the equality of opportunities of the rural people, particularly for the case of the components of their income and well-being that depend on more complete market transactions where the marginal returns on human and man-made capital improve income. However, there is still an important share of their well-being and income that depends on solving collective-action dilemmas such as in the case of resources from the commons (e.g., food, energy, water); further, other cases where contracts are incomplete (e.g., rural credit) are still relevant and critical to well-being in the agricultural sector. In these cases, inequality in general can have a significant and negative effect in solving the failures, and therefore attention should be given to public policies that are aimed at the distribution of wealth based on efficiency grounds, and aside from equity and justice arguments.

As discussed in other chapters of this volume, the results here suggest that the ratio of income sources coming from collective to individual activities does not necessarily explain the emergence of collective action in cases of overuse of the rural commons, as one could infer from the Olsonian argument of a privileged group. Although poverty increases the marginal relative value of a unit of the resource extracted from the commons, the poor can also compensate their less advantageous private alternatives with more effective community institutions to reduce the losses from the tragedy of the commons. However, these results suggest that when inequality is present in the group, other types of difficulties emerge, such as wealth and social distances within the group, that limit self-governance and cooperation.

NOTES

1. "Commons" will not be assumed here only as a common-property resource, but in a more general way, as a resource area for which there is joint use by a group. Thus, state-owned natural parks may fall within this definition, particularly if exclusion rules are very costly to enforce. Also, natural areas that provide congestible or impure public good benefits to households in the form of nonextractive benefits will coincide with the definition used here.

2. For $\gamma < w$, we would be assuming that the marginal return on the first unit of effort into extraction is less than the marginal return on a unit in the exit option which would make the commons not an option.

3. One could also make the argument that such improvement in household human and man-made capital could also improve the marginal returns on the individual extraction of the commons via changes in the parameters γ and φ. One

clear example is better fishing or logging equipment that could increase the quantity of resources extracted per unit of labor.

4. Based on the model described in equation (2), the payoffs table is derived from the following parameters. Each group consisted of $n = 8$ subjects, and each subject was allocated $e = 8$ units of time in each round. Pretesting of the experimental designs at the University of Massachusetts and at the Humboldt Institute for Biodiversity in Villa de Leyva, Colombia, led us to denominate units of time as months per year. Scale concerns and pretesting led us to choose the following final parameter values: $k = (4/16810)$, $\eta = 2$, $q^\circ = 1372.8$, $\gamma = 97.2$, $\varphi = 3.2$, $w_i = 30$, and $e = 8$. Individual payoffs were therefore calculated from the payoff function:

$$U_i(x_i, \Sigma x_j) = (4/16810) \, [(1372.8 - (\Sigma x_j)^2/2)$$
$$+ (97.2 \, x_i - 3.2(x_i)^2/2) + 30 \times (8 - x_i)]^2$$

5. Social efficiency is defined here as the ratio of actual group earnings to the maximum earnings that can be achieved by the group as a whole in one round. The maximum earnings a group can get in a round, according to the social optimum benchmark, is $\$645 \times 8 = \$5,160$ pesos.

6. The results of this regulatory treatment are not discussed here and can be read in detail in Cardenas, Stranlund, and Willis (2002). In brief, the introduction of the external regulation with imperfect monitoring had an effective but short effect on cooperation, and as rounds went by, players increased their extraction to levels even higher than those before the regulation was imposed, crowding out any group-oriented preferences.

7. These wealth measures were estimated with local prices for land, animals, and equipment and what each person reported they had in their household. At the time the exchange rate was approximately Col$\$1,300$ per US$\$$.

8. For these ten observations, a simple correlation test yields a Spearman's rho $= -0.7455$ (p-value $= 0.0133$), and a Pearson coefficient of -0.5918 (p-value $= 0.0709$).

9. The Pearson coefficient is 0.520, but the p-value is 0.123, given the small sample size.

10. It is important to compare the last rounds in both stages so that any possible learning and reciprocity effects are included in the decisions. The first rounds of both stages in these experiments usually show a heuristic process, and only after a few rounds will the players adopt a strategy based on their valuation of the incentives, their other-regarding preferences, and the norms developed during the face-to-face discussions.

11. The fixed effects estimator uses one dummy for each of the possible fixed effects, group or individual. Not only does it help solve the problem of individual round observations not being independent due to individual and group effects, but also notice the greater increase in the adjusted R^2. Nevertheless, all three models pass the overall F test of significance.

12. Some may argue that another form of frequent interactions within unequal groups is through sharecropping and rent contracts of land or other assets. While these were very scarcely observed among the players participating in the

experiments, such case, if present, would create a rather vertical type of relationship that still is less frequent, for example, for the start and finish of the contract, as opposed to more daily interactions among equals.

REFERENCES

Alesina, Alberto, and Eliana La Ferrara. 2000. "Participation in heterogenous communities." *Quarterly Journal of Economics* 115(3): 847–904.

Baland, Jean-Marie, and Jean-Philippe Platteau. 1996. *Halting Degradation of Natural Resources: Is There a Role for Rural Communities?* New York: Oxford University Press.

Bergstrom, Theodore, Lawrence Blume, and Hal Varian. 1986. "On the private provision of public goods." *Journal of Public Economics* 29: 25–49.

Cardenas, Juan Camilo, John K. Stranlund, and Cleve E. Willis. 2002. "Economic inequality and burden-sharing in the provision of local environmental quality." *Ecological Economics* 40: 379–95.

Hackett, S., E. Schlager, and J. Walker. 1994. "The role of communication on resolving commons dilemmas: experimental evidence with heterogeneous appropriators." *Journal of Environmental Economics and Management* 27(2): 99–126.

Hoffman, Elizabeth, Kevin McCabe, and Vernon Smith. 1996. "Social distance and other-regarding behavior in dictator games." *American Economic Review* 86(June): 653–60.

Kollock, Peter. 1998. "Transforming social dilemmas: Group identity and cooperation." In *Modelling Rationality, Morality and Evolution*, ed. Peter A. Danielson. New York: Oxford University Press.

Kramer, Roderick M, and Marylinn B. Brewer. 1984. "Effect of group identity on resource use in simulated commons dilemma." *Journal of Personality and Social Psychology* 46, 5(May): 1044–57.

Lawler, Edward, and Jeongkoo Yoon. 1996. "Commitment in exchange relations: Test of a theory of relational cohesion." *American Sociological Review* 61(February): 89–108.

Ledyard, John O. 1995. "Public goods: A survey of experimental research." In John H. Kagel and Alvin E. Roth. *Handbook of Experimental Economics*, ed. Princeton, N.J.: Princeton University Press.

Olson, Mancur. 1965. *The Logic of Collective Action: Public Goods and the Theory of Groups*. Cambridge, Mass.: Harvard University Press.

Orbell, John M., Alphons J.C. van de Kragt, and Robyn M. Dawes. 1988. "Explaining discussion-induced cooperation." *Journal of Personality and Social Psychology* 54(5): 811–19.

Ostrom, Elinor. 2000. "Collective action and the evolution of social norms." *Journal of Economic Perspectives* 14, 3(Summer): 137–58.

Ostrom, Elinor, Roy Gardner, and James Walker. 1994. *Rules, Games and Common-Pool Resources*. Ann Arbor: University of Michigan Press.

Sally, David. 1995. "Conservation and cooperation in social dilemmas. A meta-analysis of experiments from 1958 to 1992." *Rationality and Society* 7(January): 58–92.

———. 2001. "On sympathy and games." *Journal of Economic Behavior and Organization* 44: 1–30.

Chapter 9

COLLECTIVE ACTION FOR
FOREST CONSERVATION:
DOES HETEROGENEITY MATTER?

Eswaran Somanathan, Rajagopal Prabhakar,
and Bhupendra Singh Mehta

It is of interest to examine the role of heterogeneity in asset ownership and ethnicity in the success of community management of forests for at least two reasons. First, we would like to know under what conditions community management of forests (as compared to state management, for example), is likely to be successful in order to make policy appropriately. Second, this setting is interesting for examining some hypotheses about the role that heterogeneity plays in collective action in general.

There are at least three different arguments that can be advanced for why heterogeneity may be inimical to the success of collective action. One, proposed by Alesina, Baqir, and Easterly (1999), suggests that tastes for public goods may differ across groups, and this can reduce the willingness to pay for public goods which may not be the kind that one's own group wants. This argument does not really apply in the case of the Himalayan forests examined in this chapter, where the benefit from collective action is forest preservation and its associated benefits so that there is really not much choice as to the type of public good to be financed.

A second argument, often made by political scientists, is that social divisions may favor politicians who seek to provide private benefits to particular groups rather than providing public goods. Again, in the setting of small village forests, this argument does not apply.

This chapter is part of a larger research project for which financial support from the National Science Foundation (USA) under grants SBR-9711286 and SES-9996602 is gratefully acknowledged, as is field support from the UP Academy of Administration, and the UP Forest Dept. Much of the research was carried out at the Institute of Rural Management, Anand. We are very grateful to Preeti Rao, Sweta Patel, and Mohit Chaturvedi for excellent research assistance. James Boyce, Shanta Devarajan, Dilip Mookherjee, and seminar participants provided useful comments on earlier versions.

This leaves a third argument, perhaps the simplest, which says that heterogeneity makes it harder for communities to reach an agreement about the sharing of benefits or costs of collective action. Inequality in power, for example, may mean that equal division would be unacceptable to the powerful, while any other distribution may be subject to conflict. The basis of this argument is that heterogeneity removes a natural focal point for agreements, and simultaneously makes groups uncertain about other groups' preferences, thus making agreement less likely as each group tries to drive a hard bargain, one that may be unacceptable to the other groups. The community forest setting provides an opportunity to test this last argument.

This chapter uses satellite data to measure forest density in Himalayan forests in northern India. The forests are managed by Van Panchayats, village councils created specifically to manage village forests. A village-level survey that was carried out as part of the research provides data on heterogeneity and other variables of interest.

9.1. THE SETTING

The study area lies in the Himalayas, in the Kumaun and Garhwal regions in the state of Uttaranchal in northern India. It ranges from 300 to over 3,000 meters in altitude. Terraced agriculture, the principal occupation, absorbing 80 percent of the labor force, is found up to a height of about 1,800 meters on the gentler slopes. Owing to the mountainous terrain and the limited possibilities for irrigation, agriculture is far less productive than in the plains. The value of agricultural production per hectare in the three districts into which the study area falls is little more than half that for India.

Forests are very important for agriculture, since they are the main source of manure. This comes directly as leaf mold from broad-leaved, mainly oak, forests. The oak forests also indirectly support agriculture, being a source of fodder and grazing for cattle, whose dung is used for manure. Oak leaf fodder, in particular, is of importance since it is often the only source of green fodder in the winter months. (Himalayan oaks are evergreen, not deciduous.) Timber from oaks has traditionally been used for making ploughs.

In addition to the broad-leaved forests, from elevations of 1,000 to 1,800 meters there are *chir* pine (*Pinus roxburghii*) forests. The villagers generally perceive these to be less useful since they are not believed to be as effective in preserving the water supply and are useless for fodder, while pine needles are an inferior source of manure. Pine trees provide firewood, but their greatest use, for timber, is bound up in cumbersome regulation by the government, even in village Panchayat (council) forests.

Despite the importance of the forests, widespread degradation has taken place, owing to the problem of the commons. Up until about the 1960s, oak forests were sometimes felled for making charcoal to be supplied to the hill towns and military bases. Following felling, grazing and lopping of the new growth by villagers often prevented effective regeneration and led to degradation into scrub.

The institution that forms the principal locus of collective action to manage village forests is the Van Panchayat, literally, "forest council." About one-third of the villages in the region have Panchayat forests. The rest use reserved forests, which are managed by the state government's forest department, and civil forests, which are unmanaged village commons. Civil forests are generally very degraded (Somanathan, Prabhakar, and Mehta 2002).

The government established the Van Panchayat system in 1930 as a means of arresting the degradation that was then taking place. It was meant to enable the villagers to form officially recognized councils with the powers to frame rules for use of the forests under their control. These were to be known as Panchayat forests. Villagers could apply to create Panchayat forests out of reserved forests and those parts of their village forests that had not been reserved.

Panchayat or Council members are elected by a show of hands in front of a government official once every five years.[1] There are usually five to seven members of the Panchayat, whose chairman is called the Sarpanch. The Panchayat is empowered to make rules and regulations to restrict and manage harvesting for forest products, and to levy fines on violators. Nevertheless, it lacks the coercive authority of the state, in that if the accused refuses to pay the fine, the Panchayat's only legal recourse is to approach the courts to recover the fine, a very costly procedure that is never used. Instead, social pressure is applied to force the violator to pay. Another weakness of the system is that some Panchayats have no source of revenue other than voluntary contributions from villagers to pay for a watchman. Others may have revenue from the sale of contracts for resin-tapping from pine trees or leases for stone quarries on Panchayat land. However, the Panchayats often have difficulty in getting access to the funds from the proceeds of such activities, as their bank accounts are controlled by a state government official. These weaknesses imply that the Panchayats are strongly dependent on informal collective action and social norms.

Van Panchayats provide a favorable mechanism for overcoming the common-pool problem in village forests, at least with respect to broadleaved species. The institution is the only one of its kind in India in having permanent control over its forest, with legal recognition from the government. Villagers are far more secure in their tenure in comparison with the system of Joint Forest Management between the state forest departments and forest user groups which spread widely in India in the 1990s. In fact, Van Panchayats probably compare favorably in terms of security of tenure and community control to most such institutions in developing countries.

While agricultural productivity is low in the region, inequality is lower than in the rest of India.[2] The gini coefficient of landholdings (including landless agricultural households) is only about 0.3 for Almora and Pithoragarh districts into which most of the villages fall, and is about 0.43 for Chamoli, in which the remaining villages fall. By comparison, the Gini coefficient for India is about 0.65 and is about 0.57 for Uttar Pradesh, the neighboring state in the plains. Wealth inequality is still lower than these numbers suggest, of course, since agriculture is less productive in the hills. The low inequality is reflected in the fact that there are very few landless households in hill villages and in higher rural literacy rates, which in 1991 were above 45 percent as opposed to about 36 percent for India and 30 percent for Uttar Pradesh.

Caste heterogeneity is also lower than in the rest of India, with the index of caste heterogeneity at about 0.67 for the three hill districts being considerably lower than the mean for India or Uttar Pradesh, which are about 0.86. (These numbers are higher at the district than the village level, due to the definition of the index. See tables 9.1 and 9.2.) The largest castes are Brahmins and Thakurs or Kshatriyas as they are sometimes called, with scheduled castes being a minority. Most villages have no other castes.

9.2. ESTIMATION AND RESULTS

The effects of heterogeneity of a village in landholding and caste composition on collective action can be evaluated using different indicators of collective action. Some of these are direct measures of collective action, such as the hiring of watchmen or the annual frequency of meetings of the Panchayat. However, the efficacy of collective action ultimately depends on the net benefits from the forest.

These are of two kinds: benefits from the stock, and benefits from harvest flows. The most important direct benefit from the stock is water conservation. The forest reduces runoff during the monsoon and enables percolation of rainwater into the rock, essential for maintaining flows in springs. Water shortages are acute in many villages in the region, so the villagers see this as an important issue.

We have no data on benefits from harvest flows, but we believe that

TABLE 9.1
Variable Definitions and Units

Variable	Definition
Area	Area in hectares
CCbl	Mean proportion of area covered by tree crowns in broad-leaved part of forest (1998)
Ccpine	Mean proportion of area covered by tree crowns in pine part of forest (1998)
Propbl	Proportion of forest that is broad-leaved forest or scrub (1998)
Proppine	Proportion of forest that is pine forest (1998)
Aspect	Proportion of area that is north-facing
Altitude	Altitude in kilometers
Altsq	Square of altitude
Popdensity	Population density, persons/sq km
Roaddist	Round-trip time in hours from nearest road
Nbl	Area covered by broad-leaved tree crowns in polygons with centroids within 4-hour round trip time of polygon centroid*
Npi	Area covered by pine tree crowns in polygons with centroids within 4-hour round trip time of centroid
sh_lpg	Share of households with LPG (cooking gas) in village
sh_kero	Share of households using kerosene in village
land_equal	Ratio of minimum to maximum landholding in village
caste_heter	1 − (sum of squares of shares of households of each caste)
tot_hh	Total number of households in village
sh_wopanch	Share of women in the Van Panchayat
Watch	Dummy for watchman in Van Panchayat forest
bank_bal	Van Panchayat's bank balance in rupees
Panch_meet	Number of Van Panchayat meetings per year
Fine	Dummy for whether Van Panchayat levies fines
open_day	Number of days Panchayat forest is open in a year for any use
tot_lstock	Total livestock in village

*Data for forest cover and other geographic variables were obtained for polygons, with the union of one or more polygons comprising a Panchayat forest, reserved forest compartment, and the like.

these are increasing in the stock, which we measure. There are two reasons to believe that villagers prefer to maintain high stocks if they can achieve the necessary collective action. First, privately owned trees and groves tend to be well-maintained and lopped for fodder and wood on a sustainable basis. If villagers were liquidity-constrained and had high discount rates that rendered it optimal for them to disinvest in the forest stock, this would not be observed. Second, interviews with villagers in the course of fieldwork confirm that villagers see "successful" Panchayats as being those with higher forest density.

TABLE 9.2
Summary Statistics

Variable	Obs	Mean	Std. Dev.	Min	Max
Area	65	187.6492	518.2693	1.5586	3977.997
Propbl	65	.6563196	.2459338	.0364924	1
Proppine	64	.2629923	.2717436	0	.9633344
CCbl	65	.5519873	.2911366	.0497542	.9901401
CCpine	60	.3524733	.3071703	.0055805	.9991623
Aspect	65	.4758215	.3471274	0	1
Altitude	65	1.578867	.3754071	.8209676	2.641732
Altsq	65	2.639199	1.273442	.6739878	6.978746
habdist	65	.8272339	.4380927	.2492761	2.416653
Popdensity	65	190.6974	142.9035	15.21957	807.4767
Roaddist	65	1.729002	1.7786	.0936674	6.823395
Nbl	65	471.772	363.8833	1.256366	1551.407
Npi	65	112.5675	119.8815	0	376.6362
sh_lpg	62	.1034808	.1805171	0	1
sh_kero	62	.2182615	.2419309	0	1
land_equal	63	.1272421	.1294285	0	.9090909
caste_heter	53	.3496799	.2385456	0	.7443225
tot_hh	63	86.31746	73.484	7	286
sh_wopanch	45	.1844295	.2191394	0	1
Watch	47	.7021277	.4622673	0	1
bank_bal	48	8756.604	31934.12	0	206090
Panch_meet	46	5.630435	3.548763	0	12
fine	45	.4444444	.5025189	0	1
open_day	42	282.2143	92.18818	182	365
tot_lstock	50	682.34	794.6712	60	3500

9.3. DATA

The data on village-level variables were obtained from village surveys conducted in 1998 and 1999. Information on the caste composition of households, the maximum and minimum landholding, the numbers of households with various amenities such as cooking gas and kerosene stoves, were obtained along with some information on other village-level variables and information about the functioning of the Van Panchayat, if any.

The sample villages were selected by a random choice of thirteen 1:25,000 topographic maps from those available in the districts with significant numbers of Van Panchayats. The first ten of these that contained villages were selected and one was dropped owing to lack of time to survey it. Each valley (as we will refer to the areas from the maps) contains about ten to fifteen villages that were surveyed. In each village the

Sarpanch or one of the other panches were surveyed. The information was checked by interviewing one or two other residents.

The data on the density of forest cover in each plot of land is derived from satellite images. Since the quality of these images for earlier periods is poor, it was feasible to obtain reliable data on a large scale only for one recent year, 1998.

Other important variables constructed from maps and census data include: the mean distance of the Panchayat forest from the nearest habitation, local population density, and availability of other forest nearby that serves as a substitute, and ecological variables such as the mean aspect, altitude, and slope.

The data are examined separately for broad-leaved and pine forests. The measure of the stock that is used is the estimated proportion of the area covered by tree crowns. For the species in question, crown cover is known to be highly correlated with other measures of the forest stock such as bole biomass, total above-ground biomass, and basal cover (Tiwari and Singh 1984, 1987). Crown cover is obtained from interpretation of an IRS-1D LISS-3 image from May 31, 1998, covering an area of about 20,000 square kilometers. Details of the image interpretation procedures are given in Prabhakar, Somanathan, and Mehta (2001), so only a brief account is provided here. Information collected on the ground was used as an input to classify the image into broad-leaved forest (including scrub), pine forest, and other categories (mainly grasslands and agriculture). Crown cover was visually measured in a sample of plots using a grid placed over an April 24, 2000, 1-meter resolution Ikonos satellite image. The IRS-1D Liss-3 image was used to compute various band ratios and the normalized difference vegetation index (NDVI). Regression of these measures on a logistic transform of crown cover in the sample revealed that the NDVI and the ratio of bands 2 to 5 were most closely correlated with crown cover in broad-leaved and pine forests respectively. The NDVI and the band ratio 2/5 were used to predict crown cover in our data. Tables 9.1 and 9.2 describe the data.

The effects of inequality and caste heterogeneity on collective action are presented in regressions reported in table 9.3. The first column reports marginal effects evaluated at the means from a logit regression of the watchman dummy variable. Neither land equality nor caste heterogeneity has an effect on the probability of hiring a watchman that is statistically significant at the 10 percent level. Nor is there any measurable gender effect captured by the variable "sh_wopanch" which is the share of women in the Panchayat. The regression reported does not include several potential controls. Any variable which affects the value of the forest could affect the choice of whether or not to hire a watchman. Such vari-

TABLE 9.3
Effects of Heterogeneity on Collective Action

	Watchman	Log(Panch_meet)	CCbl	Ccpine
Land_equal	0.20	1.6667*	−0.127	0.5786189*
	(0.53)	(0.8655)	(0.246)	(0.3287293)
Caste_heter	0.43	0.8893	−0.0491123	0.0329509
	(0.54)	(1.046)	(0.1850669)	(0.2401794)
Sh_wopanch	0.04	−0.54		
	(0.30)	(0.59)		
Aspect			0.2311953**	
			(0.1031657)	
Log(tot_hh)	0.2297**	0.4742	0.0426438	−0.0095995
	(0.11597)	(0.2825)	(0.0470941)	(0.0656419)
Sh_Ha	−0.58	−1.03	−0.0208291	−0.1260322
	(0.54)	(1.23)	(0.2006364)	(0.1597859)
Nbl			0.0001476	
			(0.0001091)	
Constant		−0.80		0.2787736
		(1.29)		(0.2563678)
Wald chisq (5)	11.38**			
F(5,38)		2.42*		
R²		0.26	0.16	0.09
Observations	44	44	53	48

Note: One, two, and three asterisks (*) indicate significance at the 10%, 5%, and 1% levels respectively.

ables include ecological variables such as the proportion of the forest that is broad-leaved, the aspect, as well as variables which affect the demand for forest products and the cost of harvesting. Inclusion of these controls, however, does not affect the result.

The second column reports a linear regression of the log of the annual frequency of Panchayat meetings in the year preceding the survey on the variables of interest with the same controls. A 10 percentage point increase in land equality raises the frequency of Panchayat meetings by 16 percent. This effect is statistically significant at the 10 percent level. Caste heterogeneity has a positive and insignificant effect. The inclusion of the controls listed in table 9.1 does not weaken the result, with the co-efficient increasing to 2 although significant only at the 12 percent level. However, the land equality coefficient, though positive, is not significant in regressions with valley dummies. It could be that this is simply due to reduced variance in the explanatory variables together with an increase in the effects of measurement error.

The results on direct indicators of collective action are mixed, with no effect of caste heterogeneity on either the frequency of meetings or the presence of a watchman, while there is some evidence that land equality affects the former positively, but not the latter.

Turning to the effects on outcomes, we consider broad-leaved forests first. The third column of table 9.3 reports a linear regression of crown cover in broad-leaved parts of Panchayat forests with valley fixed effects and instruments for the neighboring stock of forests. These instruments are the predicted stock of broad-leaved and pine forests from a similar regression that excludes the neighboring stocks.[3]

Neither land equality nor caste heterogeneity has a statistically signifi-cant effect. The signs are the opposite of those in the previous regres-sions. The share of woman panches (not included in the regression re-ported here) also has no measurable effect.

This is a reduced form for a model in which the underlying exogenous variables measuring heterogeneity affect the frequency of meetings and the hiring of a watchman, which in turn affect the quality of the forest. But the difficulty in estimating the model directly is that no instruments were available for the watchman and frequency of meetings. Any vari-able that affects these is likely also to affect the value of the forest, and its quality directly.

The results on direct indicators of collective action are mixed, with no effect of caste heterogeneity on either the frequency of meetings or the presence of a watchman, while there is some evidence that land equality affects the former positively, but not the latter.

The last column of table 9.3 reports a linear regression of crown cover in the pine parts of the Panchayat forests on the explanatory variables. The coefficient on land equality, significant at the 10 percent level, is 0.56, meaning that a 10 percentage point increase in land equality raises crown cover by 5.6 percentage points. Including controls with or without valley fixed effects tends to increase the precision of the estimate, which fails to be significant at the 10 percent level only for the same specifica-tion with valley fixed effects. Nevertheless, the coefficient is always posi-tive across specifications, ranging from 0.39 up to 0.69. The other coeffi-cients of interest, on caste heterogeneity, and the share of women in the Panchayat are not significant, as before.

To summarize, there is no evidence to show that caste heterogeneity or the share of women in the Panchayat has an effect on collective action to manage the forests. The effect of land equality is less clear. On the one hand, there is evidence for the positive effect of land equality on the frequency of Panchayat meetings and on crown cover in pine forests. On the other hand, there is no effect on the probability of a watchman being hired. Nor is there any effect on broad-leaved forest cover. As pointed out earlier, villagers generally have a greater interest in the preservation of broad-leaved as compared to pine forests.

9.4. CONCLUSION

Contrary to much speculation on the role of caste in collective action, no correlation between caste heterogeneity and indicators of collective action or forest cover was found. There is some evidence to indicate a link between land equality and one of the indicators of collective action as well as between land equality and forest cover in pine forests. However, the absence of any link between land equality and forest cover in broad-leaved forests and the other indicator of collective action makes it difficult to interpret this finding. The crude measure of inequality that we possess may also obscure relations which do exist.

As pointed out in the beginning of the chapter, the community forest setting examined herein offers a test of whether heterogeneity of different kinds hinders collective action in a very direct way, making it harder for agreements to be reached. The main finding is that, at least in this region, there is no evidence that ethnic heterogeneity hinders collective action. There is some evidence that land inequality may hinder collective action. No gender effect on collective action was found. These results are in contrast to those found at larger levels of aggregation or in different contexts by various scholars. This may be because collective action in the context of village forestry may not face the hurdles that it does in other situations where collective action has to be mediated by political processes or involves choices about the types of public goods to be provided. Of course, it could also be particular to the region studied, perhaps because inequality and ethnic divisions are not as pronounced and, therefore, variable, in comparison to other areas.

NOTES

1. On the functioning of Forest Panchayats, see Anon. (1984), Saxena (1987, 1995), Ballabh and Katar Singh (1988), Somanathan (1991), Aggarwal (1996), Agrawal and Yadama (1997), Raju (1997), and Satyajit Singh (1998), among others.

2. Based on agricultural statistics from various states. Data sources for this and the following paragraph are derived from the 1931 and 1991 censuses and were provided by Rohini Somanathan.

3. For further details, see Somanathan, Prabhakar, and Mehta (2002).

REFERENCES

Agrawal, Arun, and Yadama, Gautam N. 1997. "How do local institutions mediate market and population pressures on resources? Forest Panchayats in Kumaun, India." *Development and Change* 28: 435–65.

Aggarwal, Chetan. 1996. "Boundary and property rights in Uttarakhand Forests." *Wasteland News*, Feb.–March 1996.

Alesina, Alberto, Reza Baqir, and William Easterly. 1999. "Public goods and ethnic Divisions." *Quarterly Journal of Economics* 114(4): 1243–84.

Anon. 1984. *Van Panchayaton Ki Karya Pranali Ka Moolyankan Adhyayan*. Government of Uttar Pradesh, Lucknow.

Ballabh, Vishwa, and Katar Singh. 1988. "Van (Forest) Panchayats in the Uttar Pradesh Hills: A critical analysis." Research Paper, Institute of Rural Management, Anand.

Bardhan, Pranab, and Jeff Dayton-Johnson. 2001. "Inequality and the governance of water resources in Mexico and South India." Mimeo, University of California, Berkeley.

Prabhakar, Rajagopal, Eswaran. Somanathan, and Bhupendra Singh Mehta. 2001. "How degraded are Himalayan forests?" *http://www.isid.ac.in/~som/#WP*.

Raju, Manju S. 1997. "Seeking niches in forest canopy: An enquiry into women's participation." Mimeo, Institute of Rural Management, Anand.

Saxena, Naresh C. 1987. "Commons, trees and the poor in the Uttar Pradesh Hills." Network Paper 5f, Social forestry network, Overseas development Institute. London.

———. 1995. "Towards sustainable forestry in the U.P. Hills." Centre for Sustainable Development, Lal Bahadur Sastri National Academy of Administration, Mussoorie.

Singh, Satyajit. 1998. "Collective dilemmas and collective pursuits: Community management of *van panchayats* (forest councils) in the UP Hills." Mimeo, University of Sussex.

Somanathan, Eswaran. 1991. "Deforestation, property rights and incentives in central Himalayas." *Economic and Political Weekly* 26: PE37–46.

Somanathan, Eswaran, Rajagopal Prabhakar, and Bhupendra Singh Mehta. 2002. "Community vs. state management: Forest quality in the Indian central himalayas." Mimeo, Indian Statistical Institute, Delhi.

Tiwari, Amaresh K., and Javentra S. Singh. 1984. "Mapping forest biomass in India through aerial photographs and non-destructive field sampling." *Applied Geography* 4: 151–65.

———. 1987. "Analysis of forest land-use and vegetation in a part of central Himalaya, using aerial photographs." *Environmental Conservation* 14(3): 233–44.

Vasan, Sudha. 2001. "Ethnography of the forest guard: Contrasting discourses, conflicting roles and policy Implementation." Paper presented at the Workshop, "Rethinking Environmentalism," Dept. of Sociology, Delhi School of Economics, December 6, 2001.

Chapter 10

INEQUALITY, COLLECTIVE ACTION, AND THE ENVIRONMENT: EVIDENCE FROM FIREWOOD COLLECTION IN NEPAL*

Jean-Marie Baland, Pranab Bardhan, Sanghamitra Das, Dilip Mookherjee, and Rinki Sarkar

The state of the Himalayan forests has been a major source of worry for the scientific community over the last decades. Deforestation and environmental degradation have proceeded at an alarming pace over that period, with consequences not only for the neighboring communities, but also on a much broader scale. For instance, deforestation in Nepal is held responsible for the disastrous 1988 floods in Bangladesh, due to the siltation of the Ganga River (see Metz 1991 and Myers 1986). In this chapter, we focus on a particular aspect of the issue, by examining the determinants of firewood collection in Nepal as a major cause of deforestation. It is based on the Nepal Living Standard Measurement Survey dataset carried out in 1995–6.

Our main purpose is to identify empirically the effects of various dimensions of inequality and heterogeneity across households and across villages. We examine the evidence in favor of the hypothesis that collec-

*We thank Bina Agarwal, Eric Edmonds, Marcel Fafchamps, Duncan Foley, Robert Frank, Andy Foster, Larry Kotlikoff, Elinor Ostrom, Forhad Shilpi, Giovanna Prenuschi, and participants at the September 2001 Santa Fe Institute conference on Inequality, Collective Action and Environmental Sustainability, at the Mac Arthur "Costs of Inequality" Network Meeting (Costa Rica, January 2002) and the Department of Economics, University of Pennsylvania, for helpful discussions and advice. We are especially grateful to Shiv Shaini and Nobuo Yoshida for their excellent and untiring research assistance. This research was supported by the National Science Foundation (NSF grant no. SES-0079079) and the Mac Arthur Foundation Network on Inequality and Economic Performance. We thank the Central Bureau of Statistics of Nepal and the Poverty and Human Resource Division of the World Bank for making the Nepal LSMS data available to us. Baland is also supported by the Belgian Program on Interuniversity Poles of Attraction initiated by the Belgian State, Prime Minister's Office, Science Policy Programming.

tive action is an important determinant of collection behavior in a village, as communities with a stronger "cooperative spirit" might be better positioned to evolve norms and rules of use of the forest by villagers, as well as to devise formal or informal monitoring mechanisms to enforce these (see in particular Ostrom 1990; Baland and Platteau 1996; Jodha 1997; and Bardhan 2000).

The dataset we use permits three different aspects of inequality to be distinguished: economic inequality, social heterogeneity, and economic heterogeneity. Economic inequality is measured in two ways. It first corresponds to inter-individual differences in consumption levels and living standards within a village, as measured by the Gini coefficient of consumption expenditures. It can also pertain to inter-individual differences in wealth or asset ownership within a village, as measured by the Gini coefficient of landownership. Social heterogeneity is measured by an index of social fragmentation, which represents the probability that two randomly picked villagers belong to a different caste or ethnic group. Finally, economic heterogeneity relates to the extent with which villagers can differ with respect to the costs and benefits they derive from their use of the forest. To this end, we use the standard deviation in the time taken to collect a load (a *bhari*) of firewood across households from the same village.

Two channels relate inequality to the collection of firewood. The first channel, which we call "direct," relies on the aggregation of household behavior. A household response to norms and collective regulations in the village depends on a variety of characteristics, such as its income, wealth, time taken to collect a *bhari*, and household size. A nonlinear pattern of dependence on these characteristics implies that inequality in these characteristics will affect aggregate collections at the level of the village, purely via aggregation. For instance, as discussed in other chapters of this book, the impact of income inequality hinges upon whether the marginal propensity to collect firewood is increasing or decreasing with income. When it decreases (increases), firewood collection is a concave (convex) function of household income, and, by aggregation, average collection in a village falls (rises) with inequality, since richer households have a lower (higher) marginal propensity to collect firewood.

The second channel (which we call "indirect") refers to the dependence of collective action, norms, and regulation in the village on inequality and heterogeneity. We expect average firewood collection at the village level to increase with economic heterogeneity (dispersion in collection time). The first reason is that such dispersion may originate from different abilities across households in collecting firewood and drawing benefits from the forest resource. These differentials are likely to make it more difficult to reach uniform regulation and norms in the use of the collective re-

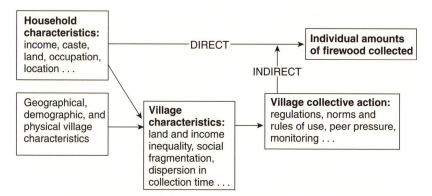

Figure 10.1. Firewood collection as a function of household and village characteristics.

source. Moreover, disparities in collection time may also reflect locational dispersion vis-à-vis proximity to the forest, which weakens their ability to monitor each other's collection activities. Similarly, it is often argued that social fragmentation tends to make collective regulation of the resource less likely and less effective (Alesina, Baqir, and Easterly 1999). Problems of asymmetric information and mistrust increase across groups of distinct preferences, and coalitional issues arise to undermine collective agreements, making the latter less likely and less stable. Moreover, monitoring, sanctions, and punishments may be limited to one's own caste, which implies less effective social sanctions in ethnically divided communities. On the other hand, the impact of economic inequality is ambiguous, as more inequality may lead to an Olsonian process whereby the economic elite bears the cost of collective action (for a discussion of this, see in particular Baland and Platteau 1997). Simultaneously, however, greater economic inequality is also associated with diverging objectives and preferences, which tends to undermine collective action.

The direct and indirect channels by which inequality can affect collection activities are depicted in figure 10.1. It is important to decompose the total impact of inequality into these two channels because only the second pertains to collective action (or local "governance"), in contrast to the first, which pertains to aggregation of "market" behavior.

However, the Nepal Living Standards Measurement Survey contains very little information on collective action, while it contains a rich description of household characteristics. As a consequence, we can estimate the direct channel operating through aggregation of household behavior. The indirect channel operating via collective action can then be interpreted as the "residual," obtained from subtracting the direct channel from the overall impact of inequality on collection levels.[1] This methodology is all the more useful as the literature tends to mix up the two channels, and often concludes in terms of collective action even when the observed phenomena result primarily from aggregation effects. In addition, our approach controls for average living standards while assessing the impact of inequality, thus avoiding spurious correlations that may arise from the correlation between inequality and per capita consumption.

The chapter is organized as follows. We first propose an extended description of the data by laying emphasis on the gross impact of various dimensions of inequality on firewood collection. In section 10.3, we present estimates of the "total" effect of inequality on village averages of collection, using the method usually followed by the literature. The results of our two-step methodology are then presented in section 10.4. In section 10.5, we turn to the results of various simulations, combining household with village estimates, to predict the total impact of various changes in inequality, and assess their relative importance. A final section concludes.

10.2. FIREWOOD COLLECTION AND INEQUALITY: A FIRST LOOK AT THE DATA

The World Bank Living Standards Measurement Survey (LSMS) for Nepal covers 274 wards, of which 215 are rural. We use only data for the rural wards, involving 2,713 households who were interviewed concerning their production and consumption activities for the year 1995–6.

Nearly one-third of the households do not collect firewood at all. On average, a household collects 5.8 *bharis* or bundles of firewood a month. This amount varies a lot from one household to another (the standard deviation across all households also equals 5.8). Both variations across households within the same village (with an average standard deviation of 3.2 *bharis*) and variations across villages contribute to this high degree of dispersion. For instance, across villages, the bottom 40 percent of the villages collect on average less than 1.33 *bharis* per household per month, while the top 20 percent collect on average more than 12 *bharis* per month. Figure 10.2 reports the distribution of villages according to the average level of firewood collection per household.

Each *bhari* takes a significant amount of time to collect, slightly more than 5 hours on average per household. Across villages, the village average time required to collect a *bhari* varies substantially, as its standard deviation is equal to 2.5. Within villages also, collection time varies across households, with an average standard deviation of 1.8 hours per *bhari* suggesting a significant extent of economic heterogeneity within villages. Moreover, higher levels of economic heterogeneity are associated with larger village average firewood collection, as shown in figure 10.3.

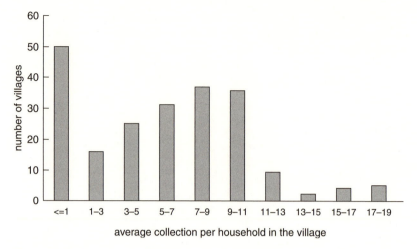

Figure 10.2. Frequency table of average firewood collection per household (total sample).

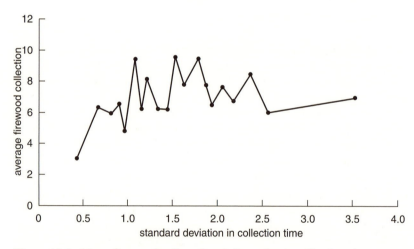

Figure 10.3. Mean firewood collected and dispersion in collection time across villages in the full sample (raw data).

Households mention adults as the principal collectors of firewood, and females somewhat more important than males in this respect (average number of adults collecting per household is 1.56, and of female adults is 0.94, so that female collection time represents 60 percent of the adult collection time within households; see also Kumar and Hotchkiss 1988). Seventy-seven percent of the households collected firewood from a government or a community forest, with the remaining households collecting

TABLE 10.1
Main and Secondary Sources of Fuel (total sample)

Type of fuel	Wood	Cowdung	Leaves and Crop Residues	Kerosene	Others: elec., Gas, Biogas, Coal, . . .
% of households using it as a primary source of fuel	72.8	18.4	6.1	1.7	0.9
% of households using it as a secondary source of fuel	5.8	8.9	26.1	1.4	0.5

either from their own lands or other sources (such as from roadsides). As table 10.1 indicates, wood fuel is the dominant source of energy for cooking and heating for 73 percent of the households.

Importantly, households in the sample make very little use of firewood substitutes, as less than 3 percent of the household used kerosene, electricity, or gas as the primary source of cooking or heating fuel. (A comparable proportion of households reported the use of a kerosene or gas stove.) By contrast, kerosene was used by 83 percent households as the principal source of lighting, so there is wide access to kerosene. The low use of kerosene or gas as a source of fuel owes either to the limited availability (or high cost) of kerosene/gas stoves,[2] the high cost of kerosene or gas in the villages, or the persistence of traditional cooking and heating practices (for related studies, see Amacher, Hyde, and Kanel 1996, and Chauduri and Pfaff 2002).

The mean annual consumption for a household was Rs 35,000. Given the average household size of 4.4 (in adult equivalent units), this consumption level corresponds to a yearly per capita income of approximately $250 (in 1996 US$).[3] Comparing across all households in the raw data, firewood collection is increasing and concave in household consumption expenditures, with a correlation coefficient equal to 0.15. Figure 10.4 illustrates this relationship, where the amount of firewood collected (number of *bharis* per household per month compared to the village median) is plotted against the corresponding percentile of household consumption expenditures (compared to the village median).[4] The 95 percent confidence interval indicates that the difference between high-income and low-income households with respect to firewood collection is large and significant. Across villages also, villages with high average

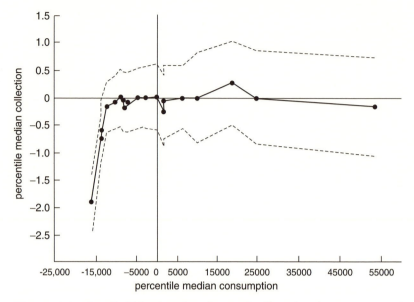

Figure 10.4. Household level median firewood collected and 95 percent confidence limits for the median of different percentiles of distribution of household total consumption (total sample differences to the village median).

levels of consumption expenditures tend to collect more firewood on average, with a correlation coefficient equal to 0.19.

Within villages, the Gini coefficient of consumption expenditures ranges from 0.09 to 0.60, and amounts on average to 0.30. Inequality in living standards therefore varies a lot from one village to another. Figure 10.5 reveals that higher levels of economic inequality within a village are associated with lower levels of firewood collection (the correlation coefficient is −0.19). This is in contrast to the association with collection time dispersion shown in figure 10.3. For those expecting a positive association with inequality owing to adverse impact on collective action, this may be somewhat surprising and would motivate an exploration to determine whether this correlation is spurious. Indeed, higher levels of consumption expenditures in a village are associated with higher inequality in consumption (the correlation between the two is indeed 0.19), so it is important to control for other possible channels of association between firewood collection and inequality.

Land is much more unequally distributed than standards of living, as Gini coefficient of landownership reaches 0.64 (ranging from 0.27 to 0.92).[5] However, its relation to firewood collection is weak, as the correlation coefficient is only 0.07. No clear relationship emerges from the raw data, as illustrated by figure 10.6.

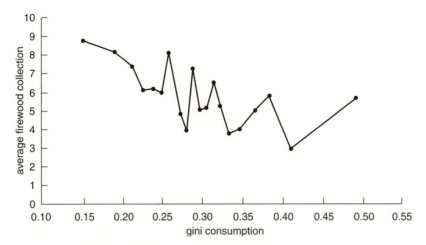

Figure 10.5. Village average firewood collection and Gini coefficients of consumption expenditures (raw data).

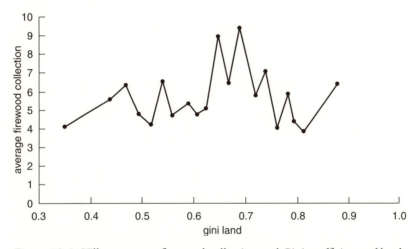

Figure 10.6. Village average firewood collection and Gini coefficients of land ownership (raw data).

In terms of religion, almost 90 percent of the households are Hindus. Religious fragmentation is low, as in many villages, all households belong to the same religion.[6] Caste and ethnic heterogeneity is much more pronounced, as 45 percent belong to upper castes (brahmin, chhetry), 28 percent to middle castes (magar, thuru, newar, tamang, rai, gurung, limbu), and 27 percent to Muslims and lower castes (kami, damai, surki). The index of social fragmentation is on average equal to 0.33,

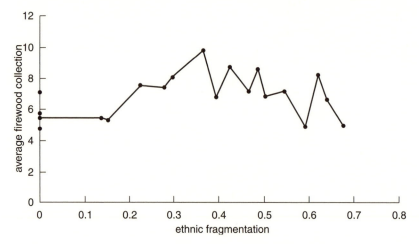

Figure 10.7. Ethnic fragmentation and village average firewood collection (raw data).

and ranges from 0 to 0.74 across villages. As figure 10.7 suggests, the relationship between the level of firewood collection in a village and its index ethnic fragmentation is weak (the correlation coefficients are both equal to 0.07).

If we turn to the other potential determinants of firewood collection, we find that education levels are low: 70 percent of household heads have no education. The majority of households (65 percent) are engaged in self-employed agricultural activities and livestock rearing, and another 16 percent of them work as agricultural wage-earners. Average village population is equal to 797 villagers, which corresponds to slightly more than 100 households, but varies from 42 to more than 5,000 inhabitants. On average, villages are fairly remote from modern transportation and communication: the average distance to dirt roads, markets, or agricultural extension services takes more than three hours to traverse, with paved roads eight hours away. They are also fairly disaster-prone, with 56 percent of the villages having experienced a natural disaster within the previous five years.

Finally, the government of Nepal introduced a community forestry scheme in 1993, handing over forest areas to be managed by local communities (for a general history of state intervention in forest management in Nepal, see Mahat, Griffith, and Shepherd 1986). The 1993 Forest Act defined "forest user groups" as autonomous corporate bodies that were assigned control over designated areas "in perpetuity." The user groups draw up to a five-year plan to manage, protect, and share forest produce. The use of forest products is subject to regulations and charges; the groups hire forest guards to monitor compliance. The groups also plan and implement reforestation schemes. Over 8,000 user groups had been created by 1999, with the government handing over 600,000 hectares to groups in 74 out of 75 districts.[7] The government plans eventually to hand over 3.5 million hectares to local communities in this way, representing 61 percent of all forest land in Nepal. Implementation of the scheme has been gradual, so many communities have yet to form forest user groups. Edmonds (2002) argues that exogenous factors such as proximity to towns and district capitals have determined the selection of communities where forest user groups have been created. In our sample, approximately 42 percent of the villages had at least one household who reported collecting from such a community forest. However, only 11 percent of households in the sample reported collecting from a community forest. Unfortunately, the Nepal LSMS did not gather more data concerning the functioning of these user groups, so we can represent the presence of local community rights only by the fraction of such households.

10.3. Firewood Collection at the Village Level: A First Approach

We first investigate the impact of different dimensions of inequality on average firewood collection in a village, controlling for village consumption levels, average collection time, and a range of possible geographical determinants of collection levels. In the second set of estimates, we control for some additional regional and distance variables, besides village demographics. Moreover, given that village average consumption expenditures and mean collection time are potentially endogenous, we follow a two-stage estimation procedure, instrumenting for these two variables.[8] The results are given in table 10.2.[9]

First, inequality in landownership, as measured by the Gini coefficient, is not a significant determinant of village average firewood collection. By contrast, the Gini coefficient in consumption expenditure continues to have a negative coefficient despite controlling for the levels of consumption. This effect could conceivably be explained by concavity of collections with respect to household living standards suggested by figure 10.4, an issue we shall investigate more fully in the next section. The impact of inequality in living standards may be large, as, in model 2, an increase by one standard deviation in the Gini coefficient (0.09) results in an decrease in firewood collection of about 25 percent in firewood collection (1.4 *bharis*). The corresponding decrease in model 1 is 13.2 percent.

TABLE 10.2
Determinants of Average Firewood Collection at the Village Level

Variables	Model 1: Reduced Form Specification	Model 2: Extended Village Specification (2SLS)
Gini land ownership	0.07 (2.00)	0.06 (2.24)
Gini cons. expenditures	−8.51*** (3.23)	−16.1*** (5.52)
SD in collection time	−0.56** (0.26)	0.54 (0.47)
Social fragmentation	1.57 (1.32)	1.41 (1.49)
Average cons. expenditures	56.6*** (20.48)	344.8*** (117.0) (I)
Mean collection time	−0.25* (0.13)	−0.50 (0.40) (I)
Fraction of households participating to a forest user group		2.05 (1.66)
Geographic and demographic variables	Some included	Included
Other village variables		Included
Number of observations	156	142

Note: *indicates significant for $\alpha = 10\%$, **for $\alpha = 5\%$, and ***for $\alpha = 1\%$. Standard errors are indicated in parentheses.

The coefficients attached to social heterogeneity are not significant. They are, however, consistently positive across the two estimates, which suggests that fragmentation may have a negative impact on collective regulation: villages with higher caste diversity, on average, may display larger firewood collections. The impact of increased economic hetero- geneity is not statistically significant.

The impact of average consumption expenditures on the average amount of firewood collected across villages is positive and very signifi- cant. An increase in the average collection time at the village level (which is itself a direct indicator of the state of the usable forest stock at the vil- lage level) is hardly significant, and negative. The existence of a forest user group in the village does not seem to matter.

These "reduced form" estimates remain difficult to interpret, however, as they represent the combined impact of household and village effects. In particular, it is impossible to distinguish here the variables that have an impact on collective action in a village, as their effects tend to be confused with their effects on the average household behavior in a village. For instance, if village firewood collection increases with consumption expenditures, is it because collective action is more difficult to organize in richer villages or because richer households tend to collect and consume more firewood? Moreover, as we argue below, the results above are statistically biased, owing to the fact that a significant fraction of households do not collect firewood at all.

To resolve those problems, we propose a two-step procedure. In a first step, we explore the "direct" channel by which inequality may affect collections, by estimating the impact of household characteristics on collection levels, while controlling for the village to which the household belonged. In other words, we exclude in this first approach all the variables that are constant at the village level (geography, collective action, prices, access to markets, population, land distribution) to focus on the determinants of intravillage differences in firewood collection between households. In the second step, we study the determinants of the differences between villages in average firewood collection, by using the residual variation in household collections that cannot be explained by household characteristics. The presence of collective action, and its potential determinants, are then assessed by comparing the two sets of estimates. This allows us to separate collective-action effects from aggregation effects in the overall impact of one variable on village-level firewood collections. The estimation procedure will also correct for biases that might result from censoring of collection levels at zero for a significant number of households.

10.4. Household and Village-Lssevel Determinants in Firewood Collection

We start with a report of the results of the first step of the estimation procedure described above, that is, the one which identifies the determinants of firewood collection at the household level, controlling for the village effect. A formal presentation of the model presented below as well as alternative estimates and a detailed exposition of the econometric methodology can be found in our companion paper (Baland et al. 2002). Among the relevant household charasterics, household consumption expenditures and the time taken to collect firewood are treated as endogenous. For instance, one may argue that household heads who are in better health may be inherently more dynamic and hard-working, collect more fire-wood, enjoy better standards of living, and need less time to collect fire-wood. The omission of the health status variable in the dataset in our esti-mates is thus capable of biasing our estimates. We accordingly use as instruments parental literacy, occupation, and inherited assets to predict household consumption. Note that the use of these parental characteristics as instruments allows us to capture the long-run components of consump-tion levels and to obtain a reasonable measure of permanent consumption. Transitory shocks in consumption are not captured by the instrumented consumption variable we use (but are in the non-instrumented version which we report in our companion paper [Baland et al. 2002]). This proce-dure is clearly more adequate to deal with such issues as collective action, poverty, or inequality. Moreover, we had to explicitly take into account the fact that some of our variables were censored: typically, the amount of firewood collected could not take values below zero, which implied the concentration of a large number of observations at zero.[10] Also, the time necessary to collect one *bhari* cannot be observed for households who did not collect, so we had to predict this variable for those households on the basis of household characteristics (such as demographics and assets owned) and instruments such as caste and migratory status. The estimation results for the amounts of firewood collected are presented in table 10.3. The baseline regression is presented without ethnicity, but this variable is then included in the alternative estimate.[11]

First, even though the significance of the coefficients estimated above remains low, we find that firewood collection is increasing and concave in levels of consumption expenditures.

Despite the lack of statistical significance, the effect of consumption is quantitatively important, as a one standard deviation increase in con-sumption level increases the amount of firewood collected by as much as 1.66 *bharis*, an increase of 29 percent over the average. We obtained similar results from many alternative estimates, which lead us to con-clude that expenditures have a strong positive and concave impact on firewood collected across households within the same village. The coeffi-cients tend to be imprecisely estimated because of the multicollinearity between the linear and square terms. An additional cause of imprecision is the use of predicted instead of actual values for consumption expendi-tures, which usually weakens the significance of the estimates.

The results obtained suggest that the relationship between collection and expenditure levels is concave, even after controlling for other rele-vant household and village characteristics. To further illustrate concav-ity, we show in table 10.4 the implied marginal propensity to collect fire-wood for different levels of expenditure using the estimated coefficients above.

TABLE 10.3
Determinants of Firewood Collection at the Household Level

Dependent Variable: Number of bharis of Firewood Collected per Month	Model 1: Coefficient (bootstrapped SE)	T-value	Impact of One SD Increase Evaluated at the Median (95%CI)	Model 2 (non-bootstrapped SE)
Consumption exp. (I) (10^6Rs)	77.71 (77.57)	1.002	1.66 (+/−2.18)	70.31 (78.41)
Squared cons. exp.(I)	−249.96 (727.83)	−0.34		−210.64 (728.21)
Collection time (I) (hours per bhari)	−0.15 (0.31)	−0.484	−0.02 (+/−0.78)	−0.15 (0.31)
Square of collection time (I)	0.02 (0.03)	0.647		0.02 (0.02)
Land owned X Collection time (I)	−0.22 (0.15)	−1.511	−0.53 (+/−0.68)	−0.23 (0.15)
Non-farm assets X Collection time (I)	−0.29* (0.16)	−1.781	−0.09 (+/−0.09)	−0.27*** 0.13)
Number of cows owned X coll. time (I)	0.01 (0.01)	0.972	0.14 (+/−0.28)	0.01 (0.01)
Years of schooling head X coll. time (I)	−0.03** (0.01)	−2.240	−0.39 (+/−0.34)	−0.03*** (0.01)
Household size	0.95** (0.42)	2.254	1.14 (+/−0.89)	0.98*** (0.45)
Household size squared	−0.05 (0.03)	−1.503		−0.05 (0.03)
Female headed household (dummy)	−0.15 (0.39)	−0.384	−0.05 (+/−0.25)	−0.18 (0.38)
Fraction children	−1.01 (3.56)	−0.283	−0.20 (+/−1.40)	−1.05 (3.52)
Fraction prime-age female	0.88 (2.84)	0.309	0.14 (+/−0.91)	0.87 (2.80)

TABLE 10.3 (*continued*)

Dependent Variable: Number of bharis of Firewood Collected per Month	Model 1: Coefficient (bootstrapped SE)	T-value	Impact of One SD Increase Evaluated at the Median (95% CI)	Model 2 (non-bootstrapped SE)
Fraction prime-age male	−0.45 (3.27)	−0.136	−0.08 (+/−1.14)	−0.48 (3.23)
Fraction old male	−0.25 (2.97)	−0.085	−0.02 (+/−0.43)	−0.22 (2.96)
Distance to the nearest market (hours)	−0.001 (0.009)	−0.073	0.01 (+/−0.34)	0.001 (0.008)
Distance to the nearest shop (hours)	−0.03 (0.02)	−1.197	−0.14 (+/−0.22)	−0.03 (0.02)
Upper ethnic group	—	—	—	0.53 (0.50)
Middle ethnic group	—	—	—	0.52 (0.54)
Lower ethnic group	—	—	—	0.54 (0.58)

p-value for chi-sq for joint significance = 0.00 (I) denotes an instrumented variable; *significant at 10%, **at 5%, and ***at 1%.

TABLE 10.4
Predicted Marginal Propensities to Collect Firewood, per Expenditure Levels (regression sample)

	Marginal propensity to collect firewood, per expenditure level and for different amounts of time required to collect firewood (impact of a 10000 Rs increase)			
Time Required	Expenditure Level			
	Rs20,000	Rs40,000	Rs60,000	Rs80,000
2 hours	0.61	0.44	0.28	0.11
4 hours	0.78	0.61	0.45	0.28

The decline in the propensity to collect firewood as income rises is rather sharp. While an increase in expenditure level by Rs10,000 results in a rise of 0.61 *bharis* collected (or 0.78 if collection time is equal to 4) for a low-income household, the increase is only 0.11 (0.28) for a high-income household. The concavity of the firewood consumption curve implies that an increase in economic inequality (as measured by household consumption expenditures) between households within a village tends to reduce the average amount of firewood collected in the village. The effect of inequality implied by aggregation of household responses is thus negative.

The positive relationship between firewood collection and consumption expenditures[12] is indicative of the absence of a well-functioning firewood market in the villages. It also tends to suggest that the income effect dominates the collection cost effect in firewood consumption, an issue which we investigate in more detail in Baland et al. (2002). This is related to the low value and the nonsignificance (across various estimates) of the coefficient attached to collection time. Collection time may have a negative impact on the amounts collected, but, rather surprisingly, the estimates are not significant, nor very important. This result is also robust across various estimates. One explanation for this lies in the absence of adequate fuel substitutes and the ability of families to shift the firewood collection burden from one member to another. Thus, in richer households, it appears that the spouse is more frequently involved than the household head in collecting firewood, whereas the reverse is true in poorer households.

However, when collection time is factored in with the level of education of the head, or the value of his non–farm business assets, the coefficients are negative and significant. This result can be explained by the fact that as the household main activity shifts away from farming, the opportunity cost of collecting firewood increases. Moreover, when occupational patterns were directly included in the regression, they were statistically significant with the expected signs.

Household size has a strong, positive, and declining impact on the amounts of firewood collected. The elasticity (computed at the median) is equal to 0.48, which suggests the presence of scale economies within families. All the other variables are less important and insignificant. Note in particular that the ethnicity of the household is not a significant determinant of firewood collection. This is important insofar as it indicates that, if ethnicity plays a role in firewood collection, it can only be through its impact on collective action. We return to this issue later.

The second step of our estimation procedure consists of evaluating the impact of inequality on the amounts of firewood collected in a village. In this approach, the dependent variable is not the average village collection as in section 10.3, but more precisely the (estimated) village effect on (latent) collections at the household level, obtained from the household regressions. There are at least three advantages for doing so. The first one has to do with statistical precision as, for each village, we usually have ten households which thus represent ten different estimates of the same village effect. Moreover, this approach allows us to take explicitly into account the problem of censoring and of unobserved data at the household level (which contaminates the village averages). Third, the household results can directly be used to analyze and interpret some of the village results. The presence of peer effects in consumption or informal social sanctions implies that one component of the village effect will be an aggregate of household responses (to the collection activities of others in the village), as elaborated in our companion paper (Baland et al. 2002). Also, as we shall see, the results obtained in this approach are close to the ones obtained with the village averages (model 2). They are, however, statistically more precise, more reliable, and more stable across alternative variants of the specification (e.g., with respect to the variables included, or treatment of endogeneity of per capita consumption or collection times).[13]

In table 10.5, we report the estimated coefficients, as well as the bootstrapped standard errors. Both village average expenditures and firewood collection time are instrumented by village averages of the corresponding instruments at the household level. (Compared to the household model, we also dropped some of the square terms, because of the high multicollinearity between a variable and its square.) In the last column, we report the impact on firewood collection of a one standard deviation increase in the variable, and the 95 percent confidence interval around this impact.

The results obtained in the complete regression model are consistent with the reduced form estimates reported in the previous section. First, inequality in land distribution does not really matter. The coefficient has the expected sign, but is small and insignificant. Note that we did not include a non-linear term in land assets in the household estimates. Assuming that higher order terms are insignificant in the household regression, a significant coefficient here would have been indicative of a collective action effect at the village level.

The Gini coefficient of consumption expenditures is negative, but not significant. The size and significance of this coefficient was robust to alternative specifications. This could be explained via the "direct" channel aggregating the concave relationships at the household level. Here, we find no evidence of a positive significant impact of inequality on collections via the "indirect" collective-action channel. If it does exist, it is overwhelmed by the "direct" channel which aggregates household responses.

Social or ethnic fragmentation significantly increases firewood collec-

TABLE 10.5
Determinants of Village-Level Firewood Collection

Dependent Variable: Village Residuals from the Household Estimates		
Random-effects tobit regression Number of groups = 133 Log likelihood = −3468.0341		Number of obs = 1369 Wald chi2(26) = 227.96 Prob > chi2 = 0.0000
Variable	*Coefficient (bootstrapped SE)*	*Impact of a one SD increase (95% CI)*
Gini land ownership	0.23 (2.78)	0.03 (+/−0.78)
Social fragmentation	3.48** (1.75)	0.78 (+/−0.77)
Gini consumption expenditures	−3.77 (3.74)	−0.34 (+/−0.67)
Standard deviation in collection time	0.73 (0.56)	0.89 (+/−1.35)
Average consumption expenditures	175.91** (84.27)	2.51 (+/−2.36)
Mean collection time	−0.43 (0.34)	−1.67 (+/−1.53)
Fraction in forest user groups	−0.22 (2.14)	−0.04 (+/−0.80)
Mean education of household heads*collection time	−0.17* (0.09)	−1.23 (+/−1.25)
Mean nonfarm business assets*collection time	−3.62 (10.94)	−0.42 (+/−2.48)
Average number of cattle heads*collection time	0.04 (0.04)	0.00 (+/−0.00)
Mean value of cultivated land *collection time	−0.71 (0.61)	−1.48 (+/−2.53)
Average poverty gap (1$ per head per day)	5.48 (4.83)	0.63 (+/−1.09)
Mean household size	−1.36** (0.59)	−0.99 (+/−0.84)
Proportion of children	20.37 (30.47)	1.34 (+/−3.94)

Table 10.5 (*continued*)

Dependent Variable: Village Residuals from the Household Estimates		
Random-effects tobit regression	Number of obs = 1369	
Number of groups = 133	Wald chi2(26) = 227.96	
Log likelihood = −3468.0341	Prob > chi2 = 0.0000	

Variable	Coefficient (bootstrapped SE)	Impact of a one SD increase (95% CI)
Proportion of young men	16.17 (29.59)	−0.85 (+/−3.06)
Proportion of young women	20.58 (28.40)	0.96 (+/−2.61)
Proportion of old women	16.32 51.18	−0.23 (+/−1.40)
Village population (1000 inh.)	−0.19 (1.39)	−0.39 (+/−1.95)
Square of village population	0.075 (0.276)	
Proportion of female-headed households	−4.76 (4.02)	−0.60 (+/−0.99)
Regional dummies and geographical variables	NS	

Note: *indicates significant for $\alpha = 10\%$, **for $\alpha = 5\%$, and ***for $\alpha = 1\%$. Standard errors are indicated in parentheses.

tion: an increase by one standard deviation in caste fragmentation increases firewood collection by 0.78 *bharis*. One may argue that this may be due to an aggregation effect, if it is the case that higher fragmentation reflects a higher fraction of ethnic minorities who collect more than others. However, our household results indicated ethnicity was not a significant determinant. This suggests that the effect of ethnic fragmentation can be interpreted as the detrimental impact of caste fragmentation on collective action, norms, and regulation at the village level.

Parallel to this, it is possible that locational heterogeneity of households, as measured by standard deviation in collection time, increases firewood collection. The coefficient is large (collection rises by 0.89 after a one SD increase) but not significant (with a *p*-value of 0.20). Once again, this effect may not be attributed to an aggregation effect, as the higher order term in collection time[14] at the household level was weak and nonsignificant. Differential proximity to the resource may create more difficulties in agreeing on a common set of regulations and in enforcing them. Many of the villages are spread out into different hamlets on different hills separated by an hour or two of walking time, in which case greater spatial separation may indeed undermine social cohesion. Analogous problems caused by differential proximity to canals have been vividly described by Wade (1988) in his study of irrigation in Andhra Pradesh (India).

The effect of forest user groups, though mildly negative, is insignificant. This is surprising, given the amount of attention and enthusiasm devoted to the community forestry scheme in Nepal. Our result also contrasts with Edmonds (2002), who finds a robust 10–12 percent decrease in the Arun Valley, after controlling for a host of household and village characteristics (see also Somanathan 1991). One explanation for this discrepancy is that our dataset covers the entire country, as against only the Arun Valley. Implementation in different regions was based on collaboration of the Nepalese government with different foreign sponsors, and Edmonds (2000) provides evidence suggesting that the UK-sponsored schemes in the Arun Valley were considerably more effective than those in other regions. Moreover, the variable we use is an imperfect measure, as it is the proportion of households who reported collecting firewood from a community forest. It therefore includes households who do not belong to a forest user group, but manage to collect some firewood from its forest, and excludes forest user group members who choose to collect from other sources. Though imperfect, it still constitutes a reasonable indicator of the importance of a forest user group in a village. (Edmonds 2002 uses the same measure.)

It may be argued that the effect of a forest user group is to redirect the source from which members collect firewood away from community or government forests. However, it turns out the opposite is the case. A much smaller fraction of households (4 out of 288) belonging to forest user groups collect from own lands or other nonforest sources, compared with households that do not belong to such groups (438 out of 1,696). Additionally, forests under a group scheme can be better managed, allowing households belonging to a forest user group to extract more produce without endangering the forest stock. Without additional information, there is however no way to discriminate among those various interpretations.

More importantly, the results indicate a significant and positive effect associated with average village consumption: richer villages tend to collect more firewood. The effect is particularly strong, as a one standard deviation increase in a village average consumption level increases firewood collection by as much as 2.51 *bharis*. This implies that, with no other changes in the village structure and economic opportunities, economic growth contributes significantly to the depletion of forest stocks. It partly reflects the aggregated impact of consumption level on collection at the household level. Besides, rising levels of prosperity may undermine social cohesion in the village and the extent to which households need to rely on forest in the long run, thus weakening local collective action with regard to forest use. In this respect, it is also worth noting that the effect of poverty is not significant.

The impact of the average time taken to collect firewood on the amounts of firewood collected is negative but not significant, thus paralleling our household estimates. This suggests that villages may not respond very actively to the depletion of the village forests, the resulting scarcity in fuel wood, and the increase in collection time by applying more restrictive norms and regulations, or more effective collective action.

The role of modernization, as represented by the interaction between some assets and collection time, is important. As explained above, these coefficients must be understood as reflecting the impact of occupational structure, since we control for the levels of consumption expenditures. First, villages with more educated people exhibit lower levels of collection. A one SD increase in the average level of education reduces the amounts collected by 1.23. This lends itself to various interpretations: higher educational levels increase the opportunity costs of time and thus reduce the time spent to collect firewood; better education facilitates collective discussions and regulation processes; it may also enhance the villagers' awareness of scarcity and their understanding of the available strategies, etc. The coefficient attached to the average value of cultivated land is also large though not significant. Related to this, some studies found that market integration, by expanding labor markets and other economic opportunities, may reduce deforestation (Bluffstone 1995; Sarkar 1998; and Amacher et al. 1996).

Village population has no impact on per household firewood collection. It implies that, contrary to the "incentive dilution" argument proposed by Olson, village population has no impact on collective action. By contrast, household size has a negative and significant impact on the average collection per household. This reflects the presence of large-scale economies in fuel wood consumption at the household level, as revealed by the household estimates (where the elasticity with respect to family size was close to one-half). The other demographic variables have little impact on village average collections, and their effects are very imprecisely estimated.

10.5. Simulating the Impact of Inequality on Firewood Collection

We now combine the effects at the household level with those at the village levels to examine the impact of different changes in inequality. For each simulation, we ignore, however, the general equilibrium effects of these changes.[15] We also incorporate the censoring effects, by allowing households which were not previously collecting firewood before the change, to switch to collecting firewood. Thus, in the first column of table 10.6, we present the number of households who switch and collect firewood after the change. In column 2, we indicate the change in the average amount of firewood collected by one household, and in column 3, we indicate the total impact of the change on the total amount of firewood collected over the 143 villages over which we ran the simulations.[16]

We examine the impact of the following eight scenarii:

Scenario 1: Reduction in Inequality in Living Standards Within Each Village.   In each village, we transfer Rs 13,500 of consumption expenditures from the richest to the poorest household in the village. This amount corresponds to one SD in household consumption expenditures.

Scenario 2: Reduction in Inequality in Living Standards Between Villages. We transfer Rs13,500 from the seventy-five richest villages (each villager contributing equally to this tax in each of these villages) to the seventy-five poorest villages (shared equally among the households in the village).

Scenario 3: Elimination of Inequality Within each Village.   In each village, we impose that living standards across all households in each village are made identical, and equal to the village mean.

Scenario 4: No Social Fragmentation.   In each village, we eradicate social fragmentation by setting it to zero. Each village is now perfectly socially homogenous. As we argued earlier, this is a direct attempt to measure the importance of collective-action effects on firewood collection.

Scenario 5: Direct Improvement in Living Standards.   We increase consumption expenditures for all households in all villages by 10 percent.

Scenario 6: Population Pressure.   We increase population in each village by 10 percent.

Scenario 7: Education.   We increase the educational level of household heads so that they all have at least primary education.

Scenario 8: Nonfarm Business Assets.   We increase in each household the value of nonfarm business assets by 20 percent.

Scenario 9: Modernization.   In each village, we increase consumption expenditures and the value of all nonfarm business assets by 50 percent,

Table 10.6
Predicted Total Change in Firewood Collection Under Various Scenarios

Scenario	Change in the Number of Households Collecting Firewood (# hh)	Change in Collection per Household, for Collecting hhold (# bharis)	Change in the Total Predicted Village Collection (# bharis and %)
Scenario 1: Reduction in inequality in living standards within each village	9	0.20	290 (3.0%)
Scenario 2: Reduction in inequality in living standards between villages	−2	0.05	65.3 (0.7%)
Scenario 3: Elimination of inequality in living standards within villages	+26	0.96	1365.9 (14.2%)
Scenario 4: No social fragmentation	−59	−0.98	−1678 (−17.3%)
Scenario 5: Direct improvement in living standards (increase by 10%)	18	0.63	982 (10.1%)
Scenario 6: Population pressure (increase by 10%)	−8	−0.03	927 (9.5%)
Scenario 7: Education (primary education for all heads)	−292	−1.69	−3883 (−40.0%)
Scenario 8: Nonfarm business assets (increase by 20%)	−1	0.07	102.1 (1%)
Scenario 9: Modernization (cons. expenditures and nonfarm business assets increase by 50%, primary education for all heads)	−88	1.01	613 (6.3%)

Number of observations: 1421, Number of villages: 143
Status quo: 88 households are not collecting, and total predicted collections are 9711

and we increase the general levels of education by imposing primary education to each household head.

The results obtained from the different scenarii are striking. The various dimensions of inequality have a very limited impact on firewood collection. Thus, the impact of reducing inequality in living standards, either within or between villages, is to raise collections by a small extent. Even if one were to eliminate all intravillage inequality, then (abstracting from general equilibrium effects) the amounts collected would increase by only 14.2 percent. The impact of social fragmentation is slightly larger. Under a drastic scenario whereby all villages are made perfectly homogenous, collections decrease by only 17 percent.

Much more important are the changes associated with the improvement in living standards and population. Thus, a 10 percent increase in living standards or in village population result in equiproportional increases in the amounts collected. This suggests that the massive deforestation witnessed over the last decades in Nepal could potentially be explained by the rising consumption standards and population levels that took place there. Even more instructive is the very large impact of education. The extension of primary education to all household heads, through its effects on the occupational structure at the household and at the village level, would result in a decline in firewood collection by as much as 40 percent. (By contrast, the impact of nonagricultural assets is negligible.) In the last scenario, where population and consumption expenditures increase by as much as 50 percent, the spread of primary education almost compensates for these changes, as the net impact on collections is a small increase of 6 percent. (The net impact is zero when population and consumption both increase by 43.5 percent, and primary education of all heads is required.) Thus, we can conclude here that the negative impact of consumption and population on deforestation can be completely counteracted by an active educational policy.

10.6. Conclusions

To conclude, this chapter uses household data concerning collection of firewood to analyze the role of inequality in the process of deforestation in Nepal. While we cannot provide direct evidence on collective action, we propose here an indirect methodology aimed at highlighting its effects on village-level firewood collection after controlling for aggregation of household behavior patterns. The results obtained provide some support for the impact of collective action on firewood collection, but none for the hypothesis that economic inequality significantly impedes collective action. In particular, social fragmentation tends to increase collections, most likely because of its damaging impact on collective action and norms at the village level (since ethnicity is not a significant determinant at the household level). The impact of other measures of inequality either is negligible or cannot be primarily attributed to the collective-action channel. The effects observed can be interpreted as the result of aggregating individual household behaviors. While land inequality has no impact, inequality in living standards has a negative impact on collections through the concavity effect at the household level. This effect largely dominates the potential adverse impact of inequality on collective action through conflicts in preferences, asymmetric information, lack of monitoring, social sanctions, and peer pressure or differential access to exit options.

The overall impact of inequality, either through collective action or aggregation effects, is negligible. It is notable that this result holds irrespective of whether or not we control for per capita consumption or aggregates of household characteristics that affect behavior at the household level. If all intravillage inequality in living standards were to be eliminated, then (ignoring potential general equilibrium effects on prices and wages) village collections would rise by only 14 percent. These effects are much less important than those associated with different aspects of growth and modernization, such as changes in population, living standards, and education. In particular, rising per capita consumption and population levels tend to raise firewood collections by a substantial amount, with an aggregate elasticity close to unity. Counteracting this is the role of primary education which raises the implicit cost of collecting firewood by offering better educated household members more lucrative occupations that reduce their dependence on the forest.

Our analysis suffers a number of shortcomings, many of which stem from the nature of the data we used. The results are based on cross-sectional differences across households and village at a point in time, whose relevance for understanding shifts over time is difficult to assess. The use of panel data over time would be a big step forward.

Other data limitations concern the absence of information on forest stock and quality: do differences in firewood collection levels drive deforestation? Is it important, compared to tree felling and conversion to agricultural land? To assess this question, we would need data concerning changes in forest stocks over time, for instance from land satellite images or forest surveys. Additionally, the relationship between forest stock and current collections in a dynamic perspective is not always clear. We have tried to control for this by using the time required to collect firewood, as the relevant measure of the forest stock for household decisions. It would be useful to seek direct evidence to support this assumption and improve our understanding.

The Nepal LSMS data are also poor with respect to information concerning prices and availability of substitutes to firewood. Also, we did not have any reliable information on the amounts of firewood actually consumed, sold, or purchased, and have instead assumed that the amounts collected were indeed consumed. Finally, in contrast to Varughese and Ostrom (2001), little or no information was available concerning informal collective action governing the use of forest products, forcing us to rely on an indirect approach. A direct analysis of the extent and effectiveness of collective action in limiting firewood collections on par with the analysis of household behavior would be preferable.

Notes

1. The methodological issues are more fully developed in our companion paper (Baland et al. 2002). Strictly speaking, there is a third alternative channel, through the general equilibrium effects of inequality within a village on wages and prices, but the nature of the data we use does not allow us to explore this empirically.

2. Thus, in only 13 percent of the villages is there at least one household reporting the use of a gas or kerosene stove.

3. Of course, PPP estimates of income per head are much higher. Thus, the World Bank estimates of Nepal PPP GNP per capita is 1170$ in 1995, much higher than the nonadjusted GNP per capita of 200$. The difference with the figure in the text comes from our use of adult equivalent units.

4. This correlation, incorporates a household size effect, as higher consumption levels are associated in our sample with larger household sizes. However, if one instead considers the plot of collection per head against consumption per head, the positive relationship is even stronger, and slightly convex. In the regressions below, we control for household size.

5. A household panel instrumental variable regression of annual consumption expenditure showed land and nonfarm business assets owned by the household as statistically significant determinants, but with small elasticities, varying between 0.01 and 0.02. Hence, neither of these assets are reliable measures of living standards; for this reason, it makes sense to use household consumption as our measure of household living standard, while keeping inequality in land ownership as an alternative measure of economic inequality.

6. The low variability in religious fragmentation explains why we decided not to study the impact of this variable on collective action and firewood collection. Its inclusion always led to insignificant estimates.

7. See "Community forest management: The nepalese experience" report by Richard Mahapatra, *Down to Earth*, Feb. 29, 2000, pp. 31–46.

8. Endogeneity of per capita consumption and collection time may arise from the existence of unobserved village geographical attributes (such as climate, soil fertility, etc.) that affect consumption levels as well as collection times. To overcome this, we use instruments that are plausibly uncorrelated with collection levels such as the village average educational and occupational status of the heads'

fathers, the amount of inherited land, the mean age of household heads, the fraction of different religious and ethnic groups in the village, and some distance variables (to town).

9. Missing values explain the difference in the number of observations between the two estimates. The first model includes altitude and past occurence of natural disasters. Model 2 includes the following variables: regional dummies, altitude, past occurence of natural disasters, time taken to various facilities, average proportions of children, young females, young males, and old men in the village households, proportion of female-headed households in the village.

10. For this purpose, we used Honore's (1992) fixed effects estimator for censored models to obtain consistent estimates at the household level.

11. Note also that in these alternative estimates, we report the estimated standard errors without bootstrapping. These standard errors are biased downward. However, as our main aim there is to show that ethnicity does not matter at the household level, the estimated coefficients would remain nonsignificant after bootstrapping.

12. Taking the average collection time (5.08), the turning point can easily be computed and is equal to Rs 126,616 which implies that for almost all households in the sample, collection is increasing in consumption expenditures, albeit at a decreasing rate.

13. The procedure, however, relies on the assumption that the village effects are additive to the household characteristics to determine individual levels of collection, as would obtain from a first-order Taylor approximation. It does not allow the use of interaction terms between village and household characteristics.

14. The square of collection time at the household level when aggregated to the level of the village corresponds to the standard deviation of collection time.

15. But we consider their direct impact on some other endogenous variables. For instance, when looking to the impact of some redistribution within a village, we explicitly compute the impact of this change on the village Gini coefficient in consumption expenditures.

16. To simplify the presentation, we report the results obtained when all the exogenous variables are kept at their observed values. The endogenous variables, in contrast, are allowed to change as a result of the change in the relevant exogenous variable. Moreover, simulations were run only for those variables which were significant in our estimates.

REFERENCES

Alesina, A., R. Baqir, and W. Easterly. 1999. "Public goods and ethnic divisions." *Quarterly Journal of Economics* 114(4): 1243–84.

Amacher, G. S., W. F. Hyde, and K. R. Kanel. 1996. "Household fuelwood demand and supply in Nepal's Tarai and Mid-Hills: Choice between cash outlays and labor opportunity." *World Development* 24(11): 1725–36.

Baland, J. M., and J. P. Platteau. 1996. *Halting Degradation of Natural Resources: Is There a Role for Rural Communities?* Oxford: Clarendon Press.

———. 1997. "Wealth inequality and efficiency in the commons, Part I: The unregulated case." *Oxford Economic Papers* 49: 451–82.

Baland, J. M., P. Bardhan, S. Das, D. Mookherjee, and R. Sarkar. 2002. "Household firewood collection in rural Nepal: The role of poverty, population, collective action and modernization." Mimeo, Boston University.

Bardhan, P. 2000. "Water community: An empirical analysis of cooperation on irrigation in South India." *Economic Development and Cultural Change* 48: 847–66.

Bluffstone, R. 1995. "The effect of labor market performances on deforestation in developing countries under open access: An example from rural Nepal." *Journal of Environmental Economics and Management* 29: 42–63.

Chaudhuri, S., and A.S.P. Pfaff. 2002. "Economic growth and the environment: What do we learn from household data?" Mimeo, Columbia University.

Edmonds, E. 2000. "Development, assistance and institutional reform." Mimeo, Dartmouth College, Department of Economics.

———. 2002. "Government-initiated community resource management and local resource extraction from Nepal's forests." *Journal of Development Economics* 68(1): 89–116.

Honore, R. 1992. "Trimmed LAD and least squares estimation of truncated and censored models with fixed effects." *Econometrica* 60(3): 533–66.

Jodha, N. S. 1997. Poverty, environmental resource degradation: Alternative explanations and possible solutions. Paper presented at the INDIA-50 Conference, University of Sussex.

Kumar, S. K., and D. Hotchkiss. 1988. "Environmental stress in the Himalaya." *Geographical Review* 75: 71–92.

Mahat, T.B.S., D. M. Griffin, and K. R. Shepherd. 1986. "Human impact on some forests of the middle hills of Nepal 1: Forestry in the context of the traditional resources of the state." *Mountain Research and Development* 6(3): 223–32.

Metz, J. J. 1991. "A reassessment of the causes and the severity of Nepal's environmental crisis." *World Development* 19(7): 805–20.

Myers, N. 1986. "Environmental repercussions of deforestation in the Himalayas." *Journal of World Forest Resource and Management* 2: 63–72.

Ostrom, E. 1990. *Governing the Commons: The Evolution of Institutions for Collective Action.* Cambridge: Cambridge University Press.

Sarkar, R. 1998. "Understanding sustainability: Study of a hill settlement." *Economic and Political Weekly*, October 31, pp. 2800–6.

Somanathan, E. 1991. "Deforestation, property rights and incentives in the central himalayas." *Economic and Political Weekly*, January 26, pp. PE 37–46.

Varughese, G., and E. Ostrom. 2001. "The contested role of heterogeneity: Some evidence from community forestry in Nepal." *World Development* 29(5): 747–65.

Wade, R. 1988. *Village Republics: Economic Conditions for Collective Action in South India.* New York: Cambridge University Press.

Chapter 11

GENDER INEQUALITY, COOPERATION, AND ENVIRONMENTAL SUSTAINABILITY

Bina Agarwal

SOME DISTINCTIONS

This chapter probes how gender inequality, as a form of inequality that is interactive with but distinct from class, caste, ethnicity, etc., might impinge on prospects of cooperation and environmental sustainability.

Consider first some distinctions.

GENDER INEQUALITY

Gender inequality, in relation to other forms of inequality such as class, caste, or race, has some distinct characteristics. One, gender inequality dwells not only outside the household but also centrally within it. Mainstream economic theory has long treated the household as a unitary entity wherein resources and incomes are pooled, and household members share common interests and preferences (Samuelson 1956), or an altruistic head ensures equitable allocations of goods and tasks (Becker 1965, 1981). Most collective-action literature is no exception in its assumptions about the household. In studying the effect of inequalities on cooperation in the management of common-pool resources (CPRs), for instance, the only inequalities recognized stem from *household-level* heterogeneity in say wealth (or class), ethnicity, or caste. Typically, these alone are treated as potentially embodying a conflict of interest, while intra-household inequalities are ignored.[1]

In recent years, however, virtually every assumption of the unitary model has been challenged effectively on the basis of empirical evidence, including assumptions of shared preferences and interests, pooled incomes, and altruism as the guiding principle of intra-household allocations.[2] Gender, in particular, is noted to be an important signifier of differences in interests and preferences, incomes are not necessarily pooled,

Paper written for the Conference on "Inequality, Collective Action and Environmental Sustainability," Santa Fe, New Mexico, September 21–23, 2001.

and self-interest resides as much within the home as in the marketplace, with bargaining power affecting the allocation of who gets what and who does what. Among other things, therefore, the household's property status and associated well-being can no longer be taken as automatically defining the property status and well-being of all household members, and especially not of women.

Two, gender inequalities stem not only from preexisting differences in economic endowments (wealth, income, etc.) between women and men, but also from preexisting gendered social norms and social perceptions, that is, the inequalities are also ideologically embedded. While norms and perceptions can also impinge on other forms of social inequality such as race and caste, gendered norms and perceptions cut across these social categories and exist in addition to other social inequalities. It is notable though that most collective-action literature, even while discussing the possible impact of social inequality, such as caste or ethnicity, on cooperation, locates the associated conflict of interest essentially in material differences, such as in economic endowments, or in occupational imperatives (e.g., herders vs. agriculturists). The inequalities embedded in social norms or in ideological constructions remain neglected.

Three, gender inequalities not only preexist in the noted forms, but they can also arise from newly defined rules and procedures that structure the functioning of the governance institution itself. For instance, the rules that guide the governance of CPR institutions can explicitly or implicitly exclude particular sections of the community, such as women, from its decision-making bodies, or its benefits. Again, much of the literature on CPR governance focuses on preexisting sources of inequalities and ignores those created or further entrenched by the institution being studied. In other words, inequality is treated as exogenous to institutional functioning, with little recognition of its potential endogeneity.

All three types of gender inequalities can impinge on prospects for cooperation and efficient local commons management.

VOLUNTARY VERSUS NONVOLUNTARY COOPERATION

A second distinction of relevance in this discussion is that between voluntary and nonvoluntary cooperation (or noncooperation). The collective-action literature essentially assumes cooperation (or its lack) to be a voluntary act: people can make free choices about whether or not to cooperate, based on their economic interests and the benefits they derive (or the costs they incur) from cooperation. This need not always be the case. It is possible, for instance, for people at the lower end of the economic and/or social hierarchy to be forced to cooperate by those at the upper end of the hierarchy. For example, the high-caste landed in an Indian village may threaten to withhold employment or credit from the low-caste landless if they fail to cooperate. Indeed, forests were often kept in good condition in feudal times by the power that the feudal lord exercised over the economic and social life of the village (Gold and Gujar 1997; Baland and Platteau 1996). Similarly, using their power, spouses or community members may threaten women with reputation loss, or even with violence if they break the rules of collective functioning. In other words, cooperation may *appear* to exist despite socioeconomic inequalities and a conflict of interest between different sections of the community, because it is imposed by some on others through the exercise of social and/or economic power. Here people might follow the rules out of coercion rather than consent, even when their costs from cooperation outweigh their benefits: these would be termed cases of nonvoluntary cooperation.

Of course, sanctions against those who break the rules (including extra-economic ones such as public reprimand) are often a part of the normal repertoire of rules in institutions governing the local commons (see, e.g., McKean 1986; Baland and Platteau 1996). But the difference here lies in the unequal and asymmetrical ways in which these penalties might be applied to particular sections of the population, predicated on the power underlying gender (or caste) relations.[3] And the sanctions may be applied without due process. Often such sanctions need not even be applied explicitly; they may merely loom large as an unspoken threat, especially in gender relations within the family.

Finally, the subdistinction *nonvoluntary noncooperation* also has a place in this discussion. For instance, as elaborated further below, some sections of the community may be excluded from participating in the activities of local institutions because of social norms. A case in point would be strict female seclusion norms which prevent women from joining a forest protection patrol or from attending village meetings, even when they would like to contribute to the effort. In other words, their noncooperation (not joining the activity) would be nonvoluntary.

The recognition of nonvoluntary cooperation (or noncooperation) is important not only for challenging simplistic assumptions about the nature of cooperation and of inequality, and the presumed relationship between the two that is dominating a burgeoning literature, but also for revealing the hidden costs and conflict of interests that could underlie the achievement of a well-preserved commons. These hidden facets are important to understand both in themselves and because they could reduce potential efficiency gains and even sustainability in the long run.

• • • • •

How might these different aspects of gender inequality impinge on the possibility of collective action and the form it takes (voluntary or nonvoluntary)? And what would be the likely outcomes for environmental sustainability? This chapter analyzes these effects in the context of local institutions for the management of forests in India.

Section 11.1 briefly provides the empirical context of the discussion. Section 11.2 elaborates on the nature of gender inequalities relevant to local commons governance in general and forest management in particular. Section 11.3 analyzes the implications of these inequalities on women's ability and incentive to cooperate voluntarily in forest management and outlines why we might expect women's cooperation to be in large part nonvoluntary. Section 11.4 focuses on the likely effects of women's forms of cooperation (or noncooperation) on the state of the forest. Sections 11.3 and 11.4 also pull together empirical evidence which establishes that institutionally created gender inequalities cannot be justified on grounds of efficiency; and further that forest quality could improve with women's greater inclusion in CPR decision-making. Section 11.5 contains concluding comments.

11.1. THE CONTEXT

Rural community forestry groups (CFGs) are among the fastest growing forms of collective action in South Asia. In India, these CFGs include: (i) groups formed under the state-initiated Joint Forest Management (JFM) program launched in 1990, in which villagers and the government share the responsibility and benefits of regenerating degraded local forests; (ii) self-initiated groups, started autonomously by a village council, youth club, or village elder and concentrated mainly in the eastern states of Bihar and Orissa; and (iii) groups with a mixed history, such as the *van panchayats* (forest councils) of the Uttar Pradesh (UP) hills (now in Uttaranchal state) initiated by the British in the 1930s. Some of them have survived or been revived by NGOs. JFM groups are the most widespread, both geographically and in terms of forest area. So far, virtually all Indian states have passed JFM resolutions which allow participating villagers access to most non-timber forest products and to 25–50 percent (varying by state) of any mature timber harvested. Today, an estimated 36,000 JFM groups exist, covering 10.2 million hectares (mha) or 13.3 percent of the 76.5 mha administratively recorded as forest land (Bahuguna 2000).[4] In addition, there would be a few thousand groups of the other types. NGOs can act as catalysts or intermediaries in group formation and functioning.

In 1998–99 I visited some community forestry sites across five states of India (Gujarat, Karnataka, Madhya Pradesh, Orissa, and the UP hills). Information was obtained mostly through unstructured interviews with villagers, at times conducted with women and men in separate groups, at other times jointly, in addition to individual interviews with key informants, especially office bearers in the executive committees of the CFGs. In addition, in the winters of 2000–1 and 2001–2, systematic data were collected for a sample of villages in three districts of Gujarat. This chapter is based largely on my 1998–99 fieldwork, supplemented by some early results from the 2000–2 fieldwork and by existing case studies.

It needs to be mentioned here that forests and village commons have always been important sources of supplementary livelihoods and basic necessities for rural households in South Asia. These common-pool resources have provided firewood, fodder, small timber, and various nontimber products. Especially for the poor and women who own little private land, they have contributed critically to survival. In India's semi-arid regions in the 1980s, the landless and landpoor procured over 90 percent of their firewood and satisfied 69–89 percent of their grazing needs from the commons (Jodha 1986). In that period, firewood alone provided 65–67 percent of total domestic energy in the hills and desert areas of India (Agarwal 1987). This situation was found to have remained largely unchanged even in the early 1990s. Firewood was then still the single most important source (and for many the only source) of rural domestic energy in South Asia, and was still largely gathered, not bought. In 1992–93, for instance, in most states of India over 80 percent of rural households used some firewood as domestic fuel, and in all states at least 45 percent of the households did so. Moreover, taking an all-India average, only about 15 percent of the firewood so used was purchased (Natrajan 1995).

This continued dependence of villagers on CPRs for daily essentials, at the time when JFM were launched in India, is a critical element in understanding how gender inequality plays out in the context of local commons governance.

11.2. FORMS OF GENDER INEQUALITY

In this discussion, we particularly need to consider two categories of gender inequalities: (1) preexisting inequalities in private property resources (such as land and income) and in gendered social norms and perceptions; (2) institutionally created inequalities embedded in the rules and procedures that govern the CFG itself. This section spells out the nature of these inequalities.

(1) PREEXISTING GENDER INEQUALITIES

(i) Inequalities in Access to Private Property Resources (PPRs): Men and women differ in their access to private property and to income-earning opportunities. Typically, women neither own nor directly con-

trol arable land (which can be an important private source of firewood, crop waste for fuel, and fodder).[5] They also have lesser access than men to employment and other sources of income (through which they might buy fuel and fodder). Given women's primary responsibility for these items, this becomes a particular constraint. Women in landless households or in female-headed households (which are more poverty prone) are placed at an obvious disadvantage. But even in male-headed households with land, although women can claim some advantage from the family's endowments in fulfilling their responsibilities, there is no guarantee of access to male-controlled income for purchasing firewood or fodder, or to family land for growing these items. (This would not even be recognized as an issue within a unitary view of the household, but within a bargaining framework all such claims are realistically recognized as subject to negotiation, with women usually operating from a weaker bargaining position.[6]) In general, therefore, gender inequalities in access to PPRs create gender differences in dependence on CPRs across most wealth and asset groups, even if in varying degree.

(ii) Gendered Social Norms.   The collective-action literature has typically emphasized the enabling and positive side of social norms;[7] but most gendered social norms have a "dark side" which constitutes a significant source of inequality. It bears emphasizing that social norms usually constitute not just a "difference" but an inequality. They permeate virtually every sphere of activity: they define what tasks men and women should perform, how they should interact in public, and so on. Consider the most significant ones in the present context.

One, the gender division of labor is both a source of inequality in terms of say the hours of daily work undertaken by men and women, and a source of difference in interest and dependence on the CPR. The more rigid the division of labor, the greater the conflict of interest this can create. In rural South Asia, typically women work longer hours than men;[8] and there is a fairly rigid division of task responsibility. Women, for instance, are largely responsible for cooking and cattlecare and for gathering fuel and fodder, and men for making agricultural implements and for house repair. In relation to the commons, therefore, women are especially concerned with firewood and fodder availability and men with small timber availability. Firewood and fodder, however, are daily needs, which create a persistent pressure on women, while small timber is an occasional need.

Two, in general, village spaces in which men congregate (such as tea stalls and the marketplace) are spaces that women of "good character" are expected to avoid (Agarwal 1994). The restriction is somewhat less for older women, but never entirely absent. These notions are often carried over to formal village meetings. A fear of reputation loss or family reprimand, or because they have internalized these norms, restrict women's mobility and their interaction in public decision-making bodies.

Three, there are female behavioral norms. The social strictures on women's visibility, mobility, and behavior, whether internalized by women or imposed on them by threat of gossip, reprimand, even violence, impinge directly on their autonomy and ability to participate effectively in CFGs dominated by men. Female seclusion norms are the most obviously restricting, but the more widespread behavioral norms are almost as pernicious. They create a range of social hierarchies which affect women's voice in private and public, in both obvious and subtle ways.

For instance, in public meetings (such as the general body meetings of CFGs), such norms often require women to sit on the floor while husbands and older village men sit on cots or chairs. Even where everyone sits on a level, often women (including executive committee members) tend to sit at the back or on one side where they are less visible. This makes them less effective in raising their concerns, while the issues raised by the more prominently seated men receive priority. Moreover, the presence of senior male family members makes women hesitant to attend meetings, or to speak up at them or publicly oppose the men. The hierarchy that marks respectful family behavior also tends to define community interactions.[9]

(iii) Gendered Perceptions. Male perceptions about women's appropriate roles and abilities are often at variance with women's real abilities. This serves as an additional source of inequality. Women are usually perceived as being less capable than men, or their participation in public is considered inappropriate or unnecessary. Some typical responses from CFGs are: "Women can't make any helpful suggestions," or that "Women are illiterate, what can they tell you?" In fact, women's illiteracy is commonly underlined to justify a disdain for their opinions, although not infrequently the men expressing such views are themselves unlettered.

(2) CREATED INEQUALITIES: GENDER IN INSTITUTIONAL FUNCTIONING

Apart from preexisting gender inequalities (both material and ideological) there can also be inequalities built into the structure of the governing institution, in particular in its rules and procedures, which can exclude women (in addition to the gender exclusionary effects of social norms), and can make for a highly gender-unequal sharing of costs and benefits.

(i) Rules of Membership.   The State-initiated CFGs broadly have a two-tier organizational structure: a general body (GB) which can potentially draw members from the whole village, and an executive committee (EC) of some nine to fifteen persons. The GB is expected to meet once or twice a year and the EC about once a month, although few CFGs are so regular. Both bodies, interactively, define the rules for forest use, the penalties for abuse, and how the forest should be protected (e.g., guards, patrol groups, etc.), the benefit distributed, and conflicts resolved. Those with voice and influence in the GB and EC thus determine how the institution functions, and who gains or loses from it.

The eligibility criteria for membership in the JFM general body and EC vary by state. Today, eight of the twenty-two JFM states for which there is information allow GB membership to only one person per household. This is inevitably the male household head. In eight others (some due to rule amendments), both spouses, or one man and one woman, can be members (Agarwal 2001). But this still excludes other household adults. Also, where the woman automatically becomes a member by virtue of her husband being a member (as in West Bengal), it is he who is seen as the primary member. In only three states (Gujarat, Madhya Pradesh, and Haryana) can all village adults become members. In the self-initiated autonomous groups, the situation is worse than under JFM, since these have replicated the customary exclusion of women from village decision-making bodies.

In the ECs within the JFM program the rules are more women-inclusive in nominal terms, since recent rule amendments in many states mandate a minimum of two or three to one-third women. But without a notable presence of women in the GB, or being selected by other women as their representatives, women brought into the EC to satisfy the mandatory requirements are less likely to be active or effective.

(ii) Rules of Closure.   Rules of forest closure can vary from a total ban on entry of both humans and animals, to restricted opening that allows the collection of specified products such as firewood and fodder and other nontimber forest products on certain days or seasons annually, to open access for some products throughout the year with a ban on others.

In most CFGs, across the board, timber and greenwood cutting is banned, although some allow highly restricted cutting of small timber for agricultural implements with permission from the EC. But CFGs vary in their rules for firewood and fodder collection and for grazing. Typically, when protection starts most villages start with the most rigid rules—banning all entry. As the forests regenerate, a less rigid closure regime could be expected. But in most cases this has not happened, even several years into protection. At best some have moved from a total ban to opening up for a few days annually. As discussed further below, these closures place a disproportionate burden on women, given their daily responsibility for procuring cooking fuel and for cattlecare. The more rigid the rules are, the greater is the burden.

(iii) Rules for Benefit Sharing. Benefit sharing has a twofold component—one is linked to the rules governing what can be extracted from the forest and how much, and the other to the method of distributing what is extracted. There can be gender inequities embedded in both components. For a start, entitlements are linked to membership (which usually requires paying a membership fee and/or contributing to protection by patrolling or helping to pay a guard's wages). Typically, non-member households are excluded from benefits. These households usually tend to be poor and so are less able to contribute toward the guard's pay or to patrolling (if men migrate out for work and women are restricted by social norms), with the exclusion disproportionately affecting women. Even for the members, the equity effects depend on the method of distribution. Strict closure, as noted, affects the poorest women the most. But where the forest is opened for a few days annually for firewood or fodder collection, some CFGs allow collection to any number of family members, others to a fixed number of family members, and yet others centralize the collection and distribute an equal number of bundles per family. While this last method ensures equality, in the first two methods, *de facto* female-headed households with few family members to help them are the most disadvantaged.

Gender disadvantage can also arise in regions where the forest produce is periodically sold. The money so obtained is in rare cases distributed, but only on the basis of one share per household even when both spouses are members. Typically, it is put into a collective fund which the EC largely controls, and the use of which it decides either on its own, or (sometimes) in consultation with the GB. Either way women tend to have little say in the use of funds.

How do these noted inequalities—preexisting and institutionally created—affect women's ability and incentive to cooperate voluntarily?

11.3. IMPLICATIONS FOR WOMEN'S COOPERATION

Cooperation in group functioning could be judged in at least two ways: one, the extent of participation in CFG activities (protection, decision-making, etc.), and two, rule compliance. Ideally both indicators should be used, rule violation being especially important since it can impinge directly on resource sustainability. However, most studies only take activity participation as an indicator.[10] Certainly it is easier to measure participation than to measure rule compliance, since few will admit to breaking the rules, and not every violation is recorded.

Moreover, as noted, cooperation (or noncooperation) can be either voluntary or nonvoluntary. Again, it is not easy to capture the voluntariness of an action, especially where power relations are involved. Nevertheless, qualitative assessments are possible, especially from what people themselves are willing to reveal, or from their actions when particular constraints are removed. Complaining (about the rules for closure, benefit distribution, and so on) could be one indicator of nonvoluntary cooperation.[11]

The noted gender inequalities can negatively affect *voluntary* cooperation on women's part by impinging on both their *ability to* cooperate and their *incentive* to do so, the former by affecting women's participation in decision-making, protection work, and so on; the latter by limiting women's options and imposing higher costs and providing lower benefits to them from forest closure.

Table 11.1 traces the potential effects of gender inequalities that we might expect first on women's ability and incentive to cooperate and then on the nature of cooperation (voluntary or nonvoluntary).

(1) ABILITY TO COOPERATE VOLUNTARILY

(i) Lower Participation in CFG Management, Especially Rule-Making. Virtually all the noted gender inequalities obstruct women from participating on equal terms with men in CFG management. For a start, the rules of membership in most states effectively exclude women from full membership, by allowing entry to only one person per household, or by recognizing women only as secondary members, or by excluding women other than spouses. The typical pattern in most CFGs is thus low female participation at all levels. In nominal terms, women generally constitute less than 10–15 percent of the general bodies in most JFM groups;[12] Even in states such as Gujarat which have the most liberal rules and all adults can be members, the percent of women in the GB is typically small; and even where NGOs are active, it seldom reaches half (see, e.g., tables 11.2 and 11.4 later in this chapter, relating to Panchamahals district, Gujarat, where a local NGO is active). The self-initiated groups and *van panchayats* tend to have even lesser female involvement.[13] A study of fifty *van panchayats* found that only nine had any women (Tata Energy Research Institute 1995).

Women are again poorly represented in the ECs, although there is some variation by context. In West Bengal, a study of 20 CFGs found

TABLE 11.1
Implications of Gender Inequality

Forms of Gender Inequality	Implications for Women's Ability and Incentive to Cooperate	Likely Effect on Cooperation	Likely Effect on Efficiency (viz. state of the forest)
A. Preexisting Sources of inequality			
1. Lesser access to private property resources (esp. land and cash)	Higher dependence on and fewer options to common-pool resources (CPRs)	Higher probability of breaking rules under strict closure: NC or NVC	If NC, effect negative; If NVC, effect neutral
2. Social Norms			
• Unequal division of labor	Higher dependence on CPRs	Higher probability of breaking rules under strict closure: NC or NVC	If NC, effect negative; If NVC, effect neutral
	Lower participation in rule-making, leading to unacceptably strict rules	NC or NVC	If NC, effect negative; If NVC, effect neutral
	Lower participation in formal protection and in other CFG activities	NVNC	Effect negative
	Higher cost incurred from closure	NC or NVC	If NC, effect negative; If NVC, neutral

• Gendering of space and behavior	Lower participation in rule-making, leading to unacceptably strict rules	NC or NVC	If NC, effect negative; If NVC, effect neutral
	Lower participation in protection and other CFG activities	NVNC	Effect negative
3. Social Perceptions	Lower participation in rule-making, leading to unacceptably strict rules	NC or NVC	If NC, effect negative; If NVC, effect neutral
	Lower participation in protection and other CFG activities	NVNC	Effect negative
B. Institutional Sources of Inequality			
1. Restricted rules of membership	Low participation in decision-making	NC or NVNC	If NC, effect negative; If NVNC, effect negative
2. Conservative rules of closure	Higher cost from closure	NC or NVC	If NC, effect negative; If NVC, effect neutral
3. Unequal rules of benefit sharing	Lower benefits from closure	Less incentive to cooperate: NC or NVC	If NC, effect negative; If NVC, effect neutral

NC = Noncooperation; NVC = Nonvoluntary cooperation; NVNC = Nonvoluntary noncooperation that 60 percent had no women, and only 8 percent of the 180 EC members were women (Sarin 1998). But in a number of other states, including Gujarat, there has been some change in recent years since it is now mandatory to include at least two women. In nominal terms, therefore, at least two get included.

There are of course also some examples of all-women CFGs or mixed CFGs with a high female presence, usually catalyzed by a local NGO, forest official, or donor, or induced by high male outmigration. But these are far from typical. Unfortunately, there are no comprehensive figures on this for India, but the 1,005 JFM groups for which I collected data through the Madhya Pradesh forest department had no all-women's groups; and of the 1,489 self-initiated groups surveyed in Orissa by a network of NGOs, only 0.5 percent were all-women.

Within the typical male-dominant mixed CFGs, women are usually ill-informed about meeting dates, and receive limited or no information about what is discussed at meetings. Characteristically, across all the regions women complain:

> Typically men don't tell their wives what happens in meetings. Even if there is a dispute about something, they don't tell us; nor do they volunteer information about other matters. (women to author, Kheidipada village, Gujarat, 1999)

> The men seldom inform us of discussions in meetings. When we ask them they say: "why do you want to know?" (women to author, Jamai village, Madhya Pradesh, 1999)

Hence, accurate information about rules, procedures, or other aspects of forest management does not always reach the women (my field visits, 1998–9, 2000–2). Similarly, male forest officials seldom consult women or seek their feedback on microplans for forest development. Some hear about the plans through their husbands, others not at all (Guhathakurta and Bhatia 1992). In regions of high male outmigration, these communication problems can prove especially acute.

Where women are GB or EC members, usually only a small percentage attend meetings. Table 11.2, based on data I collected in January 2002 from records of GB and EC meetings from eight villages in Panchmahals district, Gujarat, is illustrative. To begin with, the table shows a noticeable gap between women's nominal membership and their attendance at meetings in six of the eight villages. While in three of these villages (Asundriya, Golanpur, and Kotha) women's membership itself is low, in three others (Dehloch, Falwa, and Panchmua) nominal membership is relatively high but attendance is very low. Hence, in Dehloch, where women nominally constitute 46 percent of the GB and 36 percent

TABLE 11.2
CFG membership and Attendance in Meetings by Gender: Panchmahals District, Gujarat

Villages (Gujarat)	Women Members*		Meetings		Attendance at Meetings: Women as % of Total Attendees				
	% in GB	% in EC	Period	No	0	>0–15	>15–25	>25–33	>33
Asundriya	6.0	18.2	1999–01	5	4	1	—	—	—
Charada	52.9	27.3	2000–01	5	—	1	—	1	3
Dehloch	45.8	36.4	1992–00	16	2	5	6	2	1
Falwa	45.1	36.4	1997–01	9	3	—	5	—	1
Golanpur	15.6	18.2	1999	1	—	—	1	—	—
Kotha	1.5	18.2	2000–02	8	2	5	1	—	—
Manchod	21.9	27.3	1999–02	7	—	2	2	2	1
Panchmua	21.9	36.4	2001	1	—	—	1	—	—
Total				52	11	14	16	5	6
% of total					21.2	26.9	30.8	9.6	11.5

Note: *GB members are taken here as those listed in the letter of rights (Adhikar Patr) or whose names have been submitted in the Adhikar Patr application as having formally paid Rs 11 membership fee. Often, however, not all those so listed, especially the women, have necessarily sought membership. Some have agreed to or been persuaded to pay the fee to help the village fulfill the application requirements. In effective terms, those considered members in these villages are households who participate actively in protection by contributing to patrolling or the guard's pay. The numbers of such households fluctuate, but usually far exceed those formally listed.

Source: Author's fieldwork, 2002.

of the EC, in only one out of sixteen meetings spread over eight years did women's presence exceed one-third of those attending.[14] Falwa's record is very similar. The exception is Charada, where 60 percent of the meetings had more than one-third women attending, largely because the local NGO's staff in that area actively encouraged women's self-help groups (SHG) in the village to also join the CFGs. Hence, in Charada, of the twenty-seven women in the GB (out of fifty-one GB members), twenty-three belonged to some form of savings or health group. The minutes of Charada's meetings, however, indicate that most meetings focused on emphasizing to those present that they should take only nontimber species from the forest, rather than soliciting their opinions on significant decisions. Overall, aggregating the eight villages, women's attendance was low: out of fifty-two (EC and GB) meetings, 88.5 percent of the meetings had less than one-third women among those attending. About a fifth of the meetings had no women; and about half the meetings had under 15 percent or no women.

The gender division of labor and social norms are among the important factors underlying women's low turnout at meetings:

> If we were to attend meetings, the men will say, oh you haven't cooked my meal on time. What happened to my tea? . . . Why haven't you fed the cattle? Men make a big fuss about every small thing; so we are afraid when it comes to going out of the house for something that's not considered work. (women to author's research team, Panchmua village, Gujarat, 2001)

> The meetings are considered for men only. Women are never called. The men attend and their opinions or consent are taken as representative of the whole family—it's understood. (woman in a *van panchayat* village, UP hills, cited in Britt 1993: 148)

> Rural women and men can't sit together. But we convey our decisions to them. (man to author, Chattipur village, Orissa, 1998)

Sometimes, when asked directly, men admit that women's presence in meetings would help, but the most frequently given reason is: "Because women are the ones who cut the wood. If they came to meetings they would understand the need to protect the forests." As noted, this is also reflected in the minutes (where available) of the meetings in table 11.2 where the concern was largely to convey a message of restraint about the tree species women could take from the forest. There was rarely recognition that women could contribute to rule-making or to improved forest management.

If women do attend CFG meetings (in Gujarat or elsewhere), they seldom speak up, although the chances of them feeling emboldened to do so increase if they are present in relatively large numbers. When they do speak, however, their opinions typically receive little attention.

> Women cannot speak in front of elderly male relatives, and they have to observe *purdah*. (women to author's research team, Bambri village, Gujarat, 2001)

> People don't like it when we speak. . . . They think women are becoming very smart. (women to author's research team, Kotha village, Gujarat, 2001)

> I went to three or four meetings. . . . No one ever listened to my suggestions. . . . They were uninterested. (women in UP hills, cited in Britt 1993: 146)

Having a voice in the EC is important since this is a forum for discussions and decisions on most aspects of CFG functioning. As matters stand, they are not party to many crucial decisions. An analysis of JFM decision-making in five Gujarat villages revealed that all major decisions on forest protection, use, distribution of wood and grass, and future planning, were taken by men (Joshi 1998).

This is not to suggest that women's nominal presence does not count. Even if women are silent, it provides them information about what is happening in the CFG which they can share with other women, and it improves their sense of involvement. It is thus a necessary first step. And as the regression results presented later show, even this can have a positive effect on the state of the forest. But for effective participation, women also need to have a greater say in the decisions made.

(ii) Lower Participation in CFG Activities.   Inequalities in social norms, social perceptions, and institutional procedures also interact to restrict women's participation in other CFG activities. For instance, protection of the bounded area is a central CFG activity. In formal terms, this is usually done by employing a guard, with CFG members contributing the wage in kind or cash, or by forming a patrol group from among the member households. A male guard or an all-male patrol is typical: these two methods respectively characterized 37 percent and 22 percent of the seventy-three sites I visited in 1998–99. Female guards were rare, and only a small percentage of patrols had both sexes or women alone. Occasionally, there are shifts from all-men to all-women patrols, and vice versa (Agarwal 2001).

The gender division of labor and women's higher work burden put greater constraints on their time; fear of physical assault restricts their ability to undertake night patrolling; and in some areas where gender segregation is high, mixed patrolling is socially unacceptable.

Similarly, social norms and the perception that women have little to contribute exclude women from many other CFG activities. Women, for instance, are seldom part of teams taken on "exposure" visits to learn from other CFGs or given training in silviculture practices.

(2) INCENTIVE TO COOPERATE VOLUNTARILY

(i) Fewer Alternatives to CPRs.   Two types of gender inequalities, in particular, lead to women's greater dependence on the commons, and limit their options: one, lesser personal ownership of PPRs with no guaranteed voice in how household-level PPRs are to be used; and two, the unequal and relatively rigid gender division of labor. The implications of the first are obvious. The second places the burden of procuring items such as domestic cooking fuel mainly on women. And in the absence of well-developed rural markets for firewood (the preferred cooking fuel), this item has largely to be gathered, or substituted by equally little-monetized fuels such as crop waste or dung. Hence, even if women had the means to purchase these, in many regions they lack the option. (In rural India, 92 percent of domestic energy comes from firewood, dung, and crop residues, and only around 15 percent, 6 percent, and 3 percent of each respectively are purchased; Natrajan 1995.) On the one hand this dependency on CPRs gives women a stake in the regeneration of the resource; on the other hand it makes immediate availability imperative and reduces their incentive to cooperate within strict closure regimes.

(ii) Higher Costs of Forest Closure.   The costs of forest protection are broadly of two types: those associated with protection and management and those associated with forgoing forest use due to closure. The former would include costs such as membership fees, the forest guard's pay, the opportunity cost of patrolling time, and so on—costs largely borne by men. The latter would include the opportunity cost of time spent in finding alternative sites for essential items such as firewood and fodder, other costs (identified below) associated with firewood shortages, the loss of livelihoods based on nontimber forest products, and so on. Such costs fall largely on women. In overall terms, too, the costs tend to be higher on women.[15]

For instance, in scarcity areas typically the forest is totally closed for a start. If the area was highly degraded anyway, this need cause no extra hardship, but where earlier women could meet at least part of their fuel and fodder needs from the protected area, they were now forced to seek other options, including searching for alternative sites in the neighborhood and increasingly substituting inferior fuels such as crop waste and dung for firewood. In the early years of JFM, Sarin (1995) found that after closure, in some villages of Gujarat and West Bengal journeying to neighboring sites increased women's collection time and distances traveled for a headload of firewood several-fold: from 1–2 hours to 4–5 hours, and from 0.5 km to 8–9 km. Even this option was foreclosed when the neighbors too began to protect. But some women still felt compelled to enter protected tracts, with the risk of being caught and penalized by a patrol group or guard. Hence, the initial cost of strict closure was borne disproportionately by women. But what about changes over time, given that strict closure might be needed in some of the CFGs to ensure vegetation recovery?

Over time, with forest regeneration we would have expected a shift to less rigid regimes that allowed extractions to ease these shortages. This has hardly happened. In a majority of cases conservative regimes continue. Of the seventy-three CFGs I visited in India in 1998–99, sixty-seven had firewood available. Of these, thirty-four (50.7 percent) had a ban on firewood collection, wherein twenty did not open the forest at all and fourteen opened it for a few days annually for drywood collection, and infrequently for cutback and cleaning operations. The remaining thirty-three CFGs allowed some collection on a continuing basis, but usually only of fallen twigs and branches and sometimes only of certain types of nontimber species.

Even after years of protection, women thus reported a persistence of firewood shortages in the majority of villages across five states that I visited in 1998–99 (for a tabulation, see Agarwal 2001). In some cases, acute shortages were reported. The exceptions were regions that already had relatively good forests when protection started, as in parts of Madhya Pradesh and Orissa.

Some characteristic responses in scarce regions are given below.

We go in the morning and only return in the evening. Since the end of the rainy season, we have been going every day. I go myself and so does my daughter. Earlier too there was a shortage but not as acute. (woman EC member to author, Kangod village, Karnataka, 1998)

How will we cook if we don't get wood from the forest? What do they expect us to do? (women to author's research team, Panchmua village, Gujarat, 2001)

Usually women from both middle and poor peasant households report firewood shortages, since even the former seldom purchase firewood or have enough private trees for self-sufficiency. Where possible, women have substituted other fuels: a few could switch to biogas, but for most households gas or kerosene were not real options, hence they have to use inferior fuels such as dung, crop waste, even dry leaves. These fuels need more time to ignite and tending to keep alight, thus adding to cooking time; the additional smoke has negative health effects; and in some areas women economize on fuel by forgoing a winter fire for space heating (even in subzero temperatures), by not heating bath water in winter or heating it only for husbands, and so on. In terms of smoke, estimates by Smith, Agarwal, and Dave (1983) suggest that even when cooking with firewood on an open stove, the benzo(a) pyrene inhaled daily is equivalent to smoking twenty packs of cigarettes. This increases women's risk of cancer, tuberculosis, and various respiratory ailments (CSE 2001). Dung and crop waste are much worse offenders on this count than firewood. And even in terms of firewood, some of the species women are allowed to collect generate more smoke than the so-called timber species which they are not allowed to touch.

Women of landless or landpoor households, however, lack even the option of crop waste or dung, since they have no land or trees of their own and few cattle.[16] Indeed, closures have forced many poorer families to reduce their animal stocks (due to fodder shortages), which also reduces dung supply. As a poor woman in Khut village (UP hills) told me: "We don't know in the morning if we will be able to cook at night."

Is this cost unavoidable—a necessary price to pay for sustainable forest regeneration? Table 11.3 dramatically illustrates otherwise. In principle, for those dependent mainly on the commons, acute firewood shortages can arise both from inadequate availability of woody biomass in the protected forest and from restricted access to what is available. In practice, as table 11.3 shows, the acuteness of the shortages has much to do with restricted access. The table is based on studies undertaken by a network of ecologists, social scientists, and NGOs (and pulled together by Ravindranath, Murali, and Malhotra 2000). The studies provide information on the annual woody biomass regenerated in the protected forests, the annual firewood extraction, and the annual need for firewood in twelve villages (all with CFGs) relating to three states.[17] It is assumed, as a conservative rule of thumb, that 50 percent of the annual biomass regenerated per year can be extracted sustainably. (The estimates of annual biomass generated are themselves on the conservative side, since they exclude biomass with a girth of <10 cm, some of which is used as fuel.)

In six out of the twelve villages, less than 15 percent of the estimated firewood needed is being satisfied from the forest, and in none is more than 55 percent being satisfied. However, the point of note is that these shortages could be very substantially reduced by extracting much more than is being done. In ten of the twelve villages, extractions are far below even the conservative extractable limit, and of the two villages which show over-extraction, in one—Kharikamathani—the amount extracted is still below the total biomass produced per year.[18] In three villages, ex-

TABLE 11.3
Firewood: Sustainably Extractable, Actual Extraction, and Need

Village/State	Forest Area (ha) Protected	Protection yrs. form (in '96)	Basal Area (ha)	Growing Stock (t/ha) (t/ha/yr)	Mean Annual Increment	Sustainably Extractable (t/yr)	Actual Extraction (t/yr)	Firewood Need for Village (t/yr)	Extraction as % of Extractable	Extraction as % of Need	Extractable as % of Need
Gujarat											
Asundriya	176*	8 SC	14.4	144.5	4.10	361	35	554	9.7	6.3	65.2
Baluji na muada,	122	11 SC	44.9	343.4	9.75	595	46	511	7.7	9.0	116.0
Garda	100	6 M	1.2	58.5	1.66	83	38	264	45.8	14.4	31.4
Kunbar	188	4 M	2.0	63.7	1.81	170	61	603	35.9	10.1	28.2
Rampur	120	4 M	3.0	70.2	1.99	119	94	185	79.0	50.8	64.3
Karnataka											
Alalli	73	20 SC	13.8	140.6	3.99	146	0	416	0.0	0.0	35.0
Halakar	20	72 LC	10.5	119.1	3.38	34	107	521	169.8	20.5	12.1
Hunasar	120	100 SC	33.1	266.5	7.57	454	262	496	57.7	52.8	91.5
Kugwe	194	100 LC	24.5	210.4	5.98	580	209	697	36.0	30.0	83.2
West Bengal											
Bhagawatichowk,	53	11 SC	10.5	119.1	3.38	90	54	176	60.0	30.7	51.1
Kapasgaria	25	5 SC	11.3	124.3	3.53	44	8	139	18.2	5.8	31.6
Kharikamathani,	57	3 LC	4.0	76.7	2.18	62	87	161	140.3	54.0	38.5

Note: Basis for calculations (taken from Ravindranath et al. 2000)

Growing stock = 50.66 + (Basal area × 6.52); woody biomass with a girth of <10 cm was not included; t/ha = tons per hectare.

Mean Annual Increment (MAI) = 2.84% of the growing stock.

Sustainably extractable = (MAI × forest area)/2.

For the 4 Karnataka villages, the case study assumes firewood need to be 1.67 kg/capita/day. I have assumed the same for calculating firewood needs for Garda, Kunbar, and Rampur, since information on need was not given in the case study.

Assessments by author from information given in Ravindranath et al. (2000)

SC = Strict closure: Firewood cutting banned except for a few days per year. In some cases, collection of fallen twigs is, however, allowed all year round.

LC = Lenient Closure: Firewood extraction in the form of twigs and dry branches allowed throughout the year.

MC = Mixed Closure: A combination of LC and cutback/cleaning operations undertaken for a few days each year or every few years.

*Ravindranath et al. (2000) give a figure of 182 ha, but the forest department records show that 175.94 ha is the area registered formally as under protection.

Source: Compiled/calculated from information given in Ravindranath et al. (2000).

traction is less than 10 percent of extractable levels. If these villagers extracted up to the extractable limit, Baluji na muada could more than satisfy its firewood requirements, and Asundriya and Allali villages could satisfy 65 percent and 35 percent of their needs respectively. Hence, while firewood shortages might still persist, they would be much less acute. Currently these villages satisfy only 6 percent, 9 percent, and 0 percent respectively of their needs. The very low levels of extraction in cases such as these are due to strict closure regimes, enforced without women's acquiescence. In fact, even in nominal terms, virtually none of the villages in table 11.3 has even one woman on its EC.

Now consider table 11.4, which is based on data I collected in 2000–1 and 2002 from nineteen villages in Panchamahals district (Gujarat). In most of these nineteen villages, women report firewood shortages, as indicated by their dependence on inferior substitutes, crop waste and dung; and many report an increase in this dependence with protection.[19] However, there is some difference between villages with strict closure, that is, villages which only allow the cutting of specified (so-called firewood) species for a few days annually, and the villages with somewhat lenient closure, which too allow cutting only of specified species, but on a regular basis. In all nine strict closure villages, women report a substantial dependence on inferior fuels, which has grown with closure in several cases, while in three of the nine more lenient villages women report little or no use of inferior fuels and do not complain of firewood shortages.

What explains the difference in closure regimes? Does the presence or absence of women in the GBs and ECs affect closure rules? Table 11.4 suggests that the nature of protection might be dictated in large part by the number of segments in which the forest is divided (and the associated practical difficulties of strict monitoring), rather than by women's needs or their greater voice in decision-making. This is borne out by the results of the probit analysis presented in table 11.5. The dependent variable—the closure regime—is binary (strict closure = 1; lenient closure = 0). The three explanatory variables used are: number of forest segments (FSEG); percent women in the EC (WEC); and forest area per household (FAHH). We would expect strict closure to be associated negatively with all three. The greater the number of forest segments, the more difficult it is to ensure strict monitoring. The larger the proportion of women in the EC, the less strict we would expect closure to be, since women would have an interest in a more lenient regime. And the larger the forest area per household, the less incentive there would be to have strict closure and the more difficult it would be to monitor the resource carefully.

As hypothesized, all three coefficients have a negative sign, but only FSEG is statistically significant.[20] All the villages with strict closure have

TABLE 11.4
Details of CFG functioning in the study villages of Panchmahals District, Gujarat

Village/regulation	HHs 1991 Census[c]	Forest Area Protected (ba) Total	Forest Area Protected (ba) Per HH	Forest Segments[a]	Forest Quality Before Protection (as reported)	Forest Quality Now[d] (assessed) Scale 1–5	Protection Method	Women Members % in GB	Women Members % in EC	Use inferior Fuel Partly	Fuel Effects Women Complain of Firewood Shortages
Strict forest closure											
V₁	105	175.94	1.68	1	D	4.5	Guards	6.0	18.2	Yes	Yes (more shortage now)
V₂	660	482.25	0.73	3	D	3.5	Guards	0.5	18.2	Yes	Yes
V₃	161	310.03	1.92	3	D	4.25	Guard	1.5	18.2	Yes	Yes (some steal)
V₄	242	306.00	1.26	1	D	4.5	Guard	36.4	36.4	Yes	Yes (more shortage now)
V₅	281	53.25	0.19	1	D	4.75	Guard	45.8	36.4	Yes	Yes (women economize)
V₆	172	199.11	1.16	2	D	3.25	Hamlet F	54.9	36.4	Yes	Yes (some steal)
V₇[b]	145	546.00	3.77	3	D	3.0	Hamlet I	15.7	18.2	Yes	Yes
V₈	233	100.00	0.43	2	D	3.5	Hamlet F	21.9	27.3	Yes	Yes (more shortage now)
V₉	147	59.18	0.40	2	D	2.5	Hamlet I	0.8	18.2	Yes	Yes (acute shortage now)
Lenient forest closure											
V₁₀	100	425.00	4.25	4	D	3.0	HH I	1.8	15.4	No	No
V₁₁	83	241.71	2.91	5	D	3.0	Hamlet I	52.9	27.3	Yes	No (most; but poor Naiks report shortage)
V₁₂	66	15.27	0.23	3	D	3.0	HH I	0.0	18.2	Yes	Yes (women economize)
V₁₃	112	433.83	3.87	4	D	3.0	HH I	0.0	18.2	Yes	Yes (more shortage now)
V₁₄	95	170.00	1.79	1	D	3.75	Hamlet F	5.7	27.3	No	No'
V₁₅	60	32.00	0.53	2	D	3.25	HH I	0.0	27.3	No	No

TABLE 11.4 (continued)

Village/ regulation	HHs 1991 Census[c]	Forest Area Protected (ha)		Forest Segments[a]	Forest Quality		Protection Method	Women Members		Use inferior Fuel Partly	Fuel Effects
		Total	Per HH		Before Protection (as reported)	Now[d] (assessed) Scale 1-5		% in GB	% in EC		Women Complain of Firewood Shortages
V_{16}	249	133.83	0.54	6	D	2.5	HH I	1.1	18.2	Yes	Yes (some steal)
V_{17}	153	179.97	1.18	5	D	3.75	Hamlet I	21.9	36.4	Yes	Yes (more shortage now)
V_{18}	127	150.00	1.20	3	D	3.5	HH I	33.3	26.7	Yes	Yes
V_{19}	41	52.61	1.28	2	D	2.5	HH I	17.6	18.2	Yes	Yes (more shortage now)

Notes: **Strict protection:** Cutting of all timber species banned throughout the year; cutting of firewood species banned except when forest opened for a few specified days annually to allow such cutting under monitoring; open for fallen twigs and branches through the year except in V_1, V_5, and V_9, where this too is banned.

Lenient protection: Cutting of all timber species banned throughout the year. Cutting of firewood species and also collection of fallen twigs and branches allowed throughout the year.

Hamlet I: Hamlet-wise informal protection; Hamlet F: hamlet-wise formal patrolling; HH I: Informal protection by households near forest.

D = degraded.

[a] Segments: Two criteria were used to determine number of forest segments: (i) Noncontiguous forest parts separated by nonforest land or canal, etc;. (ii) number of sides of the village that the forest covers. Hence, where it covers three sides of the forest, it is counted as three segments even if it is contiguous.

[b] Includes the additional hamlet Hathirani na muada hhs, which has been protecting and using part of the forest.

[c] Data taken from 1991 census except for V_{15}, for which information was obtained directly from the village since census information was unavailable.

[d] Assessment of forest in comparative terms on a scale of 0 to 5:

0 = totally degraded; 1 = some growth; 5 = consistently good in terms of forest density, age (as indicated by girth and height), and overall regeneration. In between are forests which are good in parts but not consistently so.

Source: Author's fieldwork 2000–1, 2002.

TABLE 11.5
Factors Affecting Strictess of Forest Closure: Probit Results

Variable	Coefficient	Std. Error	z-Statistic	Prob.
C	1.797616	1.762546	1.019897	0.307800
FSEG	−0.626543*	0.338640	−1.850175	0.064300
WEC	−0.008060	0.051736	−0.155786	0.876200
FAHH	−0.015116	0.304199	−0.049692	0.960400
Mean dependent var	0.473684	S.D. dependent var		0.512989
Log likelihood	−10.06834	McFadden R-squared		0.233966
Restr. log likelihood	−13.14347			
LR statistic (3 df)	6.150262			
Probability(LR stat)	0.104524			
Obs with Dep = 0	10	Total obs		19
Obs with Dep = 1	9			

* Significant at the 10% level
Dependent Variable: CLR
Method: ML–Binary Probit
Sample: 1 19
Convergence achieved after 4 iterations
Covariance matrix computed using second derivatives

at most three segments of forest, and even among those with three segments, two villages (V_2 and V_3) have a continuous stretch of forest. The villages with more lenient closure mostly have more than three segments and noncontiguous patches. The scatter of the forest also affects the form of protection. All the villages with strict closure employ either guards (where there is a continuous stretch of forest) or a hamlet-wise form of protection. In the villages with more lenient closure, the forest is typically scattered in several parts, and here responsibility for protection usually vests in the households located near a given part, and occasionally with the hamlet as a whole. It is perhaps not surprising that women's presence in the EC in itself does not make a significant difference to the choice of closure regime, given that they usually have little voice in decisions. At best, from my interviews in these villages, women's complaints about strict closure helped shift some of the villages which earlier allowed no extraction at all to allowing some extraction for a few days annually.

The second major cost that falls disproportionately on women stems from the common ban on grazing, necessitating households to procure fodder in other ways and to stall-feed animals. Household responses to fodder problems can vary, but women remain in a no-win situation.

Poor households, for instance, have been selling off their cattle, which reduces dung availability for both fuel and manure. In households that have kept their cattle but cannot afford to buy fodder, women spend additional time seeking alternative sites, apart from spending time and energy on stall-feeding and stall cleaning. This is also the case among households that have replaced their goats with milch cattle. In parts of Gujarat, women report on average an extra workload of two to three hours due to stall-feeding alone. Moreover, in some Gujarat villages, where dairy cooperatives have been opened, the cattle numbers have in fact increased, and feeding and washing them has placed severe burdens on the women.[21] The milk so obtained is typically sold and not drunk by the family, and the cash returns from the sale are usually controlled by the men (author's interviews, January 2002).

(iii) Lower Benefits from Forest Closure. Given the methods used for distributing the benefits, closure typically brings fewer benefits for women than men. Some of this difference arises from the CFG's distribution rules and some from an interactive effect of the rules with unequal intra-household allocations. Benefits can derive from the distribution of forest products in kind (e.g., firewood, fodder, other nontimber products, timber, etc.); or from the use of collective funds (obtained through membership fees, fines, selling forest produce, compulsory deduction from wages received for any forest work, and so on); or from the distribution of cash benefits (in rare cases). Women benefit directly if the benefits are in kind (e.g., in the form of firewood or fodder), but the extent of benefit depends on the rules of drywood or fodder extraction. As noted above, strict closure regimes have minimized such benefits. Other nontimber products (such as tendu leaves), of which most CFGs allow collection, are seasonal, and while women collect them, men are the ones who usually sell them and control the proceeds.

Community funds are similarly controlled by male-dominant ECs. Women have little say in fund allocations. Data from twenty-nine CFGs across six Indian states that I examined, for instance, showed that most commonly, the funds were put to uses from which women were unlikely to benefit, such as youth clubhouse repair, purchasing community utensils, rugs, drums, etc. (which the men used or leased out), and travel by EC members (see also, Agarwal 2001). In some regions, such as Orissa, spending on religious functions and youth clubs was especially common (my fieldwork, 1998).

Would women spend such funds differently if they had more control? While a definitive answer is not possible in the absence of comparable information for women-dominant CFGs or all-women CFGs, related information from all-women panchayats (village councils) and other women's groups is strongly indicative. Early studies in Madhya Pradesh and Maharashtra, for instance, found all-women panchayats to differ from all-male ones in the priorities they gave to community concerns. Women placed greater emphasis on funding the provision of taps and covered toilets in Madhya Pradesh (Gandhi and Shah 1991), and to the installation of pumps on village wells, building toilets in low-caste hamlets, and filling vacancies for village school teachers in Maharashtra (Gala 1990). More recent studies reinforce these early observations: women panchayat members and chairpersons are found to pay more attention to solving problems of drinking water, children's education, roads, and electricity supply (CWDS 1999; UNDP 2001). At times, women's interventions in mixed panchayats has also led to shifts in priorities. In two Karnataka villages, five women elected representatives disagreed with the men's decision to construct a water tank, pointing out that the villages had adequate water but lacked health facilities, roads, and schools, and the funds should be spent on these needs (Narasimhan 1999). All this suggests that if women control or have a say in CFG funds, the funds are more likely to flow toward community needs and alternative priorities.

Gender-related distributional inequalities in CFGs also stem from the transfer of any cash benefits solely to men (on behalf of the household), or giving the household only one share when both spouses are members. Such transfers assume a common gender interest and deny their possible negative effect on women's incentive to cooperate. In practice, money given to men does not guarantee equal sharing or even any sharing within the family. As found in non-CFG contexts (e.g., Dwyer and Bruce 1988), here too men have been known to spend a substantial part on gambling, liquor, or personal items.[22] It is notable that when asked their preference women often opt for separate entitlements. For instance, in a meeting of four JFM groups in West Bengal in which both spouses were present, women wanted separate and equal shares for husbands and wives (Sarin 1995). I found the same in Gujarat, where women in some villages were refusing to become members unless they were entitled to their own share of benefits (my fieldwork, 1999). Being members in their own right is one way by which women could get such benefits directly, provided that the individual and not the household is treated as the unit for benefit-sharing.

Direct membership to a CFG can also bring additional financial benefits. For instance, in some Gujarat villages, a part of the daily wage earnings from tree planting goes into a savings fund. Where women are not members, the savings go into a family account (which the men effectively control). In contrast, in a few initiatives where female membership is high, savings go into separate accounts for women and men, and women can make their own decisions on how to spend this money.[23]

• • • • •

Overall therefore, there are several reasons why we would expect women by and large to not cooperate voluntarily with strict closure: their high dependence on the commons, the everyday nature of this dependence and fewer alternatives for firewood and fodder; their lack of direct participation in or even consultation on rule-making, so that their concerns get neglected in the rules men frame; and their higher costs and fewer benefits from closure. Rather, we would expect a higher probability of noncooperation (e.g., breaking rules), nonvoluntary cooperation (reflected, e.g., in complaining), and nonvoluntary noncooperation (e.g., not participating in institutional activities due to exclusion rather than choice).

(3) NONCOOPERATION AND NONVOLUNTARY COOPERATION

Nonvoluntariness in cooperation can take several forms. While a systematic assessment of this awaits more detailed empirical analysis, my fieldwork thus far provides interesting pointers. To begin with, wherever there is strict forest closure, women dislike the rules. Some break them (noncooperation); some complain but comply (nonvoluntary cooperation); and some few exit and form their own group.

(i) Noncooperation.   Almost all the villages I studied reported some cases of rule violation, at times as a frequent occurrence. Violations by men are usually for timber for self-use or sale (the latter in areas with commercially valuable trees). Violations by women are typically for firewood. Sometimes, acute need forces women into persistent altercations with the guard.[24] In one Gujarat village I found that only when the guard threatened to resign did the EC agree to open the forest for a few days annually. In Agrawal's (1999) study of a *van panchayat* village, women constituted 70–80 percent of the reported offenders between 1951 and 1991, most being poor and low-caste. It is notable that Agrawal suggests this may be due not only to their greater dependence on the forest, but also because the forest council dominated by high-caste men applies the rules more strictly to poor, low-caste women.

(ii) Nonvoluntary Cooperation.   Coexistent with noncooperation is nonvoluntary cooperation. Women in some communities state they do not break rules because of a threat of beatings from husbands (Sarin 1995; author's interviews in Gujarat, 2002). More commonly, women fear

reprimand. As some men in Manchod village told my Gujarat research team: "women have to be controlled because they are liable to cut wood." Some village bodies also seek to shame husbands if their spouses break the rules (my fieldwork, 1998). Coercion can lie too in a selective harshness in applying rules, as noted in Agrawal's (1999) study cited above.

Certainly women almost everywhere complain persistently about strict closures. Some of those who complain no doubt also break the rules, but many don't or do so rarely, as is apparent from women's fairly systematic shift to substitute fuels, even while complaining about the negative effects of using inferior fuels. Sometimes women's complaints lead to a rule change.

> After our complaints women and men had a joint meeting and decided to open the forest for a few days for firewood collection, since everyone has to cook. (women to author, Asundriya village, Gujarat, 1999).

In rare cases when they find the male-made rules too exclusionary, and if additional common land is available, women choose the exit option and set up their own CFG. In one Orissa village, for example, when I asked the women why they decided to take up their own patch for protection, they responded: "If we have our own forest, we would not need to ask the men each time for a bit of wood" (Kudamunda village, Orissa, 1998). Elsewhere they were less successful. In the UP hills, for example, women from one village closed off a patch of open grazing land for protection, but the men insisted on getting it reopened, arguing: "What right do you have to take over men's work?"[25]

(iii) Nonvoluntary Noncooperation.   Nonvoluntary noncooperation is best revealed in terms of participation in activities. There are several indications that women's lack of "cooperation" is not voluntary.

To begin with, women typically say that they would like to attend GB meetings if the situation were conducive, for instance, if the men invited them:

> We are capable like men of doing anything, but we don't get the opportunity. (women to author's research team, Bambri village, Gujarat, 2001)

> Women should be encouraged to attend meetings. If they are scolded for neglecting their housework, they will never attend. (women to author's research team, Boria village, Gujarat, 2001)

> Coming to meetings once a month is OK. If the men permit us we can come. (woman to author, Banaspur village, Karnataka, 1998)

> They don't call us, so we don't go. (women to author, Roopakheda village, Madhya Pradesh, 1999)

It is notable that women do attend meetings if they are specifically invited (since this legitimizes their bypassing social norms). Forest officials or NGOs have used their bargaining power with the community to increase women's participation in this way. In West Bengal's Bankura district, the District Forest Officer issued a circular stipulating that there should be a minimum of 30 percent women in the general body. This raised female membership in several villages to that level (Viegas and Menon 1993: 187). Again, in Haryana (northwest India), the forest department instructed its field staff to ensure that a maximum number of both men and women attend JFM meetings. The field staff would simply refuse to start meetings unless the men called the women. No excuses were accepted from the men that the women were busy with domestic chores or were unlikely to come, and women, on being invited, often turned up in force (Sarin 1998).

Similarly, where women become a cohesive group, they are themselves able to transcend some of the social norms. For instance, a number of rural NGOs in India have formed all-women groups outside the context of CFGs, such as savings-and-credit groups or more multifunctional ones, such as *mahila mangal dals* in the UP hills. Some of these group members also become CFG members. Such separate women's groups enhance women's self-confidence and experience in collective functioning in nontraditional public bodies. Sometimes, this demonstration effect alters male perceptions about women's capabilities and eases social norms which earlier defined only the domestic as legitimate female space. The following comment to me by a woman leader in Vejpur village, Gujarat, in 1999 is illustrative and typical:

> Men used to shut us up and say we shouldn't speak. Women learned to speak up in a *sangathan* (group). Earlier we couldn't speak up even at home. Now we can be more assertive and also go out. I am able to help other women gain confidence as well.

The presence of a larger number of women in village meetings can also help. Women in Panchmua village (Gujarat 2001) put it clearly: "It helps to have more women because then women will not be dominated or feel shy. After all, if there is only one woman and ten men, how will she speak? Women need each other to be able to speak up."[26]

Another indicator of women's desire to be more active in CFG work if they had fewer constraints is their setting up their own informal protection groups when the men's groups are ineffective. I came across several such groups, especially in the UP hills and Gujarat. Where not constrained by social norms, women also join fire-fighting efforts. Sometimes their vigilance alone has saved the forest (my fieldwork, 1998–99).

All of this indicates that women's limited participation in the CFG's collective activities is in large part nonvoluntary in nature.

11.4. IMPLICATIONS FOR RESOURCE REGENERATION AND SUSTAINABILITY

What effect do these factors have on prospects for resource protection and regeneration? To begin with, consider what we might expect. Table 11.1 had set out the likely outcomes of noncooperation (NC), nonvoluntary cooperation (NVC), and nonvoluntary noncooperation (NVNC), for resource sustainability.

Women's noncooperation, in terms of breaking the forest closure rules, need not automatically have a negative effect on the state of the forest. Much depends on what is collected and how much, how frequently, by what method, in what season, and so on. Firewood collection would have a neutral effect if women gathered only dried branches and fallen twigs, since that would not harm tree growth. The effect would be negative if they cut green branches or entire trees, or if their trampling through the forest damaged fresh shoots and undergrowth.

We would expect nonvoluntary cooperation to have a neutral effect insofar as women follow the rules, although under duress.

And we would expect nonvoluntary noncooperation to have a negative effect in that women's absence from CFG activities means missed opportunities for better forest management and development.

In practice, at one level, many CFGs have had notable success in forest regeneration. In some cases, replanting is undertaken, but if the rootstock is intact, even simply restricting human and animal entry can lead to rapid natural revival. For instance, within five to seven years of such restriction many severely degraded tracts in semi-arid India are found covered with young trees; and areas with little and declining vegetation show signs of good regeneration. In fact, in most ecological zones, CFGs show such beneficial results.

Table 11.3 also clearly brings this out. The growing stock (tons/hectare) and mean annual increment (MAI) of woody biomass is positive in all cases, with the MAI being more than 3 t/ha/yr in eight of the twelve villages, and as high as 9.75 in Baluji na muada. Similarly, table 11.4 shows that all the nineteen villages have moved from degraded to fair or good-quality forest. As assessed broadly on a scale of 0–5 by one of my researchers (with training in forestry) and myself, forests in sixteen of the nineteen villages fall in the range of 3 to 4.75.[27]

Hence, if our measure of efficiency of CFG functioning is solely an improvement in the condition of the forest in relation to its situation prior to protection, and its continued regeneration, then all these CFGs and many others would pass that test. But there are two problems with this assessment. One, much of this regeneration has been achieved through a highly gender-unequal sharing of the costs. Two, if our measure of effi-

TABLE 11.6
Factors Affecting Protected Forest Quality

Variable	Coefficient	Std. Error	t-Statistic	Prob.
C	0.589278	0.449045	1.312293	0.2091
LOG(FSEG)	−0.168182**	0.071276	−2.359583	0.0323
LOG(WEC)	0.244106*	0.134998	1.808222	0.0907
LOG(FAHH)	0.035020	0.042997	0.814468	0.4281
R-squared	0.455392	Mean dependent var		1.211277
Adjusted R-squared	0.346471	S.D. dependent var		0.197699
S.E. of regression	0.159822	F-statistic		4.180924
		Prob(F-statistic)		0.024467

** Significant at the 5% level; *Significant at the 10% level.
Dependent Variable: LOG(FQLT)
Method: Least Squares
Date: 04/08/02 Time: 12:52
Sample: 1 19
Included observations: 19

ciency is the gap between the gains realized and those realizable, then gender inequalities would tend to be associated with much less effective protection than possible.

First, on costs, tables 11.3 and 11.4 provide little support for claims that strict closure regimes are warranted on grounds of efficiency in forest regeneration. As table 11.3 shows, a great deal more firewood can be extracted from ten of these twelve forests without harming forest regeneration and sustainability. And MAI is reasonably high even when the closure is lenient. Table 11.4 similarly shows that on a scale of 1 to 5, although the forests with strict closure do much better, those with lenient closure are not doing badly either. In other words, there need be no conflict between gender equity and efficiency. Indeed, greater equity on this count would promote efficiency by reducing tendencies to rule-breaking or women having to cooperate under duress.

This is also borne out by table 11.6, which presents regression results with forest quality (FQLT) as the dependent variable and the number of forest segments, the percent of women in the EC, and the forest area per household as explanatory variables. We would expect FQLT to be negatively related to FSEG and positively related to WEC, while FAHH could go either way. The more the forest segments, the more difficult it is to monitor protection. The greater is women's involvement in the CFG, the better the forest quality is likely to be. On FAHH, on the one hand the more the area per household the less is the forest likely to deteriorate with extraction for basic needs. On the other hand, the more the FAHH the more difficult it would be to monitor.

The results are interesting. The coefficients of both FSEG and WEC are significant and, as hypothesized, the former is negatively related to forest quality and the latter positively. The result for WEC suggests that although women's presence in ECs does not significantly affect the nature of the closure regime, it does help improve forest quality. This is probably because it enhances women's sense of involvement in the CFG and their level of information about CFG rules and activities, information which can also flow from the EC women to other women.

This positive effect of women's presence in the EC could be enhanced further with their greater and more effective involvement in CFG activities and decision-making. In particular, this could help in three ways. One, it would help CFGs frame more acceptable rules of extraction and protection, and decrease violations. As women in the UP hills reasoned: "The male members of the committee have difficulties implementing the rules. Women could discuss these problems with the men. Perhaps more 'midway' rules would be, in the long run, more effective . . . more viable" (cited in Britt 1993: 148). Bardhan's (1999) study, although ungendered and relating to water users' groups, is again a pointer to the link between rule compliance and participation in rule formulation.

Relatedly, if women had more effective voice, firewood shortages or other hardships would be seen as a community concern and not just the concern of individual households, or of women alone. This could pressure the CFGs to not only extract more, but also find additional solutions to firewood problems, such as allocating part of the forest to fuelwood plantations; or using the community funds to subsidize alternative fuels such as biogas. This would also increase women's voluntary participation.

Two, women's greater involvement in protection work could improve protection. For example, oftentimes the male guard or patrol can fail to notice resource depletion. In several cases, women's informal patrols in Gujarat took me on their informal patrol route and pointed out illegal cuttings which the men had missed. Part of this gender difference arises from the fact that women, as the main and most frequent collectors of forest products, are more familiar with the forest than men (Agarwal 1997b).

Moreover, men alone in some areas find it difficult to catch transgressors. In most regions I visited in 1998–99, all-male patrols or male guards could not deal effectively with women intruders because they risked being charged with sexual harassment or molestation, especially where non-member women, or women from neighboring villages, were caught. In some incidents, women and their families registered false police cases against patrol members, or beat them up. Equally, however, women on their own find it difficult to patrol at night or confront aggressive male intruders. The most effective solution appears to be patrol teams that include both sexes. Recognizing this, in some regions male patrol groups have inducted women, but this is atypical.[28]

When women voluntarily form informal patrols, even where there is a male guard or patrol, protection efficiency can improve notably. In their study of twelve *van panchayats*, Sharma and Sinha (1993) found that all the four that were "robust" had active women's associations. They note (1993: 173): "If the condition of the forests has improved in recent years, much of the credit goes to these women's associations." I found that even though these associations have no formal authority for forest protection, they monitor forest use, spread awareness among women of the need to conserve forests, and exert social pressure on women who violate usage rules. However, insofar as women's groups are usually informal, they lack the authority to punish offenders who still have to be reported to the formal (typically all-male) committees. This separation of authority and responsibility can undercut women's efforts. For instance, in several cases in Karnataka and the UP hills, I found that women had abandoned their efforts, and violations had increased because the male EC members failed to penalize the culprits women caught. Women's formal involvement in protection can pay dividends especially (although not only) in the hills where male outmigration is high.

Three, efficiency can be increased by taking account of gender differences in preferences, say, regarding when grass should be cut or which trees should be planted. I found that in the rare cases when women were consulted, they often came up with alternative, more suitable, suggestions on when the forest should be opened for grass collection, taking account, for instance, of existing stocks of grass or firewood. A case in point is Simal village (UP hills) where the men had fixed a date for grass cutting, but the women, when consulted, said: "This period is not right. We have work now and also have some dry fodder left. We should be cutting when our store of fodder is depleted." So the committee rescheduled the forest opening.[29] Women also often differ from men in their preferred tree varieties (Brara 1987). Taking account of such gender differences in preferences, and including women in forest planning, could enhance the program's ability to fulfill household needs and the commitment of excluded members to the initiative.

11.5. CONCLUSIONS

This chapter has departed from most previous work on inequality and collective action, in several respects:

- In focusing on gender inequality as distinct from (even while interactive with) other forms of inequality, such as class, caste, ethnicity, and so on;
- In taking into account inequality stemming not only from economic endowments but also from social norms and social perceptions;
- In tracing the effect of both preexisting inequalities and inequalities that

arise from the structure of the governance institution itself; in other words, taking into account both exogenous and endogenous aspects of inequalities;

- In distinguishing between voluntary and nonvoluntary cooperation (and noncooperation) and identifying the likely effects on environmental sustainability.

Women are typically found to bear disproportionately higher costs and obtain lower benefits from closure than men. Overall, both the preexisting and the institutionally created gender inequalities are found to reduce women's ability to cooperate voluntarily in local forest management, as well as their incentive to do so. In particular, the substantial gender gap in economic endowments, gendered social norms and perceptions, the rules governing the institution, and the power of coercion underlying gender relations (at home and in the community) significantly constrain women's voluntary cooperation. Rather, these inequalities create tendencies among women toward noncooperation, or toward nonvoluntary cooperation and nonvoluntary noncooperation. Gender-related inequality (unless mitigated by specific measures) is therefore likely to be associated with low or failed cooperation, if we measure cooperation among all members of the community, rather than only among assumed unitary households.

The effect of this gender divergence in cooperation on the state of the resource, and on environmental sustainability more generally, could well be neutral on some counts but would clearly be negative on others. More particularly, the empirical evidence shows that this is an avoidable cost since both greater voluntary cooperation by women and greater gender equity in benefit-sharing can be promoted alongside better forest quality and sustainability, with less strict closure regimes and more gender-democratic CFG governance structures.

Appendix

Table A11.1
Descriptive Statistics

	CLR	FAHH	FSEG	FQLT	WEC
Mean	0.473684	1.543158	2.789474	3.421053	24.24737
Median	0.000000	1.200000	3.000000	3.250000	18.20000
Maximum	1.000000	4.250000	6.000000	4.750000	36.40000
Minimum	0.000000	0.190000	1.000000	2.500000	15.40000
Std. Dev.	0.512989	1.272164	1.474937	0.687450	7.606457
Skewness	0.105409	0.989993	0.585406	0.487373	0.599799
Kurtosis	1.011111	2.759230	2.493887	2.269413	1.853250
Jarque-Bera	3.166764	3.149502	1.288003	1.174742	2.180305
Probability	0.205280	0.207059	0.525187	0.555787	0.336165
Observations	19	19	19	19	19

TABLE A11.2
Correlation Matrix

	CLR	FAHH	FSEG	FQLT	WEC
CLR	1.000000	−0.199918	−0.521706	0.466388	0.132035
FAHH	−0.199918	1.000000	0.309483	−0.157717	−0.336002
FSEG	−0.521706	0.309483	1.000000	−0.510426	−0.254580
FQLT	0.466388	−0.157717	−0.510426	1.000000	0.497976
WEC	0.132035	−0.336002	−0.254580	0.497976	1.000000

NOTES

1. Occasionally, there may be a passing reference to gender (e.g., Baland and Platteau 1996; Verughese and Ostrom 2001), but without building it into the analysis.

2. For interesting discussions on problems associated with a unitary conceptualization of the household see, among others, the writings of economists Haddad, Hoddinott, and Alderman (1997); Doss (1996); Hart (1993); IDS Bulletin (1991); Katz (1997); Agarwal (1994, 1997a); Lundberg and Pollak (1993); Seiz (2000); and Sen (1990); and anthropologists Guyer and Peters (1987).

3. In McKean's (1986) study of village Japan, for instance, such sanctions were meant to be applied uniformly to all community members, although she does not say if this was also the case across the genders.

4. This figure is different from the approximately 63.3 mha under *forest cover* as shown by satellite data.

5. Agarwal (1994).

6. For elaboration on the issue of bargaining and gender relations and the factors that might affect women's bargaining power within and outside the home, see Agarwal (1997a).

7. See, e.g., Baland and Platteau (1996); Sethi and Somanathan (2001).

8. See, e.g., Acharya and Bennett (1981); Akram-Lodhi (1996); Saxena et al. (1995); and Sen (1988).

9. My fieldwork, 1998–99 and 2000–1; see also Raju (1997).

10. See, e.g., Verughese and Ostrom (2001); Molinas (1998).

11. Admittedly, this is not a fully robust indicator, since people can complain about rules even while breaking them, so that complaining could coexist with noncooperation.

12. Roy et al. (1992); Guhathakurta and Bhatia (1992); and Narain (1994); also my field visits 1998–9.

13. For the self-initiated groups, see Kant et al. (1991); and Singh and Kumar (1993); and for van panchayats, see Sharma and Sinha (1993), and Tata Energy Research Institute (1995). My field visits in 1998–9 covering both kinds of groups also indicate this.

14. There were a few more meetings during this period for which the gender breakup of those attending was not recorded.

15. For a tabular listing of potential costs and benefits by gender, see Agarwal (2001).

16. See also Jodha (1986) on differences between landed and landpoor rural households in India, in their dependence on the commons for firewood and fodder.

17. The studies covered more villages, but those that lacked complete information or had data discrepancies were not included in table 11.3.

18. This could well be the case too in the second over-extracting village, Halaker, given that (as noted) biomass of < 10 cm was not counted.

19. This is apart from an overall shortage even of crop waste due to three years of low rainfall.

20. Total forest area was also tested as an explanatory variable but turned out to be insignificant as well.

21. In their study of a Nepalese village, Thomas-Slater and Bhatt (1994) found that adding stall-fed milch cattle restricted women's mobility, lessened or eliminated their leisure time, and even caused girls to drop out of school.

22. Guhathakurta and Bhatia (1992); and my field interviews, 1998–99.

23. Personal communication, NGO project officer in Gujarat, March 1995.

24. E.g., Shah and Shah (1995); Singh and Kumar (1993); and Agarwal (1997a); also my field interviews during 1998–99.

25. Communication to the author by a group of women at a meeting at the Society for Environmental Education and Rural Development, UP hills, 1998.

26. See also Agarwal (1997b, 2000b) on the importance of a "critical mass" of women for improving their ability to cooperate and to be effective in such forums.

27. The assessment was made broadly, taking visual account of the density of tree growth, its age as indicated by the girth and height of trees, its overall regeneration, the presence or absence of stumps, etc. This assessment was made in major segments of the forest. Admittedly, the method is a rather rough one, but it appeared adequate for our purpose, which was to obtain only a broad assessment of forest quality in the nineteen villages.

28. For figures, see Agarwal (2001).

29. Personal communication, Dewan Nagarkoti, Uttarakhand Sewa Nidhi, UP hills, 1998.

REFERENCES

Acharya, M., and L. Bennett. 1981. *An Aggregate Analysis and Summary of Village Studies, The Status of Women in Nepal*, II, Part 9. Kathmandu, CEDA, Tribhuvan University.

Agarwal, B. 1984. "Rural women and the HYV rice technology in India." *Economic and Political Weekly*, March.

———. 1987. "Under the cooking pot: The political economy of the domestic fuel crisis in rural South Asia." *IDS Bulletin* 18(1): 1–22.

———. 1994. *A Field of One's Own: Gender and Land Rights in South Asia*. Cambridge: Cambridge University Press.

———. 1997a. " 'Bargaining' and gender relations: Within and beyond the household." *Feminist Economics* 1(5): 1–51.

———. 1997b. "Environmental action, gender equity and women's participation." *Development and Change* 28(1): 1–44.

———. 2000a. "Conceptualizing environmental collective action: Why gender matters." *Cambridge Journal of Economics* 24(3): 283–310.

———. 2000b. Group functioning and community forestry in South Asia: A gender analysis and conceptual framework. Working paper no. 172, World Institute for Development Economics Research, Helsinki.

———. 2001. "Participatory exclusions, community forestry and gender: An analysis and conceptual framework." *World Development* 29(10): 1623–48.

Agrawal, A. 1999. "State formation in community spaces: Control over forests in the Kumaon Himalaya, India." Paper prepared for presentation at the University of California, Berkeley, Workshop on Environmental Politics, April 30.

Akram-Lodhi, A. H. 1996. "You are not excused from cooking: Peasants and the gender division of labour in Pakistan." *Feminist Economics* 2(2): 87–105.

Bahuguna, V. K. 2000. "Joint forest management: An instrument for sustainable forest management." Paper presented at a conference on *India's Forests Beyond 2000*, Commonwealth Forestry Association (India), India Habitat Center, Delhi, April 19–21.

Baland, J. M., and J. P. Platteau. 1996. *Halting Degradation of Natural Resources: Is There a Role for Rural Communities?* Oxford: Clarendon Press.

Ballabh, V., and K. Singh. 1988. "Van (Forest) Panchayats in Uttar Pradesh Hills: A critical analysis." Research paper, Institute for Rural Management, Anand.

Bardhan, P. 1999. "Water community: An empirical analysis of cooperation on irrigation in South India." Mimeo, Department of Economics, University of California, Berkeley.

Becker, G. S. 1965. "A theory of the allocation of time." *Economic Journal* 75: 493–517.

———. 1981. *A Treatise on the Family.* Cambridge, Mass.: Harvard University Press.

Brara, R. 1987. "Shifting sands: A study of rights in common pastures." Report, Institute of Development Studies, Jaipur.

Britt, C. 1993. "Out of the wood? Local institutions and community forest management in two central Himalayan Villages." Cornell University, Ithaca, draft monograph.

Bruce, J., and D. Dwyer (eds.) 1988. *A Home Divided: Women and Income in the Third World.* Stanford: Stanford University Press.

Chopra, K., and S. C. Gulati. 1997. "Environmental degradation and population movements: The role of property rights." *Environment and Resource Economics* 9: 383–408.

CSE 2001. "Biomass: A smoky problem." *Health and Environment Newsletter* (Center for Science and Environment, Delhi) 1(1): 6.

CWDS 1999. "From oppression to assertion: A study of Panchayats and women in Madhya Pradesh, Rajasthan and Uttar Pradesh." Center for Women's Development Studies, New Delhi.

Doss, C. R. 1996. "Testing among models of intrahousehold resource allocation." *World Development* 24(10): 1597–1609.

Gala, C. 1990. "Trying to give women their dues: the story of Vitner Village." *Manushi* 59: 1–12.

Gandhi, N., and N. Shah. 1991. *The Issues at Stake: Theory and Practice in the Contemporary Women's Movement in India*. Delhi: Kali for Women.

Goetz, A. N. 1990. "Local heroes, local despots: Exploring fieldwork discretion in implementing gender redistributive development policy." Paper presented at the Development Studies Association Conference, Glasgow.

Gold, A., and B. R. Gujar. 1997. "Wild pigs and kings: Remembered landscapes in Rajasthan." *American Anthropologist* 99(1): 70–84.

Guhathakurta, P., and K. S. Bhatia. 1992. "A case study on gender and forest resources in West Bengal." World Bank, Delhi, June 16.

Guyer, J. I., and P. E. Peters. 1987. "Introduction" and other papers in Conceptualizing the Household: Issues of Theory and Policy in Africa, a special issue of *Development and Change* 18(2): 197–213.

Haddad, L., J. Hoddinott, and H. Alderman. 1997. "Introduction: The scope of intrahousehold resource allocation issues." In *Intrahousehold Resource Allocation in Developing Countries: Methods, Models and Policy*, ed. L. Haddad, J. Hoddinott, and H. Alderman. Baltimore, Md.: John Hopkins University Press.

Hart, G. 1993. "Gender and household dynamics: Recent theories and their implications." In *Critical Issues in Asian Development*, ed. M. G. Quibria, 33–74. Asian Development Bank and New York: Oxford University Press.

IDS Bulletin. 1991. "Researching the household: Methodological and empirical issues." 22(1), January.

Jodha, N. S. 1986. "Common property resources and the rural poor." *Economic and Political Weekly* 21(27): 1169–81.

Joshi, S. 1998. "Report of the Workshop on JFM and Women." Agha Khan Rural Support Programme, Netrang, Gujarat, 14 September.

Kant, S., N. M. Singh, and K. K. Singh. 1991. "Community-based forest management systems (Case Studies from Orissa)." SIDA, New Delhi; Indian Institute of Forest Management, Bhopal; and ISO/Swedforest, New Delhi, April.

Katz, E. 1997. "Intra-household economics of voice and exit." *Feminist Economics* 3(3): 25–46.

Lundberg, S., and R. A. Pollak. 1993. "Separate spheres, bargaining and the marriage market." *Journal of Political Economy* 101(6): 988–1010.

Mansingh, O. 1991. Community Organization and Ecological Restoration: An Analysis of Strategic Options for NGOs in Central Himalaya, with particular reference to the Community Forestry Programme of the NGO Chirag. MA diss., Rural Development, AFRAS, University of Sussex.

McKean, M. A. 1986. "Management of traditional common lands (Iriaichi) in Japan." In *Making the Commons Work: Theory, Practice and Policy*, ed. D. W. Bromley. San Francisco: Institute for Contemporary Studies Press.

Molinas, J. 1988. "The impact of inequality, gender, external assistance and social capital on local-level cooperation." *World Development* 26(3): 413–31.

Mukerjee, R., and S. B. Roy. 1993. Influence of social institutions on women's participation in JFM: A Case Study from Sarugarh, North Bengal. Working Paper no. 17, IBRAD, Calcutta.

Narain, U. 1994. "Women's involvement in joint forest management: Analyzing the issues." Draft paper, May 6. University of California, Berkeley.

Narasimhan, N. 1999. "Women's role in the Gram Sabha." *Kurukshetra* 48(1): 35–8.

Natrajan, I. 1995. "Trends in firewood consumption in rural India." *Margin* 28(1): 41–5.

Ostrom, E. 1990. *Governing the Commons*. Cambridge: Cambridge University Press.

Raju, G., R. Vaghela, and M. S. Raju. 1993. *Development of People's Institutions for Management of Forests*. Ahemdabad: VIKSAT.

Raju, M. S. 1997. "Seeking niches in forest canopy: An enquiry into women's participation." Mimeo, Ford Foundation, New Delhi.

Ravindranath, N. H., K. S. Murali, and K. C. Malhotra. 2000. *Joint Forest Management and Community Forestry in India: An Ecological and Institutional Assessment*. New Delhi: Oxford and IBH Publishing.

Roy, S. B., R. Mukerjee, and M. Chatterjee. 1992. "Endogenous development and gender roles in participatory forest management." IBRAD, Calcutta.

Roy, S. B. et al. 1993. "Profile of forest protection committees at Sarugarh Range, North Bengal." IBRAD Working Paper no. 16.

Samuelson, P. A. 1956. "Social Indifference Curves." *Quarterly Journal of Economics* 70(1): 1–22.

Sarin, M. 1995. "Regenerating India's forest: Reconciling gender equity and joint forest management." *IDS Bulletin* 26(1): 83–91.

———. 1998. *Who Is Gaining? Who Is Losing? Gender and Equality Concerns in Joint Forest Management*. New Delhi: Society for Promotion of Wasteland Development.

Saxena, S., R. Prasad, and V. Joshi. 1995. "Time allocation and fuel usage in three villages of the Garhwal Himalaya, India." *Mountain Research and Development* 15(1): 57–67.

Seiz, J. 2000. "Game theory and bargaining models." *Elgar Companion to Feminist Economics*. Cheltenham: Elgar Publishing House.

Sen, A. K. 1990. "Gender and Cooperative Conflicts." In *Persistent Inequalities: Women and World Development*, ed. I. Tinker, 123–49. New York: Oxford University Press.

Sen, I. 1988. "Class and gender in work time allocation." *Economic and Political Weekly* 23(33): 1702–6.

Sethi, R., and E. Somanathan. 2001. "Norm compliance and strong reciprocity." Paper presented at a workshop on "The Structure and Evolution of Strong Reciprocity," Santa Fe Institute, New Mexico, March 9–11.

Shah, M. K., and P. Shah. 1995. "Gender, environment and livelihood security: An alternative viewpoint from India." *IDS Bulletin* 26(1): 75–82.

Sharma, A., and A. Sinha. 1993. "A study of the common property resources in the project area of the central Himalaya rural action group." Mimeo, Indian Institute of Forest Management, Bhopal, Madhya Pradesh.

Singh, A., and N. Burra (eds.) 1993. *Women and Wasteland Development in India*. New Delhi: Sage Publications.

Singh, M. 1997. "Lumping and levelling: Gender stereotypes and joint forest management." Paper presented at the seminar on "The Social Construction of Community Participation in Joint Forest Management," organized by the University of Edinburgh and Indian Council of Forestry Research and Education, India International Centre, April 9–11.

Singh, N., and K. Kumar. 1993. "Community initiatives to protect and manage forests in Balangir and Sambalpur Districts." Swedish International Development Agency, New Delhi.

Smith, K. R., A. L. Agarwal, and R. M. Dave. 1983. "Air pollution and rural fuels: Implications for policy and research." Resource Systems Institute, East-West Center, Honolulu, Hawaii.

Tata Energy Research Institute (TERI). 1995. "Community participation in Van Panchayats of Kumaon region of Uttar Pradesh." Paper No. 1, Part I, TERI, Delhi.

Thomas-Slater, B., and N. Bhatt. 1994. "Land, livestock, and livelihoods: Changing dynamics of gender, caste, and ethnicity in a Nepalese Village." *Human Ecology* 22(4): 467–94.

UNDP. 2001. "Decentralisation in India: Challenges and opportunities." HRDS Discussion Paper no. 1, United Nations Development Program, Delhi.

Verughese G., and E. Ostrom. 2001. "The contested role of heterogeneity in collective action: some evidence from community forestry in Nepal." *World Development* 29(5): 747–65.

Venkateshwaran, S. 1992. *Living on the Edge: Women, Environment and Development*. New Delhi: Friedrich Ebert Stiftung.

Viegas, P., and G. Menon. 1993. "Forest protection committees of West Bengal: Role and participation of women." In *Women and Wasteland Development in India*, (A. M. Singh and N. Burra, eds., New Delhi: Sage. 171–210.

White, T. A., and C. F. Runge. 1994. "The emergence and evolution of collective action: Lessons from watershed management in Haiti." Draft paper, Center for International Food and Agricultural Policy, University of Minnesota.

Chapter 12

INEQUALITY AND ENVIRONMENTAL PROTECTION

James K. Boyce

Inequalities of power and wealth may affect the magnitude as well as the incidence of environmental protection. A growing body of literature documents that social and economic inequalities—based on class, race, ethnicity, gender, and age—often translate into environmental inequalities. This chapter suggests that the impact of inequalities affects not only how environmental quality is distributed, but also the total size of the pie.

The global environment is our common home, but not everyone lives in the same room. Clearly, many crucial dimensions of environmental quality are not private goods, exchanged in markets where the rich can buy more than the poor. But neither are they pure public goods, that when available to one person are equally available to all. Rather, many aspects of environmental quality lie in the intermediate terrain between the public and the private, a terrain where, in George Orwell's haunting phrase, some are "more equal than others."

Social and economic inequalities take many forms.[1] This chapter focuses primarily on inequalities of power, and secondarily on inequalities of income. Data on income distribution are fairly widely available.[2] Data on power distribution, by contrast, are by and large nonexistent; hence, proxies must be used to measure this dimension of inequality.

I first consider why, in theory, we can expect inequalities to have an impact on environmental protection. Section 12.1 discusses power and its role in social decisions regarding the environment. Section 12.2 formalizes this impact via a "power-weighted social decision rule," and advances two hypotheses: first, that social decisions on environmental protection will systematically favor some individuals and groups over others; and second, that a more unequal distribution of power generally will result in less environmental protection and more environmental degradation. Section 12.3 considers the effects of income distribution on environmental quality, and explains why the usual assumption that higher-income individuals have higher demand for environmental quality does not necessarily imply that a redistribution of income in their favor (that is, greater income inequality) will lead to better environmental quality.

I then turn to the empirical evidence. Section 12.4 reviews the burgeoning literature on environmental injustice in the United States, highlighting several key areas of ongoing debate. Section 12.5 summarizes a state-level analysis of the impact of power inequality on the extent of environmental protection and environmental quality in the United States. Section 12.6 reviews international evidence on the effects of inequality on environmental quality, drawing on recent literature on the "environmental Kuznets curve." Section 12.7 concludes by suggesting some potentially fruitful avenues for further research.

12.1. Power and the Environment

In analyzing environmental degradation, we can ask three basic questions:

- First, who benefits from economic activities that degrade the environment? If there were no winners—people who derive net benefits from these activities (or at least expect to do so)—environmental degradation would not take place.
- Second, who bears the costs of environmental degradation? If there were no losers—people on the receiving end of "negative externalities"—there would be no need to worry about these activities, at least from the standpoint of human well-being.
- Finally, why are the winners able to impose environmental costs on the losers?

There are three possible answers to the final question. The first is that the losers do not yet exist; that is, they belong to future generations who are not here to defend themselves. The second possibility is that the losers exist but lack information about the costs that the winners are imposing on them; even if they are aware of the costs—for example, they may see that their children are ill—they have not traced these costs to the activities of the winners. The third possibility is that the losers exist and know that the winners are imposing costs on them, but they lack the power to prevent this imposition.

In the first scenario—where the losers do not yet exist—environmental protection requires that the present generation embrace an ethic of responsibility toward future generations. In the second scenario—where the losers lack information—environmental education and right-to-know legislation can help to tip the scales in favor of environmental protection.[3]

In the third scenario—where the losers lack power relative to the winners—environmental protection requires a change in the balance of power. This third scenario is the main focus of this chapter.

Dimensions of Power

Five dimensions of power affect social decisions on environmental protection:

- *Purchasing power:* If environmental protection were a simple commodity, like orange juice, that could be bought and sold in the market, then purchasing power would be a key determinant of the extent of environmental protection. Inequalities of power would mirror inequalities in the distribution of income and wealth. The preferences of different individuals would influence social decisions insofar as they are backed by ability to pay; in effect, one dollar would buy one vote. Although environmental protection in practice has a substantial "public good" component, shifting many decisions from the market to the arena of public policy, this does not mean that purchasing power is entirely irrelevant to these decisions.

- *Decision power:* When different people prefer different public policy outcomes, those who prevail are said to wield "decision power." If the extent of environmental protection were determined by simple majority rule, each individual's preferences would count equally—one person, one vote—with the outcomes mirroring the preferences of the median voter. In practice, as every political lobbyist knows, some people wield greater decision power than others.

- *Agenda power:* Some issues never make it into the public policy arena at all. The ability to determine which do, and which do not, is termed "agenda power." This is a subtler dimension of power, in that it can determine environmental protection outcomes before overt decision power comes into play. In his classic study, *The Un-Politics of Air Pollution* (1971), for example, Matthew Crenson describes how corporate power in the steel-mill town of Gary, Indiana, kept air pollution off the local government's political agenda for years.

- *Value power:* Individual preferences do not fall from the sky. The ability to influence what other people want—what they will choose if given the opportunity to do so—is an even subtler aspect of power (Lukes 1974). As John Kenneth Galbraith (1973: 9) once observed, power can be deployed to persuade people that pollution is "palatable or worth the cost."

- *Event power:* A final dimension of power is the ability to determine the circumstances in which people make choices, rather than the choices themselves. Randall Bartlett (1989: 43) offers this hypothetical illustration: "Suppose I dig a deep pit, fill it with poisonous snakes, and throw you in.

I then stand on the edge of the pit and offer to sell you a ladder. To buy or not to buy is not the only question. What prior events made you need to buy, and my influence over them, are also relevant."

All five dimensions of power are relevant to environmental protection. When the winners from environmentally degrading economic activities wield greater purchasing power, decision power, agenda power, value power, and/or event power than the losers, we can expect less environmental protection than if the power balance is reversed.

Correlates of Power

Power, as the term is used here, is inherently relative: individuals wield power vis-à-vis others. In a world of solitary Robinson Crusoes, power would be absent (as would "externalities"). Power depends both on individual attributes and on the political framework in which these attributes are mapped into the five dimensions of power.

Correlations between individual attributes and power vary across societies. Wealth, income, race, ethnicity, gender, and age are commonly among the most important correlates. Richer individuals not only wield more purchasing power in the market for private goods and services, but also tend to be well-endowed in the other dimensions of power. For both reasons, we may expect affluent communities to receive higher levels of environmental protection than low-income communities.

Although race and ethnicity are often correlated with economic class, they may have independent effects on power. That is, holding wealth or income constant, members of disadvantaged racial or ethnic groups may wield less power (apart from the purchasing power dimension) than other groups. In the United States, for example, many studies have found that African Americans and Latinos systematically tend to bear disproportionate burdens from pollution and environmental hazards, a relationship explored further in section 12.4 below.

Gender and age can also be correlated with power, especially when these attributes interact with economic class, race, or ethnicity. For example, Bina Agarwal (1992) has documented how the degradation of forest resources in rural India has particularly severe effects on poor women, via impacts on their time, income, and nutrition. Other studies in India have found that indoor air pollution generated by cooking stoves has the most adverse effects on women and children under five (Parikh, Smith, and Laxmi 1999). Similarly, critics of inadequate regulation of pesticide use in the United States have pointed out that children are most vulnerable to their effects (Wargo 1998).

The extent to which differences in these individual attributes translate into differences in power depends on the political framework. Holding the distribution of income and other attributes constant, a society with free elections and a high degree of respect for political rights and civil liberties will have a more equal distribution of power than one with an authoritarian or totalitarian regime. Despite the relatively egalitarian distribution of income in the Soviet Union, for example, power was quite inequitably distributed, a factor that arguably contributed to its dismal record in environmental protection (Pryde 1991).

The next section analyzes how disparities in power, arising from interactions between individual attributes and the political framework, can affect both the incidence of environmental costs and the extent of environmental protection.

12.2. The Power-weighted Social Decision Rule

Formally, we can analyze the impact of the "noneconomic" dimensions of power (that is, the four dimensions other than purchasing power) by comparing actual social decisions to those prescribed by the normative rule of benefit-cost analysis (BCA). The BCA rule is:

$$\max_{i} \Sigma b_i,$$

where b_i = the net benefit to the ith individual, with costs counted as negative benefits. The outcome of this rule is "efficient" in the sense that total net benefits are maximized.[4] These benefits are conventionally measured in monetary terms, with nonmarket benefits and costs assessed using various techniques founded on the criterion of "willingness to pay." As a result, in the shadow markets of BCA as in the actual markets for goods and services, purchasing power plays a crucial role, a point to which I return below.

In many cases, social decisions can more accurately be described by a power-weighted social decision rule (PWSDR), in which benefits and costs are weighed by the power of those to whom they accrue (Boyce 1994):

$$\max_{i} \Sigma \pi_i b_i,$$

where π_i = the power of the ith individual. Whereas the benefit-cost rule addresses the normative question of what a society *should* do, the

PWSDR addresses the positive question of what a society *does*. The two correspond only in the special case where all individuals have equal power (that is, $\pi_i = \pi_j$ for all i, j). The PWSDR predicts that environmental protection decisions will systematically diverge from the "optimal" level prescribed by BCA whenever power disparities exist between the winners (those for whom $b_i > 0$) and the losers (those for whom $b_i < 0$).

Power here plays a role similar to that of "influence" in Becker's (1983) model of fiscal policy. The remedy that Becker proposes for inefficiencies arising from disparities in influence is simply to downsize the state, thereby reducing the scope for the powerful to pursue private gains at the expense of the public good. When we turn to environmental policy, however, the inadequacy of this remedy becomes evident. In the presence of externalities, inefficiencies can result not only from government action, but also from government inaction. In such cases, the only remedy for the inefficiencies caused by power inequalities is democratization, defined as movement toward a more equal distribution of power.

Power, like utility, is not directly observable. But in the same way that neoclassical microeconomic theory infers utility from preferences as revealed by individual choice, so we can infer power from the preferences as revealed by social choice. Like the utility-maximization model of individual behavior, the PWSDR yields testable predictions.

Two Hypotheses

Two hypotheses on environmental protection can be derived from the PWSDR. The first concerns how the environmental-quality pie is sliced; the second concerns its overall size.

- *H1:* Social choices regarding environmental protection will systematically favor some individuals and groups over others, reflecting their relative power.
- *H2:* The more unequal the distribution of power, the lower will be the level of environmental protection and the greater the magnitude of environmental degradation.

The rationale for the first hypothesis is straightforward, but the second requires some elaboration.

The PWSDR can result in either "too much" environmental degradation or "too little" when compared to the normative BCA rule. When the winners from environmentally degrading economic activities are powerful relative to the losers, the PWSDR predicts too much degradation; but when the losers are more powerful than the winners, it predicts too little. Figure 12.1 depicts these possibilities, labeling them *Type-I* and *Type-II* inefficiencies, respectively.

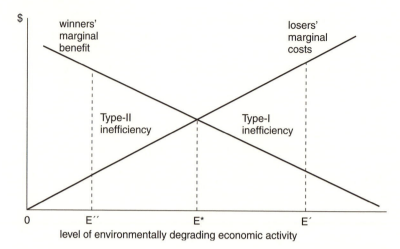

Figure 12.1. Determination of the level of environmental degradation.
E* = "optimal" level prescribed by cost-benefit analysis; E' = level under the power-weighted social decision rule when winners are more powerful than losers; E" = level under the power-weighted social decision rule when losers are more powerful than winners.

The "optimal" environmental degradation prescribed by BCA is represented by E* in figure 12.1. Beyond this level, there is too much environmental degradation in that its marginal cost to the losers exceeds its marginal benefit to the winners. This is equivalent to saying that the marginal benefit of environmental *protection* would exceed its marginal cost. To the left of E*, there is "too little" environmental degradation in the sense that the marginal benefit of the environmentally degrading activity would exceed its marginal cost.

The notion of "too little" environmental degradation may seem odd to many environmentalists. To be sure, there are good reasons to question the supposed "optimality" of the level of environmental degradation that is prescribed by BCA. As noted previously, BCA typically values benefits and costs in terms of willingness to pay, which in turn depends on preferences and ability to pay. Once we recognize the existence of value power—including propaganda that aims to persuade people that pollution is "palatable or worth the cost"—preferences become problematic as a guide to valuation. And since ability to pay is a function of the distribution of purchasing power, the BCA prescription can be regarded as optimal only if this distribution is considered optimal, too. In a society characterized by substantial inequalities of wealth and power, these considerations imply that the level of environmental degradation prescribed by BCA may be "too much."

Yet one cannot reject altogether the notion of "too little" environmental degradation on these grounds. Certainly there can be a range in which the marginal benefits of environmentally degrading economic activities exceed their marginal costs, and it is by no means inconceivable that where those who bear the costs are powerful relative to those who reap the benefits, the extent of these activities could be pushed below the "efficient" level. For example, while living in Bangladesh in 1975, I witnessed a "beautification" campaign in Dhaka, the capital, in which thousands of poor people were forcibly removed from the city. The city had experienced an influx of impoverished families in the wake of a man-made famine in the previous year.[5] The makeshift houses they had constructed on vacant lots were razed to the ground, and the residents were transported to squalid camps outside the town, far from the eyes of the city's more affluent residents and equally far from urban employment opportunities. One day, near Dhaka's General Post Office, I saw a squadron of policemen clearing the street of beggars, using batons to prod the slow or reluctant onto the truck that would haul them away. An emaciated baby sat on a rag on the sidewalk, her mother having wandered down the street begging for alms. A policeman spotted the child, picked her up, and tossed her into the back of the truck, which lumbered off in search of more human eyesores.

To the architects of the beautification campaign, the very presence of the poor in Dhaka was a kind of environmental degradation. This recalls the "externality" view of poverty:

> People must not be allowed to become so poor that they offend or are hurtful to society. It is not so much the misery and plight of the poor but the discomfort and cost to the community which is crucial to this view of poverty. We have a problem of poverty to the extent that low income creates problems for those who are not poor. (Rein 1971: 46, cited by Sen 1981: 9)

The costs to the rich may have been modest, when compared to the benefits to the poor of securing a livelihood in the city. But the expulsion of the poor reflected the balance of power in urban Bangladesh.

If, in principle, power inequalities can cause both types of inefficiencies—too much environmental degradation and too little—we must ask which is likely to be more prevalent. The answer hinges on the correlation between net benefits (b_i) and power (π_i), summed over all environmentally degrading economic activities. If the correlation is positive—that is, if the winners tend to be more powerful than the losers—then the net environmental impact of power inequalities will be more environmental degradation than would be prescribed by the BCA rule. If the correlation is negative, the PWSDR yields the opposite result.

There is good reason to expect the correlation to be positive. The benefits from environmentally degrading economic activities accrue to firms and individuals in the form of producers' surplus and consumers' surplus. The rich generally reap more of both than do the poor, by virtue of the simple facts that they own more productive assets and consume more goods and services. Hence, we can expect wealth to be correlated with net benefits. At the same time, wealth is generally correlated with power. If both benefits and power are correlated with wealth, they are likely to be correlated with each other. Type-I inefficiencies are therefore likely to be more prevalent than Type-II inefficiencies, in which case wider inequalities in the distribution of power lead to higher overall levels of environmental degradation.

12.3. INCOME DISTRIBUTION AND THE DEMAND FOR ENVIRONMENTAL QUALITY

The foregoing analysis does not imply that affluent individuals are untroubled by environmental degradation. On the contrary, it is likely that clean air, clean water, and many other environmental amenities are "normal" goods for which demand (measured by willingness and ability to pay) rises with income. "If you want a better environment," Wilfred Beckerman (1996: 27) claims, "you have to become rich."

This claim can be applied to individual households or to societies as a whole. At the household level, it implies that *within* countries, richer households are most inclined to protect the environment. At the national level, it implies that *across* countries and over time, higher average incomes will lead to better environmental quality. In this section I consider the relationship between income and environmental quality at the household level; section 12.6 considers this relationship at the national level.

In principle, changes in income distribution could alter the valuation of environmental costs. If rich people place a higher value on environmental quality than do poor people, then a regressive redistribution of income from poor to rich might translate into higher demand for environmental quality. Could this offset the impact of the inefficiencies arising from any associated shift in power inequalities, such that greater income inequality results in *less* environmental degradation rather than more?

The answer hinges on four things: first, whether demand for environmental quality rises more sharply with income among upper-income households or among lower-income households, that is, whether the demand-income relation is convex or concave; second, whether the income effect is sufficiently strong to outweigh the "price effect" arising from foregone producers' and consumers' surplus; third, the scope for substituting private environmental amenities for public ones; and fourth, the impact of inequality on collective action for the provision of public goods.

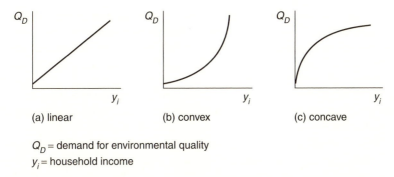

(a) linear   (b) convex   (c) concave

Q_D = demand for environmental quality
y_i = household income

Figure 12.2. Household income and demand for environmental quality.

Income and Demand for Environmental Quality

At any given level of average income, greater income inequality means not only higher incomes for the rich but also lower incomes for the poor. Assuming that environmental quality is a normal good—that is, the income elasticity of demand for environmental quality is positive—a redistribution of income from the poor to the rich will increase the demand of the rich but at the same time it will decrease the demand of the poor. The net effect on demand depends on the shape of the demand-income relation.

Three possibilities are depicted in figure 12.2. In the first panel, figure 12.2(a), demand for environmental quality increases with income at a constant rate. In this case, changes in income inequality would have no net effect on the demand for environmental quality: redistributing income from one end of the spectrum to the other does not affect total demand. In figure 12.2(b), the demand-income relation is convex. In this case, greater income inequality leads to higher total demand. In figure 12.2(c), the demand-income relation is concave. In this case, greater income inequality leads to lower total demand.

The claim that greater income inequality (as distinct from higher average incomes) leads to greater demand for environmental quality therefore hinges, first, on the assumption that the demand-income relation is convex as in figure 12.2(b).

The Price of Environmental Quality

Environmental quality has a price, in the form of producers' and consumers' surplus foregone when external costs are internalized. Pollution abatement and other measures to protect the environment raise the firm's internal costs of production. This results in lower producer incomes and/or higher consumer prices, depending on how readily the firm can pass cost increases on to its customers. A more unequal income distribution means that the rich reap a greater share of producers' and consumers' surplus. Wider income inequality thus raises the "price" of environmental protection to the rich. This price effect operates in the opposite direction of the income effect. Returning to figure 12.1, these two effects could be represented by rises in the marginal benefit and marginal cost curves, respectively. Whether the "efficient" level of environmental degradation rises or falls depends on the balance between the two.

In other words, even though richer individuals may desire more environmental quality, they also desire more of the goods and services that are responsible for environmental degradation. Faced with this trade-off, it is not obvious that their desire for environmental quality will prevail. The claim that greater income inequality leads to greater demand for environmental quality therefore hinges, second, on the assumption that the income effect outweighs the price effect.

Private-Public Substitution

Many elements of environmental quality are not pure public goods. To some extent, at least, the affluent can purchase private environmental quality (or private insulation from public bads), by living in relatively unpolluted enclaves, drinking bottled water, and taking holidays in pristine locations, and so on. The extent to which their demand for environmental quality translates into demand for the *public* elements of environmental quality depends on the scope for substitution between the private and public elements.

Studies of environmental disparities within countries and regions, some of which are reviewed in section 12.4, provide evidence that many important aspects of environmental quality indeed are not pure public goods. These studies have documented the higher-than-average levels of pollution and environmental hazards to which low-income communities and disempowered racial and ethnic groups are exposed. The flip side of this coin is that high-income communities and more powerful groups are exposed to lower-than-average levels of pollution and hazards.

Insofar as the costs from environmentally degrading economic activities can be imposed on others—separated spatially, as well as socially, from the beneficiaries—the affluent can have their environmental-quality cake and eat it too, protecting favored locations while despoiling others. Carried to its extreme, this could yield a world partitioned into "sacred groves and sacrifice zones" (Hecht 2002). The claim that greater income inequality leads to greater demand for public environmental quality therefore hinges, third, on the assumption that the scope for substituting private environmental quality for public environmental quality is sufficiently small.

Collective Action

Insofar as environmental quality cannot be purchased privately, but is indeed a public good, its provision requires more than individual demand. It also requires collective action to solve the free-rider problem. The degree of income inequality may affect a society's ability to engage in collective action. As the chapters in this volume attest, ascertaining the direction of this effect is not a straightforward matter. On the one hand, inequality may facilitate collective action by fostering the emergence of strong leaders who are able to internalize a large share of the benefits from public goods and enforce the rules of cooperation. On the other hand, inequality may corrode the bonds of sympathy and trust that constitute "social capital." The net effect may vary from time to time, and from place to place. The claim that greater income inequality leads to more environmental protection therefore hinges, fourth, on the assumption that inequality facilitates, or at least does not seriously impede, collective action.

Taken together, then, a rather restrictive set of assumptions must hold true for income inequality to have a positive effect on environmental protection. Demand for environmental quality must be convex in income. The resultant income effect must outweigh the price effect arising from the costs of environmental protection in terms of reduced producers' and consumers' surplus. The scope for fulfilling demand for environmental quality privately must be too small to displace the increased demand for the public elements of environmental quality. And the impact of income inequality on the society's ability to engage in collective action must not undermine the effectiveness of this demand. If all of these conditions hold, then higher income inequality would raise the "efficient" level of environmental protections, and this could outweigh the inefficiencies resulting from any associated increase in power disparities. Otherwise, income inequality may have an adverse effect on environmental protection. Empirical studies can shed light on which outcome is more common in practice.

12.4. ENVIRONMENTAL INJUSTICE

This section briefly reviews studies of environmental injustice in the United States, to assess whether the empirical evidence supports the hypothesis that the *direction* of environmental protection (that is, who is protected from whom) reflects power inequalities related to class, racial, and ethnic differences. No attempt will be made here to provide a comprehensive survey of this large and growing literature.[6] Instead I highlight a few key issues.

Early Studies

In the 1980s, several influential studies appeared that examined the distribution of environmental hazards along race and class lines in the United States (Bullard 1983; U.S. General Accounting Office 1983; United Church of Christ 1987; Bullard 1990). The main focus of these early studies was the correlation between the location of hazardous waste sites and the demographic characteristics of the communities in which they are located. Their general conclusion was that such sites are located disproportionately in communities with above-average percentages of African American residents and below-average household incomes.

Apart from the statistical correlations reported in these studies, "smoking gun" evidence of environmental injustice surfaced in the Cerrell report, a 1984 consultant's report commissioned by the California Waste Management Board. Noting that "political criteria have become every bit as important in determining the outcome of a project as engineering factors" and that "a great deal of time, resources, and planning could be saved and political problems avoided if people who are resentful and people who are amenable to Waste-to-Energy projects [a.k.a. incinerators] could be identified *before* selecting a site," the report recommended that "middle and higher-socioeconomic strata neighborhoods should not fall at least within the one-mile and five-mile radii of the proposed site" (Cerrell Associates 1984: 17, 31, 43).[7]

How Near Is "Near"?

One source of controversy in the subsequent literature has been the appropriate unit of analysis. Early studies often relied on fairly high levels of aggregation, such as postal zip codes. Using data at the census tract level, Anderton et al. (1994a, b) examined socioeconomic correlates of tracts with and without hazardous waste transfer, storage, and disposal (TSDF) facilities. Controlling for industrial and manufacturing employment in the tract, they found that tracts with TSDFs had below-average incomes, but not above-average percentages of African Americans or other minorities.[8] These results have been interpreted as implying that allegations of "environmental racism" lack a sound statistical basis.[9] Anderton et al. (1994b: 236) report, however, that if "near" is defined to mean census tracts at least 50 percent of whose area lies within a 2.5-mile radius from the center of a TSDF tract, "the mean percentage black population in the nearby surrounding tracts is much greater (25.7 percent) than when a comparison is drawn with all non-TSDF tracts (15.2 percent)."

In a doctoral dissertation based on the same research project, Oakes (1997) provides further details on the spatial relationships between community demographics and TSDFs. The TSDF tracts are characterized by a "remarkable" magnitude of industrialization (p. 123), with far lower population densities than the non-TSDF tracts (p. 118).[10] The percentages of minorities residing within the TSDF tracts are roughly the same as the metropolitan average, but the data for tracts located within one mile of the centroid of TSDF tracts reveals a strikingly different picture: the percentages of blacks, Hispanics, impoverished families, and households receiving public assistance are substantially higher than the average. These percentages decline as distance from a TSDF tract increases beyond the one-mile radius, falling below the average levels at around five miles (see figure 12.3). In light of the claim that the Anderton et al. findings refute the existence of environmental racism, it is worth quoting Oakes (1997: 122) at some length:

> [O]ne cannot help but be drawn to the sharp rise in the percentage of black persons in neighborhoods one mile from TSDF neighborhoods. This average rises sharply to about 30%. The average for neighborhoods two miles from TSDF neighborhoods falls to about 27%. Past the two-mile point, the average falls fairly consistently until about five miles, where it becomes less than the mean percentage black for the whole sample. The result is dramatic. While it remains true that the average percentage black persons in TSDF neighborhoods is no greater than the same average in non-TSDF neighborhoods, at least some neighborhoods near TSDF neighborhoods contain a much greater percentage of black persons. Furthermore, the average percentage of black persons in neighborhoods surrounding TSDFs falls consistently as distance is increased past two miles.

There is no obvious a priori basis for judging the "right" spatial unit of analysis—how close people must live to an environmental hazard for it to be judged relevant to their well-being, and hence relevant to analyses of environmental justice. It clearly would be rash, however, to claim that the only relevant unit is the (predominantly industrial) census tract within which the hazard is located, and that the demographic characteristics of nearby residential communities are inconsequential. Contrary to the "spin" often placed on their findings, the results of the study by Anderton et al. therefore offer strong evidence of environmental injustice along lines of race and ethnicity as well as class.

Siting Versus "Move-In"

A further issue of debate in the literature is the direction of causality. In theory, correlations between the location of environmental hazards and the demographic characteristics of nearby communities could arise not only as a result of siting decisions, but also as a result of post-siting demographic changes. After the siting of a nuisance, those who can afford to do so might move elsewhere, and at the same time falling property values might lure others to move in. Such "market dynamics" may cause or

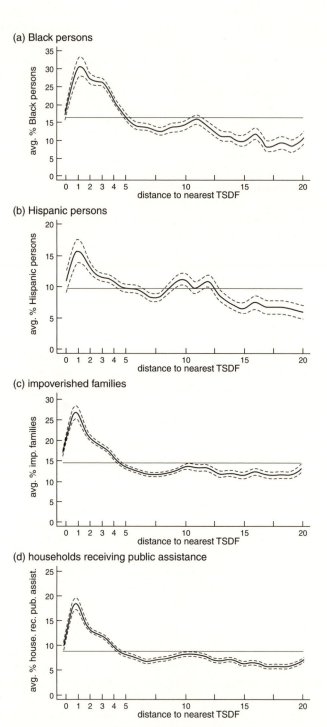

Figure 12.3. Demographic characteristics by distance to nearest TSDF tract (with 95 percent confidence intervals). Source: Oakes (1997:147).

contribute to the correlations (Been 1994). While siting decisions can be seen as unambiguous evidence of environmental inequity, move-in may seem less reprehensible, since the resulting disparities are the result of choices freely made by individuals (constrained, as in all economic choices, by their incomes) to accept lower environmental quality in return for housing that is preferable to the alternatives in other respects. In such cases, disproportionate exposure to hazards is "merely" a function of lack of income, rather than lack of power.[11]

The most thorough longitudinal study of this issue is an analysis of TSDF siting in Los Angeles County from 1970 to 1990 (Pastor et al. 2001). Examining demographic patterns before and after the siting of TS-DFs, the authors find little evidence of disproportionate move-in along racial or ethnic lines. They find strong evidence, on the other hand, that neighborhoods with above-average percentages of African Americans and Latinos and with below-average incomes *before* the siting decision were more likely to receive a TSDF. The authors conclude that "demographics reflecting political weakness" are the most reliable predictors of where TS-DFs will be sited.

Political Economy of Vulnerability

While a growing body of evidence documents that race, ethnicity, and class are correlated with the incidence of environmental costs, the mechanisms by which these characteristics affect vulnerability have yet to be explored in detail. Hamilton (1993) and Brooks and Sethi (1997) find that voter participation, a variable they interpret as a proxy for the propensity of communities to engage in collective action, is a statistically significant predictor of TSDF siting and toxic air releases, respectively. In the Los Angeles study, Pastor et al. (2001) find that neighborhoods that are fairly evenly split between African Americans and Latinos, and those that are undergoing "ethnic churning" or rapid changes in their demographic composition, are most vulnerable to TSDF siting. Pastor (2003) suggests that this arises from the relatively weak "social capital" in such neighborhoods.

Siting versus Exposure

Most environmental justice studies have focused on the location of hazardous facilities, rather than the resulting exposure to pollutants. Information on exposure or exposure risks could provide more direct evidence of environmental inequities. Such information also may help to resolve the unit-of-analysis issue discussed previously.

A new database being developed by the U.S. Environmental Protection Agency (EPA) makes such studies more feasible. Drawing on data from the Toxics Release Inventory (TRI), the EPA's Risk-Screening Environmental Indicators (RSEI) project is intended mainly to provide information for the prioritization of risk-reduction efforts. The TRI contains annual data on the volume (by weight) of toxic chemical releases by thousands of industrial facilities across the United States. The usefulness of these data for assessing hazards to nearby communities has been limited, however, by the fact that the hundreds of chemicals covered in the inventory vary in toxicity by as much as seven orders of magnitude, and by the lack of information on how these releases are dispersed by prevailing winds and water currents. The RSEI project incorporates information on toxicity and dispersal, partitioning the entire country into a one-square-kilometer grid for this purpose. A national-level analysis of these exposure-risk data reveals that the localities facing the greatest risks are inhabited by significantly higher-than-average percentages of blacks, Latinos, and Asian Americans (Bouwes et al. 2003). The disparities are even sharper when dummy variables are included to control for variations across metropolitan areas: within the nation's metropolitan areas, people of color systematically tend to live on the "wrong side" of the environmental tracks (Fetter and Ash 2004).

So What?

A final set of issues relates to the *consequences* of environmental injustice. What are the impacts of environmental burdens on the economic, physical, and emotional well-being of people who reside in the affected communities—and how important are these compared to the other problems they confront in their daily lives? There is evidence, for example, that health is affected adversely by poverty and inequality (Kaplan et al. 1996; Kennedy et al. 1996), but the role of environmental variables in this regard has yet to be explored in depth. A recent study of variations in school performance in metropolitan Los Angeles suggests that, controlling for other socioeconomic predictors, exposure to airborne toxins has a statistically significant negative effect on academic test scores (Pastor et al. 2002). Other potential effects that warrant investigation include impacts on property values, medical expenses, and days lost from work due to illness.

12.5. INEQUALITY AND ENVIRONMENTAL QUALITY: EVIDENCE FROM THE UNITED STATES

The second hypothesis derived from the power-weighted social decision rule—that inequalities in the distribution of power affect the total *magnitude* of environmental degradation—has been tested in a study of the

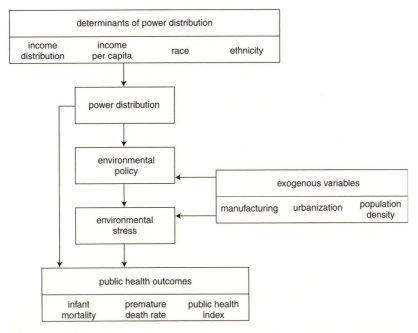

Figure 12.4. A recursive model of power inequality, the environment, and public health. Source: Boyce et al. (1999:132).

United States by Boyce et al. (1999), using cross-sectional data from the fifty states. As a unit of analysis, the state is attractive in that while all fifty states operate within the same overall U.S. political framework, the state governments play a major role in the formulation and enforcement of environmental protection policies, with considerable state-to-state variations.

The study estimates a recursive econometric model in which power inequality affects environmental policy, these policies affect environmental quality, and this in turn affects public health. The structure of the model is depicted in figure 12.4. To construct a state-level measure of power inequality, Boyce et al. combine data on four variables: voter participation, educational attainment, Medicaid access, and tax fairness. Higher voter participation is taken to indicate a more equal distribution of power. Higher educational attainment—measured as the proportion of adults who have graduated from secondary school—is taken as another indicator of a more equal distribution of power, on the assumption that there are important links between information and power. Access to the Medicaid program (which provides health care to poor families who qualify under rules that vary from state to state) and a composite measure of tax fairness are taken to reflect power disparities on the expenditure and revenue side of state fiscal policies, respectively. The common feature of this set of variables is estimated statistically as their first principal component. By the resulting measure, the state of Minnesota has the most equal distribution of power, and Mississippi the most unequal distribution.

To assess the validity of this measure of power inequality and shed light on its underlying determinants, the authors estimate the following equation, with and without regional dummy variables:

$$\pi = \alpha_1 + \beta_1 G + \beta_2 Y + \beta_3 RACE + \beta_4 ETH + \mu_1 \qquad (1)$$

where π is power inequality; G is the Gini ratio of income distribution; Y is per capita income; $RACE$ is the percentage of African Americans in the state's population; ETH is the percentage of people of Hispanic origin; and μ_1 is an independent, normally distributed error term with zero mean. The results indicate that higher income inequality, higher percentages of African Americans, and higher percentages of Hispanics are associated with greater power inequalities, and that higher average income is associated with lower power inequalities. Together, these variables "explain" more than half of the variation in power inequality across the fifty states.

The authors then analyze the impact of power inequality on environmental policies, using an environmental policy index (EP) that is based on seventy-seven indicators of the strength of state environmental policies in areas from toxic waste management, air quality and water quality to recycling, agriculture, energy, and transportation. They estimate the following equation:

$$EP = \alpha_2 + \gamma_1 \pi + \gamma_2 MAN + \gamma_3 URB + \gamma_4 PD + \mu_2 \qquad (2)$$

where the three control variables—the manufacturing share of output (MAN), urbanization (URB), and population density (PD)—are expected to generate demand for stronger environmental policies. This model "explains" about two-thirds of the variation in the environmental policy index. The estimated coefficients all have the expected signs, at levels of statistical significance ranging from 0.01 percent (in the case of the power inequality) to 5 percent (in the case of population density).

Next the authors analyze the impact of environmental policies on environmental quality, using an aggregate measure of environmental stress (ES) based on 167 indicators, including data on air and water pollution, toxic chemical releases, transportation efficiency, and the health of forests and fisheries:

$$ES = \alpha_3 + \delta_1 EP + \delta_2 MAN + \delta_3 URB + \delta_4 PD + \mu_3 \qquad (3)$$

This model "explains" roughly half the variance in the environmental stress index. The estimated coefficient on the environmental policy index has the expected sign and is statistically significant at the 0.01 percent level; manufacturing and urbanization also are statistically significant as determinants of environmental stress, but population density has no significant independent effect. A Hausman test for endogeneity of the environmental policy index is negative; after controlling for manufacturing intensity, urbanization, and population density, greater environmental stress does not appear to lead to stronger environmental policies.[12]

Finally, the authors examine the impact of environmental stress on public health by estimating the following model:

$$HEALTH = \alpha_4 + \Phi_1 ES + \Phi_2 \pi + \mu_4 \qquad (4)$$

where *HEALTH* is one of three measures of public health—infant mortality, the premature death rate, and a composite public health index. The power inequality measure is included on the right-hand side of equation (4) to allow for the possibility that it affects public health by avenues apart from environmental stress. The results indicate that states with greater environmental stress have poorer public health by all three measures, with the estimated coefficients statistically significant at the 5 percent level. When power inequality is included as an independent variable, it too has statistically significant adverse effects on all three public health variables; the adverse effect of environmental stress remains statistically significant at the 5 percent level in two of the three cases. This suggests that environmental impacts are one route by which power inequality diminishes public health, but not the only one.

In sum, the study by Boyce et al. (1999) provides empirical support for the hypothesis that greater power inequality leads to weaker environmental policies, and that weaker policies in turn lead to greater environmental degradation. This suggests that inequalities in the distribution of power operate not only to the detriment of specific groups, but also to the detriment of environmental quality in the state as a whole.

12.6. INEQUALITY AND ENVIRONMENTAL QUALITY: INTERNATIONAL EVIDENCE

International data have also been used to test the hypothesis that political and economic inequalities adversely affect environmental protection and environmental quality. Empirical research in this field confronts a number of difficulties: the paucity of internationally comparable data on environmental quality and on political and economic inequality; the pitfalls of international cross-sectional analysis, where the *ceteris paribus* assumption is always questionable; and the rather limited scope for deriving useful conclusions from time-series variations, given that the linkages between inequality and environmental quality are expected to operate over an extended time horizon.

In recent years, however, international data have become available that permit some exploration of this topic. Several recent studies have ventured into this terrain, allowing us to draw some preliminary conclusions. The starting point for this research has been analysis of the "environmental Kuznets curve," a stylized relationship suggesting that environmental quality initially deteriorates as national per capita income rises, but then goes on to improve as per capita income rises further. This section reviews the handful of such studies that have examined the role of political and economic inequalities in this relationship.

The "Environmental Kuznets Curve"

The World Bank's *World Development Report 1992*, which took the environment as its thematic focus, observed that some environmental problems "initially worsen but then improve as incomes rise," and claimed that "most forms of air and water pollution" fit into this category (World Bank 1992: 10). A number of subsequent studies, among the most widely cited of which is one by Grossman and Krueger (1995), have reported the existence of such a relationship for a number of environmental variables.[13] This pattern has been dubbed the environmental Kuznets curve (EKC) by virtue of its resemblance to the inverted U-shaped relationship between income inequality and per capita income first posited by Simon Kuznets (1955).

The EKC immediately provoked controversy, in part because it could be cast as a prescription for complacency. Just as some economists interpreted the original Kuznets curve to mean that developing countries need not worry about income distribution, but should rely instead on economic growth to solve problems of poverty and inequality, so critics feared that the EKC would offer ammunition to "gung-ho" proponents of growth by downplaying environmental concerns. To be sure, the upward-sloping segment of the EKC shows that environmental quality initially deteriorates as per capita incomes rise, up to a turning point that is often estimated to be around $5,000 per capita (roughly the level of Mexico or the Czech Republic). In the range of incomes below this level—where most of the world's nations and people are located—rising incomes would therefore be accompanied by a worsening of environmental quality. This suggests that even though environmental quality may be a "normal good" with a positive income elasticity of demand, the offsetting factors discussed in section 12.3 tend to dominate within this range. But the downward-sloping segment of the EKC suggests that eventually the deterioration in environmental quality can be reversed, and that further rises in per capita incomes help to bring this about.

Most authors agree that such reversals, if and when they occur, result from the introduction of policies for environmental protection. "There is nothing automatic about this improvement," the World Bank (1992: 10) suggests; "it occurs only when countries deliberately introduce policies to ensure that additional resources are devoted to dealing with environmental problems." Similarly, Grossman and Krueger (1995: 371–2) suggest that "an induced policy response" in the form of tougher environmental regulations, driven by citizen demand, provides the principal link between rising incomes and declining pollution, and caution that "there is no reason to believe the process is an automatic one." This echoes Kuznets' (1955: 28) conclusion regarding the relationship between per capita income and income distribution: "Effective work in this field necessarily calls for a shift from market economics to political and social economy."

The Impact of Power Inequality

Building on this insight, several studies have examined the effects of variables related to power inequality on international variations in environmental quality. Torras and Boyce (1998) examine variations in air pollution (ambient concentrations of sulfur dioxide, smoke, and heavy particles), water pollution (concentrations of dissolved oxygen and fecal coliform), and the percentages of the population with access to safe water and sanitation facilities. In addition to per capita income and income distribution, they include two explanatory variables—adult literacy and an index of political rights and civil liberties—that they consider relevant to the distribution of power. In the case of low-income countries, they find that the estimated coefficients on the rights and literacy variables have the expected signs in all cases, and are statistically significant in five of the seven cases for the rights variable and in four of the seven for the literacy variable. They obtain mixed results in the high-income countries, suggesting that rights and literacy are most important as determinants of environmental quality when average incomes are low.

Scruggs (1998) uses an index of political rights and civil liberties in an empirical exercise based on a mixed set of high- and low-income countries. He finds that greater rights have a statistically significant favorable effect on sulfur dioxide concentrations; favorable but statistically insignificant effects on particulates and fecal coliform pollution; and a statistically significant adverse effect on dissolved oxygen.

Barrett and Graddy (2000) also examine the impact of civil liberties and political rights, advancing the rationale that environmental quality depends not only on national income, but also on "citizens being able to acquire information about the quality of their environment, to assemble and organize, and to give voice to their preferences for environmental quality; and on governments having an incentive to satisfy these preferences by changing policy, perhaps the most powerful incentive being the desire to get elected or re-elected" (p. 434). They find the empirical evidence to be consistent with this expectation in the case of air pollution by sulfur dioxide, smoke, and particulates: "pollution levels are monotonically decreasing in the extent of democratic freedoms" (p. 440). In the case of water pollutants, they find the rights variables to have significant favorable effects in the cases of fecal coliform, arsenic, and lead. For several other water quality variables, including dissolved oxygen, they find no statistically significant effects.[14]

Harbaugh et al. (2000) include a "democracy index"—a 0–10 index of the extent of democratic participation in government—in a reexamination of the evidence on sulfur dioxide, smoke, and particulate air pollution, using environmental data from the same source as the World Bank (1992), Grossman and Krueger (1995), Torras and Boyce (1998), and Barrett and Grady (2000). After cleaning and updating these data, the authors conclude that "the evidence for an inverted-U relationship [between pollution and per capita income] is much less robust than previously thought" (p. 2). At the same time, however, their regression results reveal a very robust relationship between these pollutants and the democracy index: the estimated coefficients invariably have the expected sign, and they are statistically significant at the 1 percent level in twelve of the thirteen specifications tested.

Finally, Neumayer (2002) examines the impact of four different proxies for "democracy" on international environmental commitments by national governments, including their ratification of and compliance with multilateral environmental agreements and participation in intergovernmental environmental organizations. He argues that a focus on environmental commitments, rather than environmental outcomes, is appropriate given the potentially long time lags between commitments and outcomes, the difficulty of monitoring outcomes, and the sensitivity of outcomes to factors outside a government's control. While it can be argued that environmental commitments are not terribly important unless they do affect outcomes, it is certainly true that commitments tell us something about environmental protection and may be relatively easy to monitor. Neumayer finds strong evidence in favor of the hypothesis that democracies exhibit stronger environmental commitments; in most cases the estimated coefficients on the proxy variables are statistically significant, with the expected sign.

In sum, the international studies that have been carried out so far offer fairly robust support to the hypothesis that inequalities in the distribution of power lead to weaker environmental protection and greater environmental degradation.

The Impact of Income Inequality

Given the axes of the original Kuznets curve, surprisingly few EKC-type studies have explored the relationship between environmental quality and income distribution. There are two reasons why such a relationship might exist. The first is the political-economy effect arising from the correlation between the distribution of income and the distribution of power: *ceteris paribus*, countries with more unequal income distributions will tend to have more unequal power distributions. Of course, *ceteris* is seldom *paribus*, as the example of the former Soviet Union—where a highly unequal distribution of power co-existed with a fairly egalitarian income distribution—reminds us. Insofar as income inequality does translate into greater power inequality, however, the power-weighted social decision rule leads to the prediction that at any given level of average income, countries with higher income inequality will have higher levels of environmental degradation.

A second reason why income distribution may matter for the environment is that the amount of environmental degradation per unit of income may vary systematically across households ranked by income. If so, the overall level of environmental degradation will reflect not only the country's average income, but also the distribution of income across households. The sign of this "aggregation effect" depends on the shape of the relationship between household income and environmental degradation (Heerink et al. 2001). If the relation is concave—a pattern sometimes termed a "household-level environmental Kuznets curve" (Kahn 1998)—the aggregation effect implies that greater income inequality will lead to *less* environmental degradation (as income is redistributed from lower-income households with higher marginal environmental degradation per dollar to upper-income households with lower degradation per dollar). In this case, the aggregation effect runs counter to the political-economy effect, making the theoretical net impact of income inequality ambiguous. If the relation is convex, the aggregation effect implies that greater income inequality will lead to *more* environmental degradation. In this case, the two effects are mutually reinforcing.

These two possibilities are depicted in figure 12.5. As in figure 12.2, the

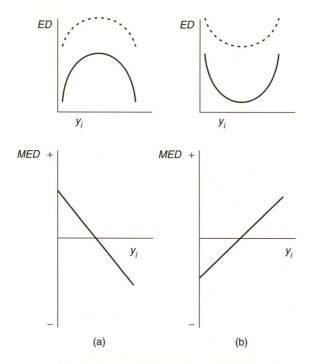

ED = environmental degradation attributable to the household
MED = marginal environmental degradation
y_i = household income

Solid line: less inequality
Broken line: greater inequality

Figure 12.5. Some possible relations between household income and environmental degradation.

horizontal axes depict household income, but instead of demand for environmental quality, the vertical axes depict the amount of environmental degradation attributable to the household (by virtue of its sources of income, pattern of consumption expenditure, or some combination of the two). In figure 12.5(a), environmental degradation is concave in household income. Marginal environmental degradation diminishes as income increases. Beyond some income level, MED may even turn negative—that is, further increments to income are associated with environmental improvements—causing total degradation to decline. In figure 12.5(b), the environmental degradation is convex in household income: high-income households generate more environmental degradation per dollar income than do low-income households.[15] The sign of the aggregation effect depends on the shape of the curve. The political-economy effect is depicted by the broken-line curves in figure 12.5: whatever the shape of the relationship between household income and environmental degradation relation, higher inequality shifts the curve upward, with higher levels of environmental degradation at each level of household income.[16]

Attempts to allocate responsibility for aggregate environmental degradation across individual households would face formidable conceptual difficulties. One approach is to allocate responsibility so on the basis of consumer expenditure: a household that buys an automobile is thus responsible for the environmental impacts generated by its production, use, and ultimate disposal.[17] A limitation of this approach is that consumers often have little information about the environmental impacts generated in the production of the goods and services they buy; it stretches the notion of "consumer sovereignty" to ascribe these impacts entirely to consumer preferences.[18] An alternative approach is to allocate responsibility on the basis of income sources: households that derive income from the production of automobiles, in the form of profits or wages, bear responsibility for the associated environmental impacts. A limitation of this approach is that decisions on pollution control are typically in the hands of managers, not workers; it would be hard to infer much about workers' environmental preferences on this basis. The practical data requirements of implementing either approach (or some combination of the two) are also formidable. The consumption-based approach requires detailed data on consumer expenditure (among households ranked by income or expenditure), input-output data on the quantities of raw materials and intermediate goods used in finished products, and data on the associated environmental impacts.[19] The production-based approach requires detailed data on wages, salaries, and profits, in addition to input-output and environmental impact data. In either case, the relationship between household incomes and environmental degradation clearly depends on more than individual demand for environmental quality, as discussed in section 12.3.

A further complication arises from the fact that some environmental degradation is caused by public-sector activities. There is no obvious way to allocate responsibility for the releases of radioactive materials at the Rocky Flats, Colorado, nuclear weapons plant, or for the dumping of bacteriological warfare agents on Vozrozhdeniye Island in the Aral Sea, across individual Americans or former Soviet citizens, ranked by their household incomes. Such cases highlight the importance of political-economy effects.

The few empirical studies that have included income distribution in EKC-type regressions have yielded mixed results. Torras and Boyce (1998) estimate the effect of the Gini coefficient of income distribution alongside the effects of adult literacy and political rights and civil liberties. Their results thus control for the impact of these aspects of power inequality on environmental quality. In the low-income countries, they find that greater income equality is associated with lower levels of air pollution from sulfur dioxide and smoke (with the estimated coefficients being statistically significant at the 1 percent level). They also find that greater income equality is associated with higher levels of access to safe drinking water, greater access to sanitation facilities, and lower levels of fecal coliform in water bodies (though the relationship is statistically significant only in the case of safe water). In the same countries, however, greater income equality was associated with worse environmental quality for two variables: heavy-particle air pollution and dissolved oxygen in water bodies.[20]

Scruggs (1998) includes income distribution as a regressor in two empirical tests. The first, using data from a mixed set of 25–29 countries, analyzes two water-quality variables (dissolved oxygen and fecal coliform) and two air-quality variables (sulfur dioxide and particulates). He finds that income equality has a statistically significant favorable effect on dissolved oxygen, and a statistically significant adverse effect in the case of particulates; in the other two cases, its effect is adverse but not statistically significant. In a second exercise, using data from seventeen OECD countries, Scruggs takes as the dependent variable a composite index based on "levels of municipal waste, fertilizer use, and sulfur dioxide, nitrous oxide, and carbon dioxide emissions" (p. 269). This is a rather curious set: the volume of municipal waste may be less relevant than how that waste is treated; how much fertilizer is used may be less relevant than what kinds, where, and how it is applied; nitrous oxide presumably is mistaken for nitrogen oxides; and the inclusion of carbon dioxide emissions is problematic since pollutants with long-term global impacts are less likely to generate policy responses than pollutants with short-term local impacts.[21] In four of five specifications, Scruggs finds that income equality has an adverse impact on this composite environmental variable, although in no case is the estimated coefficient statistically significant at the 5 percent level.[22]

Magnani (2000) examines the impact of income distribution on public research and development expenditures for environmental protection in a set of OECD countries. Using a model in which social decisions are determined simply by the preferences of the median voter, she hypothesizes that income inequality reduces pro-environmental public expenditure due to a "relative income effect," whereby greater inequality shifts the preferences of those with below-average income (including the median voter) in favor of greater consumption of private goods and lower expenditure on environmental public goods.[23] She finds that in those countries with average or above-average per capita incomes, greater income equality has a positive effect on environmental expenditures; in countries with below-average levels of per capita income her results are less definitive.

Heerink et al. (2001) include income distribution in a regression analysis of international variations in airborne sulfur dioxide and particulate concentrations, carbon dioxide emissions, access to safe water and sanitation, deforestation, and (for a sixteen-country sample of sub-Saharan African countries) the depletion of soil nitrogen and phosphorus. In six of these eight cases, the estimated coefficient on income distribution is statistically significant at the 1 percent level. In three of these cases—access to safe water, access to sanitation, and deforestation—they find that greater income equality has a favorable effect; in the other three—carbon dioxide emissions, nitrogen depletion, and phosphorus depletion—they find an adverse effect.

In sum, the limited international evidence that is now available provides empirical support for the proposition that income inequality tends to exacerbate some types of air pollution (notably smoke and sulfur dioxide), lack of access to clean drinking water and sanitation facilities, and deforestation. In each of these cases, the political-economy effect—operating via the impact of income distribution on the balance of power between winners and losers—offers a plausible explanation. The contrary findings for carbon dioxide are not surprising, since environmental impacts that are displaced onto other countries and future generations are not as likely to generate domestic pressures for national-level policies to curb emissions (Ansuategi and Escapa 2002). Other contrary findings—such as those for particulate air pollution—are inconsistent with the effect expected on political-economy grounds. Inconclusive findings are not surprising, given (i) the rather poor quality of international data on income distribution;[24] (ii) problems in the definition of environmental variables, the quality of environmental data, and sample selection; (iii) the theoretical ambiguity with respect to aggregation effects; and (iv) the possibility that income inequality simply is not a very good proxy for power inequality.

12.7. Concluding Remarks

Economic theory often treats market failure and government failure as impersonal, exogenous phenomena to be remedied by disinterested public policy. This chapter suggests that a both the magnitude and incidence of environmental degradation and environmental protection can instead be treated as endogenous phenomena, shaped by the relative power of winners and losers. The mounting evidence that low-income communities and people of color in the United States bear disproportionate environmental burdens is consistent with the hypothesis that social decisions on environmental protection systematically favor the more powerful over the less powerful. The more limited evidence available on the impact of inequality on overall environmental quality offers support for the hypothesis that greater inequality in the distribution of power leads to lower levels of environmental protection and hence greater environmental degradation.

There is much scope for further research on these issues. Among the potentially fruitful avenues for future study are the following:

- the measurement of power and power inequality, including the identification of relevant variables, alternative methods for aggregating these variables into comprehensive measures, and tests of their robustness;
- investigation of household-level relationships between income and environmental impacts, a topic important not only for assessments of the distributional incidence of environmental policies, but also for estimation of the "aggregation effect" of income distribution on environmental quality;
- exploration of differences among environmental variables, in terms of public demand for (and opposition to) environmental protection and its marginal costs;
- extension of environmental injustice research to include exposure to hazards (rather than just the location of hazardous facilities) and the impacts of such exposure on health, economic well-being, and other quality-of-life variables;
- documentation of the links between power-related variables, specific environmental policies, and specific environmental outcomes;
- estimation of the net effect of inequality on the environmental quality experienced by those who are relatively well-off, to assess whether more egalitarian distributions of power and income might bring absolute gains in this dimension of well-being even at this end of the distributional spectrum; and
- analysis of the complementarities and trade-offs between intragenerational and intergenerational equity, that is, between environmental justice and sustainability.

While much remains to be done, the broad contours of a new vision of the relationship between social justice and the environment are already visible. In the past two decades, advocates of social justice have grown increasingly aware of the importance of environmental protection, recognizing that the communities for whom they speak often bear disproportionate environmental costs. At the same time, advocates of environmental protection are beginning to recognize the importance of social justice: if inequality exacerbates environmental degradation, then advances in environmental quality will require movement toward a more democratic distribution of power and wealth.

NOTES

1. For discussion, see Sen (1992).

2. In some respects, wealth distribution provides a more robust measure of economic inequality, but data on wealth are far less common.

3. For discussions of right-to-know legislation in the United States and its impact on environmental protection, see Rich et al. (1993); Konar and Cohen (1995); and Khanna et al. (1998).

4. This does not mean that the result is efficient in the strict sense of Pareto optimality. In practice, some people typically are made worse off by decisions based on the BCA rule, notwithstanding the "potential Pareto improvement" represented by a larger economic pie. As Amartya Sen (1987: 33) remarks, "The losers could include the worst off and the most miserable in the society, and it is little consolation to be told that it is possible to compensate them fully, but ('good God!') no actual plan to do so."

5. For accounts of the famine, see Ravallion (1987) and Sen (1981: ch. 9).

6. For literature reviews, see Szasz and Meuser (1997); Bowen (2000: ch. 6), and Pastor (2003).

7. Other attributes included in the report's "personality profile" of those likely to offer the least resistance to siting decisions included "older people, people with a high school education or less, and those who adhere to a free market orientation" (Cerrell Associates 1984: 43).

8. The use of control variables for industrial or manufacturing employment (or similar proxies for the presence of industrial facilities) can be questioned on methodological grounds, since the siting of these facilities (with their associated hazards, including TSDFs) may itself be affected by the racial, ethnic, or class characteristics of nearby communities.

9. For example, Bowen (2000: 166) writes: "Thus if one used zip-code or other larger geographical areas . . . one would mistakenly conclude that minorities live closer to the sites, when in fact the demographics closest to the site show no patterns whatsoever."

10. "On average," Oakes (1997: 123) reports, "there are about 33 industrial firms in TSDF neighborhoods, while other neighborhoods typically host about 7 industrial firms. It is fair to characterize TSDF neighborhoods as industrial neighborhoods." The average population density in TSDF tracts was 724 persons/km^2, while the average in non-TSDF tracts was 2281 persons/km^2.

11. Note that the "move-in" explanation for environmental disparities is more plausible when proximity to hazards is negatively correlated with income than when it is correlated with race or ethnicity, holding income constant.

12. Whereas stronger environmental policies are expected to lead to lower environmental stress, higher environmental stress might lead to stronger environmental policies. If such endogeneity were present, this would bias the estimate of δ_1 so as to make it less (rather than more) likely that equation (3) would yield a statistically significant estimate with the expected sign.

13. For a critical review of EKC studies, see Stern (1998).

14. The authors note that "oxygen loss does not threaten human health directly" (p. 447), perhaps helping to explain the lack of significant effects in this case.

15. As in figure 12.5(a), the curves in figure 12.5(b) are drawn to allow for the possibility of negative *MED* (and thus a downward-sloping segment of the *ED* curve), in this case at lower income levels.

16. For simplicity, I have drawn this "shift effect" so as to leave marginal environmental damage (*MED*) unchanged. Uneven shifts across the income range would change the *MED* curve, too.

17. In the case of automobiles, the share of each of the three stages of the product life cycle—production, use, and disposal—in total environmental costs are estimated at 33 percent, 60 percent, and 7 percent, respectively (Kay 1997: 93).

18. Moreover, circumstantial factors can affect the resulting pattern. For example, lower-income households in the United States tend to drive older vehicles that were built when emissions and fuel efficiency standards were less stringent, whereas the rich tend to drive newer vehicles for which the standards are higher (Harrington and McConnell 1999: 22). This resulting pattern, arising from the phase-in of stricter regulations, may not generalize to other circumstances. For example, the recent boom in purchases by upper-income U.S. households of "sport utility vehicles" (SUVs) that are exempt from fuel efficiency standards may reverse the pattern.

19. Studies of the distributional incidence of environmental taxes have assembled such data for certain pollutants; see, for example, Metcalf (1999).

20. For high-income countries, the estimated impact of income inequality was generally weaker, a result consistent with Kuznets' (1963: 49) conjecture that "not only the welfare equivalents but also the power equivalents of the same relative income spread show a much wider range when the underlying average income is low than when it is high."

21. Scruggs divides emissions by national population to get a per capita measure. This too is problematic, since environmental quality is a matter of ambient concentrations and exposures, rather than emissions per capita. Higher emissions per capita in a sparsely populated country, where the emissions are widely dispersed, may be less harmful than lower emissions per capita in a densely populated country. The data presented by Scruggs (1998: 273) indicate, for example, that per capita emissions of NO_x and SO_x are twice and 5.5 times as high, respectively, in Canada as in Holland. This does not necessarily imply worse environmental quality in Canada.

22. Another curious feature of Scruggs's model for the OECD countries is the inclusion of the percentage contribution of nuclear power to the nation's energy supply as a control variable. He finds that this variable has a positive effect on his environmental quality index; as he notes, this may indicate a shift in the composition of environmental costs rather than an overall reduction.

23. Magnani (2000: 435) attributes this to the notion that "one's subjective feeling of well-being is based more on relative income than on absolute income," inferring that this translates into a desire to improve one's relative *expenditure* on private goods. The plausibility of this inference presumably depends on the distributional incidence of taxation for the provision of public goods.

24. For example, for some countries the available data refer to income distribution, while for others they refer to expenditure distribution. Measures of the latter generally show less inequality, since the expenditure/income ratio tends to decline as household income rises.

REFERENCES

Agarwal, Bina. 1992. "The gender and environment debate: Lessons from India." *Feminist Studies* 18(1): 119–58.

Anderton, Douglas L., Andy B. Anderson, John Michael Oakes, Michael R. Fraser, Eleanor W. Weber, and Edward J. Calabrese. 1994a. "Hazardous waste facilities: Environmental equity issues in metropolitan areas." *Evaluation Review* 18(2): 123–40.

Anderton, Douglas L., Andy B. Anderson, John Michael Oakes, and Michael R. Fraser. 1994b. "Environmental equity: The demographics of dumping." *Demography* 31(2): 229–48.

Ansuategi, Alberto, and Marta Escapa. 2002. "Economic growth and greenhouse gas emissions." *Ecological Economics* 40(1): 23–37.

Ash, Michael and T. Robert Fetter. 2004. "Who Lives on the Wrong Side of the Environmental Tracks?" *Social Science Quarterly* 85(2): 441–62.

Barrett, Scott, and Kathryn Graddy. 2000. "Freedom, growth, and the environment." *Environment and Development Economics* 5: 433–56.

Bartlett, Randall. 1989. *Economics and Power: An Inquiry into Human Relations and Markets*. Cambridge: Cambridge University Press.

Becker, Gary. 1983. "A theory of competition among pressure groups for political influence." *Quarterly Journal of Economics* 48(3): 371–400.

Beckerman, Wilfred. 1996. *Through Green-Colored Glasses: Environmentalism Reconsidered*. Washington, D.C.: Cato Institute.

Been, Vicki. 1994. "Locally undesirable land uses in minority neighborhoods: Disproportionate siting or market Dynamics?" *Yale Law Journal* 103: 1383–422.

Bouwes, Nicolaas W., Stephen M. Hassur, and Marc D. Shapiro. 2003. "Information for Empowerment: The EPA's Risk-Screening Environmental Indicators Project." In *Natural Assets: Democratizing Environmental Ownership*, eds. James K. Boyce and Barry G. Shelley. Washington, D.C.: Island Press, pp. 135–49.

Bowen, William M. 2000. *Environmental Justice through Research-Based Decision Making*. New York: Garland.

Boyce, James K. 1994. "Inequality as a cause of environmental degradation." *Ecological Economics* 11: 169–78.

Boyce, James K., Andrew R. Klemer, Paul H. Templet, and Cleve E. Willis. 1999. "Power distribution, the environment, and public health: A state-level analysis." *Ecological Economics* 29: 127–40.

Brooks, N., and R. Sethi. 1997. "The distribution of pollution: Community characteristics and exposure to air toxics." *Journal of Environmental Economics and Management* 32: 233–50.

Bullard, Robert D. 1983. "Solid waste sites and the black Houston community." *Sociological Inquiry* 53: 273–88.

———. 1990. *Dumping in Dixie: Race, Class, and Environmental Quality.* Boulder: Westview.

Cerrell Associates. 1984. "Political difficulties facing waste-to-energy conversion plant siting." Report prepared for the California Waste Management Board, Technical Information Series, *Waste to Energy*, chapter 3a.

Crenson, Matthew. 1971. *The Un-Politics of Air Pollution: A Study of Non-Decisionmaking in the Cities.* Baltimore, Md.: Johns Hopkins University Press.

Galbraith, John Kenneth. 1973. "Power and the useful economist." *American Economic Review* 63(1): 1–11.

Grossman, Gene, and Alan Krueger. 1995. "Economic growth and the environment." *Quarterly Journal of Economics* 110: 353–77.

Hamilton, James T. 1993. "Politics and social costs: Estimating the impact of collective action on hazardous waste facilities." *Rand Journal of Economics* 24(1): 101–25.

Harbaugh, William, Arik Levinson, and David Wilson. 2000. "Reexamining the empirical evidence for an environmental Kuznets curve." Cambridge, Mass.: National Bureau of Economic Research, Working Paper 7711, May.

Harrington, Winston, and Virginia D. McConnell. 1999. "Coase and car repair: Who should be responsible for emissions of vehicles in use?" Washington, D.C.: Resources for the Future, Discussion Paper 99-22, February.

Hecht, Susanna B. 2002. "Sacred groves and sacrifice zones: Ideologies of conservation and development." Paper presented the Inaugural Symposium of the Rock Ethics Institute, Pennsylvania State University, March.

Heerink, Nico, Abay Mulatu, and Erwin Bulte. 2001. "Income inequality and the environment: Aggregation bias in environmental Kuznets curves." *Ecological Economics* 38(3): 359–67.

Kahn, Matthew E. 1998. "A household level environmental Kuznets curve." *Economics Letters* 59: 269–73.

Kaplan, G. A., E. R. Pamuk, J. W. Lynch, R. D. Cohen, and J. L. Balfour. 1996. "Inequality in income and mortality in the United States: Analysis of mortality and potential pathways." *British Medical Journal* 312: 999–1003.

Kay, Jane Holtz. 1997. *Asphalt Nation.* Berkeley: University of California Press.

Kennedy, B. P., I. Kawachi, and D. Prothrow-Smith. 1996. "Income distribution and mortality: Cross-sectional ecological study of the Robin Hood Index in the United States." *British Medical Journal* 312: 1004–7.

Khanna, Madhu, Wilma Rose H. Quimio, and Dora Bojilova. 1998. "Toxic Release Information: A Policy Tool for Environmental Protection," *Journal of Environmental Economics and Management* 36: 243–266.

Konar, Shameek, and Mark A. Cohen. 1995. "Information as regulation: The effect of community right to know laws on toxic emissions." *Journal of Environmental Economics and Management* 32: 109–24.

Kuznets, Simon. 1955. "Economic growth and income inequality." *American Economic Review* 49:1–28.

———. 1963. "Quantitative aspects of the economic growth of nations." *Economic Development and Cultural Change* 11(2/II): 1–80.

Lukes, Steven. 1974. *Power: A Radical View.* London: Macmillan.

Magnani, Elisabetta. 2000. "The environmental Kuznets curve, environmental protection policy and income distribution." *Ecological Economics* 32(3): 431–43.

Metcalf, Gilbert E. 1999. "A distributional analysis of an environmental tax shift." *National Tax Journal* 52(4): 655–81.

Neumayer, Eric. 2002. "Do democracies exhibit stronger international environmental commitment? A cross-country analysis." *Journal of Peace Research* 39(2): 139–64.

Oakes, John Michael. 1997. *The Location of Hazardous Waste Facilities.* Unpublished Ph.D. diss., University of Massachusetts, Amherst, Department of Sociology.

Parikh, Jyoti, Kirk Smith, and Vijay Laxmi. 1999. "Indoor air pollution: A reflection on gender bias." *Economic and Political Weekly*, 27 February: 539–44.

Pastor, Manuel. 2003. "Building Social Capital to Protect Natural Capital: The Quest for Environmental Justice." In *Natural Assets: Democratizing Environmental Ownership*, eds. James K. Boyce and Barry G. Shelley. Washington, D.C.: Island Press, pp. 77–98.

Pastor, Manuel, James Sadd, and John Hipp. 2001. "Which came first? Toxic facilities, minority move-in, and environmental justice." *Journal of Urban Affairs* 23: 1–21.

Pastor, Manuel, James Sadd, and Rachel Morello-Frosch. 2002. "Who's minding the kids? Pollution, public schools, and environmental justice in Los Angeles." *Social Science Quarterly* 83(1): 263–80.

Pryde, Philip R. 1991. *Environmental Management in the Soviet Union.* Cambridge: Cambridge University Press.

Ravallion, Martin. 1987. *Markets and Famines.* Oxford: Clarendon.

Rein, Martin. 1971. "Problems in the definition and measurement of poverty." In *The Concept of Poverty*, ed. Peter Townsend, 46–63. London: Heinemann.

Rich, Richard C., W. David Conn, and William L. Owens. 1993. " 'Indirect regulation' of environmental hazards through the provision of information to the public: The case of SARA, Title III." *Policy Studies Journal* 21(1): 16–34.

Scruggs, Lyle A. 1998. "Political and economic inequality and the environment." *Ecological Economics* 26: 259–75.

Sen, Amartya 1981. *Poverty and Famines: An Essay on Entitlement and Deprivation.* Oxford: Clarendon.

———. 1987. *On Ethics and Economics.* Oxford: Basil Blackwell.

———. 1992. *Inequality Reexamined.* Cambridge, Mass.: Harvard University Press.

Stern, David I. 1998. "Progress on the environmental Kuznets curve?" *Environment and Development Economics* 3: 173–96.

Szasz, Andrew, and Michael Meuser. 1997. "Environmental inequalities: Literature review and proposals for new directions in research and theory." *Current Sociology* 45(3): 99–120.

Torras, Mariano, and James K. Boyce. 1998. "Income, inequality, and pollution: A reassessment of the environmental Kuznets curve." *Ecological Economics* 25: 147–60.

United Church of Christ, Commission for Racial Justice. 1987. *Toxic Wastes and Race in the United States: A National Report on the Racial and Socio-*

economic Characteristics of Communities with Hazardous Waste Sites. New York: Public Data Access.

United States General Accounting Office. 1983. *Siting of Hazardous Waste Landfills and their Correlation with Racial and Economic Status of Surrounding Communities.* Washington, D.C.: United States Congress.

Wargo, John. 1998. *Our Children's Toxic Legacy: How Science and Law Fail to Protect Us from Pesticides.* New Haven: Yale University Press.

World Bank. 1992. *World Development Report 1992.* New York: Oxford University Press.

INDEX

Agarwal, Bina, 7, 28, 221, 292, 317
agenda power, 316
agent-based computational models: description of, 63–65; the Janssen/Ostrom model (*see* Janssen/Ostrom model); problems of, 79; reasons for using, 61–63
Aggarwal, R. M., 102
Agrawal, A., 300–1
AI. *See* artificial intelligence
Akerlof, G. A., 124
Alesina, Alberto, 41, 209, 234
Anderton, Douglas L., 326–27
appropriation model, 17–24
artificial intelligence (AI), 64–65
Axelrod, Robert, 62, 65

Baland, Jean-Marie: collective action, 2, 36, 56n.6, 101; cultural heterogeneity, 100; firewood collection in Nepal, 3, 24, 261; models of the common good and voluntary action, 56n.8, 57n.23, 205–6
Banerjee, A., 28
Baqir, Reza, 234
Bardhan, Pranab: collective action, 36, 229; firewood collection in Nepal, 3; irrigation in India, 5, 15, 28, 41, 123; linear technology, 57n.23; public goods, 2, 16, 54; rule compliance and formulation, link between, 305
Bardhan/Ghatak/Karaivanov model: the decentralized equilibrium, 43–45; extensions of, 52–54; framework for, 36–41; limitations of, 55–56; statement of, 42–43; wealth inequality, effect of on total contributions and joint profits, 45–52
bargaining problems, 55–56, 229
Barrett, Scott, 336
Bartlett, Randall, 316–17
BCA. *See* benefit-cost analysis
Becker, Gary, 319
Beckerman, Wilfred, 322
benefit-cost analysis (BCA), 318–21, 343n.4
Bergstrom, T., 40
Bhatt, N., 309n.21

Blume, L., 40
Bowen, William M., 343n.9
Boyce, James K., 4, 28, 331–33, 335–36, 339–40
Brooks, N., 329

CA. *See* cellular automata
California Waste Management Board, 326
Cardenas, Juan-Camilo, 4–5, 25, 125
caste heterogeneity, 237, 240–43, 253. *See also* Himalayan forests
cellular automata (CA), 63–65
CFGs. *See* community forestry groups
Chambers, R., 115
children, vulnerability to pollution of, 317
Coastal Salish tribe: distributional issues and the creation of efficient institutions, 136; natural and geographic context of, 133–34; property rights of, 135–36; social organization and marriage institutions of, 134–35
collective action: community management of Himalayan forests (*see* Himalayan forests); firewood collection in Nepal (*see* Nepal); gender inequality and (*see* gender inequality); governmental authority and (*see* regulation); heterogeneity and, 25, 160–61, 191–95, 246–49; heterogeneity as inimical to, arguments for, 234–35; inequality and, 10–12, 25–31, 36–39, 207–9, 228–30, 246–49, 325 (*see also* Bardhan/Ghatak/Karaivanov model); problems of confronted in local management of irrigation systems (*see* irrigation systems); social distance based on wealth inequality, problem of (*see* experimental tests: impact of wealth inequality on cooperation). *See also* cooperation
collective goods, as public goods or common-property resources, 37
Colombia, field sites for experiments regarding cooperation and wealth inequality, 214–16. *See also* experimental tests: impact of wealth inequality on cooperation